# SLAVERY

## BY ANOTHER NAME

■   ■   ■

# SLAVERY

## BY ANOTHER NAME

■ ■ ■

THE RE-ENSLAVEMENT OF BLACK PEOPLE IN AMERICA
FROM THE CIVIL WAR TO WORLD WAR II

## DOUGLAS A. BLACKMON

DOUBLEDAY

NEW YORK    LONDON    TORONTO    SYDNEY    AUCKLAND

PUBLISHED BY DOUBLEDAY

Copyright © 2008 by Douglas A. Blackmon

All Rights Reserved

Published in the United States by Doubleday,
an imprint of The Doubleday Broadway Publishing Group,
a division of Random House, Inc., New York.
www.doubleday.com

DOUBLEDAY and the portrayal of an anchor with a dolphin
are registered trademarks of Random House, Inc.

*Book design by Ellen Cipriano*

Library of Congress Cataloging-in-Publication Data
Blackmon, Douglas A.
Slavery by another name : the re-enslavement of black people in America
from the Civil War to World War II / Douglas A. Blackmon. — 1st ed.
p.   cm.
1. African Americans—Civil rights—History—19th century.   2. African Americans—
Civil rights—History—20th century.   3. African Americans—Employment—History.
4. African Americans—Crimes against—History.   5. African American prisoners—Social
conditions.   6. Forced labor—United States—History.   7. Convict labor—United States—
History.   8. Slavery—United States—History.   9. United States—Race relations—
History—19th century.   10. United States—Race relations—History—20th century.   I. Title.
E185.2.B545 2008
305.896'073—dc22

2007034500

ISBN 978-0-385-50625-0

PRINTED IN THE UNITED STATES OF AMERICA

1 3 5 7 9 10 8 6 4 2

First Edition

*To Michelle, Michael,*
*and Colette*

*Slavery: . . . that slow Poison, which is daily contaminating the Minds & Morals of our People. Every Gentlemen here is born a petty Tyrant. Practiced in Acts of Despotism & Cruelty, we become callous to the Dictates of Humanity, & all the finer feelings of the Soul. Taught to regard a part of our own Species in the most abject & contemptible Degree below us, we lose that Idea of the dignity of Man which the Hand of Nature had implanted in us, for great & useful purposes.*

GEORGE MASON, JULY 1773
VIRGINIA CONSTITUTIONAL CONVENTION

# CONTENTS

■

# A NOTE ON LANGUAGE

■

Periodically throughout this book, there are quotations from individuals who used offensive racial labels. I chose not to sanitize these historical statements but to present the authentic language of the period, whenever documented direct statements are available. I regret any offense or hurt caused by these crude idioms.

# INTRODUCTION

*The Bricks We Stand On*

O n March 30, 1908, Green Cottenham was arrested by the sheriff of
Shelby County, Alabama, and charged with "vagrancy."[1]

Cottenham had committed no true crime. Vagrancy, the offense of a
person not being able to prove at a given moment that he or she is
employed, was a new and flimsy concoction dredged up from legal obscurity at the end of the nineteenth century by the state legislatures of Alabama
and other southern states. It was capriciously enforced by local sheriffs and
constables, adjudicated by mayors and notaries public, recorded haphaz-
ardly or not at all in court records, and, most tellingly in a time of massive
unemployment among all southern men, was reserved almost exclusively
for black men. Cottenham's offense was blackness.

After three days behind bars, twenty-two-year-old Cottenham was
found guilty in a swift appearance before the county judge and immediately
sentenced to a thirty-day term of hard labor. Unable to pay the array of fees
assessed on every prisoner—fees to the sheriff, the deputy, the court clerk,
the witnesses—Cottenham's sentence was extended to nearly a year of hard
labor.

The next day, Cottenham, the youngest of nine children born to former slaves in an adjoining county, was sold. Under a standing arrangement
between the county and a vast subsidiary of the industrial titan of the
North—U.S. Steel Corporation—the sheriff turned the young man over to

the company for the duration of his sentence. In return, the subsidiary, Tennessee Coal, Iron & Railroad Company, gave the county $12 a month to pay off Cottenham's fine and fees. What the company's managers did with Cottenham, and thousands of other black men they purchased from sheriffs across Alabama, was entirely up to them.

A few hours later, the company plunged Cottenham into the darkness of a mine called Slope No. 12—one shaft in a vast subterranean labyrinth on the edge of Birmingham known as the Pratt Mines. There, he was chained inside a long wooden barrack at night and required to spend nearly every waking hour digging and loading coal. His required daily "task" was to remove eight tons of coal from the mine. Cottenham was subject to the whip for failure to dig the requisite amount, at risk of physical torture for disobedience, and vulnerable to the sexual predations of other miners— many of whom already had passed years or decades in their own chthonian confinement. The lightless catacombs of black rock, packed with hundreds of desperate men slick with sweat and coated in pulverized coal, must have exceeded any vision of hell a boy born in the countryside of Alabama—even a child of slaves—could have ever imagined.

Waves of disease ripped through the population. In the month before Cottenham arrived at the prison mine, pneumonia and tuberculosis sickened dozens. Within his first four weeks, six died. Before the year was over, almost sixty men forced into Slope 12 were dead of disease, accidents, or homicide. Most of the broken bodies, along with hundreds of others before and after, were dumped into shallow graves scattered among the refuse of the mine. Others were incinerated in nearby ovens used to blast millions of tons of coal brought to the surface into coke—the carbon-rich fuel essential to U.S. Steel's production of iron. Forty-five years after President Abraham Lincoln's Emancipation Proclamation freeing American slaves, Green Cottenham and more than a thousand other black men toiled under the lash at Slope 12. Imprisoned in what was then the most advanced city of the South, guarded by whipping bosses employed by the most iconic example of the modern corporation emerging in the gilded North, they were slaves in all but name.


Almost a century later, on an overgrown hillside five miles from the bustling downtown of contemporary Birmingham, I found my way to one of the only tangible relics of what Green Cottenham endured. The ground was all but completely obscured by the dense thicket. But beneath the undergrowth of privet, the faint outlines of hundreds upon hundreds of oval depressions still marked the land. Spread in haphazard rows across the forest floor, these were sunken graves of the dead from nearby prison mines once operated by U.S. Steel.[2] Here and there, antediluvian headstones jutted from the foliage. No signs marked the place. No paths led to it.

I was a reporter for *The Wall Street Journal,* exploring the possibility of a story asking a provocative question: What would be revealed if American corporations were examined through the same sharp lens of historical confrontation as the one then being trained on German corporations that relied on Jewish slave labor during World War II and the Swiss banks that robbed victims of the Holocaust of their fortunes?

My guide that day in the summer of 2000 was an industrial archaeologist named Jack Bergstresser. Years earlier, he had stumbled across a simple iron fence surrounding a single collapsed grave during a survey of the area. Bergstresser was mystified by its presence at the center of what at the beginning of the twentieth century was one of the busiest confluences of industrial activity in the United States. The grave and the twisted wrought iron around it sat near what had been the intersection of two rail lines and a complex of mines, coal processing facilities, and furnaces in which thousands of men operated around the clock to generate millions of tons of coal and iron—all owned and operated by U.S. Steel at the height of its supremacy in American commerce. Bergstresser, who is white, told me he wondered if the dead here were forced laborers. He knew that African Americans had been compelled to work in Alabama mines prior to the Great Depression. His grandfather, once a coal miner himself, had told him stories of a similar burial field near the family home place south of Birmingham.

A year later, the *Journal* published my long article chronicling the saga of that burial ground. No specific record of the internments survived, but mountains of archival evidence and the oral histories of old and dying African Americans nearby confirmed that most of the cemetery's inhabitants had been inmates of the labor camp that operated for three decades on the hilltop above the graveyard. Later I would discover atop a nearby rise another burial field, where Green Cottenham almost certainly was buried.

The camp had supplied tens of thousands of men over five decades to a succession of prison mines ultimately purchased by U.S. Steel in 1907. Hundreds of them had not survived. Nearly all were black men arrested and then "leased" by state and county governments to U.S. Steel or the companies it had acquired.[3]

Here and in scores of other similarly crude graveyards, the final chapter of American slavery had been buried. It was a form of bondage distinctly different from that of the antebellum South in that for most men, and the relatively few women drawn in, this slavery did not last a lifetime and did not automatically extend from one generation to the next. But it was nonetheless slavery—a system in which armies of free men, guilty of no crimes and entitled by law to freedom, were compelled to labor without compensation, were repeatedly bought and sold, and were forced to do the bidding of white masters through the regular application of extraordinary physical coercion.

The article generated a response unlike anything I had experienced as a journalist. A deluge of e-mails, letters, and phone calls arrived. White readers on the whole reacted with somber praise for a sober documentation of a forgotten crime against African Americans. Some said it heightened their understanding of demands for reparations to the descendants of antebellum slaves. Only a few expressed shock. For most, it seemed to be an account of one more important but sadly predictable bullet point in the standard indictment of historic white racism. During an appearance on National Public Radio on the day of publication, Bob Edwards, the interviewer, at one point said to me: "I guess it's really no surprise."

The reactions of African Americans were altogether different. Repeatedly, they described how the article lifted a terrible burden, that the story had in some way—partly because of its sobriety and presence on the front page of the nation's most conservative daily newspaper—supplied an answer or part of one to a question so unnerving few dared ask it aloud: If not racial inferiority, what explained the inexplicably labored advance of African Americans in U.S. society in the century between the Civil War and the civil rights movement of the 1960s? The amorphous rhetoric of the struggle against segregation, the thin cinematic imagery of Ku Klux Klan bogeymen, even the horrifying still visuals of lynching, had never been a sufficient answer to these African Americans for one hundred years of seemingly docile submission by four million slaves freed in 1863 and their tens of millions of descendants. How had so large a population of Americans disappeared into a largely unrecorded oblivion of poverty and obscurity? They longed for a convincing explanation. I began to realize that beneath that query lay a haunting worry within those readers that there might be no answer, that African Americans perhaps were simply damned by fate or doomed by unworthiness. For many black readers, the account of how a form of American slavery persisted into the twentieth century, embraced by the U.S. economic system and abided at all levels of government, offered a concrete answer to that fear for the first time.

As I began the research for this book, I discovered that while historians concurred that the South's practice of leasing convicts was an abhorrent abuse of African Americans, it was also viewed by many as an aside in the larger sweep of events in the racial evolution of the South. The brutality of the punishments received by African Americans was unjust, but not shocking in light of the waves of petty crime ostensibly committed by freed slaves and their descendants. According to many conventional histories, slaves were unable to handle the emotional complexities of freedom and had been conditioned by generations of bondage to become thieves. This thinking held that the system of leasing prisoners contributed to the intimidation of blacks in the era but was not central to it. Sympathy for the victims, however brutally they had been abused, was tempered because, after all, they were criminals. Moreover, most historians concluded that the details of what really happened couldn't be determined. Official accounts couldn't be rigorously challenged, because so few of the original records of the arrests and contracts under which black men were imprisoned and sold had survived.

Yet as I moved from one county courthouse to the next in Alabama, Georgia, and Florida, I concluded that such assumptions were fundamentally flawed. That was a version of history reliant on a narrow range of official summaries and gubernatorial archives created and archived by the most dubious sources—southern whites who engineered and most directly profited from the system. It overlooked many of the most significant dimensions of the new forced labor, including the centrality of its role in the web of restrictions put in place to suppress black citizenship, its concomitant relationship to debt peonage and the worst forms of sharecropping, and an exponentially larger number of African Americans compelled into servitude through the most informal—and tainted—local courts. The laws passed to intimidate black men away from political participation were enforced by sending dissidents into slave mines or forced labor camps. The judges and sheriffs who sold convicts to giant corporate prison mines also leased even larger numbers of African Americans to local farmers, and allowed their neighbors and political supporters to acquire still more black laborers directly from their courtrooms. And because most scholarly studies dissected these events into separate narratives limited to each southern state, they minimized the collective effect of the decisions by hundreds of state and local county governments during at least a part of this period to sell blacks to commercial interests.

I was also troubled by a sensibility in much of the conventional history of the era that these events were somehow inevitable. White animosity toward blacks was accepted as a wrong but logical extension of antebellum racial views. Events were presented as having transpired as a result of large—seemingly unavoidable—social and anthropological shifts, rather than the specific decisions and choices of individuals. What's more, African Americans were portrayed by most historians as an almost static component of U.S. society. Their leaders changed with each generation, but the mass of black Americans were depicted as if the freed slaves of 1863 were the same people still not free fifty years later. There was no acknowledgment of the effects of cycle upon cycle of malevolent defeat, of the injury of seeing one generation rise above the cusp of poverty only to be indignantly crushed, of the impact of repeating tsunamis of violence and obliterated opportunities on each new generation of an ever-changing population outnumbered in persons and resources.

Yet in the attics and basements of courthouses, old county jails, storage sheds, and local historical societies, I found a vast record of original documents and personal narratives revealing a very different version of events. In Alabama alone, hundreds of thousands of pages of public documents attest to the arrests, subsequent sale, and delivery of thousands of African Americans into mines, lumber camps, quarries, farms, and factories. More than thirty thousand pages related to debt slavery cases sit in the files of the

Department of Justice at the National Archives. Altogether, millions of mostly obscure entries in the public record offer details of a forced labor system of monotonous enormity.

Instead of thousands of true thieves and thugs drawn into the system over decades, the records demonstrate the capture and imprisonment of thousands of random indigent citizens, almost always under the thinnest chimera of probable cause or judicial process. The total number of workers caught in this net had to have totaled more than a hundred thousand and perhaps more than twice that figure. Instead of evidence showing black crime waves, the original records of county jails indicated thousands of arrests for inconsequential charges or for violations of laws specifically written to intimidate blacks—changing employers without permission, vagrancy, riding freight cars without a ticket, engaging in sexual activity— or loud talk—with white women. Repeatedly, the timing and scale of surges in arrests appeared more attuned to rises and dips in the need for cheap labor than any demonstrable acts of crime. Hundreds of forced labor camps came to exist, scattered throughout the South—operated by state and county governments, large corporations, small-time entrepreneurs, and provincial farmers. These bulging slave centers became a primary weapon of suppression of black aspirations. Where mob violence or the Ku Klux Klan terrorized black citizens periodically, the return of forced labor as a fixture in black life ground pervasively into the daily lives of far more African Americans. And the record is replete with episodes in which public leaders faced a true choice between a path toward complete racial repression or some degree of modest civil equality, and emphatically chose the former. These were not unavoidable events, driven by invisible forces of tradition and history.

By 1900, the South's judicial system had been wholly reconfigured to make one of its primary purposes the coercion of African Americans to comply with the social customs and labor demands of whites. It was not coincidental that 1901 also marked the final full disenfranchisement of nearly all blacks throughout the South. Sentences were handed down by provincial judges, local mayors, and justices of the peace—often men in the employ of the white business owners who relied on the forced labor produced by the judgments. Dockets and trial records were inconsistently maintained. Attorneys were rarely involved on the side of blacks. Revenues from the neo-slavery poured the equivalent of tens of millions of dollars into the treasuries of Alabama, Mississippi, Louisiana, Georgia, Florida, Texas, North Carolina, and South Carolina—where more than 75 percent of the black population in the United States then lived.

It also became apparent how inextricably this quasi-slavery of the twentieth century was rooted in the nascent industrial slavery that had begun to flourish in the last years before the Civil War. The same men who built railroads with thousands of slaves and proselytized for the use of slaves in southern factories and mines in the 1850s were also the first to employ forced African American labor in the 1870s. The South's highly evolved system and customs of leasing slaves from one farm or factory to the next, bartering for the cost of slaves, and wholesaling and retailing of slaves regenerated itself around convict leasing in the 1870s and 1880s. The brutal forms of physical punishment employed against "prisoners" in 1910 were the same as those used against "slaves" in 1840. The anger and desperation of southern whites that allowed such outrages in 1920 were rooted in the chaos and bitterness of 1866. These were the tendrils of the unilateral new racial compact that suffocated the aspirations for freedom among millions of American blacks as they approached the beginning of the twentieth century. I began to understand that an explicable account of the neo-slavery endured by Green Cottenham must begin much earlier than even the Civil War, and would extend far beyond the end of his life.

Most ominous was how plainly the record showed that in the face of the rising southern white assault on black independence—even as black leaders increasingly expressed profound despair and hundreds of aching requests for help poured into federal agencies in Washington, D.C.—the vast majority of white Americans, exhausted from the long debates over the role of blacks in U.S. society, conceded that the descendants of slaves in the South would have to accept the end of freedom.

On July 31, 1903, a letter to President Theodore Roosevelt arrived at the White House from Carrie Kinsey, a barely literate African American woman in Bainbridge, Georgia. Her fourteen-year-old brother, James Robinson, had been abducted a year earlier and sold to a plantation. Local police would take no interest. "Mr. Prassident," wrote Mrs. Kinsey, struggling to overcome the illiteracy of her world. "They wont let me have him. . . . He hase not don nothing for them to have him in chanes so I rite to you for your help." Like the vast majority of such pleas, her letter was slipped into a small rectangular folder at the Department of Justice and tagged with a reference number, in this case 12007.[4] No further action was ever recorded. Her letter lies today in the National Archives.

A world in which the seizure and sale of a black man—even a black child—was viewed as neither criminal nor extraordinary had reemerged. Millions of blacks lived in that shadow—as forced laborers or their family members, or African Americans in terror of the system's caprice. The practice would not fully recede from their lives until the dawn of World War II, when profound global forces began to touch the lives of black Americans for the first time since the era of the international abolition movement a century earlier, prior to the Civil War.

That the arc of Green Cottenham's life led from a birth in the heady afterglow of emancipation to his degradation at Slope No. 12 in 1908 was testament to the pall progressing over American black life. But his voice, and that of millions of others, is almost entirely absent from the vast record of the era. Unlike the victims of the Jewish Holocaust, who were on the whole literate, comparatively wealthy, and positioned to record for history the horror that enveloped them, Cottenham and his peers had virtually no capacity to preserve their memories or document their destruction. The black population of the United States in 1900 was in the main destitute and illiterate. For the vast majority, no recordings, writings, images, or physical descriptions survive. There is no chronicle of girlfriends, hopes, or favorite songs of the dead in a Pratt Mines burial field. The entombed there are utterly mute, the fact of their existence as fragile as a scent in wind.

That silence was an agonizing frustration in the writing of this book—especially in light of how richly documented were the lives of the whites most interconnected to those events. But as I sifted more deeply into the fragmented details of an almost randomly chosen man named Green Cottenham and the place and people of his upbringing, the contours of an archetypal story gradually appeared. I found the facts of a narrative of a group of common slave owners named Cottingham and common slaves who called themselves versions of the same name; of the industrial slavery that presaged the forced labor of a quarter century later; of an African ancestor named Scipio who had been thrust into the frontier of the antebel-lum South; of the family he produced during slavery and beyond; of the roots of the white animosities that steeped the place and era of Green Cot-tenham's birth; of the obliterating forces that levered upon him and gener-ations of his family. Still, how could the account of this vast social wound be woven around the account of a single, anonymous man who by every mod-ern measure was inconsequential and unvoiced? Eventually I recognized that this imposed anonymity was Green's most authentic and compelling dimension.

Retracing the steps from the location of the prison at Slope No. 12 to the boundaries of the burial field, considering even without benefit of his words the stifled horror he and thousands of others must have felt as they descended through the now-lost passageway to the mine, I came to under-stand that Cottenham belonged as the central figure of this narrative. The slavery that survived long past emancipation was an offense permitted by the nation, perpetrated across an enormous region over many years and involving thousands of extraordinary characters. Some of that story is in fact lost, but every incident in this book is true. Each character was a real person. Every direct quotation comes from a sworn statement or a record documented at the time. I try to tell the story of many places and states and the realities of what happened to millions of people. But as much as practi-cable, I have chosen to orient this narrative toward one family and its descendants, to one section of the state most illustrative of its breadth and injury, and to one forgotten black man, Green Cottenham. The absence of his voice rests at the center of this book.

# PART ONE

■ ■ ■

## THE SLOW POISON

# I

# THE WEDDING

*Fruits of Freedom*

Freedom wasn't yet three years old when the wedding day came. Henry Cottinham and Mary Bishop had been chattel slaves until the momentous final days of the Civil War, as nameless in the eyes of the law as cows in the field. All their lives, they could no more have obtained a marriage license than purchased a horse, a wagon, or a train ticket to freedom in the North. Then a final furious sweep of Union soldiers—in a bewildering blur of liberation and terror unleashed from a distant war—ravaged the Cahaba River valley.

Henry was suddenly a man. Mary was a woman, a slave girl no more. Here they stood, bride and groom, before John Wesley Starr, the coarse old preacher who a blink of an eye before had spent his Sundays teaching white people that slavery was the manifestation of a human order ordained by God, and preaching to black people that theirs was a glorified place among the chickens and the pigs.

To most people along the Cahaba River, January 1868 hardly seemed an auspicious time to marry. It was raw, cold, and hungry. In every direction from the Cottingham Loop, the simple dirt road alongside which lived three generations of former slaves and their former owners, the land and its horizons were muted and bitter. The valley, the undulating hills of Bibb County, even the bridges and fords across the hundred-yard-wide Cahaba sweeping down from the last foothills of the Appalachians and into the flat fertile plains to the south, were still wrecked from the savage cavalry raids of Union Gen. James H. Wilson. Just two springs earlier, in April 1865, his horsemen had descended on Alabama in billowing swarms. The enfeebled southern army defending the state scattered before his advance. Even the great Confederate cavalry genius Nathan Bedford Forrest, his regiments eviscerated by four years of war, was swept aside with impunity. Wilson crushed the last functioning industrial complex of the Confederacy and left Alabama in a state of complete chaos. Not three years later, the valley remained a twisted ruin. Fallow fields. Burned barns. Machinery rusting at the bottoms of wells. Horses and mules dead or lost. The people, black and white, braced for a hard, anxious winter.

From the front porch of Elisha Cottingham's house, two stories stacked of hand-hewn logs and chinked with red clay dug at the river's edge, the old man looked out on his portion of that barren vista. The land had long ago lost nearly all resemblance to the massive exuberance of the frontier forest he stumbled upon fifty years earlier. Now, only the boundaries and contours remained of its carefully tended bounty of the last years before the war.

He had picked this place for the angle of the land. It unfolded from the house in one long sheet of soil, falling gradually away from his rough-planked front steps. For nearly five hundred yards, the slope descended smoothly toward the deep river, layered when Elisha first arrived with a foot of fertile humus. On the east and south, the great field was hemmed in by a gushing creek, boiling up over turtle-shell shapes of limestone protruding from the banks, growing deeper and wider, falling faster and more furiously—strong enough to spin a small grist mill—before it turned to the west and suddenly plunged into the Cahaba. He named the stream Cottingham Creek. An abounding sense of possibility exuded from the place Elisha had chosen, land on which he intuitively knew a resourceful man could make his own indelible mark.

Yet in the aftermath of the war Elisha Cottingham, like countless other southern whites in 1868, must have felt some dread sense of an atomized future. They knew that the perils of coming times constituted a far greater jeopardy than the war just lost. A society they had engineered from wilderness had been defeated and humiliated; the human livestock on which they had relied for generations now threatened to rule in their place. In the logical spectrum of possibilities for what might yet follow, Elisha had to consider the terrifying—and ultimately realized—possibility that all human effort invested at the confluence of Cottingham Creek and the Cahaba River would be erased. The alacrity that infused their achievement was lost. More than a century later, the last Cottingham would be gone. No trace of the big house, the slave cabins, or a waterwheel would survive. None of the fields hacked from the forest remained at plow. Only the creek and sunbleached gravestones clustered atop the hill still bore the Cottingham name.

Elisha had arrived at the banks of the Cahaba, barely a man himself, in an Alabama territory that was still untamed. It was 1817, and Elisha and his three brothers faced a dense wilderness governed by the uncertainties of Indian territory and the vagaries of an American nation debating the precepts of eminent domain that would ultimately expand its borders from the Atlantic to the Pacific Ocean.[1] Alabama would not be a state for two more years.

Elisha's brother Charles soon decamped to the newly founded county seat of Centreville, where in short order shallow-draft riverboats would land and a trading center would be established.[2] Another brother, William, moved farther south. But Elisha and his younger sibling, John, stayed in the wilderness on the Cahaba. In the four decades before the Civil War, they staked out land, brought in wives, cleared the lush woodlands, sired bountiful families, and planted season upon season of cotton. The engines of their enterprises were black slaves. In the early years, they imported them to Alabama and later bred more themselves—including Henry—from the African stock they bought at auction or from peripatetic slave peddlers who arrived unbidden in springtime with traces of ragged, shackled black men and women, carrying signs advertising "Negroes for Sale." Manning farms strung along a looping wagon road, the brothers and their slaves cleared the land, raised cabins, and built the church where they would pray. Harnessing their black labor to the rich black land, the Cottingham brothers became prosperous and comfortable.

Some neighbors called the Cottingham section of the county Pratt's Ferry, for the man who lived on the other side of the Cahaba and poled a raft across the water for a few pennies a ride. But the Cottinghams, God-fearing people who gathered a congregation of Methodists in the wilderness almost as soon as they had felled the first timber, adopted for their homestead a name marking the work not of man but of the Almighty. Where the clear cold creek gurgled into the Cahaba, a massive bulge of limestone rose from the water, imposing itself over a wide, sweeping curve in the river. To the Cottinghams, this place was Riverbend.

The Cottinghams demanded a harsh life of labor from their bondsmen. Otherwise, what point was there to the tremendous investment required of owning slaves. Yet, especially in contrast to the industrial slavery that would eventually bud nearby, life on the Cottingham plantation reflected the biblical understanding that cruelty to any creature was a sin—that black slaves, even if not quite men, were at least thinly made in the image of God.

Set among more than twenty barns and other farm buildings, Henry and the rest of the slaves lived in crude but warm cabins built of rough-hewn logs chinked with mud. Heat came from rock fireplaces with chimneys made of sticks and mud. Elisha recorded the ownership of thirteen slaves in 1860, including four men in their twenties and thirties and six other male teenagers. A single twenty-year-old female lived among the slaves, along with two young boys and a seven-year-old girl.[3]

Given the traditions of isolated rural farms, Elisha's grandson Oliver, raised there on the Cottingham farm, would have been a lifelong playmate of the slave boy nearly his same age, named Henry.[4] When Elisha Cottingham's daughter Rebecca married a neighbor, Benjamin Battle, in 1852, Elisha presented to her as a wedding gift the slave girl who likely had been her companion and servant. "In consideration of the natural love and affection which I bear to my daughter," Elisha wrote, I give her "a certain negro girl named Frances, about 14 years old."[5]

Those slaves who died on the Cottingham place were buried with neat ceremony in plots marked by rough unlabeled stones just a few feet from where Elisha himself would be laid to rest in 1870—clearly acknowledged as members in some manner of a larger human family recognized by the master. Indeed, Elisha buried his slaves nearer to him by far than he did Rev. Starr, the man who ministered to all of the souls on the Cottingham place. The Starr family plot, with its evangelical inscriptions and sad roster of infant dead, was set down the hill and toward the road, even more vulnerable to the creeping oblivion of time.

Long generations hence, descendants of slaves from the plantation still recounted a vague legend of the generosity of a Cottingham master—giving permission to marry to a favored mulatto named Green. That slave, who would remain at Elisha's side past emancipation and until the old master's death, would become the namesake of Henry and Mary's youngest son.

But even as Elisha had allowed a strain of tenderness to co-reside with the brutally circumscribed lives of his slaves, he never lost sight of their fundamental definition—as cattle. They were creatures bought or bred for the production of wealth. Even as he deeded to daughter Rebecca the slave Frances, Elisha was careful to enumerate in the document the recognition that he was giving up not just one slave girl, but a whole line of future stock who might have brought him cash or labor. Along with Frances, Elisha was careful to specify, his newlywed daughter received all "future increase of the girl."[6]

The marriage of Henry, now twenty years old, and Mary, one year his junior, in 1868 was the first among Cottingham people, black or white, in two seasons. Another slave, Albert, had wed, and left for good in the middle of the first picking time after the destruction of the war—amid the chaos and uncertainty when no one could be sure slavery had truly ended.[7] Albert didn't wait to find out.

Now, two years later, the coming marriage surely warmed Elisha at some level. But as Henry prepared to take a wife and become a man of this peculiar new era, everything the old white man had forged—everything on which that gift to his daughter twenty years before had been predicated—hung in the fragile limbo of a transformed social order. Whatever satisfaction the filial ties gave the white master at the wedding of his former bondsman would have been tempered by the poverty and grief that had overwhelmed him.

Most of Elisha's slaves remained nearby. Some still worked his property, for wages or a share of the cotton crop. But the end of the war had left the white Cottinghams at a point of near desolation. The hard winter threatened to bring them to their knees.


As Henry and Mary's wedding approached in 1868, whites across the South strained to accept the apparently inevitable ignominies descending from the war. The loss of fortunes, the war's blood and sorrow, the humiliation of Union soldiers encamped in their towns, all these things whites had come to bear. They would bear them a little longer, at least until the instant threats of hunger and military force receded.

But these abominations paled against the specter that former slaves, with their huge mathematical majorities in Louisiana, Mississippi, southern Alabama, south Georgia, and South Carolina, would soon vote and rule governments and perhaps take their masters' lands. This vision was a horror almost beyond contemplation. It poisoned the air for Elisha and other white landowners with prospects for even greater disaster.

In the last days of fighting, the U.S. Congress had created the Freedmen's Bureau to aid the South's emancipated slaves.[8] New laws gave the agency the power to divide land confiscated by the federal government and to have "not more than forty acres of such land . . . assigned" to freedmen and black war refugees for a period of three years. Afterward, the law said former slaves would be allowed to purchase the property to hold forever. President Andrew Johnson rescinded the provision a few months later, but emancipated slaves across the South remained convinced that northern soldiers still garrisoned across the region would eventually parcel out to them all or part of the land on which they had long toiled.

The threat that Elisha's former slaves would come to own his plantation—that he and his family would be landless, stripped of possessions and outnumbered by the very creatures he had bred and raised—was palpable.

The last desperate rallying calls of the Confederacy had been exhortations that a Union victory meant the political and economic subjugation of whites to their black slaves. In one of the final acts of the Confederate Congress, rebel legislators asserted that defeat would result in "the confiscation of the estates, which would be given to their former bondsmen."[9]

Already, forty thousand former slaves had been given title by Gen. William Tecumseh Sherman to 400,000 acres of rich plantation land in South Carolina early in 1865. It was unclear whether blacks would be able to retain any of the property, but rumor flared anew among blacks across the South the next year at Christmastime—the end of the annual crop season—that plantation land everywhere would soon be distributed among them. The U.S. Congress debated such a plan openly in 1867, as it drew up the statutes to govern Reconstruction in the southern states. And again as harvest time ended that year, word whipped through the countryside that blacks would soon have land. At one point the following year, in 1868, during a period of intense speculation among freed slaves that land was soon to be provided to them, many blacks purchased boundary markers to be prepared for the marking off of their forty-acre tracts.[10]

Forty miles to the west of the Cottingham farm, in Greene County, hundreds of former slaves filed suit against white landowners in 1868 demanding that the former slave masters be compelled to pay wages earned during the prior season's work. Whites responded by burning down the courthouse, and with it all 1,800 lawsuits filed by the freedmen.[11]

Despite Bibb County's remote location, far from any of the most famous military campaigns, the Civil War had not been a distant event. In the early months of fighting, Alabama industrialists realized that the market for iron sufficient for armaments would become lucrative in the South. In 1860 only Tredegar Iron Works, a vast industrial enterprise in Richmond, Virginia, driven by more than 450 slaves and nearly as many free laborers, could produce battle-ready cannon for the South. The Confederate government, almost from the moment of its creation, set out to spur additional capacity to make arms, particularly in Alabama, where a nascent iron and coal industry was already emerging and little fighting was likely to occur. During the war, a dozen or more new iron furnaces were put into blast in Alabama;[12] by 1864, the state was pumping out four times more iron than any other southern state.

Across Alabama, individual property holders—slaveholders specifically—were aggressively encouraged to attempt primitive industrial efforts to support the Confederate war effort. The rebel government offered generous inducements to entrepreneurs and large slave owners to devote their resources to the South's industrial needs. With much of the major plantation areas of Mississippi under constant federal harassment, thousands of slaves there were without work. Slave owners willing to transport their black workers to the new mining regions of Alabama and dig coal could avoid conscription into the southern armies.

After seeing their homes and stockpiles of cotton burned, W. H. and Lewis Thompson, brothers from Hinds County, Mississippi, and the owners of large numbers of slaves, moved to Bibb County midway through the war to mine the Cahaba coalfields for the Confederacy. They opened the Lower Thompson mine, and later another relative and his slaves arrived to dig another mine. The coal was hauled eleven miles to Ashby and then shipped to Selma. The mining was crude, using picks and hand-pulled carts. The slaves drained water from the shafts by carrying buckets up to the surface.[13]

A neighbor of the Cottinghams, local farmer Oliver Frost, regularly took his slaves to a cave on Six Mile Creek to mine saltpeter—a critical ingredient for gunpowder—for the Confederate army, often remaining there for weeks at a time. The Fancher family, on a farm three miles north of the crossroads community called Six Mile, regularly hauled limestone from a quarry on their property to a Bibb County furnace during the war.[14]

The centerpiece of the Alabama military enterprises was a massive and heavily fortified arsenal, naval foundry, ironworks, and gunpowder mill located in the city of Selma. To produce its weapons and metal plating for use on ironclad ships critical to the Confederacy's limited naval operations, the Selma works relied on enormous amounts of coal and iron ore mined and forged in nearby Shelby and Bibb counties.[15] Alabama iron was particularly well suited to use in the revolutionary new development of fortifying battle ships with steel plates. Iron forged at Alabama's Cane Creek Furnace, in Calhoun County, had been utilized for a portion of the armor used to convert the hull of the captured USS *Merrimac* into the CSS *Virginia*, the southern entrant in the famous March 8, 1862, battle of ironclads.[16] The Confederacy was hungry for as much of the material as it could get.

Of particular strategic value were ironworks established by local investors in 1862 in the village of Brierfield. Nine miles from the Cottingham place, the Brierfield Iron Works produced the plates that adorned the Confederate vessel CSS *Tennessee*, which during the battle of Mobile Bay on August 5, 1864, withstood the barrage of seventeen Union vessels without a single shot penetrating her hull.[17] Bibb County iron quickly became a coveted material.

As the war escalated, maintaining production required an ever increasing number of slaves. Agents from major factories, Brierfield Iron, and the Shelby Iron Works, scoured the countryside to buy or lease African Americans. Foundries routinely commissioned labor agents to prowl across the southern states in search of available slaves. In 1863, the Confederate government purchased the Brierfield operation for $600,000, so that it could directly control its output. The purchase encompassed "its property of all kinds whatsoever," including thousands of acres of land and a catalogue of dozens of wagons, wheelbarrows, coal sleds, axes, and blacksmith tools. On the list of livestock were seventy mules, forty-one oxen, and nine black men: "John Anderson, aged about 35, Dennis, about 38, George, about 30, Charles, about 47, Perry, about 40, Curry about 17, Matthew, about 35, Mose, about 18, and Esquire, about 30 years."[18]

The Confederate government began construction of a second furnace at the site shortly after acquiring the property. All of its output went to the Selma Arsenal, fifty miles by railroad to the south, where the iron was used for armor and for naval guns, including the state-of-the-art eleven-inch Brooke rifled cannon, with a capacity of firing a 230-pound shell more than two thousand yards.[19]

By the standards of the antebellum South, the Brierfield Iron Works was a spectacle of industrial wonder. The adjacent village held church in a schoolhouse surrounded by the tenements and small housing for three hundred workers. Two massive brick blast furnaces, each forty feet high, belched a thick brew of smoke and gases at the top and a torrent of lique-fied iron at the base. Nearby was a rolling mill where the molten iron was formed into crude one-hundred-pound "pigs" for shipment to Selma, and loaded onto a railroad line extended into the factory yard. One hundred yards away sat a kiln for firing limestone, ten tons of which was fed each day into the furnaces. Beyond the kiln was a quarry for the endless task of repairing the stone furnaces, a sawmill, and then seven thousand acres of forest from which fuel for the constantly burning fires was cut.[20]

The nine slaves owned by the ironworks were an anomaly. Few indus-trial enterprises wanted to actually purchase slaves. They were too expensive at acquisition, and too costly and difficult to maintain. Too unpredictable as to when they might become uncooperative, or die. Far preferable to the slave-era industrialist was to lease the slave chattel owned by other men.

In 1864, however, few such workers could be found anymore. Instead, the Confederate officer commanding the Brierfield iron production opera-tion, Maj. William Richardson Hunt, rented two hundred slaves to perform the grueling tasks necessary to continue equipping the rebel army.[21] Late in the war, as the need for the area's coal and iron capacity grew dire, the Confederate government began to forcibly impress the slaves held by whites in the county. A son of Rev. Starr's—a doctor and also a resident of the Cottingham Loop—became the government's agent for seizing slaves.[22] There is no surviving record of which black men were pressed into service. But by war's end, Scipio Cottingham, the sixty-three-year-old slave who had shared the farm longest with master Elisha, had come to identify himself as a foundry man. Almost certainly, he had been among those rented to the Brierfield furnace and compelled to help arm the troops fighting to preserve his enslavement.

As the war years progressed, ever larger numbers of local men from near the Cottingham farm left for battle duty. Two of Elisha's sons fought for the Confederacy. Moses and James, both husbands and fathers, each saw gruesome action, personal injury, and capture by the Union. Elisha's grandson Oliver, too young to fight with the troops, joined the Home Guard, the ragtag platoons of old men and teenagers whose job was to patrol the roads for deserters, fleeing slaves, and Union scouts.

In the beginning, large crowds gathered at the stores in the crossroads settlement of Six Mile to send them off, and groups of women worked together to sew the uniforms they wore. Soldiers on the move through the area were a regular sight, crossing the Cahaba on the ferry near the mouth of Cottingham Creek, and traversing the main road from there toward the rail towns to the east.[23]

Confederate soldiers camped often on the Cottingham farm, stretching out in the big field near the river, foraging from the plantation's supplies and food, exchanging spent horses for fresh ones. At one point late in the war, an entire regiment set camp in the field, erecting tents and lighting cooking fires.[24]

The appearance of Confederate soldiers must have been an extraordinary event in the lives of the black members of the Cottingham clan. The war years were a conflicted period of confused roles for slaves. They were the subjects of the Union army's war of liberation, and the victims of the South's economic system. Yet at the same time, slaves were also servants and protectors of their white masters. In the woods near the Cottingham home, slaves guarded the horses and possessions of their white owners, hidden there to avoid raids of northern soldiers. Some slaves took the opportunity to flee, but most stayed at their posts until true liberation came in the spring of 1865.

The foundry and arsenal at Selma and the simple mines and furnaces around the Cottingham farm that supplied it with raw materials had taken on outsized importance as the war dragged on. The Alabama manufacturing network became the backbone of the Confederacy's ability to make arms,[25] as the Tredegar factories were depleted of raw materials and skilled workers and menaced by the advancing armies of Ulysses S. Grant. Preservation of the Alabama enterprises was a key element of a last-ditch plan by Jefferson Davis, the southern president, to retreat with whatever was left of the Confederate military into the Deep South and continue the war.[26]

For more than a year, Union forces in southern Tennessee and northern Alabama massed for an anticipated order to obliterate any continued capacity of a rump Confederate government to make arms. Small groups of horse soldiers made regular probing raids, against minimal southern resistance. In April of 1864, Alabama's governor wired Confederate Lt. Gen. Leonidas Polk, commander of rebel forces in Alabama and Mississippi, imploring him to send additional troops. "The enemy's forces . . . are fortifying their position with their cavalry raiding over the country. . . . It is certain that the forces will work way South and destroy the valuable works in Central Alabama. . . . Can nothing be done?"[27]

Finally in March 1865, a mass of 13,500 Union cavalrymen swept down from the Tennessee border, in one of the North's penultimate death blows to the rebellion. Commanded by Gen. James H. Wilson, the Union army, well drilled and amply armed, split into three huge raiding parties, each assigned to destroy key elements of Alabama's industrial infrastructure. Moving unchallenged for days, the federal troops burned or wrecked iron forges, mills, and massive stockpiles of cotton and coal at Red Mountain, Irondale, and Helena, north of Bibb County. On the morning of March 30, Union soldiers slogged down the rain-drenched roads into Columbiana, destroying the machinery of the Shelby Iron Works, shoving its equipment into local wells and streams, and freeing the slaves critical to its operations.

Against nearly hopeless odds, Nathan Bedford Forrest, a former slave dealer who had become the South's most storied horseman, met the blue advance at a point south of the town of Montevallo. Skirmishing along

Mahan Creek, just miles from the Cottingham farm, Forrest's disorganized command could only harass Wilson's advance. Northern troops took the Brierfield furnace on March 31, and left it a ruin.

Outmanned and outfought, with flooding creeks blocking his maneuvers, Forrest, himself slashed by a saber in savage fighting on April 1, retreated for a final stand at Selma. The next day, Wilson's troops charged the fortified industrial complex in Selma, and routed Forrest's remaining four thousand men. The Confederate general slipped away with an escort of one hundred soldiers, massacring as he made his escape most of a contingent of twenty-five sleeping Union scouts he stumbled upon in a field.

Federal forces captured nearly three thousand of Forrest's men, along with more than sixty pieces of field cannon, scores of heavy artillery guns, nine factories, five major iron forges, three foundries, twenty locomotives, immense quantities of military supplies, and 35,000 bales of cotton. The arsenal, factory shops, and foundries at Selma were systematically destroyed. Perhaps most shocking to local whites, before moving on to attack Georgia, Wilson's officers quickly raised a one-thousand-man regiment of black troops, placed under the command of the Third Ohio Cavalry.[28]

With the remaining Confederate armies commanded by Gen. Robert E. Lee and Gen. Albert Sydney Johnston unable to unite, Jefferson Davis's hope to continue the rebellion as a guerrilla struggle collapsed. Cut off from his remaining troops, his Alabama munitions system destroyed, deprived of the last regions of relative security in the South, he attempted to flee to Texas or Mexico. Under hot pursuit by detachments of General Wilson's troops, he was captured by Union forces in Georgia weeks later. The war came finally to its end.

Alabama had suffered losses totaling $500 million—a sum beyond comprehension in 1865. The total value of farm property was reduced during the war from $250 million to less than $98 million, including the loss of slaves. All banks in the state had collapsed. Agricultural production levels would not match that of 1860 for another forty years.[29]

But the final days of the war proved to be only the beginning of a more inexorable and anarchic struggle. A vicious white insurgency against the Union occupation and the specter of black citizenship began to take shape,

presaged by the conduct of Home Guard patrols like the one Oliver
Cottingham had joined. The patrols, uncoordinated and increasingly contemptuous of any authority during the war, had come to be known more as
bandits and thugs than defenders of the Confederacy. After four years of
conscriptions verging on kidnappings, violence perpetrated against critics
of rebellion, and ruthless seizures of supplies and property, the Home
Guard was in many places as despised as the Yankee troops. But in the aftermath of a sudden—and in much of the South, unanticipated—surrender, no
clear central authority existed in the domestic affairs of places too small or
remote to warrant a detachment of northern troops. In the Deep South,
that meant nearly everyplace outside state capitals and economic centers.

The result, in the two years preceding Henry and Mary's wedding, was
a spreading wave of internecine violence and thievery by returning Confederate soldiers, particularly against those southerners who had doubted the
war. Deserters, who had been far more numerous than southern mythology
acknowledged, began settling old scores. The increasing lawlessness of the
postwar years was, rather than a wave of crime by freed slaves as so often
claimed, largely perpetrated against whites by other whites.

The Cottingham farm sat in the middle of this unrest. One gang of
deserters in Bibb County, made up of men believed to have abandoned the
armies of both the North and the South, called themselves the Uglies, and
marauded through the countryside during the war, robbing farms and
threatening Confederate supporters. Another gang inhabited the Yellow
Leaf swamp on the border with adjoining Chilton County. A paramilitary
band of men near the town of Montevallo, calling itself Blackwell's Cavalrymen, hunted the countryside for Confederate deserters before the southern
surrender and continued as an outlaw gang after the war. The group eventually murdered a total of seventeen local men. White lawlessness was so
rampant in Shelby County that less than a year before Henry and Mary's
wedding, Union military officials in the Alabama capital threatened to send
troops into the area to restore peace.[30]

Chilton County had been a hotbed of such guerrilla activity throughout the war and emerged as a refuge for Confederate deserters and southerners who remained loyal to the Union. A local plantation owner, Capt.
James Cobb, who had been sent home from duty with the southern army
due to poor health, was assigned the task of breaking up the gangs of

deserters. The effort spawned vendettas that would outlast the war. On June 3, 1865, nearly two months after the surrender, Cobb was seized by a group of thirty whites and hanged from a tree on his property. Afterward, they ransacked his home, killing or stealing his livestock. The former Confederate officer was accused of having named seven of the mob's members as deserters. The Blackwell group subsequently captured the seven and summarily executed them.[31]

Of the handful of Union soldiers sent to Bibb County to oversee a nominal local court system during the first two years after the war, one was killed on a Centreville street corner by a Confederate veteran wielding an axe handle.[32] Two agents of the Freedmen's Bureau were assigned to the area in January and February of 1866. The men, named Beard and Higgenbotham, were promptly whipped by local whites and driven from the county. Not long after, rumor spread that two former slaves named Tom Johnson and Rube Russell had been seen around the county sporting fine clothes paid for by Freedmen's Bureau agents. The emancipated slaves planned to "live like white folks and marry white wives," according to a newspaper account. Johnson was promptly hanged from a tree on Market Street. A few mornings later, passersby found Russell dangling dead, in a tree not far from the scene of the earlier lynching.[33]

Yet even as southern whites like those in Bibb County made their rejection of the new order so apparent, no alternative was clear either. The loss of slaves left white farm families such as the Cottinghams, and even more so those on expansive plantations with scores or hundreds of slaves, not just financially but intellectually bereft. The slaves were the true experts in the tasks of cotton production on most farms; in many cases it was slaves who directed the gangs of other slaves in their daily work. Slavery had been introduced into the southern colonies in the 1600s with the argument that whites, operating alone, were incapable of large-scale cotton production. The concepts of sharecropping and farm tenancy hadn't yet evolved. The notion that their farms could be operated in some manner other than with groups of black laborers compelled by a landowner or his overseer to work as many as twenty hours a day was antithetical to most whites.

Moreover, the sudden willingness of millions of black laborers to insolently demand cash wages and other requirements to secure their labor was an almost otherworldly experience for whites such as Elisha Cottingham. Former slaves were suddenly mobile too, seeking new lodging away from the farms of their slave lives and attempting to put white farmers into competition with one another for their work.

In the absence of any means to supply freed slaves with land, the Freedmen's Bureau and northern military commanders stationed in the South encouraged blacks to enter into labor contracts with whites. The results were written agreements between whites and black farmhands filled with provisions aimed at restoring the subjugated state of African Americans. One agent of the Freedmen's Bureau wrote that whites were unable to fathom that work "could be accomplished without some prodigious binding and obligating of the hireling to the employer."[34]

Some white plantation owners attempted to coerce their former slaves into signing "lifetime contracts" to work on the farms. In one South Carolina case in 1865, when four freedmen refused such agreements, two were killed and a third, a woman, was tortured.[35] More common were year-to-year contracts that obligated black workers to remain throughout a planting and harvest season to receive their full pay, and under which they agreed to extraordinarily onerous limitations on personal freedom that echoed slave laws in effect before emancipation. They agreed not to leave the landowner's property without a written pass, not to own firearms, to obey all commands of the farmer or his overseer, to speak in a servile manner, and in the event of a violation of the rules to accept whatever punishment the farmer deemed appropriate—often the lash.[36] Most of the early contracts adopted in the South in 1865 and 1866 were dissolved by commanders of the occupying Union troops. But they framed a strategy that southern whites would return to again and again.

When Elisha's sons arrived home from the war, they found only the barest gleanings of the earlier time with which to restart their lives. The thriving farmland world of their boyhoods no longer existed. After four years of steadily inflated Confederate scrip, now entirely worthless, the value of a man's land and tools, even of a bale of cotton, was nearly unknowable. Elisha's property was worth the substantial sum of nearly $20,000 before the war. The great bulk of that was invested in his slaves, and now they were his no more. The Cottinghams had not even the cash to buy cotton seed and corn, much less the labor of the former slaves they had so recently owned.

In February 1868, Elisha, perhaps sensing his own mortality more acutely in the postwar chaos, began dividing much of the plantation among his four sons, John, James, Moses, and Harry.[37] At the same time, his daughter, Rebecca Battle, bought two hundred acres of the property for $600.[38]

Later that month, Moses Cottingham borrowed $120 from a cotton buyer in the town of Randolph, an outpost in the other end of the county on the edge of the wide-open cotton lands of southern Alabama. For collateral, Moses promised two five-hundred-pound bales of cotton at the end of the season.[39] From another man, he borrowed $120, securing that note with one six-year-old mule and a ten-year-old horse.[40] The following January, 1869, Moses borrowed again, mortgaging for $150 his ever older horse and three other mules. The crop that fall wouldn't be enough to pay off the loan, and Moses couldn't clear his debt until 1871.[41]

A sense of paralysis was pervasive among whites. Elias Bishop, a prosperous farmer with a spread of several hundred acres under plow in another rich bend of the Cahaba downstream from the Cottinghams, was in similar straits. In the fall of 1869, Bishop, South Carolina–born and another of the county's earliest settlers, borrowed a little more than $50 against one hundred bushels of corn and mortgaged a portion of his land for $37.60. He never paid it back.[42] The next summer, wife Sarah Bishop borrowed $150 against two bales of cotton from John C. Henry, the cotton buyer at Randolph who had become the county's de facto banker and financier. She settled the debt after the harvest of 1870, but immediately had to assume another loan.[43]

The Bishops, like Elisha and his family, were devout Wesleyan Methodists.[44] Along with their slaves, the Bishops had attended the Mount Zion church near their farm in the south end of the county, where the family lived in a house overflowing with daughters.[45] The Bishops and Cottinghams, white and black, would have known each other well through the close-knit circles of the Methodist circuit. John Wesley Starr, as a circuit-riding clergyman, was a regular feature before both congregations. Elias Bishop had accumulated an even more impressive collection of slaves than Elisha, with ten black men and three black females old enough to work in the fields at the beginning of the war. A half dozen young children rounded out the slave quarters. On the day of emancipation in 1863, the Bishop slave girl named Mary, who five years later would become Henry Cottinham's wife, was fourteen.[46]

In the wake of the war, one episode in the lives of white Cottinghams became the defining anecdote of the family's suffering and resurrection. Elisha's son Moses, who had migrated to Bienville Parish, Louisiana, a few years before secession, lost his land and the life of his wife, and had been forced to send his children on a harrowing journey through the battle zones of Mississippi with only a slave and a geriatric preacher to protect them. The saga resonated through generations of white Cottinghams and blacks descended from their slaves.

After Moses enlisted in January 1862, his pregnant wife, Nancy Katherine, grew ill and then died during childbirth. Moses returned home from the front to bury Nancy and make arrangements for their six surviving children. Elisha Cottingham sent a Baptist minister to Louisiana to bring his grandchildren back to Alabama for the duration of the war. With the southern railroad system already in shambles and most trains impressed into military service, the preacher and one of Moses' two slaves, Joe, set out in an ox-drawn wagon. "That was the hardest trial I had ever had to go through, to leave my little children to be carried off to Alabama," Moses recounted to descendants years later.[47]

For three weeks, the odd expedition inched across the war-disrupted South. The preacher and the old African American, a scramble of children foraging for turnips and cornmeal, the oldest daughter, Cirrenia, still a child herself, feeding two-month-old Johnny, the infant whose birth had killed their mother, with a gruel of baked sweet potatoes. In November 1862, the ragged band arrived at Elisha Cottingham's farm on the Cahaba River. The fate of Moses, still at war, was unknown. "We never knew whether he was dead or alive till one day, after the war was over, we saw him coming," Cirrenia later wrote. Moses started over, resettling on nearby land along Copperas Creek, marrying the daughter of another former slaveholding family and begetting another seven children.

The losses suffered by Moses and the slow rescue of his family in the heat of war could have been a parable for how white southerners perceived the destruction of the South they had known. Physical and financial devastation, death and grief, followed by a transforming struggle to survive and rebuild. But the story also underscored the terrifying vulnerability whites like the Cottinghams discovered in being forced to place the fate and future of Moses' family in the hands of a descendant of Africa. After the war, as the Cottingham slaves brazenly asserted their independence, the journey of Joe and the children across the South came to symbolize a reliance on blacks that southern whites could never again allow. Regardless of their intertwined pasts, the rehabilitation of the South by whites would not just purposefully exclude blacks. As time passed and opportunity permitted, former slaves would be compelled to perform the rebuilding of the South as well— in a system of labor hardly distinguishable in its brutality and coercion from the old slavery that preceded it.

If one looked out from Elisha's porch in December 1868, across the crop rows and down past the creek, the only green in a nearly colorless winter landscape was in the short scruffy needles of twisted cedars he had planted long ago, along the wagon drive from the road to the house. The slave cabins, nearly two dozen of them, were mostly empty now. Even Scipio, the old man slave who had worked Elisha's farm nearly as long as the white master himself, was gone down the road. Already, weather and uselessness were doing the shacks in.

Crisp brown leaves heaped at the feet of a line of high pines and bare hickories that framed the boundaries of the main field between the river and the house. The walls of yellow limestone rising up abruptly from the eastern bank of the Cahaba looked pale and gray.

The big field, long devoid of its hardwood forest, was striped with lifeless rows of cotton stalks and corn husks standing against the low, sharp-angled rays of winter sun. In every direction, thousands of bedraggled slips of lint still clung to broken cotton bolls—wisps of that portion of the harvest that time and weather and, in Elisha's mind, the obstinancy of "his Negroes" had conspired to leave behind. All winter long they would hang there, limp and wet, layering the dead fields with a hazy whisper of white and goading Elisha Cottingham in their waste.

How differently lay the land for Henry Cottinham and Mary Bishop. They had been reared on farms within a night's walk of the plain country church where now they would marry, and the hills and fields and forests fanning out from the Cahaba eastward along Six Mile Road had been the width and range of life to these two slaves. Contrasted against that circumscribed existence, the extraordinary events in the aftermath of emancipation—no matter the deprivation or arduousness—must have been bathed in a glow of wonder and astonishment.

It was slaves who had created the Cottingham plantation and civilized the Cahaba valley and all of rugged central Alabama. Bibb County was a place where there were no flat places. A freshly cleared tract of forest ground displayed a roiling surface of earth, a scene more like swells pitching in a rolling sea than fields beckoning the plow. It was the first generation of slaves, like Scipio, who hacked and burned the woods, sawing down the great virgin forests, digging out and dragging away the stumps and stones left behind, breaking by plow for the first time the rich, root-infested soil, smoothing and shaping the land for seed. For the generations of slaves that followed, it was the traces of a mule-drawn plow that demarked the boundaries of hour upon hour spent restraining the iron blade from plunging down hillsides or struggling to drive it up the impossible inclines that followed.

As well as Scipio and the black families that surrounded him had come to know the shape and contours of the Cottingham farm, never, until well into the years of war, had they even imagined the possibility that they could someday own the land, grow their own harvests, perhaps even control the government. Now, all those things, or some luminous variant of them, seemed not just possible but perhaps inevitable.

Whatever bitterness Elisha Cottingham carried on the day of Henry and Mary's wedding must have been more than surpassed by the joy of the plantation's oldest former slave, Scipio, the grandfather of Henry. Almost seventy years old yet as robust as a man a third his age, Scip, as he was called, had witnessed near unearthly transformations of the world as he knew it. He had been born in Africa, then wrenched as a child into the frontier of an America only faintly removed from its eighteenth-century colonial origins. Through decades spent clearing forest and planting virgin fields, he watched as the unclaimed Indian land on which he found himself evolved into a yet even more foreign place. In the early years of the Cottingham farm, Cherokee and Creek Indians still controlled the western bank of the Cahaba's sister stream, the Coosa River. Choctaw territory extended to within fifty miles of the plantation.[48] Steadily, as the years passed, the natives of Alabama receded, and the frontier outposts swelled into settlements and then little, aspiration-filled towns. As the Civil War years approached, the Cottingham plantation fell finally into a steady rhythm of stability and cotton-driven prosperity.

Whether the child who came to be a Cottingham slave called Scipio knew the specific place of his origins, who his parents were, what African people they were a part of, how they came to be compelled across the Atlantic and into slavery—what his native name had been—all was lost.

The erasure of his history was completed by the moniker placed on him by white captors. Scipio was a classic slave name, one of a catalogue of cynical, almost sneering, designations rooted in the white South's popular fetish for the mythology of the classic cultures. It came from the name of a second-century general who governed Rome as Scipio Africanus. For the Roman Scipio, this was a tribute to his victory over Hannibal in the year 201, extending Roman control over Carthage and all of northern Africa. His reign had also seen the brutal suppression of the first great Roman slave revolt, in which on one occasion more than twenty thousand rebelling slaves were crucified. The context of such a name might have been lost on an African slave barred from learning Western history, but to educated whites the mocking irony would have been obvious.[49]

Scipio at least knew that he had been born in Africa, unlike nearly every other slave that entered the Cottingham farm, and that he believed the year of his birth was 1802. Perhaps he came directly to Cottingham from an Atlantic slave ship. Possibly he was first enslaved in Virginia or North Carolina, and then resold to the Deep South in the great domestic slave trading boom of the early nineteenth century. Shipping manifests at the port of New Orleans contain an entry for a teenage slave boy named Scipio arriving from a plantation in Virginia in 1821. Whatever his origins, Scip would hold defiantly until the end of his life to his identity as an Africa-born black man.[50]

Even bound into the agony of a quotidian life of forced labor, Scip must have conversely thrilled to the rise of the bountiful tribe of men and women who sprang from his Atlantic passage. The white people who brought him here had purchased other slaves, particularly in his boyhood, and housed them in the quarter of log-and-mud cabins down the hill from Elisha's house. But since Scip had grown to manhood, it was he who had sired slave after slave. First came George in 1825 (who would become the father of Henry) and Jeff in 1828. Then, in 1830, arrived Green, whose likely namesake, born more than fifty years later, would be delivered to Slope No. 12 mine in 1908.

They were all sturdy boys, and as much as any man might expect in a hard life. But in the final years before the Civil War, Scip surprised any of the other freed slaves who might have thought old age was setting upon him. He took up with Charity, a teenage girl almost forty years his junior. Whether the union was coerced or by choice, it was consummated in slavery and continued in a sweet freedom. Charity would stay with Scip until the end of his long life, deep into the years of emancipation, and for nearly twenty years bear to him sons and daughters with the regularity of cotton bolls and swollen spring streams.

Years before emancipation, Scip had seen the first signs of the epochal transformation about to infuse his world. Exotic new enterprises began to appear in the former frontier of Bibb County. On creeks surrounding the Cottingham farm, small forges were built in the 1830s, early precursors to the massive steel and iron industry that would come to dominate Alabama by the end of the century. In 1850, at a location a few miles from the Cottinghams', a massive boiler-driven sawmill began operation, pumping from the still virgin forests a fantastic stream of sawn planks and timbers. More ominously, Bibb Steam Mill Company also introduced to the county the ruthless form of industrial slavery that would become so important as the Civil War loomed.

The mill acquired twenty-seven male African Americans, nearly all strapping young men, and kept them packed into just six small barracks on its property. The Cottingham slave cabins would have seemed luxurious in contrast.[51]

The founders of Bibb Steam, entrepreneurs named William S. Philips, John W. Lopsky, Archibald P. McCurdy, and Virgil H. Gardner, invested a total of $24,000 to purchase 1,160 acres of timbered land and erect a steam-powered sawmill to cut lumber and grind corn and flour.[52] In addition to the two dozen slaves, Bibb Steam most likely leased a larger number of slaves from nearby farms during its busiest periods of work.

The significance of those evolutions wouldn't have been lost on a slave such as Scipio. By the end of the 1850s, a vigorous practice of slave leasing was already a fixture of southern life. Farm production was by its nature an inefficient cycle of labor, with intense periods of work in the early spring planting season and then idleness during the months of "laid-by" time in the summer, and then another great burst of harvest activity in the fall and early winter, followed finally by more months of frigid inactivity. Slave owners were keen to maximize the return on their most valuable assets, and as new opportunities for renting out the labor of their slaves arose, the most clever of slave masters quickly responded.

Given all that had changed in Bibb County in the years leading up to the southern rebellion, it would have been no surprise to the old slave that he found himself during the war in the service of the Confederacy, making iron for cannons and rebel ships in the ironworks at Brierfield.

Perhaps it was a comfort to Scip that joining him at Brierfield was the pastor who had been for so long a part of life at the Cottingham plantation. After thirty years of itinerancy among scattered churches, Rev. Starr was posted in 1864 to the Bibb Iron Works, a gesture on the part of the Methodist circuit to allow the old preacher to finish out his days at a congregation close to the home he cherished on Cottingham Loop.

Starr was the archetypal backwoods Methodist. He had completed hardly any formal schooling. Indeed, Starr was so profoundly uneducated that when as a man barely twenty years old he first began to preach at little churches not far from his south Georgia birthplace, even his friends doubted privately that he could ever carry off a career as a professional minister. But Methodism was a young and evangelical sect in the 1830s. The rough Alabama countryside, and especially the masses of still heretical slaves who made up much of its population, was a major target for missionary work.

The life of a Methodist circuit rider, traveling in a grinding, repetitive loop from one settlement chapel to another, was an entrepreneurial task of establishing churches and converting the unwashed. A vigorous iconoclast such as Starr could overcome academic ignorance with a fundamentalist fervor for the Bible and a resounding voice from the pulpit. Starr had done that, winning postings at a string of small Methodist congregations across Georgia and then Alabama.[53]

Through the years, he had been formally assigned to nearly twenty different congregations in the circuits orbiting the Bibb County seat of Centreville. Along with each of those churches had come responsibility for still more gatherings of the faithful who worshipped in the homes of scattered landowners or in remote rustic settlement chapels. That duty had delivered Starr to the home of Elisha Cottingham, and eventually the preacher bought a small piece of Cottingham land to which he hoped someday to retire.

The people of Riverbend, free whites and black slaves, had met for services on Elisha's plantation for so long that in minutes of the meetings of the Methodist circuit, the congregation was known simply as "Cottingham's." After nearly twenty years, its members raised a spare one-room church in the 1840s on the adjacent land of Elisha's brother, John Cottingham. Built on immense timber joists, resting on pillars of limestone rock, it would stand against the wind and shifting times for nearly a century and a half. The builders dubbed it Wesley Chapel.[54]

Starr preached there many times, and as age and dropsy slowed his step, it was to this corner of Bibb County that he was drawn to rest. One of the preacher's sons, Lucius E. Starr, grown and ready to raise a family of his own, became a physician and made a name for himself in the county seat. The Cottinghams were good to Rev. Starr and his wife, Hannah, and after a lifetime of near constant motion it must have been a relief to him in 1860 to buy land right beside the family that had treated them so well.[55] The Starr home was within walking distance of the spare country chapel and the Cottingham family cemetery, where Starr already hoped to be buried. They called the farmhouse the "preacher's sanctum."

By the final months of the war, the old firebrand knew well life's most bitter stings. His namesake son, also a Methodist minister, died in an epidemic of yellow fever a few years before secession. One of his youngest, Wilbur Fisk, another likely playmate of the slave Henry and Elisha's grandson Oliver, became a sergeant in the Alabama 29th Infantry before seeing his unit decimated in savage fighting across north Georgia. He died soon after during the long defense of Atlanta in 1864.

As an unschooled man, Starr, in his day, had a particular appeal for the raw country folk that predominated the rutted back roads of the South. That translated as well into an affinity for slaves. As a young pastor on the circuits of Georgia, Starr was praised for his ministrations to the souls of

black folks as he galloped among the plantations and camp meetings of
south Alabama.[56] So it was fitting that the final church appointment of his
long career, where he would wait out the end of the war, was to the ironworks at Brierfield where slavery was being practiced in its most raw and
brutalizing form. There, Scip and the preacher Starr toiled at their respec-
tive tasks, until General Wilson's army descended.

A few months after the surrender of the Confederacy, the U.S. government
sold the wrecked ironworks at Brierfield to the man who during the war had
been responsible for arming the entire southern military, Josiah Gorgas, the
architect of the slave-driven Alabama wartime industrial complex. Gorgas, a
Pennsylvania native who married the daughter of a former Alabama governor, had become a committed Confederate, rising to the rank of general by
war's end. After the surrender, he worked tirelessly to return the furnaces to
full use and profitability.

But the ravaged state of Alabama that surrounded him made that plan
nearly impossible. The cost of paying market rate wages to black men such
as Scip who had worked as slaves during the war totaled a bankrupting $200
per day. Those black laborers Gorgas could pay and keep on hand were
repeatedly harassed by marauding bands of Ku Klux Klan members. Gorgas, like Elisha Cottingham and so many other whites bewildered by both
the ramifications of black emancipation and the continuing venality of
renegade whites, was disconsolate. The South they first dreamed of making
an independent republic grounded in slavery—and then dreamed of rebuilding as a rival to the North—appeared irretrievably broken. "What an
end to our great hopes!" he wrote in his diary. "Is it possible that we were
wrong?"[57]

Scip Cottinham, having learned the skills of a foundry worker during
the war, must in his own way also have been baffled by the extraordinary
turn of events that left him a free man in the twilight of his life.

Neither he nor Henry would likely have known what to say to so
strange and moot a white man's question as the one posed by Gorgas to his
diary. But they would have had no doubt as to whether Gorgas and the Cottingham brothers, and the hundreds of thousands of other southern men
who had taken up arms during the war, had been wrong.

Before Union troops arrived in Bibb County, the night hours had permitted Henry his one limited taste of freedom within the confines of chattel life. It was after sundown that the slaves of Riverbend and other farms could slip quietly through the forests to see and court one another.

Now freedom had turned darkness into light. Henry, young and strong at the very moment of the rebirth of his people, no longer had to wait for the passage of the sun into the horizon. His feet could carry him flying down the dusty track to the Bishop place, in plain daylight for all to see, past old Elisha's cabins, past the store at Six Mile, past the broken iron furnace at Brierfield, to Mary.

For Henry and Mary, freedom was a tangible thing, and January was a fine time for a wedding. Both raised on the banks of the Cahaba, they were as attuned to the seasonal swells of the river and the deep soil on its edges as the great stretches of spidery white lilies that crowded its shoals each spring and retreated into its depths every winter.

Picking last fall's crop of cotton in the valley had gone on until nearly Christmas. In another two months, it would be time to begin knocking down the brittle cotton stalks left from last year, harnessing the mules and plows, and breaking the crusted soil for a new crop. Planting season came hard on the heels of that, and before long it would be summer, when mule hooves and plow blades and bare black feet, slavery or no slavery, would march between the furrows, without rest, for nearly every hour of every day. So that January, bitter as was its wind, arrived for them sweet and restful.

Like Henry and Mary, all of Alabama, and the South—indeed at one level all of the United States—was setting up housekeeping in the winter of 1868. Redefined by war, grief, deprivation, death, and emancipation, America was faced with the challenge of repairing and reordering a collective household.

Some of the old slaves said they too weren't sure what "freedom" really was. Henry likely couldn't explain it either, but he had to know. This wedding day was emancipation. It was the license from the courthouse and big leather-bound book that listed his marriage right beside those of the children of the old master. It was his name on the piece of paper, "Henry Cottinham." No more was he one of the "Cottingham niggers."

To Henry Cottinham and Mary Bishop there could be no better time to marry. They marched the few steps to the house of Rev. Starr, down to the Cottingham chapel around the curve, and took their vows as free citizens.[58] Henry Cottinham was a man, with a name, spelled just the way he had always said it. Freedom was an open field, a strong wife, and time to make his mark. Mary's "increase," like the product of all their labor, would be theirs—not Elisha Cottingham's. Henry would plant his seed, in soil he knew and in Mary his wife. In a few years, they would have a son named Green. Henry would raise up the offspring of the land and of his blood.

Surely, that was freedom.

# II

# AN INDUSTRIAL SLAVERY

*"Niggers is cheap."*

Across the South, white southerners were baffled. What to do with freed slaves like Henry Cottinham and his grandfather Scip? They could not be driven away. Without former slaves—and their steady expertise and cooperation in the fields—the white South was crippled. But this new manifestation of dark-skinned men expected to choose when, where, and how long they would work. Those who could not find employ wandered town to town, presumptuously asking for food, favors, and jobs.

To get from place to place, or to reach locations where work had been advertised, they piled onto the empty freight cars of what few trains still ran. They formed up at night around campfires in the shadows of train depots and cotton warehouses on the fringes of towns. In the face of hostile whites—the Ku Klux Klan and members of other suddenly flourishing secret white societies—they brandished guns and were willing to use them. Beyond gall to their former masters, these meandering swarms of illiterate men also expected to be allowed to vote.

The breadth of white venom toward freed slaves—and the decades of venality that followed it—belied the wide spectrum of perspectives on slavery shared by white southerners before the war. From the earliest years of the North American colonies, whites struggled to resolve vastly differing views even among slaveholders of the place and position of blacks in the new society.

Colonial America began as a place uncertain of the abject subjugation of native Indian populations and thousands of African slaves pouring into the Western Hemisphere. Many were perplexed by the concept of categorizing humans by race and skin color, versus the long-standing European tradition of identification rooted in nationality and place of origin. In the first decades of colonization in the 1600s, "slave" and "Negro" were not synonymous in the American colonies. Slaves were as likely to be Indians as Africans. Some early owners of black slaves were themselves black. Free Africans in Virginia were permitted to vote well into the 1700s. Many indentured white servants were coerced into extending their labor contracts until death—effectively making them light-skinned slaves.

Dispelling that confusion and ensuring the dominant position of whites in general—and Englishmen in particular—colonial legislatures, especially in Virginia, South Carolina, and, later, Georgia, began in the 1650s to systematically define residents by color and lineage. The intentions were twofold: to create the legal structure necessary for building an economy with cheap slave labor as its foundation, and secondly, to reconcile bondage with America's revolutionary ideals of intrinsic human rights. Blacks could be excluded from the Enlightenment concepts that every man was granted by God individual freedom and a right to the pursuit of happiness because colonial laws codified a less-than-fully-human status of any person carrying even a trace of black or Indian blood. Instead of embracing the concept that regardless of color "All men are created equal," with no king or prince born to higher status than any other, colonial leaders extended a version of "royal" status to all whites.

Still, vast swaths of the region, including the rock-strewn Appalachians stretching from northern Alabama, across Georgia, and up through the Carolinas and Virginia, contained virtually no slaves at all. Indeed, in some of those places, companies of men had gathered after secession, armed themselves, and marched north to join with the Union armies moving upon the South.

In other places, men who owned hundreds or thousands of slaves nonetheless wrestled without resolution with the subtle moralities of human bondage and the trafficking of men. Robert Wickliffe, owner of more slaves than any other person in Kentucky and likely anyone in the United States, argued passionately against the exportation of slaves from the coastal regions of the United States to the comparative horrors of Deep South plantations in Georgia and Mississippi. The 1860 census counted among four million blacks in the South more than 250,000 free African Americans in the slave states, more than fifty thousand of them in Virginia. In Louisiana, a handful of black freedmen owned dozens of slaves. In the intricately hued tapestry of New Orleans, more than three thousand free blacks owned slaves themselves.[1]

But in what came to be known as the Black Belt—a long curve of mostly alluvial cotton farmland stretching across the fertile flatlands ranging from South Carolina through the lower reaches of Georgia and Alabama, and then extending across Mississippi and Louisiana—antebellum society had been built wholly on true chattel slavery. Millions of slaves came to live there under the ruthless control of a minority of whites. Here, the moral rationalization of slavery—and the view of slaves as the essential proof of white men's royal status—became as fundamental to whites' perception of America as the concept of liberty itself. A century later, this was the paradox of the post–Civil War South—recognition of freed slaves as full humans appeared to most white southerners not as an extension of liberty but as a violation of it, and as a challenge to the legitimacy of their definition of what it was to be white.

The destruction of slavery in the Civil War didn't settle this contradiction. Instead, it made more transparent the fundamental question of whether blacks and whites could ever cohabit peacefully—of whether American whites in any region could recognize African Americans as humans. Faced with the mandated equality of whites and blacks, the range of southern perspectives on race distilled to narrow potency. Even among those who had been troubled by—or apathetic toward—slavery before the war, there was scant sympathy for the concept of full equality. By overwhelming majorities, whites adopted an assessment of the black man parallel to that in the great crescent of cotton country.

The Civil War settled definitively the question of the South's continued existence as a part of the United States, but in 1865 there was no strategy for cleansing the South of the economic and intellectual addiction to slavery. The resistance to what should have been the obvious consequences of losing the Civil War—full emancipation of the slaves and shared political control between blacks and whites—was so virulent and effective that the tangible outcome of the military struggle between the North and the South remained uncertain even twenty-five years after the issuance of President Abraham Lincoln's Emancipation Proclamation. The role of the African American in American society would not be clear for another one hundred years.

In the first decades of that span, the intensity of southern whites' need to reestablish hegemony over blacks rivaled the most visceral patriotism of the wartime Confederacy. White southerners initiated an extraordinary campaign of defiance and subversion against the new biracial social order imposed on the South and mandated by the Thirteenth Amendment to the U.S. Constitution, which abolished slavery. They organized themselves into vigilante gangs and militias, undermined free elections across the region, intimidated Union agents, terrorized black leaders, and waged an extremely effective propaganda campaign to place blame for the anarchic behavior of whites upon freed slaves. As the United States would learn many times in the ensuing 150 years, a military victor's intention to impose a new moral and political code on a conquered society was much easier to wish for than to attain.

Bibb County, home of the Cottinghams, was edged on the south by that great fertile prairie of plantation country where by the 1850s slaves accounted for the majority of most local populations. Bibb whites harbored no equivocation about the proper status of African Americans in their midst. There had been no agonized sentiment of doubt in this section of Alabama regarding the morality of slaveholding. No abolitionist voices arose here. In the 1840s, when the northern and southern branches of the Methodist Church divided over the issue of slavery, its Bibb County congregations—certainly including Cottingham Chapel—emphatically went the way of the southern church.[2]

There were no free blacks there before the war. The explosion in slave numbers in the adjoining counties—where tens of thousands of black men and women populated plantations strung along the Tennessee, Alabama, and Tombigbee rivers—offered a huge inventory of readily available African Americans and sustained a thriving local traffic in slaves.[3]

In Montgomery, the state capital seventy miles from the Bibb County seat, a huge wholesale market in slaves preoccupied the commercial life of the bustling city. Richard Habersham, a Georgian traveling through the town in 1836, described a sprawling slave market with scores of black men and women and crowds of white men closely inspecting them. "I came suddenly upon ranges of well dressed Negro men and women seated upon benches. There may have been 80 or 100 all in different parcels. . . . With each group were seated two or three sharp, hard featured white men. This was the slave market and the Negroes were dressed out for show. There they sit all day and every day until they are sold, each parcel rising and standing in rank as a purchaser approaches. Although born in a slave country and a slave holder myself and an advocate of slavery, yet this sight was entirely novel and shocked my feelings."[4] Twenty-five years later, three months after the opening of the Civil War, a correspondent for the *Times* of London watched a twenty-five-year-old black man sold for less than $1,000 during a day of slow bidding at the same market. "I tried in vain to make myself familiar with the fact that I could for the sum of $975 become as absolutely the owner of that mass of blood, bones, sinew, flesh, and brains as of the horse which stood by my side," wrote W. H. Russell. "It was painful to see decent-looking men in European garb engaged in the work before me. . . . The negro was sold to one of the bystanders and walked off with his bundle God knows where. 'Niggers is cheap,' was the only remark."[5]

Elisha Cottingham might have acquired Scipio at the Montgomery market, or from one of the speculative traders who moved between the big urban slave markets at Montgomery and Mobile, Alabama. They traveled the crude roads of the backcountry, acquiring lots of slaves and then pushing "droves" of them shackled together from town to town. They pitched their tents in crossroads settlements to showcase their wares, and paraded slaves before landowners in need of labor.

During the 1850s, a man named J. M. Brown styled himself as "not a planter but a Negro raiser," growing no cotton on his Bibb County plantation but breeding slaves on his farm specifically for sale on the open market.[6] On the courthouse steps, Bibb County sheriffs routinely held slave auctions to pay off the unpaid taxes of local landowners. County officials authorized holding the sales on either side of the Cahaba River for the convenience of potential buyers in each section of the county.

The South's highly evolved system of seizing, breeding, wholesaling, and retailing slaves was invaluable in the final years before the Civil War, as slavery proved in industrial settings to be more flexible and dynamic than even most slave owners could have otherwise believed.

Skilled slaves such as Scipio, churning out iron, cannons, gun metal, rifled artillery, battle ships, and munitions at Selma, Shelby Iron Works, and the Brierfield foundry, were only a sample of how thousands of slaves had migrated into industrial settings just before and during the war. The extraordinary value of organizing a gang of slave men to quickly accomplish an arduous manual task—such as enlarging a mine and extracting its contents, or constructing railroads through the most inhospitable frontier regions—became obvious during the manpower shortages of wartime.

Critical to the success of this form of slavery was dispensing with any pretense of the mythology of the paternalistic agrarian slave owner. Labor here was more akin to a source of fuel than an extension of a slave owner's familial circle. Even on the harshest of family-operated antebellum farms, slave masters could not help but be at least marginally moved by the births, loves, and human affections that close contact with slave families inevitably manifested.

But in the setting of industrial slavery—where only strong young males and a tiny number of female "washerwomen" and cooks were acquired, and no semblance of family interaction was possible—slaves were assets to be expended like mules and equipment. By the early 1860s, such slavery was commonplace in the areas of the most intensive commercial farming in Mississippi and parts of Alabama.

It was a model particularly well suited to mining and first aggressively exploited in high-intensity cotton production, in which individual skill was not necessarily more important than brute strength. In those settings, black labor was something to be consumed, with a clear comprehension of return on investment. Food, housing, and physical care were bottom-line accounting considerations in a formula of profit and loss, weighed primarily in terms of their effect on chattel slave productivity rather than plantation harmony.

On the enormous cotton plantations unfolding in the antebellum years across the malarial wasteland of the Mississippi Delta, absentee owners routinely left overseers in charge of small armies of slaves. In an economic formula in which there was no pretense of paternalistic protection for slaves, the overseers drove them mercilessly.

Frederick Law Olmsted, traveling through the South prior to the Civil War, wrote of the massive plantations of Alabama and Mississippi as places where black men and women "work harder and more unremittingly" than the rest of slave country. "As property, Negro life and Negro vigor were generally much less encouraged than I had always before imagined them to be."[7]

Another observer of Mississippi farms said that on the new plantations "everything has to bend, give way to large crops of cotton, land has to be cultivated wet or dry, Negroes to work hot or cold."[8] Under these circumstances, slave owners came to accept that black laborers would also die quickly.[9] "The Negroes die off every few years, though it is said that in time each hand also makes enough to buy two more in his place," wrote planter James H. Ruffin in 1833.[10]

An English traveler visiting the great plantations in the final years of slavery described African Americans who "from the moment they are able to go afield in the picking season till they drop worn out in the grave in incessant labor, in all sorts of weather, at all seasons of the year without any change or relaxation than is furnished by sickness, without the smallest hope of any improvement either in their condition, in their food, or in their clothing indebted solely to the forbearance and good temper of the overseer for exemption from terrible physical suffering."[11]

Even large-scale slave owners who directed their business managers to provide reasonable care for slaves nonetheless advocated harsh measures to maintain the highest level of production. "They must be flogged as seldom as possible yet always when necessary," wrote one.[12]

An overseer's goal, a Delta planter said, was "to get as much work out of them as they can possibly perform. His skill consists in knowing exactly how hard they may be driven without incapacitating them for future exertion. The larger the plantation, the less chance there is, of course, of the owner's softening the rigor of the overseer, or the sternness of discipline by personal interference."[13]

Scip saw those changes coming. In the 1830s, a water-driven cotton mill was constructed on a creek seven miles north of the county seat, not far from the Cottingham plantation.[14] Employing several dozen white laborers, the mill ginned cotton and spun it into thread and rope. Of far more portent for Scip's future, and that of his descendants, had been a chance discovery in the 1820s by a white settler named Jonathan Newton Smith. On a hunting trip near the Cahaba, Smith was surprised when large stones pulled from a creek to encircle a campfire ignited. Smith had tripped across the massive deposits of coal abounding in Alabama, and over the next fifty years would be a pioneering exploiter of the serendipitous proximity of immense brown iron ore deposits scattered across the ridges and, beneath the surface, the perfect fuel for blasting the ore into iron and steel.[15] It was a combination that would transform life in Alabama, reshaping Scip's last years of slavery and radically altering the lives of millions of individuals over the next century.

Smith ambitiously assembled thousands of acres of land containing mineral deposits, and by 1840, he and others had opened small iron forges on all sides of the Cottingham farm. One was built on Six Mile Creek, a few miles down the mail road toward the nearest settlement. Another was across the Cahaba River. A third was constructed on a tributary of the big river just north of the plantation.[16] These were crude mechanical enterprises, belching great columns of foul smoke and rivers of effluent. But they were marvels of the frontier in which they suddenly appeared. A giant water-powered wheel first crushed the iron ore, which was fed into a stone furnace and heated into a huge red molten mass. The "hammer man," working in nearly unbearable heat and using a red-hot bar of metal as his tool, then maneuvered the molten iron onto an anvil where a five-hundred-pound hammer, also powered by the waterwheel, pounded it into bars. Primitive as was the mechanism, the rough-edged masses of iron were the vital raw material for blacksmiths in every town and on every large farm to craft into the plows, horseshoes, and implements that were the civilizing tools of the Alabama frontier.[17]

In addition to Smith, two other white men living near the Cottingham farm, Jonathan Ware and his son Horace, were aggressively expanding the infant industry.[18] To Smith's geological observations, Horace Ware, a native of Lynn, Massachusetts, brought a keen instinct for the market among southern cotton planters for locally forged iron. He had learned the iron trade from his father, and bought land near the Cahaba coalfields and on a rich vein of iron ore in 1841. He put his first furnace into blast in 1846.[19]

Slaves were the primary workers at the earliest recorded coal mines in Alabama in the 1830s. Moses Stroup, the "father" of the iron and steel industry in Alabama, arrived in the state in 1848, acquired land on Red Mountain just south of present-day Birmingham, and erected his first furnaces. By the early 1850s, he was constructing a much larger group of furnaces in Tuscaloosa County, entirely with slave labor.[20]

Indeed, nearly all of the early industrial locations of the South were constructed by such slaves, thousands of whom became skilled masons, miners, blacksmiths, pattern makers, and furnace workers. Slaves performed the overwhelming majority of the raw labor of such operations, working as fillers, who shoveled iron ore, limestone, and coal into the furnaces in carefully monitored sequence; guttermen, who drew off the molten iron as it gathered; tree cutters, who felled millions of trees, and teamsters to drive wagons of ore and coal from the mines and finished iron to railroad heads.[21] Alabama's first recorded industrial fatality was a slave named Vann, killed in the early 1840s by falling rock in an iron ore pit near Alabama's earliest known forge.[22]

Southern railroads also became voracious acquirers of slaves, purchasing them by the hundreds and leasing them from others for as much as $20 per month in the 1850s.[23] By the beginning of the Civil War, railroads owned an estimated twenty thousand slaves.[24]

All of the early iron masters of the region relied on slaves for the grueling menial work of clearing their property, constructing hand-hewn stone and brick furnaces and forges, and gathering the ore and coal exposed on outcrops or near the surface.[25] As the forges went into production, slaves were trained to perform the arduous tasks of the blast furnace. Quickly, the Wares and other budding industrialists began a traffic in the specialized category of slaves trained in the skills of making iron.

During the late 1830s, the Wares took on as an apprentice from a businessman in Georgia a slave named Joe. Five years later, Jonathan Smith purchased the slave at auction for $3,000, and set him to work as the hammer man in one of his Bibb County forges.[26] By the late 1850s, the Wares, having shifted their iron-making operations to adjoining Shelby County, operated the largest metal works in the Deep South, largely with skilled slaves. Horace Ware's son, John E. Ware, would later reminisce about the most valued slaves at the forge. He recalled that "Berry, Charles, Anderson, Clark and Obediah" held key positions.[27]

The Hale & Murdock Furnace near Vernon, Alabama, was built in 1859 and then dramatically expanded to meet war needs in 1862 by a force of 150 men, most of whom were slaves.[28] In December 1862, a Montgomery businessman began work on an iron ore mine and furnace north of the Cane Creek forge using a force of two hundred slaves moved from Tennessee as federal forces advanced from the North.[29] Shortly after the operation was fully under way, Union general Wilson's raiders wrecked it.

In 1860, a year before the Civil War erupted, Jonathan Smith launched his most ambitious effort ever, the enormous ironworks at Brierfield, less than nine miles from the Cottingham farm. A partner of Smith's, Col. C. C. Huckabee, was a planter and longtime major slaveholder. His forced workers were a key element of his investment in the enterprise, and in its expansion during the war. Enormous numbers of men were needed to provide the quantities of wood, ore, and limestone required by a nineteenth-century furnace. "I set all my niggers to work in the woods," Huckabee later recalled, "and for many a day after that, the axes sounded like thunder in the pines."[30]

At the Wares' Shelby Iron Works, slaves were the salvation of the operation's ability to continue supplying thousands of tons of iron to the Confederacy. Perhaps owing to his New England origins, Ware had never seriously considered extensive use of black labor in the first fifteen years of business. In 1859, however, he inquired about the industrial use of slaves in a letter to Joseph R. Anderson, manager of the Tredegar Works and perhaps the most famous southern industrialist of the era. Anderson responded enthusiastically and offered to sell Ware some of Tredegar's well-trained factory slaves.[31]

Ware didn't buy any of the African Americans available from Virginia, but he did bring in as partners several of Alabama's most prominent proponents of industrialism.[32] They in turn began to acquire black laborers aggressively. Soon, Shelby Works, with dozens of African American forced laborers on its balance sheet, was the largest owner of slaves in the county.

Nearby, the Alabama Coal Mining Co. owned another dozen slaves, all men aged twenty-six to sixty.[33]

In 1862, the Shelby Works contracted with the Confederate government to produce the vast quantity of twelve thousand tons of iron a year for the war effort, effectively placing the operation under the control of the Confederate chief of ordnance in Richmond, Col. Josiah Gorgas, and his iron agent at the rebel arsenal and munitions factory in Selma, Col. Colin J. McRae. For the course of the war, the Shelby Works attempted to keep its furnaces in near constant blast—producing huge quantities of iron to be shipped to gun barrel makers in Mississippi and Georgia,[34] and to the cannon and plate armor manufacturers at Selma. A second furnace was added in 1863 to boost the war effort.[35]

With most of the white male population already mustered or conscripted into fighting units, the company's only option for fulfilling its obligations was to rely almost entirely on slaves. Borrowing from the practices of railroads and the few other industrial systems already familiar to businessmen of the South, the Shelby Works quickly came to rely on "leased" slave labor that would prove both extraordinarily effective and resilient.

To procure the slaves, the Shelby Works hired a labor agent named John M. Tillman to lease African Americans from plantation owners in central Alabama, northeastern Mississippi, and eastern Georgia. Tillman's duties also included acquiring as many mules as possible, and the feed corn to feed both the four-legged and two-legged creatures he collected.[36]

Leased slave laborers typically cost $120 a year near the beginning of the war, but their cost more than doubled by the crisis years of 1864 and 1865. Slaves with a particularly useful skill, such as carpentry or prior ironmaking experience, fetched $500 or more per year. The great majority were men aged twenty to forty-five, engaged in the back-breaking work of cutting timber in nearby forests and digging iron ore and limestone. They were supplemented by a much smaller number of women and their children who performed menial tasks such as cooking and cleaning. Soon, Ware was the master of between 350 and 400 slaves. His company remained hungry for more.[37]

Ware's slaves worked under the control of a white overseer, mostly in gangs of men assigned to specific tasks. Under terms of the contracts, owners received quarterly payments, and their slaves were provided with basic food, clothing, and shelter. If a slave escaped, it was the responsibility of the company to pay a fee for the slave's arrest and return to the ironworks. As an incentive to work hard and follow rules, slaves were permitted to earn small amounts of cash for themselves—typically less than $5 a month—by agreeing to perform extra tasks such as tending the furnace at night, cutting extra wood, or digging additional ore.[38]

The company overseer, called "boss" or "captain" by the slaves, was not empowered to severely discipline the leased slaves in his charge. Punishment remained the province of the owner. When slaves attempted to flee, stole, or refused the orders of the overseer, Shelby Works wrote the owner for instructions on how to handle his property. The punishments meted out by plantation masters to the slaves who worked under their direct employ were often harsh in the extreme, even torturous by modern sensibilities. But few slave masters encouraged the forge operators to treat their valued stock with brutality, particularly when the efficiency of the slave had no bearing on his financial return to the owner. Slaves who at Christmas reported to their owners that the managers of the ironworks had abused them often were not made available to the company again. Moreover, slaves with wives still living back at the plantations from which they had come were allowed to return home periodically, sometimes several times a year.

Industrialists were embracing the same practices across the South. An advertisement placed by the Empire State Iron and Coal Mining Company of Trenton, Georgia, in the Huntsville, Alabama, *Confederate* in 1863 sought to "hire or buy, 100 able-bodied hands, to be employed at their works . . . 20 miles southwest of Chattanooga."[39]

In 1862, an Alabama engineer named John T. Milner and his business partner, Frank Gilmer, convinced the Confederate government to finance the construction of a blast furnace on Red Mountain in Jefferson County to produce iron for the war effort. The plant, constructed and operated primarily by slaves, marked the birth of the vast industrial complex that would surround the new city of Birmingham by the end of the century. By the time the Red Mountain furnace was in operation in 1863, Milner and Gilmer had also opened a complex of mines operated with slave labor near the town of Helena, Alabama.[40] Within a decade after the war, the Helena mines would be manned entirely by convict forced laborers and set an early standard for the depredations against ostensibly emancipated African Americans.

Everywhere in the South that could produce coal or iron during the war, southern industrialists were being pressured to increase production at existing mines and furnaces, or to seize and reopen idled business. In a · move that would hang ominously over the descendants of the Cottingham slaves, southern industrialists in 1861 took over a mining company near Tracy City, Tennessee, previously controlled by a syndicate of northern investors.

With the outbreak of war, the formerly New York–controlled mines of Tennessee Coal, Iron & Railroad Co. were placed in the hands of Confederate-sympathizing businessmen. Arthur S. Colyar, the southerner who took over management of the company in 1861, immediately placed forty slaves in the concern's Sewanee Mines. He was quickly pleased with their performance, telling a newspaper reporter: "In a few months they were doing good service and not one of the party failed in the effort to learn to dig coal."[41]

The business would become the largest commercial enterprise in the South, and a half century later the largest subsidiary of U.S. Steel, and the company that would acquire Scip's grandson Green Cottenham four decades later.

To the enterprising industrialists who would reshape the southern economy in the half century after the Civil War, the new concepts of industrialized black labor had taken firm hold. Long before the end of chattel slavery, Milner was in the vanguard of that new theory of industrial forced labor. In 1859, he wrote that black labor marshaled into the regimented productivity of factory settings would be the key to the economic development of Alabama and the South. Milner believed that white people "would always look upon and treat the negro as an inferior being." Nonetheless—indeed for that very reason—blacks would serve a highly useful purpose as the clever mules of an industrial age, "provided he has an *overseer—a Southern man*, who knows how to manage negroes."[42] Milner's intuition that the future of blacks in America rested on how whites chose to *manage* them, whether in slavery or out of it, would resonate through the next half century of national discourse about the proper role of the descendants of Africa in American life.

Milner was no mere theorist. He was a dogged executor of his vision. It was men like Milner who would seize the opportunity presented by convict leasing to reclaim slavery from the destruction of the Civil War. As Alabama began selling its black prisoners in large numbers in the 1870s, he scrambled to acquire all that were available—plunging them by the hundreds into a hellish coal operation called the Eureka mines, and later illegally selling hundreds of these new slaves in the 1880s, along with another coal mine, to the Georgia Pacific Railroad Co.

In every setting that Milner employed convict slaves in the late nineteenth century, he and his business associates subjected the workers to almost animalistic mistreatment—a revivification of the most atrocious aspects of antebellum bondage. Records of Milner's various mines and slave farms in southern Alabama owned by one of his business partners—a cousin to an investor in the Bibb Steam Mill—tell the stories of black women stripped naked and whipped, of hundreds of men starved, chained, and beaten, of workers perpetually lice-ridden and barely clothed.

Milner took center stage in Alabama's new industrialization, urging southerners to "go to work . . . eradicating the diseases that are destroying us." Part of that eradication would be to successfully re-regiment freed slaves. "I am clearly of the opinion, from my own observation, that negro labor can be made exceedingly profitable in rolling mills," Milner had written of steel production in 1859. "I have long since learned that negro slave labor is more reliable and cheaper for any business connected with the construction of a railroad than white."[43]

Milner and others had seen his theory of the black slave as an effective industrial forced worker vividly fulfilled during the war. The system emerging with the end of Reconstruction would mimic it repeatedly. African Americans driven by the right men, in the correct ways, could be the engines of far more complex enterprises than the old bourbon-soaked planters would ever have believed possible. Black laborers might not quite be men, the industrialists reasoned, but they recognized that African Americans were far more than apes. The renting of slaves, as much as anything, had taught them that masses of black laborers brought under temporary control of a commercial enterprise could be powerfully leveraged in commerce.

The attitudes among southern whites that a resubjugation of African Americans was an acceptable—even essential—element of solving the "Negro question" couldn't have been more explicit. The desire of white farmers to recapture their former slaves through new civil laws was transparent. In the immediate wake of emancipation, the Alabama legislature swiftly passed a measure under which the orphans of freed slaves, or the children of blacks deemed inadequate parents, were to be "apprenticed" to their former masters. The South Carolina planter Henry William Ravenel wrote in September 1865: "There must . . . be stringent laws to control the negroes, & require them to fulfill their contracts of labour on the farms."[44]

With the southern economy in ruins, state officials limited to the barest resources, and county governments with even fewer, the concept of reintroducing the forced labor of blacks as a means of funding government services was viewed by whites as an inherently practical method of eliminating the cost of building prisons and returning blacks to their appropriate position in society. Forcing convicts to work as part of punishment for an ostensible crime was clearly legal too; the Thirteenth Amendment to the Constitution, adopted in 1865 to formally abolish slavery, specifically permitted involuntary servitude as a punishment for "duly convicted" criminals.

Beginning in the late 1860s, and accelerating after the return of white political control in 1877, every southern state enacted an array of interlocking laws essentially intended to criminalize black life. Many such laws were struck down in court appeals or through federal interventions, but new statutes embracing the same strictures on black life quickly appeared to replace them. Few laws specifically enunciated their applicability only to blacks, but it was widely understood that these provisions would rarely if ever be enforced on whites. Every southern state except Arkansas and Tennessee had passed laws by the end of 1865 outlawing vagrancy and so vaguely defining it that virtually any freed slave not under the protection of a white man could be arrested for the crime. An 1865 Mississippi statute required African American workers to enter into labor contracts with white farmers by January 1 of every year or risk arrest. Four other states legislated that African Americans could not legally be hired for work without a discharge paper from their previous employer—effectively preventing them from leaving the plantation of the white man they worked for. In the 1880s, Alabama, North Carolina, and Florida enacted laws making it a criminal act for a black man to change employers without permission.

In nearly all cases, the potential penalty awaiting black men, and a small number of women, snared by those laws was the prospect of being sold into forced labor. Many states in the South and the North attempted to place their prisoners in private hands during the eighteenth and early nineteenth centuries. The state of Alabama was long predisposed to the idea, rather than taking on the cost of housing and feeding prisoners itself. It experimented with turning over convicts to private "wardens" during the 1840s and 1850s but was ultimately unsatisfied with the results. The state saved some expense but gathered no revenue. Moreover, the physical abuse that came to be almost synonymous with privatized incarceration always was eventually unacceptable in an era when virtually every convict was white. The punishment of slaves for misdeeds rested with their owners.

Hardly a year after the end of the war, in 1866, Alabama governor Robert M. Patton, in return for the total sum of $5, leased for six years his state's 374 state prisoners to a company calling itself "Smith and McMillen." The transaction was in fact a sham, as the partnership was actually controlled by the Alabama and Chattanooga Railroad. Governor Patton became president of the railroad three years later.[45] Such duplicity would be endemic to convict leasing. For the next eighty years, in every southern state, the questions of who controlled the fates of black prisoners, which few black men and women among armies of defendants had committed true crimes, and who was receiving the financial benefits of their re-enslavement would almost always never be answered.

Later in 1866, Texas leased 250 convicts to two railroads at the rate of $12.50 a month.[46] In May 1868, four months after Henry and Mary's wedding, the state of Georgia signed a lease under which the Georgia and Alabama Railroad acquired one hundred convicts, all of them black, for $2,500. Later that year, the state sold 134 prisoners to the Selma, Rome and Dalton Railroad and sent 109 others to the line being constructed between the towns of Macon and Brunswick, Georgia.

Arkansas began contracting out its state convicts in 1867, selling the rights to prisoners convicted of both state crimes and federal offenses.[47]

Mississippi turned over its 241 prisoners to the state's largest cotton planter, Edmund Richardson, in 1868. Three years later, the convicts were transferred to Nathan Bedford Forrest, the former Confederate general, who in civilian life already was a major planter and railroad developer. In 1866, he and five other former rebel officers had founded the Ku Klux Klan. Florida leased out half of the one hundred prisoners in its Chattahoochee penitentiary in 1869.

North Carolina began "farming out" its convicts in 1872. After white South Carolinians led by Democrat Wade Hampton violently ousted the last black government of the state in 1877, the legislature promptly passed a law allowing for the sale of the state's four hundred black and thirty white prisoners.

Six years earlier, in 1871, Tennessee leased its nearly eight hundred prisoners, nearly all of them black, to Thomas O'Conner, a founding partner along with Arthur Colyar of Tennessee Coal, Iron & Railroad Co.[48] In the four decades after the war, as Colyar built his company into an industrial behemoth, its center of operations gradually shifted to Alabama, where it was increasingly apparent that truly vast reserves of coal and iron ore lay beneath the surface.

Colyar, like Milner, was one of those prominent southern businessmen who bridged the era of slavery and the distinct new economic opportunities of the region at the end of the nineteenth century. They were true slavers, raised in the old traditions of bondage, but also men who believed that African Americans under the lash were the key to building an industrial sector in the South to fend off the growing influence of northern capitalists.

Already, whites realized that the combination of trumped-up legal charges and forced labor as punishment created both a desirable business proposition and an incredibly effective tool for intimidating rank-and-file emancipated African Americans and doing away with their most effective leaders.

The newly installed white government of Hale County—deep in the majority-black cotton growing sections of Alabama—began leasing prisoners to private parties in August 1875. A local grand jury said the new practice was "contributing much to the revenues of the county, instead of being an expense." The money derived from selling convicts was placed in the

Fine and Forfeiture Fund, which was used to pay fees to judges, sheriffs, other low officials, and witnesses who helped convict defendants.

The prior year, during a violent campaign by Ku Klux Klansmen and other white reactionaries to break up black Republican political meetings across Alabama, a white raiding party confronted a meeting of African Americans in Hale County. Shots were fired in the dark and two men died—one white and one black. No charges were brought in the killing of the African American, but despite any evidence they caused the shooting, leading black Republicans R. H. Skinner and Woodville Hardy were charged and convicted of murder. They were sent to the Eureka mines south of Birmingham in the spring of 1876.[49]

By the end of 1877, fifty convict laborers were at work in Milner's Newcastle Coal Company mine outside Birmingham. An additional fifty-eight men had been forced into the Eureka mines he founded near Helena. A total of 557 prisoners had been turned over that year to private corporations by the state of Alabama.[50]

By the end of Reconstruction in 1877, every formerly Confederate state except Virginia had adopted the practice of leasing black prisoners into commercial hands. There were variations among the states, but all shared the same basic formula. Nearly all the penal functions of government were turned over to the companies purchasing convicts. In return for what they paid each state, the companies received absolute control of the prisoners. They were ostensibly required to provide their own prisons, clothing, and food, and bore responsibility for keeping the convicts incarcerated. Company guards were empowered to chain prisoners, shoot those attempting to flee, torture any who wouldn't submit, and whip the disobedient—naked or clothed—almost without limit. Over eight decades, almost never were there penalties to any acquirer of these slaves for their mistreatment or deaths.

On paper, the regulations governing convict conditions required that prisoners receive adequate food, be provided with clean living quarters, and be protected from "cruel" or "excessive punishment." All floggings were to be recorded in logbooks, and indeed hundreds were. But the only regularly enforced laws on the new slave enterprises were those designed primarily to ensure that no black worker received freedom or experienced anything other than racially segregated conditions. In Alabama, companies were fined $150 a head if they allowed a prisoner to escape. For a time, state law mandated that if a convict got free while being transported to the mines, the sheriff or deputy responsible had to serve out the prisoner's sentence. Companies often faced their strongest criticism for allowing black and white prisoners to share the same cells. "White convicts and colored convicts shall not be chained together," read Alabama law.[51]

In almost every respect—the acquisition of workers, the lease arrangements, the responsibilities of the leaseholder to detain and care for them, the incentives for good behavior—convict leasing adopted practices almost identical to those emerging in slavery in the 1850s.

By the late 1870s, the defining characteristics of the new involuntary servitude were clearly apparent. It would be obsessed with ensuring disparate treatment of blacks, who at all times in the ensuing fifty years would constitute 90 percent or more of those sold into labor. They were routinely starved and brutalized by corporations, farmers, government officials, and small-town businessmen intent on achieving the most lucrative balance between the productivity of captive labor and the cost of sustaining them. The consequences for African Americans were grim. In the first two years that Alabama leased its prisoners, nearly 20 percent of them died.[52] In the following year, mortality rose to 35 percent. In the fourth, nearly 45 percent were killed.[53]

# III

## SLAVERY'S INCREASE

*"Day after day we looked Death in the face & was afraid to speak."*

H enry and Mary did not wait long to begin their increase. Cooney, a
little girl, came to them before the end of another harvest season had
passed.[1] The arrival of an infant, even more so a first child, to a pair of former slaves in the first years after emancipation must have been an event of
sublime joy. A young black family of the early 1870s already knew that the
presumptions of full freedom that had accompanied the end of slavery were
being gravely challenged in the South. But surrounding and overwhelming
the anxieties triggered by those obstructions—violence by the Ku Klux
Klan and other paramilitary groups and the machinations of white political
leaders—was the astonishing range of possibilities now at least theoretically
available to a newly born child.

While Cooney was still a babe, the northern states by overwhelming
majorities ratified the Fourteenth and Fifteenth amendments to the Constitution, abolishing with absolute clarity the institution of slavery as it had
existed for the previous 250 years and granting full citizenship and voting
rights to all black Americans. A black toddler in central Alabama would
learn his first words at a time when black men were gathering regularly
with others to elect those who would govern their counties and states.

Cooney was seven years old when the U.S. Congress passed its first
Civil Rights Act, further guaranteeing the right of African Americans to
vote on the same terms as whites and to live as full citizens in the eyes of the

law. The new state legislatures of the South, now including substantial numbers of black Republicans, passed laws mandating for the first time in the southern states that children, whether black or white, be afforded some semblance of basic education. By 1871, more than 55,000 black children were attending public school in Alabama.

Henry and Mary knew there would be trouble, yes, plenty of it. But the young man and woman, illiterate, provincial, and unskilled, had every reason to expect nonetheless that in the expiring of ten or twenty years, their daughter and the boisterous brood of boys and girls who would follow her would live lives in a world so transformed from their own as to be utterly unrecognizable.

By the time Cooney turned two, as Thanksgiving approached in 1870, the most defining feature of the old Cottingham world, Elisha, the white man who had sculpted the landscape onto which Cooney was born and then seen it disintegrate, was dead.

Elisha was laid to rest at the top of the red-clay hill, surrounded by what was left of the stand of beech and oak that had greeted his arrival in the wilderness. As his life had been on the landscape stretched out around him, Elisha's plot was squarely in the center of the graveyard, with his wife, siblings, and kin fanning out to each side. One body length away, just within arm's reach, lay in death a long row of the slaves he had governed for most of a century in life.[2]

Old Scip, once Elisha's most reliable slave, was not easing gently toward his natural end. Freedom had taken tangible form for the former slaves of the Cottingham farm. Old Elisha's former slaves separated into three groups. The first, beginning with young Albert Cottingham, abandoned Bibb County and the place of their enslavement as quickly as it had become clearly established that they were in fact free to go wherever they wished.

Three other black families—each of them led by one from the generation of middle-aged slaves who had spent the longest spans of their lives as Cottingham slaves—chose to remain close by the old master, likely still residing in the slave quarters a short distance from Elisha's big house and later in simple tenant cabins erected to replace them. The elder Green Cot-

tinham, a partly white slave now forty years old, along with his wife, Eme-
line, and their baby boy, Caesar, remained on the farm. Likely Green's
mulatto line connected him directly to the white Cottinghams, but no record
survives to indicate whether that was so. Another slave father to remain on
the place was Jeff Cottingham, forty-eight, who continued to spell his name
as his former master did, and who was raising in his home an eight-year-old
boy named Jonathon, who was also partly white.[3] Also staying behind was
Milt, another of the older crew of slaves.

On the other side of the big house, away from the slave cabins, lived the
youngest of Elisha's sons to reach adulthood, Harvey, also forty years old,
with his wife, Zelphia, and seven children. Slightly farther down the wagon
road, J. W. Starr's widow, Hannah, remained in the preacher's house,
though her son Lucius had become the master of the household. Next door
to them, a Starr daughter and her family farmed on another portion of the
dead reverend's land.

A few miles away, beyond Cottingham Loop, at the edge of the Six
Mile settlement around which the lives of all the Cottinghams had come to
orbit, Scip and the third group of former slaves settled themselves in a life
overshadowed by their former enslavement but clearly distinct from the
controlled lives they had formerly led.

At the center of those former slaves remained Scipio, still defiantly
insistent that his birth as an African and the African origins of his mother
and father be fully recorded whenever the census taker or another government official inquired as to his provenance. He took the name Cottinham.

Six Mile had the vague makings of a real town, with a small school and
a weekly newspaper that boasted of a cluster of homes, two stores, and a
sawmill. On one boundary of the settlement lived George Cottinham, now
forty-five, and next door lived Henry, twenty-two years old, and Mary, with
the little girl Cooney. George and Henry, as father and son, farmed rented
property, probably owned by the white Fancher family nearby.

Two houses away, Scip was ensconced with Charity, his junior by
thirty-eight years, and the five children they had under the age of fourteen.
The effort by General Gorgas to rebuild the Brierfield furnaces had collapsed, and the weary Confederate industrialist turned over the operation
to another ex-rebel officer turned entrepreneur.

Scipio worked under his supervision at the Bibb furnace where he had spent so much of the wartime years, still laboring at the task Elisha had sent him to learn in the effort to save the Confederacy. He traveled daily to the furnaces, several miles away, usually in the company of four much younger black men who boarded in a small house near the dry goods store in Six Mile. Sometimes, Scip would spend the night near the furnace in rented lodgings with two of the men, Toney Bates, twenty-two, and Alex Smith, nineteen.[4]

The free lives of Scip, George, and Henry were hardly easy. But for the first time they were truly autonomous of Elisha Cottingham and his kin. How long such black men in the post-emancipation South could remain so would become the defining characteristic of their lives.

As slaves, men such as Scipio and Henry were taught that their master was a palpable extension of the power of God—their designated lord in a supremely ordained hierarchy. In the era of emancipation, that role—now stripped of its religiosity and pared to its most elemental dimensions of power and force—was handed to the sheriff.

This was a new capacity for local law enforcement officers, and the small circles of elected officials who also played a part in the South's criminal and civil justice systems. Prior to the Civil War, all of government in the region, at every level, was unimaginably sparse by modern standards. In Alabama, an elected board of county commissioners oversaw local tax collections and disbursements, primarily for repairs to bridges, maintenance of the courthouse, and operation of a simple jail. The sheriff, also chosen by the people, usually spent far more time serving civil warrants and foreclosing property for unpaid debts than in the enforcement of criminal statutes. The arbiter of most minor legal disputes and alleged crimes would be a justice of the peace, normally a local man appointed by the governor to represent law and government in each "beat" in the state. In an era of exceedingly difficult transportation, beats were tiny areas of jurisdiction, often limited to one small quadrant of a county. One rural Alabama county elected thirty justices of the peace in 1877.[5] But within those boundaries, the justice of the peace—more often than not the proprietor of a country store or a large farm—held tremendous authority, including the power to convict defendants of crimes that carried potential sentences of years of confinement.

In most southern states, county sheriffs and their deputies received no regular salaries. Instead, the law enforcement officers, justices of the peace, certain court officials, and any witnesses who testified against a defendant were compensated primarily from specific fees charged to those who voluntarily or involuntarily came into the court system. A long schedule of approved fees designated the cost of each official act those officials might undertake: 50 cents for serving a warrant in a lawsuit over a bad debt; $1 for making an arrest on an indictment; 35 cents for a clerk who certified a court document. Payment was enforced at the resolution of every court proceeding, with the accumulated fees lumped into whatever other penalty was ordered by a judge. After the advent of widespread convict leasing, the fees—which usually amounted to far more than the actual fines imposed on defendants—were paid off from the payments made by the company that acquired the prisoner.

Before the war and immediately afterward, the cases brought before the county judge and his fellow commissioners in most rural southern counties were drearily routine, and rare. In the great majority of cases in Bibb County and similar places, the penalty for guilt was a fine of $1, regardless of the offense. The point of the prosecution and conviction was not so much to mete out justice from the government but to establish definitively that an offense had been committed and compel the guilty party and the victim to resolve their differences. If a drunken man injured a neighboring farmer's cow, then the court's role was to ensure that the drunk paid for the loss. Incarceration was an expensive and impractical outcome in a society where cash rarely changed hands.

Already, the practice had become established of one man acting as "surety" for the fine imposed on another. Traditionally, this meant the father, brothers, or neighbors of a man convicted of a crime coming into court to pay his fines and assure the court of his future good conduct. In many cases, the surety would actually be the victim of the crime, agreeing to resolve a dispute in return for a contract with the accused to work as payment for the damages he had done.

The county was interested in neither rehabilitation nor long-term punishment, particularly in an era when every man was needed to staff the farms and enterprises of the county. With the exception of those men who clearly merited the noose, most miscreants could be rendered harmless if they simply stayed at whatever lonely place on a muddy road they had appeared from. Those guilty of serious felony crimes were the business of the state, anyway—tried and sentenced by state circuit court judges and incarcerated however and wherever the state saw fit. The local sheriff was a referee in the world of misdemeanors, calling fouls and separating fighters.

Where sheriffs exercised their greatest power was in the enforcement of debts. In Shelby County, where Green Cottenham would ultimately be arrested three decades later, Amos M. Elliott owned a store on a backcountry road, and by the 1870s had become a stalwart citizen of his corner of the county. Merchants such as he were as much bankers as retailers. Nearly every purchase was made on credit to be repaid when a farmer's crop was sold at the end of a season. More often than not, the store owner would be the buyer of the crop as well, meaning that the man who had plowed the fields and picked the cotton or corn might never actually see hard currency. His debts, payments, and profit or loss were recorded only in the ledgers of the store. This was even more so the case for a black man.

Elliott was also justice of the peace—the most visible presence of government authority in the crude world of country life, empowered to perform marriages, formalize contracts between parties, and otherwise represent law and order. In the late 1870s, Elliott's docket was filled with cases involving disputes over amounts ranging from $5.85 to $7.45. A judgment—ordering payment to a particular party or a term of forced labor in lieu of one—often triggered a busy trade in betting on the future of the convicted man. Judgments were treated like securities, and were resold at discounts based on the likelihood, or not, of the losing party being able to pay them.

In every case, the sheriff and Elliott, as the presiding justice of the peace in his beat of the county, received a portion of the settlement as a fee. Many times, Elliott himself agreed to pay a defendant's judgment and then take a mortgage in the same amount on the man's property. In nearly every one of the 225 cases he heard between 1878 and 1880, Elliott ordered that

"all of the defendants [*sic*] personal property is therefore liable to the satisfaction of this judgment."[6]

In July 1882, Elliott ordered Harman Davis to pay a $30.88 judgment
on a three-year-old debt. Elliott paid the amount himself, and Davis signed
a mortgage to repay the money to him with interest. The consequences of
losing a case over a $5 debt could be catastrophic. Alf Barrett was sued for
$5 on September 6, 1879, and then failed to appear at the trial Elliott con-
vened. Elliott declared the man to be in default and ordered that he pay
the plaintiff $5.07, 60 cents each to the sheriff and himself, and 50 cents
each to three witnesses. Two months later, to clear the obligations, the
sheriff seized every article of property to which Barrett could lay claim,
"one lounge, 1 Round Table, 1 Lamp, 1 looking Glass, 4 Picture frames &
Pictures, 3 chairs, 2 Wash Tubs, Wash Stand, Bowl & Pitcher, 1 Lantern, &
3 Sad Irons."

The jeopardy attached to minor violations of the law would soon
become much more serious than to be stripped of every possession. The
South's judicial tradition of using the criminal courts to settle civil debts,
and of treating a man's labor as a currency with which to pay fines and
mortgages, was being recognized, ominously, by the new commercial
engines of the era. In Alabama, the nexus of new economic mechanisms, old
legal patterns, and antebellum traditions of industrial slavery occurred
more naturally than in any other place.

The system of leasing convicts soon radically altered the implications
of the debt enforcement process and the significance of each official
involved in it. County sheriffs and judges had dabbled with leasing black
convicts out to local farmers, or to contractors under hire to repair roads
and bridges, beginning almost immediately after the Civil War. But as the
state turned ever larger blocs of African Americans over to private companies, an organized market for prisoners began to evolve. Soon, labor agents
for the mining and timber companies were scouring the countryside to
make arrangements for acquiring able-bodied black laborers—just as John
Tillman had done to locate slaves for the Shelby Iron Works during the
war, just as Rev. Starr's son was doing when Scip Cottinham was leased to
the Brierfield furnaces in the 1860s.

Instead of slave owners, the men who now controlled squads of black
laborers available to the highest bidder were sheriffs. The key distinction,

however, between the sheriff and the old slave masters was that since these African Americans were not his or anyone else's permanent property, he had no reason for concern about how they were treated by their new keepers or whether they survived at all. By the early 1880s, twenty-nine of Alabama's sixty-seven counties were leasing their prisoners.[7] The trade in black workers continued to swell. Because of the financial benefits of leasing convicts rather than sending them to state officials, some counties opted to prosecute men accused of felonies on misdemeanor charges—solely so the sheriff and other locals could receive the proceeds of the prisoner's lease. County prisoners eventually far surpassed the number of men pressed into forced labor by the state.

Control of those county convicts was lucrative, for both the companies who acquired them and the sheriffs who supplied them. In addition to the fees they received from defendants, sheriffs also kept any amount left over from daily feeding fees paid for each prisoner by the state. As a result, Alabama's sheriffs were financially motivated to arrest and convict as many people as possible, and simultaneously to feed them as little as they could get away with.

In counties where large numbers of convicts were sold to the mining companies, such as Jefferson County, where Birmingham was located, a speculative trade in convict contracts developed. The witnesses and public officials who were owed portions of the lease payments earned by the convicts received paper receipts—usually called scrips—from the county that could be redeemed only after a convict had generated enough money to pay them off. Rather than wait for the full amount, holders of the scrips would sell their notes for cash to speculators at a lower than face amount. In return, the buyers were to receive the full lease payments—profiting handsomely on those convicts who survived, losing money on the short-lived. In Jefferson County, the financial arrangements on each convict were recorded in ledger books showing earnings due to each official and then a subsequent calculation of the final rate of return on each prisoner after his release, escape, or death.[8]

The job of a county sheriff became a heady enterprise, often more akin to the business of trading in mules than law enforcement. Sheriffs and their local judges developed special relationships with local companies and preferred acquirers of their prisoners. Arrests surged and fell, not as acts of

crime increased or receded, but in tandem to the varying needs of the buyers of labor. Companies, commissioners, justices of the peace, probate
judges, and sheriffs issued offers of rewards for escapees. Constables
arrested men on speculation that they might be wanted elsewhere, seizing
them on the basis of rumors, and then inquiring whether there might be
reward money available in the county from which they hailed. Town bullies
and rural store owners such as Elliott became bounty hunters verging on
extortionists.

Swift, uncomplicated adjudication was the key to the system. Trials
were discouraged; lawyers for black misdemeanor defendants were scant.
Indeed, the fee system—with its additional charge for each act in the judicial process or appearance of another witness or official—was a built-in disincentive to prisoners who knew that each added dollar of their final fine
and costs would ultimately equate to additional days held in forced labor.
The span of time from arrest to conviction and judgment to delivery at a
slave mine or mill was often no more than seventy-two hours. The most
common penalty was nine months to a year in a slave mine or lumber camp.

All of this was predicated on the absolute defenselessness of black men
to the legal system, and the near certainty that most would be unable
to bond themselves out of jail or pay fines imposed upon them. Across
Alabama, northern Florida, and Georgia, a bewildering world of casual
judicial process emerged in which affidavits were scribbled on scraps of
notebook paper, half-official judges and strongmen assuming the authority
to arrest resided every few miles, men were identified and arrested on the
basis of meaningless physical descriptions, and hardly anyone could sign
their own name. Increasingly, it was a system driven not by any goal of
enforcement or public protection against serious offenses, but purely to
generate fees and claim bounties.

The county convict leasing system, with its efficient mechanisms for
forcing black men to do the bidding of white business operators, soon
leached into the process of collecting debts of any kind. White farmers who
advanced money to black tenants at the beginning of a crop season began to
enforce their debts not by evicting those black men who fell behind, but by
swearing out criminal warrants accusing them of fraud. Facing certain conviction by a local white judge, most laborers willingly agreed to accept their
white landlords—who had brought them to court in the first place—

as their "sureties." The defendants typically would "confess judgment," an archaic legal concept under which the accused confesses his responsibility before being tried. The local judge then accepted payment and forfeiture of a bond from the white surety, rather than render a verdict on the alleged "crime." In return, the African American farmer would sign a contract to work without compensation for the white landlord for however long it took to pay back the amount of the bond.

The instances of confessing judgment spread rapidly through the farming regions of the South, according to local court dockets of the 1880s and 1890s. This was especially true as southern states adopted more statutes intended to criminalize routine black behaviors—such as carrying a weapon, riding on empty freight train cars—or violations of racial etiquette such as speaking loudly in the presence of white women. On its face, the arrangement appeared similar to other practices that would remain common in the courts for the next century and beyond—granting mercy to a criminal partly in exchange for a commitment to repair the damage of their crimes, and place themselves under the close supervision of a trusted party.

Occasionally, confessing judgment in the 1880s was precisely just such a legitimate, humane resolution of a legal matter. But only rarely. The records of thousands of prosecutions show it was vastly more likely that an arrested black man—knowing he had no possibility of true due process, or acquittal—agreed to confess judgment specifically to avoid the far more dire alternatives that he knew lay in wait. It was the nineteenth-century equivalent of modern plea bargains, in which a defendant agrees to a lesser sentence ahead of trial in order to be spared any possibility of the most severe punishment. The exception being that in the variation of this practice in the 1880s, it was a nearly foregone conclusion that the man under arrest would be found guilty of *something*. Often, his only hope for moderating the blow was to negotiate the most bearable form of forced labor.

The black men who confessed judgment avoided being sold into the slave mines, but traded that fate for onerous labor contracts closer to home or working under men they had at least elementary knowledge of—their present landlord, or often with the same farm families under whom they or their slave forebears had worked in antebellum times. The result was that black tenant farmers and sharecroppers often returned as uncompensated convict laborers, subject to imprisonment, shackles, and the lash, to the same fields where a few days earlier they had worked as independent, free men. White farmers often continued to claim that the convict laborer was incurring additional debts for necessities such as visits by a doctor, medical care, clothing, damaged implements, or housing. Once captured by a contract under which the black man was not free until all his debts were paid, the "convict"—who in fact might never have been found guilty of a crime— could be held almost indefinitely. Moreover, almost any white person who became involved in the resolution of a black man's legal situation could casually add his own "costs" to the balance of a prisoner's debt and compel him to labor for an even longer period.

When a black man named Sevi Pearson was accused in Tallapoosa County of battery against a woman named Cora Iverson in April 1885, he confessed judgment to an elderly notary public named Luke Davenport as part of an arrangement with John W. Pace, an active acquirer of black men through the courts. Davenport, whose legal credentials were limited to a stint as an acting justice of the peace three decades earlier, had the legal power to order Pearson to pay a total of $70.50. Pace paid the penalty for him instead, and Pearson signed a contract under which he agreed to work for Pace for nine months. Ominously, the contract included a provision that the black laborer "further agrees that he will take such treatment as other convicts."[9]

In November 1887, the county clerk of Wilcox County wrote the state official in charge of the system for leasing prisoners into mines and lumber camps, to outline arrangements related to the anticipated gubernatorial pardon for two black convicts named Cats Sellers and Lewis Walker. "My fees for this and forms [and] applications are contingent on the negroes working with John Pritchitt after their liberation. He having paid for their attorneys fees, notices," wrote the clerk, Thomas L. Cochran.[10] Only the slimmest fraction of men forced into Alabama's slave mines ever gained a governor's pardon. Even for many of them, freedom did not mean being free.

In its full bloom, the misdemeanor convict leasing system solved two critical problems for southern whites. It terrorized the larger black population into compliance with a social order in which they willingly submitted to complete domination by whites, and it significantly funded the operations of government by converting black forced labor into funds for the counties and states.

Most scholars of American history have accepted that the repressive legal measures and violence of the post–Civil War era were the result, at least in part, of the lawless behavior of freed slaves. Charitable, if patronizing, iterations of this picture attributed the supposed criminal inclinations of freedmen to the psychic injuries of their generations of bondage, or simply to the difficulty of any emancipated people in adjusting to the dynamics of a life in freedom.

The reality of crime in the era, based on the actual arrest records of many counties in Alabama, Florida, and Georgia, is that true crime was almost trivial in most places. In the Bibb County of January 1878, where African Americans still had the legal right to vote, the biggest criminal threat to the peace of the county was a band of Gypsies plying their wares from an encampment near Columbiana and wandering the muddy wagon rut roads in the country. To move them along, the sheriff brought charges of vagrancy and of trading goods between the hours of sunrise and sunset— an "offense" that would increasingly be used to prevent freed slaves from buying goods from anyone other than their white landlords. Before the case could be heard, the idle Gypsies moved on. Peace was maintained.

Later that year, during the summer, James Cottingham, one of Elisha's many white grandsons and a regular troublemaker in the postwar years, was convicted of assault and battery with a weapon. His fine was $1 plus court costs. He paid it and was free.

In neighboring Shelby County, the arrest log of 1878 shows only twenty-one prisoners brought to jail for the year. There were three homicides in that time, and a woman named Lucy Cohill was arrested for adultery—a charge that in almost all instances stemmed from sexual relations between a black and a white. But few other cases even registered in the public eye. The total fees charged to all those arrested amounted to $80.80.[11] Little changed over the next two years, with the number of inmates in the county jail never exceeding twenty.

All of that transformed as the value of leasing black convicts became more apparent. County after county was adopting the practice. The attraction was not just that local officials could fob off most of the cost and trouble of housing and guarding prisoners. By the end of the 1870s, the opportunity represented by forcing black laborers into the mines was being richly fulfilled at Milner's Newcastle Coal Co., operating just north of where the Pratt Mines were then being developed, and Shelby County's Eureka mines.

The Eureka mine complex consisted of two operations, one manned by free miners and the other by convicts. Managing the forced labor was J. W. Comer, a descendant of one of Alabama's great prewar slave-owning families and a brother to Braxton Bragg Comer, who would become Alabama's governor in 1907. Under Comer, the Eureka Iron Works thrived on a cruel mix of primitive excavation techniques and relentless, atavistic physical force.

State inspectors sent to the convict work camps wrote repeatedly during the 1870s that the "convicts everywhere were being properly cared for and guarded . . . humanely treated."[12] Similarly facile characterizations would be issued repeatedly by other examiners over the decades of convict leasing, often the result of payoffs between the acquirers of forced laborers and their supposed supervisors.

The reality of conditions inside the Eureka mines was documented with rare clarity as a result of a brief state inquiry in 1881 into Comer's operations and Milner's Newcastle mines. More significantly, vignettes of Comer's conduct were also recorded as a result of the presence of a prisoner able and willing to complain of conditions named Ezekiel Archey, and the tenure of a nominally sympathetic Alabama official in charge of guarding the welfare of leased prisoners, Reginald H. Dawson.[13]

Archey, a prisoner leased into Comer's Eureka mines, wrote that the convicts lived in a windowless log stockade, their quarters "filled with filth and vermin." Gunpowder cans were used to hold human waste that periodically "would fill up and runover on bed" where some prisoners were shackled in place at night. Prisoners left for the mine at 3 A.M. in chains, forced to march at a quick trot. The grueling task of boring rock for dynamite, exploding sections of a seam of coal, and shoveling tons of the remains into cars lasted until 8 P.M.[14]

"Every Day some one of us were carried to our last resting, the grave.

Day after day we looked Death in the face & was afraid to speak," Archey wrote. "We can go back to '79 and '77 all these years of how we sufered. No humane being can tell . . . yet we hear. Go ahead. Fate seems to curse a convict. Death seems to summon us hence." Indeed, between 1878 and 1880, twenty-five prisoners died at the Eureka mines, most dumped unceremoniously into shallow earthen pits on the edge of the mine site.[15]

During hearings held by the special legislative commission in 1881 to inquire into the conditions and operations of the convict leasing system, a witness named Jonathon D. Goode testified that Comer ordered a recaptured black escapee to lie "on the ground and the dogs were biting him. He begged piteously to have the dogs taken off of him, but Comer refused to allow it."

Then, Comer "took a stirrup strap, doubled it and wet it, stripped him naked, bucked him, and whipped him—unmercifully whipped him, over half an hour. The Negro begged them to take a gun and kill him," Goode continued. "They left him in a Negro cabin where . . . he died within a few hours."[16]

An assistant superintendent at the mine, James O'Rourke, testified that guards whipped prisoners with "a leather strap or stick about an inch broad and two foot long." For offenses as generic as "disobeying rules," state law allowed up to thirty-nine lashes. Punishment was far more severe for infractions as minor as fighting, tearing bedding, or insolence toward guards. One witness told of the use of water torture at Eureka, on convicts for whom whipping was deemed insufficient. Such prisoners were physically restrained. Then, "water [was] poured in his face on the upper lip, and effectually stops his breathing as long as there is a constant stream."[17] Over the next thirty years, variations of this medieval water torture technique were repeatedly employed in southern slave labor camps, in some cases supplanting whipping as a preferred method of punishment. Many convict managers chose this terrifying method because the convict was able to more quickly recover and return to work than after a severe flogging.

The commission also investigated Milner's Newcastle mines, where both state and county convicts were at work. Milner was already one of the key industrial pioneers of Alabama, having mapped and directed the effort to build one of the state's most important railroad routes prior to the Civil War. Milner had grown up in a slave-owning family, and in early adulthood owned "a little negro of his own named Steve, who followed him about like a shadow," according to one contemporary. Milner put his Steve and several other slaves to work prospecting for gold in the 1840s to earn his tuition for college.[18] Elected to the state Senate in 1866, Milner, short of height but a deliberate speaker, was a key figure in the later ouster of African Americans from all political participation and authored a widely distributed statement titled, "White Men of Alabama Stand Together." He was one of the founders of the city of Birmingham in the 1870s.

By 1881, Milner was already one of the state's most substantial industrialists. His primary company, Milner Coal and Railway Company, developed extensive mines at Coalburg and Newcastle, north of Birmingham. At Newcastle, Milner played the part of a self-aggrandizing antebellum slave master. The complex featured its own private railroad, more than 150 forced laborers acquired from the state and various counties, and an elaborate system of high-temperature beehive ovens used to make coke—a derivative of regular bituminous coal from which impurities had been baked out. A quarter mile from the mine, Milner presided over his family and received political and business visitors in a spacious house featuring a detached kitchen, smokehouse, and barns. Orchards and rose gardens crowded the home.[19]

It was a different scene in the prison mine not far away. A description of Milner's mine by *The New York Times* in December 1882 told of black prisoners packed into a single cramped cabin like slaves on the Atlantic passage. The building had no windows. Vermin-ridden bunks stacked three high were covered with straw and "ravaged blankets." "Revoltingly filthy" food was served cold from unwashed coal buckets, and all 150 black convicts shared three half-barrel tubs for washing. All convicts were forced to wear shackles consisting of an "iron hoop fastened around the ankle to which is attached a chain two feet long and terminating in a ring."[20]

The powerful utility of slave labor as a weapon against the unionization of free laborers began to become most apparent in 1882, when hundreds of skilled and unskilled workers refused to continue work at the Pratt Mines, the steadily enlarging labyrinth of shafts on the edge of Birmingham. The miners objected to a sharp wage reduction and the company's growing reliance on convict laborers. Rather than relent to the strikers' demands, the company leased the mines to Comer, who filled them with legions of convicts at his disposal. The strike was crushed.[21] The same year, Alabama collected $50,000 in revenue from the sale of convict leases.[22]

The impact of that relatively brief labor event and its correspondence with payments equal to approximately $860,000 in modern currency, when adjusted for inflation, would be felt for decades. It forged in dramatic fashion the consensus that the coal and steel industry of Birmingham would thrive only with a central reliance on forced labor. That would not change for a half century.

Later in 1882, state inspectors, writing the first candid official assessment of convict camps, said the private prisons were "totally unfit for use, without ventilation, without adequate water supplies, crowded to excess, filthy beyond description." Prisoners were "poorly clothed and fed . . . excessively and sometimes cruelly punished; there were no hospitals; the sick were neglected; and they were so much intimidated that it was next to impossible to get from them anything touching on their treatment."[23]

Milner also operated a slave mine at the aptly named Coalburg. The place was no town, but a ramshackle mining camp adjacent to a shaft into a seam of coal that would be exhaustively mined for more than eighty years. The prison at Coalburg, and its nearby successor, Flat Top, were synonymous with the most wretched conditions that could develop in the forced labor mines. The Coalburg prison had no floor or toilets; prisoners were fed only meat and bread. Many men were being held long past the expiration of their ostensible sentences. In the late spring of 1883, eight out of one hundred prisoners died—a rate that the state prison inspector extrapolated to be 30 percent a year.[24]

Milner had no compunction about his view that black prisoners purchased from the state and from county sheriffs were his to do with as he saw fit. True, they were no longer mortgaged slaves, as were Steve and the blacks he had owned in the 1850s. But he was as much their lord and master as he had been over the African families. Shortly after the war, he warned fellow southerners of the importance of combating the "unthrift, idleness, and weeds" that were certain to follow the emancipation of the slaves.[25]

Milner became the central figure in an orbit of shrewd but brutal southern industrialists who shared his views on the best means of managing black laborers. Beginning before the Civil War, Milner teamed up with William Hampton Flowers to operate slave-driven timbering operations near Bolling, Alabama. Using mostly hand tools and enormous exertion, the slaves fashioned thousands of crossties for the railroads then under construction across southern Alabama.

After the war, Flowers purchased a half interest in Milner's timber operation. The partnership, Milner, Caldwell & Flowers Lumber Co., built a state-of-the-art sawmill and came to control tens of thousands of acres of prime forestland. From the 1880s through the turn of the century, the company relied on thousands of convict laborers leased from counties and the state of Alabama to produce vast quantities of turpentine and millions of linear feet of cut lumber and crossties.

In the spring of 1883, Milner was made an offer by the entrepreneur behind an ambitious railroad under construction from Atlanta. Milner quickly sold to the Georgia Pacific Railroad part of his Coalburg mine operation and, in an overtly illegal aspect of the transaction, a lot of one hundred black convicts. The buyer of both the mine and the forced laborers was Capt. James W. English, a powerful Atlanta politician who also headed Chattahoochee Brick Company in Atlanta, the biggest and arguably most abusive buyer of forced laborers in Georgia.

In 1883, Alabama's prison inspector, Reginald Dawson, began to visit prisons populated with men convicted of state crimes, and a commission of the state legislature undertook an investigation to ensure that the prisoners were being humanely treated. The moves were made not out of humanitarian concerns but as acts of preservation for the system. In some other states, notably Tennessee, public criticism of barbaric conditions among prison laborers had threatened the entire practice of convict leasing. In Alabama, the system was already proving uniquely well suited to the needs of mine owners, coke oven operators, foundries, and lumber and turpentine camps. The men in charge were committed to preserving the system against any criticism.

Shortly before Milner's transaction flouting the laws that superficially governed Alabama's prison mines, Dawson became "chief inspector" of the state Board of Inspectors of Convicts. He was a South Carolina native, born in 1838 to an illustrious lawyer and planter father. The family moved to Dallas County, Alabama, in 1842, and Dawson studied to become an attorney. A lieutenant in an Alabama infantry regiment during the war, he was wounded and came home in 1864.[26]

Dawson distinguished himself as one among a small number of southerners who were troubled by the obvious contradictions between the convict leasing laws and the realities of the forced labor system that it spawned. He repeatedly gave officials an unvarnished assessment of the situation, apparently in the sincere belief that with full exposure, the apparatus of Alabama's traffic in African Americans could be reformed.

After becoming chief convict inspector, Dawson visited prison encampments scattered across the state. In addition to examining the destinations of state convicts, a law passed the previous year also allowed state officials to inspect the larger, but even less regulated, county convict system. An early stop was at J. W. Comer's plantation in Barbour County. Dawson described the men held there on misdemeanor charges in a desperate condition, poorly clothed and fed, and "unnecessarily chained and shackled."[27]

At the Pratt Mines, then also under the management of Comer and his business partner, William McCurdy, Dawson observed extremely high death rates. He termed conditions at two drift mines as having "miserable accommodations, unfit for men to be kept in."[28] Like Comer, McCurdy was a south Alabama man with a long track record, first in slaves, then in convicts, on his Lowndes County farm. On McCurdy's plantation in Lowndes County, seventy black convicts leased from the state and an unknown number of county prisoners were held in two pens called the upper and lower cells.[29] The farm would operate with forced laborers for at least fifty years.[30]

Despite the conditions and the appalling number of maimed and "disabled men" that Dawson found at the mines operated by Comer, Milner, and the other forced labor entrepreneurs in 1883, there was little he could do. Comer and McCurdy, as well as the Pratt Mines, held binding contracts under which the corporations had effective ownership of two hundred prisoners each.

Dawson wrote repeatedly in his diary during the hot summer of that year that he was "stronger than ever in the conviction that the convicts should not be worked in the mines."[31] The inspector also began to write country judges across Alabama urging them to cease the transfer of local prisoners to the desperate mines near Birmingham. Dozens received such letters, including one on September 10, 1883, to Simon O'Neal reporting that prisoners at the Pratt Mines "are not well clothed." He added: "I think the work required of some of the convicts is excessive." Two weeks later, Dawson wrote R. A. J. Cumlie: "The appalling amt of deaths that have occurred at the mines, both from disease and accidents, the great number of cripples, the men broken down by disease to be found there should convince the public that they should not be forced to incur the augers incident to this sort of work."[32]

After Dawson inquired into the circumstances of a convict from Lee County being held by Comer and McCurdy at one camp, the inspector realized that although the man had been in custody since 1875—eight years—he wasn't listed in official records as a prisoner. Comer "never reported him," Dawson wrote to the Lee County judge. "Comer and McCurdy have had him near two years. . . . You have no idea how many such cases I have worked up."

Dawson appealed to Governor Edward A. O'Neal for help. "Convicts have been hired out and lost sight of, others are in possession of contractors and no bond or contract on file. Others have been found in possession of parties different from those to whom hired."[33]

Dawson's pleas had little effect. By March 1883, twenty-nine counties were leasing their prisoners to mines. Altogether, in excess of four hundred such men were being forced into labor, the vast majority of them because of their inability to pay fines imposed for minor or spurious offenses.[34]

Similarly, Dawson discovered multiple county prisoners at the Newcastle and Coalburg prison mines owned by Milner who had never been paid for by the company and were never listed on the rolls of prisoners that Milner was required by law to maintain. The benefit of never showing a prisoner on the official registers of convicts was tremendous. The company holding him could ignore its obligation to make monthly payments to the county of the prisoner's arrest. Far more ominously, the prisoner could be held indefinitely. The end effect, by almost any definition, was to reduce the convict to a slave. After a visit to Coalburg in July 1885, Dawson wrote in his diary: "Still a great deal of sickness. There is much dissatisfaction and complaints here. The convicts are demoralized and the management is bad."[35]

Dawson could never determine how many such cases occurred. He wrote that his investigation never truly "probed to the bottom." Even inspectors such as Dawson rarely considered an even more troubling dimension of the system: that much larger numbers of the prisoners—whether listed on the official registers or not—had committed no real crime.[36]

A woman named Annie Tucker was convicted of a misdemeanor and sold into the Pratt Mines in 1883. She later testified during a legislative inquiry that she "cooked, washed and ironed at mines."[37] At some point that year, P. J. Rogers, an official at the prison who later became sheriff of Jefferson County, so severely whipped Tucker that the Board of Inspectors censured him. Dawson wrote in his diary that Tucker "ran away from Mr. McCurdy's house—was caught and carried to the prison. Col. Bankhead whipped her himself—not severely—After he left, by order of Mr. McCurdy, P. J. Rogers stripped her, had her held down, and inflicted 56 lashes upon her with a heavy strap."[38]

After a meeting on November 14, 1883, with two white men who had recently visited Comer's Pratt Mines, Dawson wrote in his personal diary: "Disgusted with what they found at shaft—men eating out of coal shovels. Notified Col. Ensley to furnish men things to eat out of—and other necessaries—Reported to Governor the neglect of sick men . . . and also cruelty."

A week later Dawson visited the Shaft mine himself. "Found things not at all improved—men lousy, filthy and dirty. Had no change for near two months—beds scarce and dirty. One very sick man in a cell in a miserable condition."[39]

The plantation operations of J. W. Comer were no better. After a visit to the Comer farm in Barbour County, Dawson wrote: "Things in bad order. No fireplace in cell. No arrangements for washing . . . no hospital. Everything filthy—privy terrible—convicts ragged—many barefooted—very heavily ironed."[40]

Elected officials responded by adopting new rules governing the leasing of convicts. Companies that acquired forced laborers were mandated to provide "clean quarters" and adequate food. Guards were prohibited from using "cruel" or "excessive punishment." The new rules also dictated that if the body of a dead prisoner was not taken by a family member, the company was responsible for an orderly internment.[41]

Except for the requirements of racial separation, operators of the slave labor camps roundly ignored the rules. Between 1882 and the end of 1883, the number of convicts in the Pratt Mines increased from ninety-two state prisoners and an unknown number of county convicts to more than five hundred slave laborers in its Slope and Shaft mines, about half its total workforce.[42] One of Dawson's deputies wrote him in December 1883 that conditions at the Pratt Mines were severely deteriorating. "Most of the Negroes have not had a change of clothing in from three to nine weeks and are as lousy as they can be," wrote Albert T. Henley, citing "the filthy condition of things."[43]

In 1884, Archey, still imprisoned at the Eureka mine, wrote to Dawson decrying the treatment he and other black men continued to receive. "Comer is a hard man. I have seen men come to him with their shirts a solid scab on their back and beg him to help them and he would say let the hide grow back and take if off again. I have seen him hit men 100 and 160 [times] with a ten prong strop, then say they was not whiped. He would go off after an escape man come one day with him and dig his grave the same day.

"We go to cell wet, go to bed wet and arise wet the following morning and evry guard knocking beating yelling Keep in line Jumping Ditches," Archey wrote.[44]

In 1885, when Dawson personally appealed to Milner to unchain his permanently shackled laborers at the Newcastle mines for some portion of each day or night, Milner reacted contemptuously. "My best and longest mine men," Milner wrote back, "will get away & then ruin my business here."[45]

For its part, Shelby County, though home to some of Alabama's most glaringly abusive slave mines, moved cautiously, reconsidering each year whether to partake in the profits offered by the new trade in laborers or to stick with working prisoners on the muddy country roads and collapsing bridges across the county. On December 13, 1880, the county commission split the difference, ordering that prisoners convicted of crimes in the following year be hired to an outside labor agent, but that the men be "employed on public works." The labor agent was the firm of Comer & McCurdy.

The requirement for prisoners to be used on the public roads was only temporary, however. Late in 1881, the commissioners authorized the probate judge to hire local convicts to "a farm, coal mine or Iron works," with the nearby Shelby Iron Works production facility or Comer's Eureka mines obviously in mind. Immediately the character of law enforcement in the county changed profoundly.[46]

In November of that year, the jail suddenly filled with forty-five prisoners, six charged with burglary, ten accused of carrying a concealed weapon, six for petit larceny, and, notably, a woman named Mollie Stubbs was accused of vagrancy. It was the first use of the old-fashioned "idleness" charge in many years, almost certainly the first since the end of the Civil War. Stubbs was ordered to work forty days at hard labor to pay off a $12 fine.[47]

Now engaged in the business of black labor, the Shelby County jail stayed a busy place from then on. A month rarely passed in which there were fewer than twenty prisoners. Charges such as vagrancy, adultery, using obscene or abusive language, and obtaining goods under false pretenses suddenly became common, and were almost always filed against African Americans.

In July 1883, Shelby County recognized that the initial restrictions placed by local officials on prisoner leasing were limiting the revenue that could be generated. The commission named Amos Elliott, the county's best-known and longest-standing storekeeper and justice of the peace, to act as its agent in the management of prisoners. Elliott was given virtual carte blanche as to the fate of men arrested in Shelby County, receiving authorization to hire out prisoners to "persons or corporations" in accordance with state laws revised earlier that year. The one caveat was that Elliott was also to "make the necessary arrangements for the safe keeping and proper care of Convicts," and, in accordance with the rules of treatment the state had adopted along with its newest statute on prisoner labor, Elliott was bound to "scrutinize and enquire into the management and treatment of said Convicts."[48]

Elliott, already well acquainted from his many years as a justice of the peace with the pecuniary benefits of the Alabama fee system,[49] energetically took up the first order of the commission. There was no indication that he did on the second.

Despite the Shelby commissioners' initial reluctance to see their prisoners dispatched to commercial enterprises, the lure of private sector payments was simply more than any paternalistic good intentions could resist. In February of 1884, the commission approved payments to Elliott of $273.93 for his work in hiring out prisoners and judging cases. Approval was also granted for $94 paid to James T. Leeper for his help in placing convicts, and F. A. Nelson, the county sheriff, was authorized to receive $173 for having arrested them.[50] Like Elliott, the men engaged in the county's trade of forced labor weren't marginal or disreputable figures. The sheriff was a popular elected official. J. T. Leeper was the county solicitor, and worked as a lawyer in partnership with W. B. Browne, president of the Columbiana Savings Bank and on several occasions mayor of the town.[51]

The number of men arrested, and the fees paid to such prominent local white men, escalated swiftly, even as the particularities of the ostensible judicial process deteriorated. Between late summer of 1884 and the spring of 1886, more than two hundred prisoners passed through the jail and then into private hands. In county ledgers, the nature of the charges against most of them, or the amounts of the fines they were ordered to pay, weren't recorded.[52]

Five years earlier, with the passing of New Year's Day 1881, the people of adjoining Bibb County found themselves under the extraordinary power of a new county judge. Jonathon S. Gardner, veteran county commissioner, had been elevated to the nearly omnipotent position. From a shiny straight-back chair in the courthouse, Judge Gardner controlled both the judicial and administrative functions of local government, with the power to tax citizens, build roads and bridges to their farms, convict them of crimes, decide their punishments, and incarcerate them as he saw fit.

Gardner succeeded attorney Thomas J. Smitherman, descendant of one of the county's most prominent families, a major holder of property, and a neighbor and longtime acquaintance of the Cottinghams. In August

1865, Smitherman, also a Confederate veteran, had been authorized by the provisional governor of Alabama to give oaths of allegiance to residents of the county wishing to restore their citizenship rights.

While the power of the county judge's position whenever it intersected with the life of a specific individual was almost boundless, there was in fact little in the way of meaningful philosophical policy shifts that the new county judge could effect. Which roads and bridges to rebuild after each year's spring downpours, in what order, and by whom among the small coterie of local men who lived primarily off the odd jobs of the county, were the judge's most consistent questions and demonstrable executive power.

They were mundane decisions, but often were the determining factor between which farmers would thrive and which would wither in isolation. A passable road was critical to the primitive task of moving to market a five-hundred-pound load of cotton—the sole goal of most small-acreage farmers. A washed-out bridge, unrepaired, might be insurmountable.

Crime and punishment was the judge's other realm of discretion. While the number of men brought up on even the smallest of criminal charges in the nineteenth century was inconsequential—no more than a dozen a year—the county judge's method of response was virtually unlimited. It was here that the new judge Gardner would make his mark.

Six months after Gardner took office, Bibb County joined the rising tide. Two days after the county's Independence Day celebrations that July, Dave Wilson was charged with assault and battery and the equally serious crime of using "abusive and insulting language in the presence of females." Found guilty, Wilson, a twenty-one-year-old black farmhand, was sentenced to ten days of hard labor, under the supervision of the sheriff, plus the cost of the court proceeding.[53]

A few months later Abram Griffin, an itinerant black farmhand from Montgomery,[54] faced charges of carrying a concealed weapon and assault and battery. Guns carried by black men were becoming an increasingly potent issue among white southerners. Across the South, but nowhere more intensely than in Alabama, public campaigns were under way to ban the possession of firearms by any African American. In an era when great numbers of southern men carried sidearms, the crime of carrying a concealed weapon—enforced almost solely against black men—would by the turn of the century become one of the most consistent instruments of black incarceration. The larger implications of disarming black men, at a time when they were simultaneously being stripped of political and legal protections, were transparent.

Griffin's assault, whatever it was, little interested the Bibb County judge in 1881. He was convicted but fined only $1. On the charge of carrying a weapon, however, the man faced a serious penalty. Unable to pay the court a $50 fine and costs, Griffin instead was forced by Judge Gardner to work at hard labor 188 and one half days.[55]

Later that year, Judge Gardner presided over the case of Milton Cottingham, one of the former slaves Elisha had watched come of age on the banks of the Cahaba and likely another son of Scipio. Milton was still working a portion of the land he had farmed as a slave for Elisha, though by 1880 he was a sharecropper on a plot next to Rev. Starr's old home on the Cottingham Loop. Like Scip, he had married after slavery to a woman half his age, and lived with Julie and their two-year-old son, Gabe, just steps from the slave cabins Milt had known as a boy.

On Halloween day of 1881, Milton came before Judge Gardner, charged with malicious mischief. The prosecutor was Thomas Smitherman, the former judge. At issue was an alleged injury to some cows owned by A. B. McIntosh.

Only the barest details of the accusation survive in court records, but it was not uncommon in the South at the time for a white landowner to accuse a tenant farmer of overworking or otherwise harming a mule or cow furnished along with the land. Ostensible injuries to the livestock could be another basis for landowners to withhold additional amounts from their sharecroppers when it came time to settle accounts at the end of the year. Whatever the specifics in Milt Cottingham's case, he pleaded not guilty.

Judge Gardner heard testimony on the alleged incident and ruled the former slave before him guilty. He levied a fine of $24. The vast majority of African Americans in the county—or the entire South for that matter—in 1881, given the same outcome, would have faced a Faustian bargain. Twenty-four dollars was a huge sum, the equivalent for most laborers of three months or more of wages. Without cash, the typical freedman would have had to choose between spending a year or more held by the county in a primitive jail, and working a chain gang on the roads each day. Or he could agree to work for an even longer period as the near-property of a white man willing to pay the fine on his behalf.

Milt Cottingham enjoyed a rare advantage. The community of former Cottingham slaves remained sufficiently intact—and had prospered enough during Reconstruction—that Milt's brothers, James and George, appeared on his behalf, with $24 in hand. The black Cottinghams had not yet been crushed. Milt was set free.[56]

On February 13, 1893, the Bibb County Commission voted to "hire out convicts of the County that have heretofore and may hereafter be convicted." The probate judge, M. Y. Hayes, was made the labor agent for the county and ordered to enter into a two-year contract under which convicts would be leased out for $4 per month "per head," and $2.50 to cover the county court costs of each prisoner.

Two years later, in 1895, the commission authorized Hayes to continue leasing "as in his discretion he deems best." At the same meeting, the commission approved a proposal for upgrading and repairing a local road—perhaps the modest government's single most important function in encouraging the prosperity of its rural residents. The road to be improved that winter was the one leading to the farm of Elisha's son whose children had been forced to trek across the war-riven South in 1862, Moses L. Cottingham.[57] When the cotton came in later that year, the white Cottingham would have no trouble getting to market.

# IV

# GREEN COTTENHAM'S WORLD

*"The negro dies faster."*

In the two decades after Henry and Mary Cottinham exchanged vows at Wesley Chapel, the pair had successfully established their own self-sustained lives apart from the old Cottingham plantation. They and many of the other former slaves who had banded together with Scipio and lived in proximity at the crossroads of Six Mile eventually moved into the settlement at Brierfield, the remnants of the town surrounding the old furnaces where Scipio had worked as a slave and a freedman and the location of a basic school for black children.

The Cottingham slaves scratched out a tenuous self-reliant life. But the years did not pass easily. Mary's *increase*, as Elisha Cottingham had called the future offspring of the slave girl Francis when he gave her away in 1852, had been great, but leavened with pain and sorrow. She carried nine children to birth. Only six survived early childhood. Cooney, the little freedom baby who had arrived with such expectation, was not among them.

The last of Henry and Mary's children, a fourth boy, came in May of 1886. Henry called him Green, the same name as Henry's mulatto uncle born on Elisha Cottingham's plantation more than fifty years earlier.

Beyond the confines of the family's strained domesticity, little else was evolving in the way that Henry and Mary, and millions of other black southerners, had imagined at the dawn of freedom.

As Green grew into school age and then adolescence, the family increasingly felt the repercussions of two convulsive crescendos building toward a climax early in the next century. First was the progressively more overt effort to obliterate all manner of black independence and civic participation in the South—the effective reversal of the guarantees of the Thirteenth, Fourteenth, and Fifteenth amendments. Then came a fevered movement to follow the great American territorial expansions of the nineteenth century with an era of unprecedented government-engineered social and economic uplift almost wholly reserved for whites. The two campaigns arrived like successive storms on a shore—the first violent wave smashing any creation of man, the second scouring what had been, scattering the remains, and saturating the soil with salt.

The totality of the destruction to be wrought on American blacks was underscored by a remarkable and little acknowledged facet of southern life in the final two decades of the 1800s. African Americans, by the most critical economic measures, were not significantly disadvantaged in comparison to the great mass of poor whites that surrounded them in the South. Of 4.4 million black southerners, poverty was abject and daunting. But millions of white southerners shared the same plight. And while more than half of southern blacks—about 2.5 million—could not read, there were 1.3 million whites among their neighbors who also were illiterate.

The prolonged economic inferiority and social subjugation of African Americans that was to be ubiquitous in much of the next century was not a conclusion preordained by the traditions of antebellum slavery.

Indeed, optimism and an expansive sense of opportunity pervaded black life in the years surrounding Green Cottenham's birth in 1886. African Americans still felt strongly that they were on the cusp of authentic integration into mainstream American life. Inspired by the moral force of the Civil War victory and the pronouncements of evangelical uplift, self-reliance, and personal improvement offered by an army of black pastors and statesmen of abolition such as Frederick Douglass, and soon Booker T. Washington, black Americans were poised to assimilate fully into American society. Already, African Americans were seeing concrete dividends from the black public schools established during Reconstruction.

The challenges of freedom's aftermath remained surmountable, and the United States, just beginning to emerge as a truly modern nation, was embarking upon an unparalleled period of strategic social uplift. Blacks and poor whites alike were ready to exploit the opportunities of what would become a fifty-year campaign by federal and state governments to dramatically elevate the horizons of tens of millions of Americans living in crude frontier towns, urban tenements, and the isolation of remote rural farms.

By World War II, millions of white southerners had been raised from profound poverty, illiteracy, and ignorance to at least modest middle-class status. Free public schools, consistent medical care, passable roads, clean tap water, electricity, even the concept of regular hourly wage work—all still rarities across the South and much of the rest of the nation at the dusk of the nineteenth century—were promulgated upon millions of the most dispossessed of Americans with a speed and efficacy that in hindsight made the Great Society initiatives of the 1960s appear timid and indolent.

Even as southern whites rampaged violently and blacks suffered a grinding series of legal and political reverses, African American men continued to save meager funds to buy farms, mules, and plows. Black land ownership surged. New communities were established. Additional schools were opened against extraordinary odds. Most African Americans were resigned to the reality that whites would hold a dominant position in southern society, but found it incomprehensible that they and their descendants might be relegated again to a permanent, inferior social and legal position. Many, probably a majority, were reconciled to the likelihood of second-class citizenship. But, as argued by Booker T. Washington, they saw this status as a way station to full participation in society—a time to build economically and overcome the most obvious vestiges of slavery. Tens of thousands of blacks continued to exercise their vote, and a not insignificant number of white leaders still accepted, even if reluctantly, that the equal citizenship of former slaves could not be constitutionally revoked. The legal construct of separate-but-equal segregated government services—which would define the long era of Jim Crow in the twentieth century—had not yet been clearly established. Even the practice of identifying in government records every citizen as either "Negro" or "White"—a nearly obsessive American compulsion by early in the next century—in many areas had not yet become routine.

But the succeeding years would come as if the masses of poverty-stricken whites and blacks were twin siblings of a parent indulgent to one and venomous to the other. A new national white consensus began to coalesce against African Americans with shocking force and speed. The general white public, the national leadership of the Republican Party, and the federal government on every level were arriving at the conclusion that African Americans did not merit citizenship and that their freedom was not valuable enough to justify the conflicts they engendered among whites. A growing body of whites across the nation concluded that blacks were not worth the cost of imposing a racial morality that few in any region genuinely shared. As early as 1876, President Ulysses S. Grant, commander of the Union army of liberation, conceded to members of his cabinet that the Fifteenth Amendment, giving freed slaves the right to vote, had been a mistake: "It had done the Negro no good, and had been a hindrance to the South, and by no means a political advantage to the North."[1] "The long controversy over the black man seems to have reached a finality," wrote the *Chicago Tribune*, approvingly. Added *The Nation:* "The Negro will disappear from the field of national politics. Henceforth, the nation, as a nation, will have nothing more to do with him."[2] That the parent had once sacrificed enormously to rescue the less favored child only made its abandonment deeply more bitter.

By the end of the 1940s, when Green Cottenham might have been easing toward a workman's retirement, it was only his white peers who approached old age as the first American generation with socially guaranteed security. Emerging among the children and grandchildren of those whites was a level of modest wealth, educational attainment, and personal achievement unimaginable to anyone in the South of 1886. For the first time in U.S. history, a geographically broad and stable national middle class had evolved—an anchor of sustained wealth and shared values that would sculpt American life through the end of the twentieth century. But it would be defined in white-only terms.

The South was in the midst of an economic and cultural convulsion, one that should have offered an opening for a radical redefinition of the roles of blacks and whites in American life. A terrible depression in the 1870s had finally eased as the South began to emerge from economic ruin. In the dis-

puted presidential election of 1876, white southern political leaders leveraged the electoral college system to rob the winner of a huge majority of
the popular vote, Samuel J. Tilden, of the White House. In return, the
Congress and the administration of the fraudulent new Republican president, Rutherford B. Hayes, finally removed the last Union troops from the
South and ended a decade of federal occupation of the region.[3] An era of
southern economic revitalization appeared to be at hand. In 1886, Henry
Grady, the dynamic young editor of the *Atlanta Constitution*, famously
declared the creation of a "New South"—one in which industrialism would
replace agriculture and in which the conflicts of region and race that had
paralyzed the nation for more than twenty-five years were at an end.

In some places, the economic evolution was truly phantasmagoric. In
1880, large portions of Alabama remained as sparsely populated as the
newest western territories of the United States. Most of the state averaged
fewer than twenty residents per square mile. A decade later, nearly all of
Alabama was as thickly populated as most states to the east.

Birmingham illustrated the tectonic forces at work in U.S. society more
than any other place. The booming city erupted out of abandoned forest in
the 1870s and suddenly became a national center for the making of iron and
steel. As coal production in Alabama surged from 10,000 tons in the early
1870s to 400,000 tons in 1881, the city built thousands of new homes, laid
streets, installed the infrastructure of a major capital, and opened schools,
churches, and colleges. Jefferson County, center of the boom, nearly
quadrupled from fewer than 25,000 residents in 1880 to nearly 90,000 ten
years later. By 1900, the number approached 150,000.[4]

The entire U.S. economy was surging with industrial fervor, generating
a ravenous appetite for Alabama's coal and iron ore. Wall Street financiers
joined with the South's new generation of industrialists, men such as Col.
James W. Sloss, James DeBardeleben, and Truman Aldrich, to aggressively
exploit the deposits of iron ore and apparently limitless seams of coal that
riddled the Appalachian foothills of northern Alabama. In 1878, Sloss—
one of the original lessors of Alabama prisoners sixteen years earlier—
DeBardeleben, and Aldrich formed the Pratt Coal and Coke Co., and took
over what would become the underground behemoth known as Pratt Mines.

Recognizing the vast potential of the mineral deposits, the Tennessee

Coal, Iron & Railroad Co. soon moved its center of operations from Nashville to the coalfields of Alabama. The coming economic boom, unprecedented in the South, would require thousands of men, working deep in the earth, in a never-stopping excavation.

In 1886, Sloss sold his massive Birmingham furnace complex to a group of New York–backed investors. A year later, with additional financial backing from the North, the new owners formed a corporation that would come to be known as Sloss-Sheffield Iron and Steel Company. The corporation quickly purchased the territory and mining operation at Coalburg owned by John Milner.

Production boomed. The crude mines and simple furnaces of Bibb County now paled in the glow of this industrial revolution. The old shafts and digs were being abandoned. The work they represented to families such as the black Cottinghams melted away. Word spread that soon there would be no work except in the new city exploding less than fifty miles away—Birmingham. The family's center was slipping too. Sometime in the 1880s the old slave Scipio, the man who had carved a world from the wilderness, had fathered and grandfathered so many in slavery but defiantly never forgotten his African roots, died at Brierfield.

The furnaces near Six Mile, where Scipio, Henry, and their clan had sustained a measure of economic independence, ceased operations. Only the families of grandson Henry and his much younger half-brother Elbert remained in the community. Most of the former Cottingham slaves and their descendants, many now using the more phonetically correct names Cottinham or Cottenham, had already been pulled toward the lure of activity and wealth of Birmingham. Huge numbers of other poor blacks and whites from across the South were pouring into the city. Henry and Mary could not resist the inexorable current of the new era, tugging them toward the bulging, smoky new metropolis.

Yet already, the opportunity for the rise of new industries to open substantial new doors for black citizenship and economic advancement was being ignored. Even black leaders such as Booker T. Washington were urging blacks to accept a deferential, second-class position in American society, in return for less racial violence by whites. African Americans increasingly found themselves trapped between the accommodationist retreat of Washington and the hollow claims of harmony and goodwill by white men such as Henry Grady.

Few companies riding the southern boom saw any value in integrating black workers into their expanding enterprises. African Americans' value in the new order was greatest as a defense against unions attempting to organize free workers—especially in Alabama's coalfields. The utility of forced labor as a bulwark against disruptions of the South's biggest enterprises was obvious. Coal mines, timber camps, and farms worked by imprisoned men couldn't be shut down by strikers, or have wages driven up by the demands of free men. The new slave labor provided an ideal captive workforce: cheap, usually docile, unable to organize, and always available when free laborers refused to work.

By the end of the 1880s, at least ten thousand black men were slaving in forced labor mines, fields, and work camps in the formerly Confederate states.[5] The resubjugation of black labor was a lucrative enterprise, and critical to the industrialists and entrepreneurial farmers amassing capital and land.

In Georgia, near the town of Athens, former state senator James M. Smith held hundreds of debt slaves on a farm that stretched thirty miles from the town he named after himself: Smithonia. In the post–Civil War economy, Smith nurtured a small farm into the state's largest plantation. He became a major buyer of convicts soon after Georgia's Reconstruction government was toppled by a campaign of voter fraud and Ku Klux Klan violence.

On thousands of acres, he raised cotton, corn, sorghum, and timber, and operated small factories.[6] For workers he relied on an army of terrified convict slaves, including many African Americans he had owned before the war or their descendants. John Hill, a former slave who said his relatives had been held at Smithonia for decades after the end of slavery, described the farm in an interview given in the 1930s: "He had what they called chain-gang slaves. He paid them out of jail for them to work for him," Hill recounted. "He let them have money all the time so they didn't never get out of debt with him. They had to stay there and work all the time, and if they didn't work, he had them beat."

If workers tried to flee, Smith relied on deputy sheriffs to recapture them and his own overseers to inflict brutal punishments. "They had dogs to trail them with so they always got caught, and then the whipping boss beat them almost to death," Hill said. "It was awful to hear them hollering and begging for mercy. If they hollered 'Lord have mercy!' Marse Jim didn't hear them, but if they cried, 'Marse Jim have mercy!' then he made them stop the beating. He say, 'The Lord rule Heaven, but Jim Smith ruled the earth.' "[7]

Another former governor and U.S. senator of Georgia, Joseph E. Brown, worked hundreds of black forced laborers in his coal mines in the northern mountains of his state. Other slave laborers helped rebuild Brown's iron furnaces that had been destroyed by Union troops in the Civil War. In North Carolina, the tracks of the critical, state-owned Western & Atlantic Railroad were being laid by huge gangs of black men compelled by sheriffs to work for the company. In Louisiana and Mississippi, thousands of impoverished African Americans were building levees and working massive cotton plantations under the lash.

In Atlanta, an expert in the prewar use of slaves to build railroads, John T. Grant, and his son William Grant leased nearly four hundred of Georgia's state and county convicts to perform the extraordinarily harsh work of building a seventy-one-mile railway line between the towns of Macon and Augusta. Despite reports of terrible abuse and high mortality among the forced laborers, the business—Grant, Alexander & Company—soon controlled nearly all of Georgia's prisoners. Though the Civil War was nearly a decade past, Grant, Alexander was soon laying track on projects across the state—all of it performed with slave labor.[8]

Meanwhile, John Grant's railroad building partner from before the war, Col. Lemuel P. Grant, was developing his extensive landholdings into the city's first major suburb, called Grant Park. The colonel, an engineer and railroad builder unrelated to John Grant, had directed construction of the extensive fortifications surrounding Atlanta during the Civil War using slave labor. The neighborhood surrounded the growing city's first substantial green space, a Frederick Law Olmsted firm–designed park that would permanently bear the colonel's name. Nearby, Joel Hurt—one of the state's wealthiest men and a major leaseholder of convicts for his Georgia Iron and Coal Company—was building another of the city's finest residential enclaves.

The bricks used to pave the streets and line the sidewalks of these flourishing new Victorian areas were sold in lots of a million to the Atlanta City Council by former mayor James W. English. His brick-making concern, Chattahoochee Brick Co., would by the end of the century churn out 300,000 hot red rectangles of hardened clay every day—all made by forced laborers. On Sunday afternoons, white men frequently met in the yard of the English brick factory to swap or buy black men, little changed from the slave markets of a half-century earlier.[9]

As leases for forced laborers proliferated across the South, whites readopted a sense of ownership reminiscent of antebellum days. After the death of a partner in Stevens Bros. & Co., a pottery factory in Georgia's Baldwin County, in 1890, an auction was held to sell off all the assets. The newspaper advertisement for the sale could just as well have been from the world of Elisha Cottingham in the 1850s. "Will be sold . . . to the highest bidder . . . Eleven mules, 1 horse, 1 bull, 800 bushels of corn . . . lease of 30 convicts with various terms to serve, 1 grist mill."[10]

Thousands more forced laborers slaved on extraordinarily profitable farms stretching across the old slavery belt of Texas, where prisoners were chained at the neck and held in boxcars at night. Working from sunup to sundown, they survived on "food buzzards would not eat" and suffered sadistic punishments. Hundreds of men charged with petty crimes were simply worked to death and then buried unceremoniously wherever they fell. To escape that fate, Texas convicts mimicked the desperate tactics of slaves before them—slicing their heel strings, hacking off their hands, or gouging out their eyes. A few chronicled their nightmares in the written word. I spent "the prime of my life . . . as a slave," exclaimed one prisoner, while another lamented that he was "buried alive . . . dead to the world."[11]

Speaking to a gathering of prominent black writers and thinkers on the twentieth anniversary of the Emancipation Proclamation in 1883, Frederick Douglass, the aging black leader of pre–Civil War years, lamented that despite the bloody sacrifice of black soldiers in the fight for liberation, "in all relations of life and death, we are met by the color line. It hunts us at midnight . . . denies us accommodation . . . excludes our children from schools . . . compels us to pursue only such labor as will bring us the least reward."[12]

A few months later in 1883, the U.S. Supreme Court ruled that the Civil Rights Act of 1875, the one federal law forcing whites to comply with the provisions of the Fourteenth and Fifteenth amendments—awarding voting and legal rights to blacks—could be enforced only under the most rare circumstances. Civil rights was a local, not federal issue, the court found.

The effect was to open the floodgates for laws throughout the South specifically aimed at eliminating those new rights for former slaves and their descendants. Justice John Marshall Harlan, the only member of the court to oppose the opinion, publicly worried that the amendments representing the ideals of equality and freedom articulated by Lincoln in the Gettysburg Address, as well as the arching moral justification for the carnage of the Civil War, had been renounced.

Douglass, despondent, wrote to an acquaintance: "We have been . . . gruesomely wounded . . . in the house of our friends."[13] In the wake of the Supreme Court ruling, the federal government adopted as policy that allegations of continuing slavery were matters whose prosecution should be left to local authorities only—a de facto acceptance that white southerners could do as they wished with the black people in their midst.

The significance of those legal and political developments can hardly be overstated. The era of Reconstruction and black political control on any statewide level in the South had ended fifteen years earlier, but in the early 1880s, large numbers of African Americans continued to vote, particularly in majority-black cotton-growing counties. As a result, even deeply racist white politicians were compelled to temper—or at least consider—their rhetoric and positions with racial implications. Funding for public schools remained equally apportioned to black and white children, and African Americans in many places maintained at least some level of access to local courts and other government services. But a declaration by the country's highest courts that the federal government could not force states to comply with the constitutional requirement of the equal treatment of citizens, regardless of race, opened a torrent of repression.

.  .  .

In 1888, Tennessee Coal, Iron & Railroad entered into its first contract
with the state of Alabama to lease convicts into the Pratt Mines. The big
company took over operations from J. W. Comer, who had long held
thousands of forced laborers in his farm fields and mines. After acquiring
Pratt Mines, the Tennessee company competed for the lease on all state
prisoners in an auction against companies representing nearly every major
economic figure in Alabama or the South. Other bidders included Sloss-
Sheffield, several companies controlled by Milner, and a partnership between DeBardeleben and Comer's sometime associate, Lowndes County
planter William D. McCurdy. Within five years, more than one thousand
men, nearly all of them black, were working under the whip at the Pratt
Mines, and Tennessee Coal, Iron & Railroad Co. in effect owned all state
convicts for the next quarter century.

Fueled by access to this large pool of forced laborers and fresh investment from New York, the company began a dramatic expansion. By the end
of 1889, there were eight major mine openings in the Pratt complex, producing 1.1 million tons of coal in that year alone—a nearly 25 percent
increase over the prior year. Each shaft descended several hundred feet, and
then branched into passageways following a seam of coal. Off the passageways, miners excavated "rooms," leaving columns of coal at specific inter-
vals to hold up the roof of the mine. A few men returned to the same room
each day, removing more coal using varying combinations of picks, levers,
dynamite, and hydraulic jackhammers. The coal was loaded into small cars
running on narrow gauge rails through the passageways back to the bottom
of the main shaft, where the cars were consolidated into larger wagons.
There, a mechanized hoist, powered by a steam engine on the surface,
hauled the wagons out into daylight.

The coal was pulled to the "tipple," a huge wooden structure atop a
railroad trestle, and tipped. The coal was dumped into much larger railroad
cars waiting below. A steam locomotive hauled the trainload from there to
one of several nearby sites where the company operated more than eight
hundred ovens to produce the dense-carbon coke used as fuel by the growing number of steel and iron furnaces in and around Birmingham. In addi-

tion to nearly one thousand forced prison laborers regularly on hand, the company soon employed another two thousand free miners, the majority of whom were also black, many of them former convicts.[14]

Forced laborers were priced depending on their health and their ability to dig coal. Under state rules, a "first-class" prisoner had to cut and load into mine cars four tons of coal a day to avoid being whipped. The weakest inmates, labeled "fourth-class" or "dead hands," were required to produce at least one ton a day. A first-class state convict cost a company $18.50 a month, according to a convict board financial report. A dead hand cost $9. The leasing of convicts soon was generating in excess of $120,000 a year for the state of Alabama, an extraordinary sum for a state whose total general tax revenue—and budget—at the time barely exceeded $1 million.

To boosters of southern industry, the rapidly expanding operations at Pratt Mines were the fulfillment of a once impossible fantasy. The success not only defied caricatures of the slumbering rural South, but actively challenged a citadel of northern capitalism. "Nothing has ever been done in the South that looks so much like being a real competitor of Pennsylvania in the iron business," boasted the *Nashville Union*.[15]

In 1889, the Pratt Mines moved their prisoners into new barracks in the company's wooden stockade at the Shaft No. 1 mine. In a report to the governor, mine inspectors said the prison, designed to hold 480 men, was "as neat and clean as . . . the best regulated hotels" and that "the drinking water is filtered and in warm weather is cooled with ice."[16] A second prison was opened at Slope No. 2 later in 1889, nearly doubling the number of convicts the company could house. The company claimed to have spent $60,000 building the structures and surrounding compound.

For the men beneath the surface, the view was very different. Pratt Mines was a scene of nightmarish human suffering and brutal retaliation. Subjected to squalid living conditions, poor medical treatment, scant food, and frequent floggings, hundreds died—the victims of mine explosions, rock falls, fires, neglect, and, most commonly, recurring outbreaks of disease. Many more left the mines and work camps alive but physically shattered. If unclaimed by relatives, those who died were quickly interred in crude burial places adjacent to the prison camps or incinerated in one of the company's coke ovens.

In hushed tones, survivors recounted to friends and relatives how slave miners labored under ghastly conditions, working in pools of putrid water that seeped out of the rock or leaked from equipment used to soften the coal. The seepage was contaminated by mineral residues and the prisoners' own body waste, but was often the only water available to drink. The contaminated seepage frequently triggered waves of dysentery, a painful malady caused by drinking water contaminated with human waste. Dysentery causes inflammation of the large intestines, terrible stomach pains, and uncontrollable diarrhea that leads to severe dehydration and, ultimately for many, death. Dozens died each year during epidemics of diarrhea and intestinal sickness that swept through the mines with grim regularity, according to death registries maintained at some mines. Gas from the miners' headlamps and smoke from blasts of dynamite and gunpowder choked the air. Deadly methane, which occurs naturally in seams of coal, accumulated in poorly ventilated sections of mines. An 1890 convict inspector described "more sickness" at the Pratt Mines "than any other place."[17]

An unintended distinction between antebellum slavery and the new forced labor system became increasingly clear—and disastrous for the men captured into it. Slaves of the earlier era were at least minimally insulated from physical harm by their intrinsic financial value. Their owners could borrow money with slaves as collateral, pay debts with them, sell them at a profit, or extend the investment through production of more slave children. But the convicts of the new system were of value only as long as their sentences or physical strength lasted. If they died while in custody, there was no financial penalty to the company leasing them. Another black laborer would always be available from the state or a sheriff. There was no compelling reason not to tax these convicts to their absolute physiological limits.

The private guards who staffed the slave labor mines and camps were vulgar, untrained, and often inebriated. Placed under the complete control of the companies and businessmen who acquired them, the laborers suffered intense physical abuse and the deprivation of food, clothing, medical care, and other basic human needs. Guards, rarely supervised, hung men by their thumbs or ankles as punishment. Convict slaves were whipped for failure to work at the rate demanded by their overseers, commonly receiving as many as sixty or seventy lashes at a time. Accounts of men or women lashed until skin literally fell from their backs were not uncommon. Convicts who attempted repeated escapes were subject to many of the same torturous restraints as their slave forebears—shackles, balls and chains, or objects riveted to iron cuffs or collars to limit their mobility. A convict recaptured after escaping a labor camp in Muscogee County, Georgia, had a steel ring placed around his neck to which "was fixed a spike, curling inward, so that rapid running was impossible."[18]

Underfed and overworked convicts traveled from the Pratt Mines stockade to the mine through an underground manway before dawn each day, and back through the same tunnel after dark. Only on Sundays, when mining ceased for a day, would the prisoners see sunlight. An 1889 report by Alabama legislators reported an "immense amount of whipping" of inmates at Pratt and other prison mines.

During 1888 and 1889, seven of the black laborers forced into the Slope No. 2 mine were children under the age of ten. Prison inspection reports indicated that among nearly 1,100 men brought there, only one third could read. Fewer than forty had prior criminal records. Of the 116 prisoners who died, a large number were teenagers.

The official registry of casualties listed the death of twelve-year-old Arthur Easter in March 1888 for unknown reasons. Fifteen-year-old George Wolfork, a waiter before being seized into the prison, died in May 1888 of typhoid after first being stabbed in the arm. Malachi Coleman, a sixteen-year-old trained as a bricklayer, serving a four-month term, died in May after having his "leg mashed." Luther Metcalf, sixteen years old, died of unknown causes in October. John Cotton expired in November, six weeks after arrival. The cause of death was listed as "arm off below shoulder." Other common causes of death from just one page of the registry included: "yellow fever; abscess lower jaw; shot in neck; shot in shoulder and finger; right eye out; skull fractured."[19]

Volatile mixtures of fumes or combinations of "afterdamp"—air with dangerously elevated levels of carbon monoxide and other gases—and coal dust collected in the poorly ventilated shafts, sometimes igniting to cause huge explosions. Gas ignited in Shaft No. 1, killing eleven men in one 1891 incident, all but one of whom were forced workers. At other times, gas did not explode but began burning as it passed out of the coal—igniting the seam itself and turning the mine passage into a tunnel of literally flaming rock.[20] Some fires could only be extinguished by flooding the mine shafts entirely.

Under such execrable conditions, prisoners attempted increasingly brazen escapes, with almost monthly frequency. More than once, convicts themselves attempted to set fire to the mine in hopes of breaking free during the ensuing melee. Invariably, escapees or others died in the plots. The company reported one such breakout in May of 1890, claiming that three white prisoners and one black convict staged a fire alarm in the middle of the night. "In the terror and confusion, while the officers were trying to restore quiet," the four broke free of the stockade, guards said. One prisoner remained free for some time; a second was mortally shot. Two others—Bob Crawford and Noah Marks—were immediately recaptured, most likely by the prison's bloodhounds.[21]

In the meantime, the pent-up hostilities of the stockade erupted into riot. "It became necessary for us to adopt some prompt and severe measures to reduce the insubordinates to subjection. But everything was settled in a short time," read the company report. It is not difficult to imagine what those measures were. Mine officials said Crawford, a white man from outside the South, "committed suicide on the day afterwards."[22]

Conditions at Sloss-Sheffield's Coalburg slave camp were even worse than at the Pratt Mines. Several hundred prisoners purchased from judges and sheriffs in twenty-three Alabama counties—including the Cottingham homeplace of Bibb—had been acquired along with the purchase of the mines. In 1889, an epidemic of measles and dysentery swept through the men.

"The sickness hung on as if loathe to give up its hold upon this unfortunate place," wrote one state inspector. He called the place "disastrous." Of 648 forced laborers at the mine in 1888 and 1889, 34 percent did not survive. At the Pratt Mines, 18 percent died. All but a handful were black.[23] Another visitor in the same period wrote the Alabama governor that every slave worker who had been in the mine for at least six months had contracted dysentery. He called the death rate "enormous, frightful, astonishing."[24]

Convicts in Sloss-Sheffield's prison compound reached the mine by shuffling through a long, low-ceilinged shaft extending from inside the walls of their prison compound.[25] A special committee of the Alabama legislature studying the convict system in 1889 reported that "many convicts in the coal mines . . . have not seen the sun shine for months." In the first two weeks of June of that year, 137 floggings were given to the 165 forced laborers at the mine.[26]

Conditions were so demoralizing at the Coalburg mine, the convicts so beaten and bedraggled, that laborers did not even choose to attend church services on Sundays—the one regular diversion permitted forced workers. "There are but few of the convicts that manifest any interest in any kind of religious services," wrote Evan Nicholson, a chaplain at the camp in 1890.[27]

The horror of the mortality rates and living conditions was underscored by the triviality of the alleged offenses for which hundreds of men were being held. At the end of the 1880s, thousands of black men across the South were imprisoned in work camps only for violations of the new racial codes, completely subjective crimes, or no demonstrable crime at all. Among the "felons" sold to the Pratt Mines in 1890, seven men were working for the crime of bigamy, four for homosexuality, and six for miscegenation—an offense almost solely prosecuted against black men who engaged in sex with white women. Many others had been arrested and sold for ostensible crimes that explicitly targeted blacks' assertions of their new civil rights: two for "illegal voting" and eleven on a conviction for "false pretense," the euphemism for new laws aimed at preventing black men from leaving the employ of a white farmer before the end of a crop season.[28]

The application of laws written to criminalize black life was even more transparent in the prisoners convicted of misdemeanors in the county courts. Among county convicts in the mines, the crimes of eight were listed as "not given." There were twenty-four black men digging coal for using "obscene language," ninety-four for the alleged theft of items valued at just a few dollars, thirteen for selling whiskey, five for "violating contract" with a white employer, seven for vagrancy, two for "selling cotton after sun set"—a statute passed to prevent black farmers from selling their crops to anyone other than the white property owner with whom they sharecropped—forty-six for carrying a concealed weapon, three for bastardy, nineteen for gambling, twenty-four for false pretense. Through the enforcement of these openly hostile statutes, thousands of other free blacks realized that they could be secure only if they agreed to come under the control of a white landowner or employer. By the end of 1890, the new slavery had generated nearly $4 million, in current terms, for the state of Alabama over the previous two years.[29]

By then, local sheriffs, deputies, and some court officials also derived most of their compensation from fees charged to convicts for each step in their own arrest, conviction, and shipment to a private company. The mechanisms of the new slavery reached another level of refinement, as trading networks for the sale and distribution of blacks emerged over wide areas. Sheriffs were now incentivized to arrest and obtain convictions of as many people as possible—regardless of their true guilt or whether a crime had been committed at all. Ever larger numbers of other whites also began to seek their own slice of the growing profits generated by the trade in compulsory black labor.

"It is plain that [prisoners] are fed as cheaply as possible in order that the sheriffs may have wide margin of profit," wrote one jail inspector, Dr. C. F. Bush. "I have had several sheriffs to admit to me that, without profit from the feed bill, they would not have the office, as it was one of their greatest sources of revenue."

Another official said the system "legalized graft" and "resulted in starvation." A third prison doctor wrote that men held in the county jails routinely "made their appearance pale, weak and anemic, and the bodies covered with ulcers due to have been confined in vermin ridden, insanitary and poorly ventilated jails and the lack of a sufficient amount of . . . food."[30]

In J. W. Comer's remote home territory, Barbour County, in the cotton country of southern Alabama, nearly seven hundred men were leased between June 1891 and November 1903, most for $6 a month, each logged elegantly into a leather-bound *Convict Record*. Most were sent to mines operated by Tennessee Coal, Iron & Railroad or Sloss-Sheffield.[31]

Steady streams of telegrams and letters radiated from sheriffs, labor agents, and company executives in a furious search for additional laborers or to induce men in positions of petty power to arrest ever more men under any circumstances. Offers to bring in a particular black man for sale or pleading that certain African Americans be seized for sale poured into the office of Shelby County sheriff Lewis T. Grant in 1891. G. Bridges, an agent of the Louisville & Nashville Railroad, wrote Grant on February 24, complaining about the number of itinerant men near the station in the town of Calera, one stop away from Columbiana. "We are suffering from a surplus of loafing negroes and white tramps, and car breaking and pilfering is frequently indulged in. . . . Perhaps you might have a lot of them arrested for trespassing on the property of the Railroad Co."[32]

Bridges was less than thrilled when Sheriff Grant suggested that the railroad pay him for the arrest of the unwanted men. "Thank you for the offer of services you so kindly make," the railroad man responded a day later. He suggested that instead the sheriff's deputy be sent out. "Would it not be more convenient and expeditious, to call on him to arrest trespassers?" These were business transactions, not law enforcement.[33]

Escambia County sheriff James McMillan wrote on March 13 asking Grant to watch out for a seventeen-year-old "yellow" boy and an accompanying woman with a little girl. "Please get them up for me and if they fail to make bond which I expect they will I will come or send after them."

Jefferson County sheriff P. J. Rogers telegrammed on April 9 to "look out for Andrew Cubes a yellow negro about 22 years old who escaped from guards at Calera last night while in transit to our place from Selma, $50 reward."[34]

Sloss-Sheffield sent preprinted fill-in-the-blank postcards to sheriffs in every county, announcing the escape of convicts and the reward placed on their head. "$25 REWARD!" read the card mailed on April 21, 1891, seeking 175-pound Dan Homer, a twenty-two-year-old county convict with dark black skin, black whiskers, and scars on his left thumb and left hand.[35]

Often the sheriffs' correspondence reflected a simple gamble by some treacherous white man that if he pointed out a promising black laborer, a sheriff or deputy would find a reason to arrest him and share the financial benefits. "There is a negro up there at the Public Works by the name of Peter McFarland . . . he is a ginger cake color Black hair Black eyes hair cut close . . . he is wanted for Burglary if you will arrest him and put him in jail. I will give you $10 . . . wire me at once if you get him," wrote F. E. Burfitt, from Selma, on May 26.

The next day, Calhoun County deputy sheriff John Rowland wrote Grant: "Is there a reward for one Will Riddle wanted in your county for disturbing public worship?"

W. B. Fulton of Pensacola, Florida, wrote the Shelby County sheriff on November 23, 1891, asking if a black man with the last name of Elliott had perhaps stabbed a man at the Shelby Iron Works some years earlier. "Look into the matter and see if there is any Reward for him, and if so I will bring him to you and divide the Reward. I know where he is and can get him any-time. Hoping to hear from you at your earliest convenience."[36]

A week later, a telegraph to Grant on November 29, 1891, from the constable in Waverly, Alabama, warned that he had arrested an African American named Frank Hubbard but "will not hold unless there is an ample reward." Scores upon scores of such letters—some penned in refined script of educated men, more often in the scrawl of county brutes, some-times crisp and terse telegrams—piled in heaps in a drawer of the sheriff's wooden desk.[37] Scattered among them were reminders from Jefferson County's Sheriff Rogers, who later became general manager of convicts for the Tennessee Coal, Iron & Railroad Co., to send along bills and receipts related to the transportation of prisoners from Columbiana to the Pratt Mines—by then the ultimate destination of nearly every one of the hun-dreds of black men unfortunate enough to encounter Sheriff Grant.[38]

The opportunities for abuse in these dealings were immense and obvi-ous. Blacks who fell into the disfavor of white officials anywhere in the South could be swept into the penal system on the most superficial pre-tense. The ability of blacks to resist these developments became more and more circumscribed.

The sudden rise of this new threat was shocking to blacks at a time when thousands still actively participated in southern political life. But that too was soon under a new and corrosive attack. In the Alabama election of 1892, the political dynamics of the state were cloaked in what appeared to be a clash of ideals between a new populist rhetoric aimed at uniting agrar-ians and laborers against the "Bourbon" alliance of plantation owners and industrialists who controlled the Democratic Party—a theme echoing across the South.

The Alabama populists were led by gubernatorial candidate Reuben Kolb. It was widely believed that his victory in the previous election had been stolen in 1890, when Democrats stuffed the ballot boxes with thousands of ostensible African American votes in overwhelmingly black counties. The result had been the fraudulent but irreversible coronation of Governor Thomas Goode Jones, a former Confederate who a decade later would play a pivotal role on the issue of continuing the South's new slavery.

In 1892, both Kolb and Jones ran for the governor's office again. Kolb promised to support crop prices and regulate the abusive railroad cartels that imposed high freight fees on farm goods being shipped to market. Philosophically, he had the support of new activist black farmer's groups who shared the populist concerns over laws and practices that abused poor people, sharecroppers, and tenant farmers. In a nod to black voters, Kolb, the former state agriculture secretary and a Confederate veteran as well, also said he opposed the practice of leasing convicts.

Governor Jones vowed to revive the state by encouraging the explosive growth of Birmingham and continuing to help wealthy cotton plantation owners in the state's predominantly black, southern counties. Whites were in turmoil over the choice, with poorer hill country counties breaking for Kolb and whites in the rich flatlands once again supporting Jones. To win reelection, Jones knew he had to once more pack the voting polls with thousands of black Republicans on his side. Despite their shared economic interests with black sharecroppers and tenants, Kolb's poor-farmer white followers responded to Jones's currying of African American voters with the most shrill white supremacist rhetoric.

Jones's conservative Democrat backers, including the state's major newspapers, shamelessly turned the tables—accusing Kolb populists of supporting black political rights and dubbing him the candidate of the "nigger party." Kolb's supporters reacted with even more odious anti-black invective. The South was tracing out the lines of the violent racial ideology and vernacular that would consume it for the next seventy-five years.

John Milner, the Alabama industrialist who had so aggressively pushed for the state to adopt laws helping him fill his mines with forced black labor, published a pamphlet denouncing even the vaguest suggestion of allowing black political rights.

Titled "WHITE MEN OF ALABAMA, STAND TOGETHER!," the pamphlet blared: "It would be better . . . if left in the control of their negroes, that Alabama . . . sink beneath the waves and be forever lost."[39]

That was the real substance of the campaign. Most of the philosophical clash between the two sides was a sham, as the South was swept by the latest wave of white animosity toward African Americans. Whites realized that the allies of blacks in the North appeared to be abandoning the former slaves. A time had come to settle scores and relay the foundations for a society based on the harshest racial divisions. Further inflaming the passions of 1892 was the Federal Election Bill sponsored by Massachusetts representative Henry Cabot Lodge. The act, known to opponents as the "Force Bill," mandated that black voting rights be protected in the South through federal supervision of elections. Two years earlier, the measure was approved by the House of Representatives but failed in the Senate. The new version raised the sensational specter of reintroducing federal troops in the southern states to force compliance.

In reality, the Force Bill was the last gasp of the dwindling numbers of Civil War–era Republican idealists in Washington to compel adherence to the mandates of the constitutional amendments granting citizenship to African Americans. The measure was doomed from introduction. But its consideration left southern whites seething at the vision of another Union invasion and a return of power to blacks. It spurred the push to eliminate African American political activity once and for all. On election day in Alabama, there was virtually no doubt that Kolb outpolled Governor Jones. But once again, thousands upon thousands of ballots purportedly cast by blacks who clearly were no longer being allowed to vote turned the balance for Jones. He was declared the winner, after official returns showed 127,000 votes for Jones to the challenger's 116,000.

The reelection was followed by an astonishing surge of activity against African Americans. The opening of the next session of the state legislature marked the beginning of the final push to end all black political involvement, to consolidate the segregation codes that would define the Jim Crow era, and to begin cutting African Americans out of the most important efforts of government to improve public life. Legislators voted to join seven other southern states that already mandated segregated seating for blacks and whites on trains. Public education, a new but increasingly popular government function, was the most critical target of the racial attack.

Whites had chafed at the notion of black education as long as Africans had been imported to the United States. Instruction of slaves was illegal in the antebellum South. After emancipation, government-collected property taxes were used to open new schools for all children. Whites gawked at the schools opened for blacks during Reconstruction—even the crude one-teacher variations that predominated in the region. Per pupil spending on education for black children and white children was essentially identical, leading to wide resentment among whites—especially in the cotton plantation regions where whites owned the vast majority of land and paid nearly all the taxes, but were enormously outnumbered by African Americans in population. That "white taxes" were spent for the education of black children, rather than solely their own, was infuriating.

White leaders began to openly espouse that schools for blacks were bad for the emerging new economic order. "Education would spoil a good plow hand," opined a state legislator, J. L. M. Curry, in a speech to the Alabama General Assembly.[40] Most worrisome to leading whites was that schooling illiterate blacks would encourage "the upper branches of Negro society, the educated, the man who after ascertaining his political rights, forced the way to assert them."[41]

In the 1880s, the Alabama legislature attempted to enact laws specifying that school funds would be apportioned on the basis of which taxpayers contributed them: whites would fund white schools, blacks would fund black schools. Federal courts quickly declared that openly discriminatory scheme in violation of the Fourteenth Amendment.

As the popularity of state-funded free public schools surged, the friction caused by black education grew. The number of white children attending public schools in Alabama raced from 91,202 to 159,671 between the 1870s and late 1880s. At the same time, the number of black pupils increased from 54,595 to 98,919. But the amount of funding spent for every student was declining, and attempts to raise taxes were doomed. Whites saw the money spent in black schools as the only viable source of additional funds for their own children.

In the legislative session of 1892, white leaders simply changed the law so that school taxes were no longer distributed among all schools in equal per pupil allotments. Instead, the total number of students, white and black, would determine how much funding a county or town received from the state. But it would be up to local officials to divide the money among schools "as they may deem just and equitable." The author of the bill was hailed by another elected official who said he "deserved a vote of thanks from the white people of the state."[42] The effect on blacks was catastrophic. Overnight, white schools came to receive the vast majority of all funds for education. In one predominantly African American county, the total budget for black teachers' salaries in 1891 was $6,545—in approximate parity with what was being spent per student at white schools in the county. After turning over control of funding to local officials, black teacher salaries were slashed. Later the length of the black school year was cut to just six months—reducing costs and eliminating school as an excuse for African American children not to work in the fields during planting and harvest. Forty years later, the total salaries for teachers instructing 8,483 black children in the county had risen negligibly to just over $8,000. The budget for white teachers, with fewer than two thousand pupils, had climbed by a factor of almost 30, to nearly $60,000.[43]

If any doubt remained about the intentions of southern whites in 1892, vigilante and mob violence soon dissolved it. More lynchings of blacks occurred in the United States in 1892 than in any other year—in excess of 250. Executions peaked in Alabama the following year, with the deaths of twenty-seven blacks.

At the same time, the region's biggest industrial concerns continued to expand explosively. In December 1892, Tennessee Coal, Iron & Railroad bought outright the Cahaba Coal Mining Company and its 44,000 acres of coal-rich property—some of it extending to within a few miles of the old Cottingham plantation in Bibb County. In addition to the coalfields, the company acquired a fifteen-mile railroad, nearly five hundred coke ovens, much of the town of Blocton, and seven mines producing up to three thousand tons of coal a day.[44] The number of men forced into Alabama slave mines surged with the growth, swelling by half to 1,200 in 1892 from 845 just three years earlier.

As labor strife surged in the early 1890s, company officials privately worked on plans to shift even more of the company's operations to captive forced laborers. One Tennessee Coal, Iron & Railroad official visiting Montgomery wrote to the superintendent of the Pratt Mines: "[T]he probability is we will have to arrange to take care of a great many more convicts."[45]

On the fourteenth day of February 1893, a new era opened for the black men of Shelby County—where Green Cottenham would be arrested fifteen years later. Four men were loaded onto the Birmingham train, headed to the new buyer of Shelby's prisoners. Ben Alston, Charles Garnes, and Issac Mosely had each been convicted of assault six weeks earlier. Henry Nelson was arrested the previous day for using "abusive language in the presence of a female"—a phony charge available for arresting "impudent" black men. Scratched into the record of prisoners was the same entry for all four men, a destination so new that the jailer hadn't yet learned to spell it: "sent to prats mines."[46]


Voices of opposition to what was happening in the South were dying. Some reform-minded activists protested the physical abuses of prison labor, but the explicitly racial aspect of the new forced labor system was often largely unacknowledged. White southerners responded with galling mendacity to the occasional criticism expressed by northern newspapers. Many whites were thrilled by the patina of legitimacy presented by Charles Darwin's new concepts of human evolution, which were being twisted to offer a genetic, seemingly objective rationale for black inferiority. The dark-skinned race was capable of learning less, so blacks needed fewer and smaller schools, according to this logic. Blacks could work effectively only under threat of a whip.

In a speech to the National Prison Congress in Cincinnati, Ohio, in October 1890, Alabama's new inspector of convicts, W. D. Lee, coolly defended the appalling conditions at the mines in Coalburg and Pratt City. Virtually all criticism of Alabama's and the South's forced labor system were "exaggerations" and "falsehoods," he said.

The prisons were clean, the prisoners well fed and humanely treated. The hounds used to track escapees were "nothing more than the fox or deer hounds that have been used in the South for the chase from time immemorial, trained to run the human track." Never once had a dog injured a convict, Lee maintained.

Prisoners in Alabama received generous amounts of corn bread, bacon, fresh meat, bread, coffee, and tobacco. "Hundreds of convicts have been sent to the penitentiary with diseases of which they would have died at home for want of medical attention, who have been cured and sent home, at the end of their terms, sound men," Lee continued.

He said he was mortified by allegations that the prisoners were underfed and overworked. "In some form or other I have had the management and control of negroes ever since I came to the years of discretion," Lee said. "In the days of slavery, I fed, clothed and worked them, and since they became free, I have employed and managed them on the plantation. I see what, as free men, they have to eat and wear, and the houses they live in. And I assert here, without fear of successful contradiction, that the negro convicts . . . are better housed, better fed, better clothed, and receive better medical care and treatment in sickness than do the majority of the same class, as free men, in their homes."[47]

The truth was that African Americans were trapped in a catch-22 between the laws criminalizing the mores of black life and other laws that effectively barred them from assimilating into mainstream white American society or improving their economic position.

Even ostensible friends of African Americans succumbed to the increasingly mandatory dismissal of black intellectual faculties. "The population of our prisons is mostly a population of negroes. These people are proverbially weak, improvident, credulous—the victims of impulse and circumstances. Many of those in the prisons have been guilty of only trivial offense; and many of these offenses are not in themselves criminal, or even immoral, but which have been made penal simply by statutory enactment," wrote Jerome Cochran, state health officer, in 1892.

"It is the peculiar misfortune of the negro," Cochran continued, "that his investment with the privileges of citizenship, and of the elective franchise has also subjected him to the operation of laws made by men for the government of white men—law which he does not understand, and the moral obligations of which he is not able to appreciate."[48]

In 1895, Thomas Parke, the health officer for Jefferson County, investigated conditions at Sloss-Sheffield's Coalburg prison mine. He found 1,926 prisoners at toil. Hundreds had been charged with vagrancy, gambling, carrying a concealed weapon, or other minor offenses, he reported. In many cases, no specific charges were recorded at all. Dr. Parke observed that many were held for minor infractions, fined $5 or $10, and, unable to pay, leased for twenty days to Sloss-Sheffield to cover the fine. Most then had another year or more tacked onto their sentences to cover fees owed to the sheriff, the clerk, and the witnesses involved in prosecuting them.

"The largest portion of the prisoners are sentenced for slight offenses and sent to prison for want of money to pay the fines and costs. . . . They are not criminals," Dr. Parke wrote in his formal report.

Male prisoners were barracked in a primitive wood-plank prison beside the putrid Five Mile Creek, near a row of coke ovens. The miners spent nearly half of each twenty-four hours in the mine, six days a week. The shaft was minimally ventilated; coal cars were pushed out of the earth by the miners themselves, rather than with mechanized equipment. Medical care was dispensed occasionally from a primitive shack; scores of miners worked with serious illnesses, including untreated and open wounds inflamed with infected boils and pus. Parke's tally of prisoners held at Coalburg in 1895 included at least five hundred workers not accounted for in the state's official records at the time—indicating that hundreds of laborers had been sold into the mine through extralegal systems. More than a hundred forced laborers died at the mine during the two years prior to Parke's visit.

The physician, even one burdened with intensely racist perspectives, was shocked by the inhumanity. He asked whether "a sovereign state can afford to send her citizens, for slight offenses, to a prison where, in the nature of things, a large number are condemned to die."

Embarrassed by the publication of Parke's report, Sloss-Sheffield commissioned the physician it paid to care for the forced laborers, Dr. Judson Davie, to write a response. He claimed the extraordinary rate of mortality among blacks was their own fault. But even his apologia for health conditions at Coalburg was telling. He said many convicts, once injured, tried not to become well to avoid a return to the mine. "Some eat soap; some rub poisonous things into their sores or cuts; but by far the greater obstacle to their making quick and good recoveries is the mental depression of the new men," he wrote. He added that many miners chose to drink the polluted "seep water" in which they worked "of their own accord in preference to going to springs or other usual places of getting drinking water." He also contended that nearly every black man contracts syphilis by adulthood. No blame for that could be ascribed to the mine, he contended.

The larger issue, Davie wrote, was genetic: "It is a fact that the negro

race is inferior to the white race physically as well as mentally and morally—
their powers of resistance, so far as a great many diseases are concerned,
notably tuberculosis, does not compare at all favorably with the white race."

Still, Dr. Parke's criticism of the lethal conditions in Sloss-Sheffield's
slave mine embarrassed the company enough that a month later its president, Thomas Seddon, sent a letter to local officials defending his treatment of black workers. He summed up the explanation neatly: "The negro
dies faster."[49]

Sentiments like that were hardly rare in the three decades after the
Civil War. Yet throughout that difficult time, African Americans still clung
at some level to the idea that whatever white men such as Parke said or did,
the United States as a whole still stood squarely to the contrary. This, the
Civil War proved, was immutable.

Then, in 1896, the U.S. Supreme Court denied a thirty-year-old white
shoemaker with a trace of African blood, named Homer Plessy, the right to
ride in the white compartment of an East Louisiana Railroad train. On its
face, the ruling sanctioned only the newly conceived concept of "separate
but equal" public facilities for blacks and whites. But its actual import was
vastly greater. *Plessy v. Ferguson* legitimized the contemptuous attitudes of
whites like the top executives of Sloss-Sheffield. Moreover, it certified that
any charade of equal treatment for African Americans was not just acceptable and practical at the dawn of the twentieth century, but morally and
legally legitimate in the highest venue of white society.

It was a signal moment in America's national discourse. From the lowli-
est frontier outposts to the busiest commercial centers, Americans had
shared a consensus that the highest definition of a citizen was his veracity,
that truth telling and fulfillment of a man's commitments were the highest
measures of virtue. The near cult of honesty that pervaded public discussions was quaint by the sensibilities of more than a century later. But in a
still new nation born of the eighteenth-century Age of Reason, it was an
utterly sincere expression of a fundamental national creed.

That allegiance to logical purity, combined with the basic tenets of
equality embodied in the philosophies of the Revolution, had impelled the
nation toward civil war during the antebellum decades, as the inherent contradiction between the new republic's noblest ideals and slavery grew more
apparent. In spite of the prevailing view among all white Americans that

blacks were in some manner lesser to them, the nation nonetheless made war upon itself at devastating cost, in a conflict ultimately justified as a struggle to end the bondage of slaves. Northern soldiers who had doubted whether emancipation was worth the blood it required were transformed by scenes of new freedom they encountered in the South. The morally bewildering sacrifice of the war became a concrete demonstration that a nation could steadily mold itself toward the "more perfect union" of the Declaration of Independence. The surrender of the South, the emancipation of the slaves, and passage of the civil rights amendments of the 1870s were the zenith of that vision.

The Supreme Court's endorsement in 1896 of the flagrantly duplicitous doublespeak of Jim Crow segregation represented a resignation of America's white institutions to the conclusion that the emancipation of black slaves had been folly. Most agreed that the elimination of slavery per se was an adequate remedy to the past abuses of blacks. In the eyes of the vast majority of white Americans, the refusal of the southern states to fully free or enfranchise former slaves and their descendants was not an issue worthy of any further disruption to the civil stability of the United States. Black Americans were exchanged for a sense of white security.

There had always been lies and misrepresentations in U.S. politics, but the new consensus represented by *Plessy v. Ferguson* marked an extraordinary turning point in the political evolution of the nation. Thousands of northern whites had fought not because of their fondness or empathy for African Americans but because the principles of the Declaration of Independence coupled with the American compulsion for honesty demanded it. The abandonment of that principle, and embrace of an obviously false mythology of citizenship for black Americans, brought an end to the concept that abstract notions of governance by law and morality could always be reconciled to reality. It marked a new level of unvarnished modern cynicism in American political dialogue. And it established a pattern over the ensuing twenty years in which almost any rationalization was sufficient to excuse the most severe abuses of African Americans.

Emboldened by the betrayal from the nation's most eminent legal minds, the men controlling the mines and labor camps of the South adopted even more flimsy ruses of justification for black men's imprisonment. The level of physical coercion increased terrifyingly. At the Pratt

Mines, an observer for a special Alabama legislative committee in 1897 wrote a report describing 1,117 convicts, many "wholly unfit for the work," at labor in the shaft.[50] In an 1898 convict board report, the largest category in a table listing charges on which county convicts were imprisoned was "Not given."[51] No one even bothered to invent a legal basis for their enslavement.

In a 1902 report, one man was in the mines for "disturbing females on railroad car." More than a dozen were incarcerated for "abusive and obscene language." Twenty convicts were digging coal for adultery, twenty-nine for gambling. Dozens of prisoners were at labor for riding a freight train without paying for a ticket.[52] In 1902 and 1903, local officials in Jefferson County prosecuted more than three thousand misdemeanor cases, most of them yielding a convict to work in a Sloss-Sheffield mine—the vast majority of whom were black.[53]

One of those convicts was John Clarke, a miner convicted of "gaming" on April 11, 1903. Unable to pay, he ended up at Sloss-Sheffield. Working off the fine would take ten days. Fees for the sheriff, the county clerk, and the witnesses who testified against him required that Clarke spend an additional 104 days in the mines. Sloss-Sheffield acquired him from Jefferson County for $9 a month. One month and three days later, he was dead, crushed by "falling rock."[54]

At least 2,500 men were being held against their will at more than two dozen labor camps across Alabama at the time Clarke died. More than nine hundred were in the Pratt Mines. Sloss-Sheffield held nearly three hundred. The McCurdys still controlled nearly one hundred in Lowndes County. Scores more were imprisoned in the turpentine and lumber camps of the Henderson-Boyd and Horseshoe Bend lumber companies and other remote prison compounds scattered deep in the forests of southern Alabama. Payments to the state that year exceeded a half million dollars, the equivalent of $12.1 million a century later and a figure nearly equal to 25 percent of all taxes collected in Alabama.[55]

As the dark cloud of the new slavery was descending on those men and the hundreds of thousands of friends, acquaintances, and family members across the South, the descendants of the old slave Scipio struggled to maintain emancipated lives. Abraham Cottingham and his sons Jimmy and Frank, descendants of Mitt, another son of Scipio, were among nearly four hundred black voters who still participated in Shelby County elections in 1892. Defiant, even as the vast majority of other black men in the county were intimidated or obstructed from the polls, Abraham paid an increasingly onerous poll tax and complied year after year with burgeoning requirements established by the state of Alabama for blacks to qualify for a ballot. Each election year, under hostile eyes, he signed his name boldly in the register of voters maintained in the worn-brick county courthouse across the street from the jail.[56] But even Abraham could not resist the new state constitution adopted in 1901, under which virtually no black person could again vote in Alabama. No black Cottingham would cast a ballot for at least six decades.

Sometime in the 1890s, Henry Cottinham died. The circumstances of his death weren't recorded. In June of 1900, Mary Cottinham abandoned Brierfield, where so many black descendants of the Cottingham farm had once congregated, leaving behind only Henry's younger brother Elbert, with his own wife and ten children.

Struggling to survive, Mary, the former slave girl from the Bishop farm, moved the remaining family to Montevallo, a town just inside Shelby County, where a new mining company was expanding quickly. She found work as a washerwoman. Her two daughters, Ada and Marietta, sixteen and twenty, were anxiously hoping for marriage. Soon, the girls would leave home, and Mary was alone with her youngest. Her baby boy, Green, was fourteen and had learned to read and write.[57] Surrounded by the terrible tempest of hostility engulfing black America, he was rising into the muscle, hair, and boisterous curiosity of a teenage man.

# PART TWO

■ ■ ■

## HARVEST OF AN
## UNFINISHED WAR

# V

# THE SLAVE FARM OF JOHN PACE

*"I don't owe you anything."*

The last thing John Davis should have been doing in the second week of September 1901 was a long hike across the parched fields of cotton stretching endlessly along the Central of Georgia Railway line running from the Georgia state line to the notorious town of Goodwater. Millions of crisp brown cotton bolls, fat and cracking at the seams with bulging white fiber, waited in the fields and river flatlands of central Alabama calling out to be picked. The task would take weeks and demand the labor of virtually every available man, woman, and child for hundreds of miles.[1]

Davis needed to be in his own patch of cotton—the lifeline of his tiny farm near Nixburg, a wisp of a town twenty miles south of Goodwater. For him to maintain any glimmer of independence in the South's terrifying racial regime, Davis had to produce his single bale of cotton—the limit of the physical capacities of one farmer and a mule and just enough to pay a share to the owner of the land he farmed and supply his family with enough food and warmth to pass the cold months soon to set in.

But as he struggled to reach the tight bend in the rails more than ten miles from his farm, where freight trains were forced to slow and itinerant travelers knew there was a chance to leap aboard empty freight cars, John knew he needed just as badly to see his wife, Nora. She was ill—so sick it had become impossible for him to care for her and the young couple's two children—especially at the very time of the season when he, like hundreds of thousands of men working small farms across the South, had no choice but to remain in his fields from dawn to dusk.

John and Nora had been married for only three years. At twenty-five, she was two years older. She came to the marriage with two children born when Nora was little more than a child herself. John treated the youngsters as his own. The husband and wife had come of age just miles apart on the outskirts of the rough-edged railroad town of Goodwater and married there in 1898. Eleven-year-old Albert certainly was already John's most important helpmate in the fields. At harvest time, he would have also needed ten-year-old Alice and Nora picking the rows.[2] Sending them all to Nora's parents' house meant John would have to pull every boll himself. But it must have seemed the only way.

John stayed behind working furiously to bring in the crop. But Nora remained desperately ill. Her husband had to see her now. So Davis made his way on September 10, 1901, to the big railroad curve outside Alexander City and waited with the other men wandering the rails for the No. 1 train. The fall sun was just beginning to falter as the train eased out of the little mill town at 5:31 P.M. each day. Half an hour later, he would be on the outskirts of Goodwater.

As the train ambled forward, Davis must have felt a contradictory set of worry and relief as panoramas of cotton fields flashed by in a gentle blur on each side of the tracks, bobbing across the low foothills at the southernmost base of the Appalachian range. He would have to hurry to see Nora and the children, and still return to Nixburg in time to save his cotton. He prayed he was not going to Goodwater to bury his wife. He had to know he might not make it home before his fields were ruined.

Still, the dust-choked freight car rattling across the landscape was in its own way a respite from the torturous tasks of the harvest. Gathering a season's cotton was excruciating work. Davis, like nearly every black man and woman in Alabama, had spent most of his waking life pawing through such fields. The passing crop rows soon would be choked with laborers: strapping young men coursing through the rows with swift, nimble expertise; young mothers with babies towed atop long sacks of cotton dragging behind them; nearly feeble old men and women—African Americans whose lives were grounded immutably in the seasonal rhythm of growing, tending, and picking cotton for other men.

The eldest in the fields were slavery's children—the toddlers and adolescents and near adults of the emancipation time—who had experienced the full exuberance of freedom and citizenship and then the terror of its savage and violent withdrawal. Now they moved slowly behind their young people, picking with thin leathery fingers whatever fiber had been missed by the others, while the toddling children of this sour new era of oppression scrambled alongside, heaving their own sacks. Albert and Alice would absorb for themselves the same unchanging equinoxal cycle of cotton growing and cotton picking, but in their lives—at least until old age—it would never be sweetened or leavened by even the flash of freedom that the children of slavery days had briefly known three decades earlier.

On the plants, blanketing the fields and rising in the most fertile places as much as six feet high, supple green buds that had swollen beneath small graceful flowers were by now turning hard and brittle. Split open and dried dark brown, the outer skin of each pod was sharp to the touch. As the strongest field hands moved down the furrows, pulling the cotton and passing it into their sacks, fingers and palms began to crack and bleed from the pricks and slices of thousands of bolls. Depending on the weather and condition of the cotton, harvest season might well begin in September and drag past Christmas, long after the cotton stalks had frozen and died.

With every passing week in that span and each downpour of rain, the crop grew less saleable and more vulnerable to swings in the prices offered by the ginners who consolidated the local harvests for sale to cotton brokers in Montgomery or Columbus, Georgia. At critical junctures in the picking season, poor weather or lack of sufficient laborers could destroy an entire year's crop. For the white men who owned cotton land in 1901, mobilizing every available black worker—man, woman, and child—into the fields at picking time was the single most crucial challenge of the entire season. Even the most progressive and generous white men in America, whether in the South or the North, almost universally agreed that blacks were preternaturally skilled at this particular task, and naturally and spiritually ordained to perform it. That it might be wrong to coerce or compel African Americans to work the fields when the crop was in danger rarely occurred to any white man.

White farmers needed similar numbers of black workers in the early weeks of the following spring, when seed was being planted and bright new shoots of cotton had to be carefully tended, each furrow regularly hoed to keep weeds from smothering the fragile seedlings. Once the cotton was up, and stretching toward the sky, and all through the hot months of summer, there could be fewer hands. Nearly all the women and children were idled during the humid months. So long as rain and sun came in the correct proportions, the cotton would stretch higher and fuller. In some years, it grew as tall as a man's shoulders, thick and impenetrable, straining with the weight of blossoms. After the cotton was picked in the fall, there was once again little work to be done. African Americans faced the long, hungry "lay by" of winter.

This conundrum of farm labor management—the need to satisfy radically spiking demands for labor and the absolute peril of failing to do so—had been the most compelling impetus for slavery in the nineteenth century. There were many other reasons that slavery survived in the Deep South too, some economic and some cultural. But in the end, it was the particular nature of cotton production, requiring absolute access to armies of laborers for brief periods at crucial points in the calendar, which made slavery a superbly successful economic mechanism. By holding laborers captive, plantation men could dragoon every worker, regardless of age or strength, at those urgent junctures and marshal them into highly efficient gangs of field workers—all without worry that they might ever drift away in search of better circumstances during the lean months in between.

In the nearly four decades since emancipation of the slaves, white farmers in the South had evolved only negligibly in their abilities to manage enterprises with free labor. Concepts of industrial labor practices—such as set working weeks and fixed hourly wages—remained foreign to most late-nineteenth-century southerners. They were mystified and offended by the demands of former slaves—encouraged by agents from the federal government in the immediate wake of emancipation—that they be paid regular, set amounts and receive guarantees of certain working conditions through a written contract with white farmers. Even sharecropping—in which black farmers lived on and worked small parcels of land in return for keeping a portion of their harvest—and straightforward renting of farm land to African Americans required a form of business acumen and honest dealings that few southern whites were capable of fulfilling in their relations with blacks. White landowners in the South almost universally believed that management of their farms could be successful only if, in one way or another, "their Negroes" could be tied to the land. Coercion and restraint remained the bedrock of success in the cotton economy—and the cornerstone of all wealth generated from it.

To establish a serflike status for blacks, whites relied on a bitterly repressive new social code. Few would hire a black worker who did not have the express approval of his or her former white employer to change jobs. Off the farms, only the most menial work could be awarded to African Americans—a convention that both blacks *and* whites violated only at risk of their own physical harm. Black public behavior beyond the "bumbling Negro" caricature acceptable to whites—whether in attitude, dress, or visible aspirations—also invited economic ostracism by whites, at best, and physical injury at worst. The possibility of mob violence against any African American who blatantly rejected the unwritten code lingered in the background of black life, a relatively infrequent but omnipresent threat.

Just as ubiquitously undergirding the new conventions of black and white relations—and overshadowing every aspect of the lives of young black men—was "the Lease," as most southerners generically called the new system for seizing and selling African Americans. In addition to the black men compelled into slave mines and lumber camps, thousands of white landowners and local businesses in the countryside and in provincial towns like Goodwater, Nixburg, and nearby Columbiana regularly purchased black men from local sheriffs and judges who participated in or turned a blind eye to the process.

There was also no longer any possibility that blacks might obstruct the new trade in forced labor through political participation. As of 1901, nearly every African American had been effectively stripped of all elective rights in Alabama and virtually every southern state. After passage of a new state constitution in 1901, Alabama allowed the registration only of voters who could read or write and were regularly employed, or who owned property valued at $300 or more—a measure clearly aimed at complete elimination of blacks from voting. In Mississippi, only those who were able to pay a poll tax of up to $3 and who could, according to the voting registrar's personal assessment, read or understand any clause in the U.S. Constitution could register. Louisiana permitted only those who could read and write or owned at least $300 worth of property. (However, any person who could vote on January 1, 1867, or his descendants, was allowed to continue voting regardless of reading skills. This literal "grandfather clause" guaranteed continued voting rights for illiterate and impoverished whites.)

South Carolina required literacy or property ownership. North Carolina charged a $2 poll tax and required the ability to read. Virginia, after 1904, allowed to vote only those who had paid their annual $1 poll tax in each of the three years prior to an election and who could fill out a registration form without assistance. Veterans from either the armies of the Union or the Confederacy were exempted of the requirements—though few of the thousands of African Americans who fought in the Union army were acknowledged as veterans.

During the same legislative gathering at which the new Alabama constitution was drafted, a delegate from Chambers County named James Thomas Heflin came to prominence. Over the next thirty years, he would be the state's most influential figure, serving as a U.S. senator and an early master of the rhetoric of white supremacy that would be emulated across the South by men such as Theodore Bilbo in Mississippi, Strom Thurmond in South Carolina, and Bull Connor and George Wallace in Alabama. During debate over how completely blacks should be blocked from the vote, Heflin argued that there should be no possibility of African Americans casting ballots, regardless of their individual intelligence or wealth. Standing in the elegant legislative chambers of the state capitol in Montgomery—a building that forty years earlier had served as the first seat of government of the Confederacy—he boomed: "I believe as truly as I believe that I am standing here that God Almighty intended the negro to be the servant of the white man." Anticipating eventual war between the races, Heflin continued: "I do not believe it is incumbent upon us to lift him up and educate him on an equal footing that he may be armed and equipped when the combat comes."[3]

When debate turned briefly to whether the whipping of prisoners leased to coal mines and lumber camps should be prohibited, a representative from Sumter County summed up the position of the constitutional convention:

"Everybody knows that the great bulk of convicts in the state are Negroes," he said. "Everybody knows the character of a Negro and knows that there is no punishment in the world that can take the place of the lash with him. He must be controlled that way."[4] The laws remained unchanged.

. . .

As Central of Georgia No. 1, carrying John Davis on a car close to the rear, approached the final wide curve of the tracks on the outskirts of Goodwater on that Tuesday in September 1901, the conductor blew his whistle and slowed dramatically as the engine eased past Sterling Lumber Company. For almost thirty years, this had been the point of disembarkation for the scores of impoverished men—mostly black and a few white—who used the freight trains of the South routinely to move from town to town and job to job. The railroad bed was itself the handwork of forced laborers, as was the case for nearly all southern rails built before the Civil War or in the first decades after. Goodwater was a place of rich opportunity for men seeking menial work. It had grown into a flourishing commercial center as the hub of the cotton economy in the verdant plain of farmland that rippled between the Coosa and the Tallapoosa rivers—which plunged on parallel currents, eighty miles apart, out of the Appalachians and into the Black Belt of south Alabama. As the picking season progressed each fall, farmers pulled their cotton in long trains of mule-powered wagons from outlying settlements to the gin and rail station at Goodwater. From there, the compressed bales of lint were shipped by train southeast through a succession of other Alabama towns to Columbus, Georgia, sixty miles away. River barges took them down the Chattahoochee River to ports on the Gulf of Mexico at Pensacola and Apalachicola, Florida.

For the paying passengers on the line, Goodwater was a welcome respite from the dusty rails. The town had been the final stop on the line in the railroad's first years of operation, feeding a flourishing local economy of hotels, restaurants, and carriage rentals to continue the journey to the new city of Birmingham. Goodwater's Pope House hotel was a nineteenth-century culinary landmark. The nearby Palace Hotel and Argo Saloon were famous as outposts of comfort and vice. After the rails were extended the remaining distance to Birmingham in the 1880s, nearly every train on the line continued to stop at Goodwater to rest passengers and load cotton, coal, and water for the steam engine.

After the final whistle before the train neared Sterling Lumber, John Davis and the other informal travelers deftly hopped off. It would soon be dusk, and Davis began making his way by foot toward the home of Nora's parents. As he arrived at the first cluster of houses near the Goodwater train station, within earshot of the Pope House and its dinnertime banter drifting in the late-day quiet, a white man suddenly appeared in the road ahead.

"Nigger, have you got any money?" he shouted.[5]

The man was Robert N. Franklin, one of the town's appointed constables and keeper of a dry goods store perched at the top of the muddy dirt street that led through Goodwater's commercial district. Davis certainly would have known who Franklin was. Short-necked and rotund, Franklin and the store he ran had been fixtures in Goodwater for at least a decade. There were no black-owned enterprises in Goodwater, and Davis's parents would have traded regularly at the store owned by Franklin. The very overalls that Davis wore that day almost certainly came from Franklin's store or one of the other white-owned mercantile shops facing Main Street.

That mattered little at the moment Franklin appeared from the shadows. The question he belligerently posed was a simple but perilous provocation. However Davis answered was fraught with jeopardy. Under the new racial statutes and conventions of the South, demanding whether an itinerant black man had money was tantamount to asking him to prove his right to freedom, or his right even to live. A black man traveling alone in Alabama could be arrested and charged with vagrancy on almost any pretense. To have no money in hand demonstrated his guilt without question and, worse, was seen as absolute proof of his worthlessness. Almost every possible consequence of admitting indigence or joblessness—much less of having ridden for free on a freight train—was terrible.

Yet given the vulnerability of every black man among whites—even more so a white with some measure of official authority and community respect—to reveal that he possessed cash exposed him to more grave risk. Vulgar whites like Franklin could rob or harm a black man with impunity, against which he had no recourse. Contrarily, to accept the risk of a vagrancy charge and lie to a local official might be the beginnings of even more serious trouble. Davis had only to glance around as the light faded that evening to be reminded of his vulnerability. The road ahead ran from the edge of town, alongside the tracks, rising slowly up a long hill. It passed the open gallery of the Pope House and its two stories of painted wooden clapboards—all off limits to African Americans. Railroad Street continued first past the crude one-room brick lockhouse that passed for the town jail, and then the enormous Goodwater train depot, and finally to a crest where Franklin's store looked over the settlement. At the train station, as a score or more of white passengers disembarked, local black men hustled to unload baggage and fill the freight cars with freshly ginned bales of cotton. All but a few came from farms owned by white men but worked by black men.

A partly blind African American man clad in threadbare overalls, called "Bad Eye" Bradley, furiously refilled the steam engine's boilers with water and its fuel car with coal. He was one of the few black men in the town with a job paying regular wages. Across the street from Franklin's store, Davis could have seen the plate glass windows on the front of the saloon and the balustrade of the second-floor balcony of the Palace Hotel—both destinations of relative luxury that no black man would ever dare enter as a customer. Tethered out front were the one-horse carriages and open-bed wagons that only the rarest African American owned.

Out of sight from Davis, except for their cluttered rear entrances, stood a succession of new brick buildings extending south from Franklin's store for several hundred yards. Among them were businesses operated by the mayor, Dave M. White, and his close friend, justice of the peace Jesse L. London, as well as the vacant lot where construction of the new town hall was to begin in a few months. Only to the north, across the railroad tracks, among a ramshackle collection of shotgun houses and unpainted bungalows where most of the town's black population lived, was there a place of refuge for an African American man. Davis had prayed to reach it before Franklin appeared in the street. Now it was too late.

With his single hostile query—"Nigger, have you got any money?"—Franklin distilled the smothering layers of legal and economic jeopardy that defined black life in the twentieth-century South. Davis was pinned.

"No, I have not got any money," the black man stammered. Then, gambling on what Franklin was up to, he corrected himself. "I have some, but not for you."

"When are you going to pay me the money you owe me?" Franklin pressed.

"I don't owe you anything," Davis said.

The two men stood facing each other in silence for a moment. Then Franklin went on his way, but Davis knew the incident wasn't over. He crossed the iron rails and made his way to the home of Nora's parents as quickly as he could. For a few hours, there was a quiet reunion of the farmer, his children, and the stricken wife and mother.

But later that evening, the constable showed up again. He called for Davis to come outside.

"I want that money, or I will arrest you," Franklin shouted.

"You will have to arrest me. I do not owe you anything," Davis said, clinging to the hope that a higher authority would see through Franklin's ruse.

Galled by the black man's resistance, Franklin left again. But soon another local constable arrived, Francis M. Pruitt, a burly mass of man who sported a bushy western mustache and a wide-brimmed black hat. He said he held a warrant for Davis's arrest.

"Let me see it," the black man said.

"Come up town and I will let you see it," Pruitt rejoined.

There was little else Davis could do. Earlier in the day, he might have escaped by catching another railroad car and fleeing the county as quickly as possible. But the chance for that was passed now. Docile cooperation was Davis's only reasonable recourse, his only chance of seeing Nora again, of ever returning to his fields. It was still conceivable that he could weather this scrape with no harm, that a reasonable voice would come to his aid. If necessary, he would simply submit to whatever the white men demanded. It was a dance every black man in the South was being forced to learn. To resist only invited far worse.

Davis trudged to the center of town with Pruitt, who locked him in the calaboose near the train station, not far from where his encounter with Franklin had begun. Four other African Americans seized by Franklin and Pruitt in the previous forty-eight hours were already there. Davis never saw the ostensible warrant for his arrest, and would have been unable to read it if he had. Later Jesse London, the justice of the peace, would testify that Pruitt himself had sworn out a warrant claiming Davis "obtained goods under false pretenses" from him—rather than Franklin—and that Davis willingly pleaded guilty to the charge.[6] London claimed he ordered Davis to pay a fine and the costs of his arrest and trial, though no one involved could later recall what the amount of the sentence had been.

The next morning, Pruitt retrieved Davis and the others from the calaboose and hustled them onto the train platform to board the No. 3 train from Birmingham at 9:55 A.M.—one of two daily runs rattling from Alabama's booming new industrial center, down through the prosperous provincial towns of Sylacauga, Goodwater, Dadeville, and beyond to either Montgomery, the state capital, or the river port at Columbus.

"We are going to carry you over to Mr. Pace's," Pruitt informed Davis.

"I don't know Pace's," Davis replied.

"We know," the white man replied.[7]


John Davis had been snared in the web. In the section of Alabama where Davis traveled that fall, at least two dozen local white men were actively involved in a circuit of traffic in human labor orbiting a seventy-five-mile stretch of the Central of Georgia rail line, with the town of Goodwater as its epicenter.

Pruitt and Franklin were the most regular procurers of stout-backed black workers for men of means in the surrounding towns and counties who needed a steady stream of compliant hands. Nearly every sheriff and town marshal in southern Alabama made his primary living in some variation of this trade in human labor—some through formal contracts between the counties or towns and the big mining companies and timber and turpentine operations. Others limited themselves to the less organized, clandestine capture and sale of black men along the railroads or back roads—such as John Davis. Pruitt and Franklin and many others operated with a measure of official police power given by local governments. Even more men—typically brutish plantation guards or the young adult sons of large landowners—acted as "special constables" or temporary deputies appointed to serve arrest warrants concocted to justify the capture of a particular black man.

To give the arrests an imprimatur of judicial propriety, Franklin, Pruitt, and others relied on the judges of what were called Alabama's "inferior" courts. In these lower courts, town mayors, justices of the peace, notaries public, and county magistrates had authority to convene trials and convict defendants of misdemeanor offenses. A relic from the frontier era, every Alabama town or rural community had such local judges appointed by the governor or locally elected. Most were store owners or large landowners—men of limited substance but in the context of their world the most substantial men of the community. In the town of Goodwater, the amateur judiciary consisted of Mayor White and Jesse London. Once appointed justice of the peace by one governor, such men retained their powers almost in perpetuity, either by routine reappointment from successive governors or so long as local citizens accepted their continuation in unofficial "ex officio" capacities. By the turn of the century, Alabama had thousands of such judges scattered through every community and at almost every major crossing of roads, so many that no one in the state capital even maintained a comprehensive list of who they were.

Mayor White's dry goods store was a few doors down Main Street from Robert Franklin's. London, whose mercantile business was nearly adjacent to the mayor's, was almost as young as White's oldest children, and he was married to a cousin of White's wife. The two wives, both reputed to be marvelous cooks, at times managed the Pope House hotel near the train station.[8]

Mayor White, the son of a blind farmer, had grown up without education under difficult circumstances in the countryside of another rural Alabama county. To his death in 1935, his tastes never deviated from the poor people's fare of squirrel, opossum, and chitterlings. Yet in spite of those origins, White moved to Goodwater intent on lifting himself from the coarse life of frontier Alabama through sheer labor and willpower. He had no patience for games or those he considered loafers. "By the eternal, if you need exercise, get a hoe and do something constructive with it," White liked to tell children. Over time, he acquired farms and a livery stable in addition to the store. With success, he took on the air of a benevolent businessman, donning a daily uniform of a pinstripe shirt, gray suit, black bow tie, and a black hat. At Christmastime, he secretly passed out food and paid for medical care for poor whites in the town. He was active during the turmoil of Alabama's late-nineteenth-century political battles, eventually winning election to the Alabama Senate and the Executive Committee of the state Democratic Party.[9]

But the emergence of a place like Goodwater, or a man such as White, into the first degrees of twentieth-century sophistication was not entirely what it seemed. Long into middle age, White would fight any man he believed insulted him. He impressed his children with his gallon-by-gallon consumption of moonshine whiskey, and ability to chain-smoke cigars. On one occasion, he survived a gunshot wound received during a political argument at a rally in Dadeville. He was an early proponent of the defiant "states' rights" agenda that would consume southern Democrats, and in the next generation fuel segregationists like Strom Thurmond and in the following generation George Wallace. He made bitter enemies in politics and business, and believed there were "parasites" threatening the society that whites like him had wrested from the tailings of the previous century. He was contemptuous of the notion that African Americans deserved the full citizenship of the Fifteenth Amendment.

Yet it was this man—uneducated and crude—who held power in Goodwater, conducting rudimentary trials on the boardwalk in front of his store, maintaining a clumsy "city court" docket of warrants and verdicts behind his counter, and extending his legal authority in support of the county's busy slaving network. Under White's acquiescence, his friend Jesse London summarily found John Davis guilty of a misdemeanor—despite the fact that Franklin and Pruitt couldn't agree on what charge they were claiming to bring against him.

In adjoining Tallapoosa County, the man most relied on to sentence free men to hard labor was a justice of the peace named James M. Kennedy, a civic jack-of-all-trades who extracted a steady income from a collection of overlapping, periodic public appointments. He had been an election inspector for the area in 1892, and not infrequently was made a special temporary deputy sheriff to serve warrants in civil and criminal cases. Most important, Kennedy was named by Governor William Oates in 1894 a justice of the peace and notary public for the remote section of Tallapoosa County where he lived—though a decade later he was no longer certain by which governor or in which year his tenure as a judge had begun.

Few of the part-time judges such as White and London had any legal or academic qualifications beyond better than average handwriting. Even that skill was not often apparent. There were no clear guidelines for the proper operation of the inferior courts or clear case law defining their parameters and jurisdiction. Like so much of the legal and administrative systems of regions only decades removed from wilderness status, the lower courts of Alabama were policed mainly by citizens' innate sense of justice. The power of these ill-defined casual judges, particularly over illiterate and impoverished citizens, was immense.

Above men like Kennedy, White, and Franklin, at the top of the pyramid of players in the rural forced labor networks, were large landowners,
entrepreneurs, and minor industrialists—just as they had been in the years
before the Civil War. In Coosa and Tallapoosa counties, the trade in African Americans relied on three powerful families, all of whom in turn at least
periodically employed or conducted business with most of the other men
involved in the buying and selling of black men.

The two most prominent buyers, John W. Pace and James Fletcher
Turner, together held a contract to "lease" every prisoner sentenced to hard
labor by the two counties. Turner and sometimes Pace also leased from the
city of Dadeville all prisoners who had been convicted under the town
ordinances.[10] Sometimes in conjunction with each other, sometimes operating independently, Pace and Turner actively purchased African Americans
through every official and unofficial means available. Both operated farms
with hundreds of acres under till, large sawmills, and mining or quarrying.
In 1900, Pace paid $2,600 to expand his holdings to include a five-hundred-
acre plantation near his main farm.[11] He ran the farm from a large and comfortable country home—where he had become well known in the county
for his lavish hospitality—and maintained a second residence in town, less
than a block from the Dadeville square.

Turner, known to acquaintances as Fletch, owned a large farm four
miles outside the town limits, in a place called Eagle Creek, a booming
sawmill at a settlement called Camp Creek, and a major stake in a limestone
quarry at Calcis opened by his father and managed by his younger brother
Eliza. Even measured against the wide scope of human horror being perpetrated in the slavery operations of Pace and Turner at their farms and
sawmills, the quarry near the newly founded town of Calcis stood alone as
a place of notably perverse abuse.

Situated thirty-five miles northeast of Goodwater, the quarry was half-
way up the rail line to Birmingham. Inside its compound, workers heaped
huge quantities of shattered limestone into two thirty-foot-high cylindrical
kilns, which superheated the rock with blasts of burning coal piled into
a lower chamber. Under intense heat, the limestone turned to quicklime,
a highly caustic powder that when moist turned instantly into a burning,
potentially explosive acid.

Eliza Turner was a man of questionable mental stability—claiming later in life that he had invented the radio, the X-ray, and the Teletype, only to have been robbed in each case by Guglielmo Marconi and others.[12] Laborers who survived the Calcis quarry told frightening stories of tubercular men and sexually abused women quarantined to a sick house hidden deep in the adjoining woods. Equally horrifying were the fates of workers who accidentally came into contact with quicklime unintentionally mixed with water. The few who lived left the quarry with terrible, disfiguring acid scars.

Despite the dangers in making quicklime, the substance was a critical component in the blasting of iron ore into steel and fetched lucrative prices from the iron companies expanding at breakneck speed in Birmingham. By the time the Turners' five-year-old quarry and kiln was operating at full capacity in 1903, its sole customer was Tennessee Coal, Iron & Railroad Co.—the company fast becoming the most powerful commercial interest in the state and the keeper of more than a thousand forced laborers at its Pratt Mines.

The Turner quarry hired skilled free laborers to run the locomotive that dragged tons of limestone up from the quarry pit and coopers who made barrels to ship the powder. But for the back-jarring task of wielding picks and sledgehammers in the bottom of the pit, and the unremitting task of piling thousands of tons of stone into the stone kilns, the Turners relied on Franklin, Pruitt, and the others to supply dozens of slave laborers crowded into a crude log and stone "pen" at the edge of the quarry.

Turner himself lived in a spacious farmhouse at the Eagle Creek farm with his extended family, including a volatile eighteen-year-old son, Allen, who took charge whenever his father was away.

Not far from Pace's farm were George D. and William D. Cosby, two middle-aged brothers with large landholdings who frequently repurchased black workers from Pace and Turner. The Cosbys, along with W.D.'s twenty-seven-year-old son, Burancas, worked the black men and women they acquired on their own farms and also engaged in a sideline of reselling workers to smaller-scale farmers nearby.

Between the fall of 1901, when John Davis was arrested in Goodwater, and the spring of 1903, the three families—Pace, Turner, and Cosby—bought at least eighty African American men and women. Like the hundreds of undocumented forced workers tallied in the Sloss-Sheffield mine in 1895, none of those captured near Goodwater ever appeared among the thousands of "official" convict laborers sold by the state of Alabama and its counties. The true total seized by the three families was almost certainly far higher.[13]


A day after his arrest, John Davis still didn't know what charge he had been convicted of, or how much money Robert Franklin falsely claimed he owed. After a one-hour rail ride to Dadeville and then a ten-mile trip by horse and wagon to a five-hundred-acre farm at the meeting of the Tallapoosa River and Big Sandy Creek, Davis faced the hoary form of John W. Pace.

Pace was a towering figure. He loomed over most men, more than six feet tall and weighing at least 275 pounds. Despite his fortune, he still rou- tinely appeared in town in a collarless, homespun shirt, homemade shoes, and a broad-brimmed black hat—his face was flush from a life of work out- doors. By 1900, he showed signs of gout and walked awkwardly—which he explained as the result of severe frostbite to his feet in the past.[14]

Davis was pulled from the wagon and forced to stand before the old farmer. Pace, further confusing the contradictory bogus charges, pro- claimed that the black man owed Pruitt $40 for goods purchased at a store in Goodwater. Now he claimed Davis also owed Franklin $35 for fines and costs from his conviction.[15] Davis had two choices, Pace said: to pay $75 immediately or agree to be taken under his control.

Davis had no choice. He had no money at all. Pace promptly produced a two-page handwritten contract on which Davis, who could not read or write his name, scrawled an "X." The contract signed, Pace paid Pruitt and Franklin $75. The coerced contract was a sham, and illegal on its face. Court decisions already in force made it clear that even if Davis had been legitimately convicted of a crime, he could not legally be held on the con- viction once his fine had been paid—as Franklin and Pruitt claimed they had done.

Regardless, Davis knew only that he had marked a document that he was told obligated him to work at any task Pace demanded for ten months, to repay the $75 Pace had "advanced" him to pay the fines. Most signifi- cantly, Davis had unwittingly agreed to language that appeared in dozens of such contracts that Pace and others intimidated black laborers to sign.

Under the documents, the blacks Pace acquired "agree[d] to be locked up in the cell at night" and submit to "such treatment as other convicts."[16] The contracts further authorized "that should the said Pace advance me anything over and above what he had already furnished me, I agree to work for him under this contract until I have paid for same in full." The additional charges explicitly included any costs resulting from a laborer attempting to escape the farm. Most ominously, the documents allowed Pace to "hire me out to any person, firm or corporation in the state of Alabama—at such sum as he may be able to hire me at for a term sufficient to pay him all that I may owe him."[17]

For all practical purposes, Pace owned John Davis.


John Pace arrived in Tallapoosa County at the age of twenty-five in 1879, a time when settlement towns and farms were still being carved from unmarked forests. Most land was dense red clay, flecked with shards of igneous rock, layered upon the flanks of infertile ridgelines cutting asymmetrically to the north and east. Gold was mined there in the 1830s and the 1840s, and the flurry of early wealth established one aspiring country town, Dadeville. Almost ten miles from the deep Tallapoosa River, Dadeville had a railroad station, a few stores, and a livery stable. Setting it apart from other hard-edged outposts was a small medical institute—a source of southern physicians since before the Civil War.

By the 1880s, the rich mineral veins were tapped out. The allure of cotton had replaced the magnetic attraction of gold. Farmers and tradesmen like Pace were slipping in from Georgia and other parts of Alabama to begin a new, more orderly domestication of the land. Growing numbers of them worked in exasperation to clear the trees and scratch crops out of rocky fields on the low ridges. But along the Tallapoosa River lay a wide spine of rich alluvial soil running through the center of the county. On that bottomland plain, where a creek called Big Sandy emptied into the Tallapoosa, spread one great tableau of flat, fertile land. Pace set out to obtain all of it he could, and make his fortune there.

Pace had never been troubled by slavery, or any other manner of the white man's control of blacks in the odd postwar world. For that matter, hardly any man Pace had ever met objected. He had been only nine years old when his family's slaves were emancipated from their Georgia farm during the Civil War. One of them, a girl named Catherine, only a few years younger than he, never departed. She took the Pace family name and, despite freedom, grew to middle age as a servant in his Tallapoosa County home.

There were no illusions in this section of Alabama about the nature of relations between black men and white. No one laid claim to the stylized hoop-skirt vision of antebellum life embraced in the Old South fantasies that were becoming the vogue in the rest of the United States. Eastern Alabama had never been suited to vast plantations where paternalistic slave masters and contented black servants supposedly lived before the war. Black men and women in Tallapoosa County were there to be worked, worked hard like mules. Notwithstanding whatever the Thirteenth Amendment said about slavery, if white people wanted to buy "Negroes" like mules, sell them, trade them, or whip them, there was nothing wrong about that to Pace either.

Before the war, a slave owner named Gum Threat owned another Tallapoosa river plantation not far from where Pace established his first farm. He handled his slaves in the final years before emancipation with indifferent brutality. "Iffen they ever was a devil on this earth it was Gum Threat," recalled one of his former slaves a half century later. "He jest didn't have any regard for his slaves. He made 'em work from daylight to dark and didn't give them any more food and clothes than they could possibly git along with. He beat them for everything they done and a lot they didn't."

After an escaped slave named Charles Posey was dragged back to Threat's plantation, the master stood above him on the edge of his front porch and kicked the man under the chin. "You could hear his neck pop. He fell to the ground and kicked around like he was dying," recalled the former slave who witnessed the punishment. "They brought him to and then Gum Threat stripped him to the waist and took him into an old building, stretched him out and fastened his feet and hands wide apart. Then he took a live coal of fire as big as your hand and laid it in the middle of his bare back. I remember seeing the scar there and it was about one-eighth of an inch deep."[18]

John Pace recognized the value of restoring forced black labor as soon as he arrived in Tallapoosa. Soon after the Civil War's end, the probate judge in Dadeville, who ran the county government, adopted the practice of parceling out arrested blacks to farmers who were willing to pay for them. Pace successfully ran for county sheriff and quickly absorbed how profitably black men could be rounded up and put to work in his own commercial interest, and what little glimmer of judicial process was necessary to hide slavery behind a guise of prisoners working off legal penalties for actual crimes.

By 1885, just six years after buying his first two hundred acres of Tallapoosa river bottom, Pace reached an agreement with the county judge to lease every prisoner sentenced to hard labor, as well as any unable to pay fines and court costs. As in almost every Alabama county, that amounted to nearly every black man arrested.

Fifty years after Gum Threat's assaults on his slaves, life was little changed for the new slaves of Tallapoosa County. Not far from Pace's spread, a man named B. S. Smith operated a large farm and timber operation on the banks of the Tallapoosa. He contracted directly with the state of Alabama to acquire several hundred men found guilty in state courts of felony offenses. In addition, Smith and his wife, Elizabeth, aggressively sought scores of other forced laborers from counties across Alabama. After the couple wrested the contract for Autauga County prisoners away from W. D. McCurdy in 1883, Mrs. Smith complained to the county sheriff that one worker had disappeared during the transfer from McCurdy's notoriously brutal Lowndes County farm to hers.[19] By the mid-1880s, the Smith plantation degenerated into a miserable compound of rampant disease and death.

In 1886, a black prisoner named Alex Crews died at the Smith convict farm from complications of severe frostbite to his feet. A state physician visited on January 30, 1886, and reported back to the state Board of Inspectors of Convicts. "I found the clothing of the convicts very defective, being thin and worthless, insufficient for protection during the cold weather. Many of them had no shoes beyond a sole tied to their feet, there being no uppers and some with no protection for the feet except rags tied around them. I told Mr. Smith that the clothing and sanitary condition of the men were miserable and outrageous."[20]

A reporter for the *Montgomery Daily Dispatch*, a black newspaper in the state capital, wrote that one of its reporters had asked Crews on his deathbed whether there were other men on the Smith farm as ill as he. "Oh, yes, boss,"

Crews replied. "Some of them are a heap worse." The following month, the president of the Board of Inspectors of Convicts, Col. Reginald H. Dawson, visited the farm and reported back to Governor Edward O'Neal that he found "seven convicts more or less frostbitten, and that one of them . . . will probably die."[21] The state took no action.

Pace operated his slave farm little differently, extending his landholdings and his purchases of black men in tandem proportions. As his operations grew, he employed a growing number of white men to manage various enterprises and portions of the farm. In the spring of 1892, he hired the justice of the peace, James Kennedy, who had just married the younger sister of Pace's wife, Mollie. Pace had raised Mollie almost as a daughter, and Kennedy became in effect his first son-in-law. After a few months spent running a limestone quarry in the adjacent county, Kennedy settled into a house 150 yards from that of Pace and took over the older man's sawmill and its squads of black hands.

Six years later, Pace added Anderson Hardy to the payroll, a man just a few years his junior but the new husband of Pace's nineteen-year-old daughter, Elizabeth. He lived in a house adjacent to Pace's and acted as a foreman of the farm, guard, and, frequently, the designated whipping boss to lash noncompliant workers.

Pace had become a great landowner by the standards of the province and his era, with nearly a thousand acres of property under till at the Big Sandy Creek farm and ownership of several blocks, including a second home, in downtown Dadeville.[22] Like many in Tallapoosa County, he also harbored visions that gold might once again be found in the area, and purchased a half interest in May 1894 in a labor-intensive mining venture at his end of the county.[23]

Powered by the flow of the Big Sandy Creek, the Pace sawmill teemed with the black laborers he acquired from throughout Alabama, working under conditions and with technology little changed from the Bibb Steam Mill a half century earlier. Kennedy oversaw the operation with cold indifference, and soon began to branch into other duties desired by Pace.

Thin, ever clad in an inexpensive rumpled jacket, balding severely except for a few twisted locks at the crown of his forehead, his voice high-pitched and nasal, Kennedy struck an unattractive profile, a southern Ichabod Crane, unaccustomed to and ill-equipped for power. Any of the men and boys imprisoned on the place, and most likely all of the women, could have knocked him to the ground. But armed with a buggy whip and his obscure appointment as a justice of the peace, and backed by the wealthy white men who paid him, Kennedy was transformed into a terrifying figure.

Using his status as justice of the peace to convict and sentence men for misdemeanor offenses, Kennedy became the on-site judge for Pace's forced labor business. When the Cosby family wanted to take control of a particular black man, one of the Cosbys would order an employee to swear out an affidavit accusing the African American of a crime—usually failure to pay for goods, breaking a contract to work for the entire planting season, or a charge as generic as "fighting." Often, the bogus warrants were signed by Jack Patillo, the young son of a related white family; J. Wilburn Haralson, another white employee of the farm; or one of several black workers who lived permanently under the control of the Cosbys.

Whatever the charge, the Cosbys seized the black man and took him and their affidavit to Pace's farm, where Kennedy would hold the semblance of a trial. These proceedings never lasted more than a few minutes, and rarely was any record of the charge or outcome preserved. There was never an acquittal, according to later statements by Kennedy. The defendant was always found guilty and ordered to pay a fine he could not produce, usually $5 plus the costs of the arrest and trial—a total of about $20. For a black laborer at the turn of the century in Alabama, $20 was a sum equal to at least three months' work. The Cosbys, who had seized the black man to begin with, would claim to pay Kennedy the ostensible fine and fees, and force the prisoner to sign a labor contract agreeing to work a year or more under guard to pay them back.

The system worked almost flawlessly. Soon the Cosbys were acquiring so many black men and women that, within a few years, Kennedy said he could no longer recall most of their names and faces.[24]

The efficiency of having Kennedy convict any black man or woman desired by a white buyer was also obvious to Pace. There was no need to remit any portion of the fines to the county courts or to submit to even the superficial supervision that was sometimes demanded for the prisoners he purchased directly from the county jail. Most useful was that when a black man's term of labor neared an end, Pace, Turner, or the Cosbys could swear out a new warrant for another supposed crime. Kennedy would obligingly convict again, and sentence the worker to another six months or year of hard labor. Soon, the Cosbys arranged for William D. Cosby to be named a notary public as well. After that, in order to further the ruse of court oversight, the trials were divided between the two slave farms in a carefully structured theater.

"W. D. Cosby would try Pace's negroes. I would try Cosby's negroes," Kennedy later explained. "Whenever the time of a man working for J. W. Pace or W. D. Cosby or G. D. Cosby was about out, they would send somebody before me, if one of Cosby's negroes, to have an affidavit against him on some trumped up charge; and, if working for Pace, somebody would go before W. D. Cosby and make an affidavit against him."[25]

Except for Pace, Turner, and the eldest Cosbys, nearly all of the men engaged in this labor-selling network were in their twenties or thirties. Most had recently begun their own families. Many were born during or just after the Civil War and had grown up steeped in the stories of the roles their fathers or grandfathers played during the conflict and the chaotic years that followed. They were not descendants of the white ruling class, but hardscrabble country whites whose previous generation had fought to defend slavery but whose members had rarely owned slaves themselves. All came of age during the years when African Americans exercised their greatest level of freedom and political participation in the South. As children or teenagers they witnessed or heard the stories of the violent campaigns carried out by their fathers to reestablish white hegemony in the 1870s and 1880s.

These men emerged into adulthood just as the political parties of the South were finally articulating, without reservation, and with only scant criticism from elsewhere in the country, a rhetoric of complete white supremacy and total black political exclusion. They explicitly embraced as personal responsibility a duty to preserve the new racial regime. The rising young men of Goodwater and Dadeville also were motivated by their understanding that unlike the long-ago era of full-scale slavery—in which their fathers gained almost nothing from richer white men's ownership of slaves—the economic benefits of the new system of black forced labor were available to nearly every white man.

The buyers in the new system grasped that lesson better than any. It was they who had forged the new racial order of the South, through two decades of strife between whites and blacks and among whites who could not agree on how best to reassert their control over the region. Pace and Turner had been in the thick of that fight.

A decade before John Davis was delivered to Pace's farm, as the April primary election in the pivotal year of 1892 approached, Pace and Turner led opposing factions amid the tensions flaring in Tallapoosa and every county seat across the state. Borrowing from the leading newspaper in Birmingham, the local *Tallapoosa Voice* bellowed against the continued participation in elections by black voters in counties where African Americans made up a majority or large minority of the population. "The one issue before the white people of Alabama is to maintain the integrity of the white man's democratic party. This is the one thing to which the party organization should look. That is the one thing the voter should address himself to," said one editorial.[26]

Pace declared himself a backer of Reuben Kolb, along with the rest of the local Democratic leadership. The rallying call of the Kolb populists became the denunciation of any black participation in the primary election. Another newspaper allied with Pace's group, the *Alliance Herald*, mocked the reliance on black votes by the Bourbon coalition led by Governor Jones. "Oh yes; you are terribly concerned about white supremacy! While you are . . . pretending to be so much exorcised [*sic*] on the subject, your friends and allies in Sumter county are preparing to have negro votes carry that county for Jones. Negro votes in Marengo and negro votes in Sumter! No negro has voted for Kolb in this contest."[27]

Kolb carried the party primary in Tallapoosa County, but lost the statewide election. Infuriated by the wave of black voting—some of it fraudulent—that sealed Jones's nomination, the populists abandoned any pretense of sympathy to African American farmers. Kolb continued his bid for governor under the flag of a new third-party "Agrarian" alliance. To rally voters, his supporters adopted the most virulent white supremacist invective.

Quoting from a Republican newspaper in Washington, D.C., the *Voice* warned local whites of the "feast" that awaited them if full citizenship was allowed for blacks:

*More than twenty negro Representatives from the South will render the
Republican control of the future Congresses absolutely safe and sure.
Heavy taxes should be laid upon the property of the whites to develop and
extend the public school system of these States. Separate schools of the two
races would be abolished, and the plan of bringing the youth of both
colors into close and equal relation in school and churches given a fair
trial. . . . The State laws against the intermarriage of the races should
be repealed, and any discrimination against the blacks in the matter of
learning trades or obtaining employment should be a criminal offence—
while the colored man's rights to hold office should be sacredly protected
and recognized.*[28]

The irony that this description was exactly the vision of American life
promised by the U.S. Constitution escaped nearly all southern whites.
Against that backdrop of fury, Tallapoosa County Democrats met in July
1892 to make official the county's support for Kolb, the populist candidate
who had won the earlier primary. As the formalities were concluded, the
county's most prominent Confederate veteran, Brig. Gen. Michael J. Bulger, a southern hero of Gettysburg, the war's most decisive battle, was asked
to regale the crowd at the mass meeting in Dadeville. But ten minutes into
Bulger's stemwinder on the heroism of the county's storied Civil War units,
Fletch Turner and a rump committee of supporters for incumbent governor
Jones barged in and seized the podium. Through a series of parliamentary
maneuvers, Turner's group took charge of the county party organization and
endorsed a new slate of party nominees—including the local superintendent of education substituted for Pace in the race for county sheriff.[29]

Jones carried the statewide election by a vote of 127,000 to 116,000,
winning twenty-nine counties versus thirty-seven for Kolb. Despite Fletch
Turner's party coup, Tallapoosa stayed in the Kolb camp. Jones retained the
governorship.

Pace and Turner would not argue politics again. A century of complete
white domination of the South was under way. The two men forged a commercial partnership grounded on the same white supremacist principles.
On the issue of black men, they agreed completely. Pace and Turner
became partners in the business of buying and selling African Americans.
Together they signed a new contract with Tallapoosa County and with the

probate judge of adjoining Coosa County to acquire all the prisoners of
both jurisdictions. Their forced labor network began to thrive.


As the long spare frame of James Kennedy ambled from house to house
down Red Ridge Road in the dusty southern end of Tallapoosa County in
April 1900, the fields were teeming with black farmhands planting the
cotton that would be harvested the following fall. In another of his remunerative government sidelines, Kennedy was the appointed federal census
taker for the Red Ridge beat—the section of the county controlled by his
employer and brother-in-law, John Pace. He spent his days that spring
busily listing the 1,250 residents of every household in the district.[30]

On the approach to the Pace family compound, Kennedy's task became
both more familiar and unsettlingly grim. After listing the members of his
own family and the white farmers who adjoined the sawmill he managed,
Kennedy arrived at the crude farm of Jessie Lisle, a forty-eight-year-old
father who worked mostly as a guard over the blacks held at Pace's farm.
Lisle rented a patch of property from Pace too and with an overgrown family scratched out a coarse life from a garden and a few pigs and chickens.

Next came the household of Anderson Hardy, the new son-in-law of
Pace. The marriage was only two years past, but Elizabeth Hardy had
already given birth to a child and seen it die. Sharing the house with the
Hardys was Joseph G. Smith, another guard, renting a bed, and Mary Smith,
a thirty-seven-year-old black women listed as a servant. Hardy kept four
black men aged twenty-eight to thirty-two years locked in a cell nearby.
Finally, there was the prisoner Maurice Cunningham, an illiterate ten-year-
old black "water carrier," who spent his days sprinting from man to man on
the farm with a simple wooden bucket of water and dipper made from a
dried gourd.[31]

The last residence before reaching the big house where John Pace lived
was the home of James H. Todd, a guard on the plantation who rented a
room to Arther Berry, a forty-year-old overseer who acted as Pace's whipping boss.

When Kennedy arrived at the main house on the plantation, he listed
the members of Pace's family in the same straightforward fashion as he
had at almost every other home on Red Ridge Road. There was John,

forty-six years old, his wife of twenty years, Mollie, and a sixteen-year-old
son, Fulton—a studious boy who was already working as a teacher in the
nearby school for white children. Also living in the home was Catherine,
the black cook who had grown up from slavery times with John Pace.

Beyond the inner circle of the blood-related family members, converting the sordid particulars of the farm and its other inhabitants onto the
clinical grids of a census bureau enumeration form wasn't simple. How, for
instance, to categorize the rest of the Pace farm population's relationship to
John Pace, the head of household? Or of the five African Americans held in
the crude cell at Hardy's place? Kennedy could not call them slaves—slavery
was abolished. The census bureau's old "Slave Schedules," listing unnamed
human chattel by sex and age, hadn't been used since 1860. Yet for all practical purposes that was what these black workers were. Kennedy could not
call them "boarders," as paid farmworkers living on a worksite were commonly called on government forms. That was the term used for Pace's various guards rooming with nearby white families. In his first pass through
the paperwork, Kennedy simply skipped the column altogether.

Beneath the names of the Pace family members, Kennedy first listed
the eleven men then on the property who had been delivered by the sheriffs or other authentic police officials of Tallapoosa or Coosa county, ostensibly for committing misdemeanors. Most were young, single, strong adults.
All of them were black. Most could read and write at least a little. Henry
McClain, twenty-two years old, Milledge Hunter, eighteen, Erwise Sherman, thirty, Harry Montgomery, twenty-one, Jim Miles, thirty-two, Eman-
ual Tripp, a twenty-six-year-old Arkansas boy now very far from home.
Familiarity exempted no black man from the fates of the Pace farm: Green
Lockhart, aged twenty-four, was almost certainly a descendant of slaves for-
merly owned by a white family of the same name at the other end of Red
Ridge.

Mixed in with the young men were other African Americans with
larger lives and responsibilities waiting for them elsewhere. Isom Mosely
and Alwest Hutchinson were both thirty-one years old and married. Mosely
had three children somewhere. Willie Ferrell, twenty-nine, had ten young-
sters at home. Henry Wilson, at fifty years old the dean of these men and
the father of nine children, had owned a farm of his own at the time of his
capture.

Each of them came under the labor and control of Pace through at least a semblance of a formal judicial process, though the legitimacy of all the misdemeanor arrests and convictions was doubtful. Kennedy listed those men as "convicts." But in addition, Pace was also holding seven other blacks. Augusta Wright, thirteen years old, was listed as a housemaid. Two sets of brothers were being worked in the fields: Archer Lewis, aged twelve, and Q. F. Lewis, just ten. Luke Tinsley was thirteen, and Henry Tinsley was ten. None had learned to read or write.

Pace had seized the Tinsley brothers as soon as they grew big enough to pick cotton—to begin paying off a debt he claimed was owed by their mother for a fine he paid on her behalf three years earlier, in 1897.[32] Luke, already bulking into the young frame of a man, could swing a hoe as well as almost any other laborer. Henry, a small boy with smooth dark black skin and chocolate hair, skittered across the field to keep up with his brother and avoid the gruff shouts of the two adult African Americans overseeing the children in the fields. Both adults were former slaves, now almost certainly being held by force: P. Johnson, a forty-five-year-old man born in Virginia, and Josephine Dawson, a thirty-five-year-old wife and mother. On his second pass, Kennedy described the group being held against their will as "servants."

The largest fields of the Pace farm had long been cleared of forest and tamed into productive cotton. But on the boundaries, and in adjacent property he acquired in the 1890s, Pace's enterprises were a crude blade cutting into the raw of the land. His holdings included huge swaths of vestigial forest, still choked with the same massive timber that greeted the first frontier settlers. Removing the towering stands of oak, hickory, and pine, excavating and burning the tremendous root systems they left behind in the river's ancient alluvial deposits, releveling the ground, ditching to drain the new fields: these were the monumental tasks required to continue expanding Pace's small empire. The means and methods of turning the land to production were hardly changed from the times of Elisha Cottingham nearly a century earlier—axes and cross-saws, mules and slaves.

The economic incentives for Pace were twofold. Clearing the land expanded the range of his cotton production. But more immediately, there was a buzzing market for the lumber he could produce in clearing the giant trees of the property. Sawmills were busy in every section of Tallapoosa County, and Pace needed a constant flow of new laborers to perform the backbreaking tasks of clearing the "new ground" and keeping the sawmill in near-continuous operation.

When John Davis arrived at the Pace farm a year after the census enumeration, few of the African Americans recorded by James Kennedy had escaped. Some, like Davis, had been fraudulently snared as they traveled country roads and sold to Pace by ad hoc constables, for amounts ranging from $40 and $75. Others were arrested in towns and formally convicted in the county seat for allegedly violating some petty offense, most often vagrancy. For most, there was little or no record made of their alleged crimes, when their "sentences" would expire, or in some cases, even who they were. Davis was held with men called "Tallasee" and "Gypsy," whose identities and origins were never clear to him. No official records of their "arrests" were ever created.

Each was coerced into signing a contract like the one entered into by John Davis—agreeing to be held essentially as a slave for approximately a year, locked as "a convict" at night, chained during the day if Pace desired it, and obligated to continue working past the expiration of the contract for as long as Pace claimed was necessary to pay for medical or any other extra expenses over the term of the agreement—including the cost of recapture if the prisoner tried to escape. Occasionally, a friend or relative of a Pace prisoner would appear and purchase their freedom. In the case of highly productive laborers, Pace nearly always asserted a basis for keeping them far longer than the original term—often extending from two years up to ten.

The simplest method of adding additional time to a man's contract was to accuse him of another made-up charge. A typical ploy was to claim that a black worker had violated his or her contract by eating food they weren't entitled to, or rearresting them as they departed at the end of the contract on a claim that they were leaving with clothes that actually belonged to Pace. Another theatrical "trial" would be held before one of the various justices of the peace. If one of the other white men was interested in obtaining a particular African American, Pace routinely sold them for a premium over what he had originally paid. In those cases, Pace made a profit in addition to the value of the year or more labor received. The black worker was then compelled to sign a new contract with his buyer—usually agreeing to work another year or more to pay off his new "debt" to the white man.

To resist the system was more than foolhardy. Arther Berry, the man Pace most often relied on to discipline his laborers, was like most southern white men in his belief that black workers could only be fully productive if frequently subjected to physical punishment. Berry's tool of choice was a three-inch-wide leather strap. The whipping end was eighteen inches long, attached to a wooden handle. Berry, or one of the other guards, ordered laborers to lower their pants and lie on the ground while being whipped with the strap on the buttocks, back, and legs. Those who resisted were held down at the hands and feet by other laborers, often stretched across a barrel or the stump of a tree. In the crude environment of the farm's timber-cutting operations, Berry would whip with any available object if his strap was not handy, cutting a switch from a tree or using a sapling the size of a broom handle.[33] Other whipping bosses on the farm were his brother, Jesse Berry, and the thuggish guard James Todd.

One prisoner described in an affidavit how the obedience of laborers was enforced: "I was mistreated bad sometimes," said Joe Patterson, who became an object of particular cruelty. "Mr. Todd whips the hardest. Sometimes Mr. Todd would tie [a convict's] hands together and put them over the knee and put a stick in between the legs and whip him with a big buggy trace, pulled the clothes down so he would be naked. Sometimes he would hit over one hundred licks, sometimes fifty, or seventy-five times, sometimes thirty—never less than thirty. . . . The whipping would take place in the field or stockade, no doctor present and nobody to count the licks, or time it."[34]

In another bitter echo of antebellum years, any effort to escape the slave farm risked not just the laborer who attempted to flee but any black person he or she encountered. After a black man named Dave Scott ran away, Pace tracked him down with dogs and then arrested everyone on the property where he was taking refuge. Pace ordered that Scott's wife, four other family members, and two more blacks found nearby be brought back for "harboring" the runaway slave.

After being found guilty by James Kennedy, the half dozen workers were sold to George Cosby, who held them in a stockade surrounded by guard dogs and beat them regularly. When the sentence of one of the workers, Lum Johnson, was about to expire, he was rearrested and charged with stealing potatoes from another nearby white farmer, Bob Patillo. Cosby took him back to his farm, claiming he'd paid an $18 fine on his behalf. Johnson was forced to sign another labor contract and returned to the stockade.

Nearly all the black residents of Tallapoosa and the surrounding counties had heard stories about atrocities on the farms of Pace and other forced labor enterprises in the area. Everyone knew black men faced medieval-era punishments for any failure to work; black women faced the double jeopardy of being required to submit both to the cotton fields and kitchens, as well as the beds of the white men obtaining them.

A black neighbor near the farms named M. J. Scroggins said the Cosbys starved their forced laborers and were violent. "They would feed the negroes on nothing but a little corn bread and syrup. Go barefooted in cold weather, women and men," Scroggins said. "The white people would be afraid to go by the Cosbys. Some people had gotten killed out there, and never could prove who did it. The Cosbys are pretty bad folks. If a strange negro walked along the road they would catch him up and put him on the chain gang." The Turner farm was particularly notorious for sadistic inflictions upon sexually defiant black women. At one point, an African American woman named Hazel Slaughter suddenly reappeared in Dadeville after a months-long disappearance. She showed other women in the community how her stomach was scarred and raw from an attack by dogs used to track her down after an attempted escape from the farm of Fletch Turner. In whispered tones, Slaughter said she had run away after watching Turner's teenage son, Allen, use a spade to beat to death another black prisoner, named Willie Ferrall. Bloodhounds were set on her track. They tore through the woods behind her as she fled, finally running her down miles from the farm. Before guards caught up on horseback and began dragging Slaughter back to service on the Turner farm, the dogs had torn the clothes from her body and ripped open her stomach.

The account was more than plausible. Stories circulated in the county months earlier that Allen Turner had killed a young black woman on the farm named Sarah Oliver. Another black woman, Cornelia Hammock, was arrested in Dadeville and charged with larceny on May 20, 1902, according to the rudimentary trial docket erratically maintained by the town's mayor.

She pleaded innocent, but was immediately declared guilty by the mayor and fined a total of $16.40. Unable to pay the fine, Hammock was ordered to the farm of Fletch Turner to work until November 1903—a total of eighteen months. She survived only two days. No cause of death was recorded. Her death was never investigated.[35]

"It is the general talk of the colored people in and about Dadeville," swore a local black leader a year after the killing. The stories were "reported to colored people by other colored people who have been there that these practices are carried on there all the time. . . . Colored people believe it."[36]

Tallapoosa County had become the embodiment of the casual new slavery flourishing across the South. White southerners had clearly won the national debate over who would decide the future of the country's black population. As southerners had insisted for more than a decade, the nation's "Negro problem" would be dealt with using the southern, white man's solution. None of the ostensible allies of black citizenship would act meaningfully to stop it.

From the perspective of most white Americans, the new racial order had been affirmed formally and informally at the highest levels of society. The U.S. Supreme Court ruling four years earlier in *Plessy v. Ferguson*, sanctioning "separate but equal" public facilities for blacks and whites, sanctified the wave of new legislation and business practices requiring disparate treatment of blacks and whites. The ruling's effects went far beyond the courts and legislative chambers. The open willingness of the highest court to base its seminal ruling on claims that were so clearly false—that train cars designated for blacks were no different from those of whites—sent a profound message to all Americans. So long as whites performed at least the bare rituals of due process and cloaked their actions behind claims of equality, the crudest abuses of blacks and violations of their protections under law would rarely ever be challenged.

The neo-slavery of the new century relied on a simple but extraordinary ruse that the Supreme Court's ruling implicitly endorsed. Men such as Franklin, Pruitt, Kennedy, Berry, and Todd, in places like Goodwater and Tallapoosa County, could safely force a black man into servitude for months or years as long as they pretended that the legal rights of those black men had not been violated. The implications were as deeply absorbed by black people as were the rhythms of farming in the era of old slavery. This long era of false trials and arrests would taint the African American view of legal processes and guarantees for generations to come.

In the larger scheme of what was happening across the South, the capture of John Davis was a routine, inconsequential event. John Pace acquired a steady stream of mostly anonymous black men throughout the year leading to the seizure of Davis. Pace and his son-in-law Anderson Hardy bought Jack Melton in February 1901, using the pretext of a fake warrant signed by James Kennedy accusing Melton of the ubiquitous allegation of "violating a written contract." In April of that year, Elbert Carmichael was seized. Then came Ed Burroughs, on an allegation no one could later recollect. He was followed by Joe Hart and Otis Meyers. Just before Halloween—a month after Davis was kidnapped and sold—Pace bought Lewis Asberry for $48.

Through the winter and approaching spring planting of 1901, the seizures of black men continued steadily.[37] After the turn of the year came Joe Patterson, the defiant black man sold for $9.50 to Anderson Hardy, who in turn resold him to Pace. Patterson had been arrested in Goodwater and convicted by "Judge" Jesse London, the same storekeeper who "convicted" John Davis the previous fall.

On January 17, 1902, Franklin and Pruitt were back at the Pace farm offering a young boy named W. S. Thompson, convicted at Goodwater of carrying a concealed pistol. Pace paid $50 for him. The so-called witness to Thompson's signature on a contract agreeing to work for Pace for one year to pay off his fines was Lewis Asberry—the black man seized three months earlier. Ten months later, Pace sold Thompson back to his mother.[38]

Near the end of February, Turner wrote a check to John G. Dunbar, the Goodwater town marshal, against his account at Tallapoosa County Bank in the amount of $40. On the memo line, Turner scratched: "Cost of fines for 3 Negroes." In March, Robert Franklin delivered to Pace a black man named Hillery Brooks and traded him for $35.

The seizure of black men on the back roads of the South was no longer even a brazen act. Note Turke, a young black man from the Tallapoosa County hamlet of Notasulga, held a job as a free worker with Tennessee Coal, Iron

& Railroad in Birmingham. After a visit home, he was walking down a dirt road outside Dadeville on the way to catch a train back to Birmingham on a harshly cold day in the middle of November 1902. Suddenly Burancas Cosby, the son of W. D. Cosby, appeared on the road and tackled Turke without provocation.[39]

"Where are you going?" Cosby shouted.

"To the depot," Turke replied.

"Do you want a job?"

"I already have one. I'm on my way to it."

"Where are you from?" Cosby asked.

Turke explained where he lived, who his family was, and even rattled off the names of white people he knew, all in a vain effort to demonstrate that he was a black man who deserved not to be molested or harmed. The result was only to convince Cosby that Turke was a worker worth having.

"You are a very good nigger. You better stop over with me," Cosby proclaimed, pointing to his house up the road. Cosby mounted his horse and continued on his way.

Turke knew better than to go to the white man's house. He hurried toward the train station, still miles away. Cosby, no doubt uncertain of whether he could manhandle Turke in a one-on-one struggle, stayed behind. But soon Cosby caught back up, this time accompanied by a boisterous crowd of other white men.

"Turn around and go back with me," Cosby shouted.

Turke could do little else.

Cosby took him to the farm of his uncle, George Cosby, and locked him inside a corncrib. The next morning, a black farmhand named Luke unlocked the door and took Turke before George Cosby.

"Hello, young man, what are you doing here?" the elder Cosby asked through the slats holding Turke and the bulging harvest of the farm's corn crop.

"I don't know. They have got me here. I don't know what for."

"What are you going to do about it?" Cosby said.

"I don't know. I am a stranger here. They stopped me and got me here. I cannot help myself," Turke said.

"Young man, didn't you know they would do things like that? There are grand rascals about here. Do you want me to go your bond?"

Turke was flabbergasted. "I have not done anything for you to go my bond."

Cosby, playing out the thin charade of a kind and reasonable white man, told Turke that he should plead guilty to whatever charge the white men claimed against him. "If they call on you, you plead guilty," Cosby said. "If you say you want me to go, I will get you out of this thing and work you."

"Plead guilty of what?" Turke asked. "I am guilty of one thing, that is going on the public road, and I thought that was free for everybody."

"You plead guilty and you will get off light," Cosby reassured him.

"I am in a strange county," Turke replied. "But if you will allow me a chance to write or telegraph home . . ."

"No, we don't want that at all, you go ahead and plead guilty—whenever they get their hands on you they are going to do what they like with you. You just plead guilty."

Turke finally told the older white man that he and his son would have to do whatever they chose—kill him or imprison him—but that he would not plead guilty to a crime dreamt up by others. "Kill me or do what you please," Turke said. "I propose to do what is right."

As dark fell, Burancas Cosby and the gang of white men returned and took Turke into the night. They dragged him outside a window at the home of another white man who was a justice of the peace. Turke never heard his name. Talking beneath the raised sash of the window, the justice astonishingly said he wouldn't play along with the ruse that night. "Men, I can't have anything to do with this thing," the justice said. "I have had a lot of those things before me, and I told you not to come before me any more with such things as that."

The mob took Turke back to the log crib. The next day, they returned, on horseback, buggies, and wagons, and took Turke to a small warehouse where another ostensible justice of the peace waited. He dutifully pronounced Turke guilty, though it wasn't clear of what crime, and fined him $15 plus unspecified costs.

Turke had already been robbed by one of the white men of the $5.41 and a pocketwatch he carried on the first day of his kidnapping. He had nothing with which to pay. George Cosby appeared and proclaimed he had paid the fine. He took the silent black man back to his farm and the corn-crib and its iron lock.


The system by which John Pace and Fletch Turner obtained black men for their farms, sawmills, and limestone quarry was more refined than the Cos-bys' brutish tactics. The two men often spent their days on the square in downtown Dadeville, awaiting word via telegraph of their various enter-prises and the frequent arrival of regular procurers of black labor, who arrived daily on the two train runs stopping at the town depot.

Robert Franklin and Francis Pruitt, the two men who seized John Davis, were the county's most important traders in black men. At forty-six years old, Franklin was the most atavistic of the half dozen constables and deputies who were routinely on the prowl for black men on behalf of Pace and Turner. In addition to his store, Franklin was commissioned as a night watchman, paid $30 a month by the town of Goodwater. He made easily as much again in the trafficking of black laborers.[40]

Pruitt, thirty-six years old, also worked as a night watchman in Good-water and operated a livery stable as a sideline. He received $42 a month to police the town and collected a $2-per-family annual tax for upkeep of the unpaved streets. Altogether, he eked out enough to maintain his widowed mother and wife, adult sister and brothers, and two toddling sons, in a com-pact wood frame house near the center of town.

The two men's ostensible police supervisor, Goodwater marshal John G. Dunbar, also regularly offered black men for sale, as did the town's other constable, Laray A. Grogan, who busily transported black forced laborers from Goodwater to the Turner lime quarry and kiln in the town of Calcis. Grogan, thirty years old, lived with his young wife and three children under age six next door to Mayor White.[41]


Early in April of 1902, Franklin and Pruitt got word that runaways had fled the Samples Lumber Company sawmill outside the nearby town of Hol-lands. Samples, like virtually all lumber cutting operations in southern Ala-bama, Georgia, and Florida at the time, was a spectacle of horrifying abuse.

Young black men—and occasionally whites—were routinely lured to remote timber camps deep in the forests with promises of solid wages and good working conditions. As often as not, the camps became prisons, where men and boys were held against their will for months or years, fed and housed miserably, worked under brutal circumstances, and paid little or nothing. Hundreds of other black men were purchased from jails across the state. Since black men knew they enjoyed no protection from these abuses from local sheriffs or judges, they relied on word of mouth in African American neighborhoods or among other itinerant workers to identify which camps fulfilled their advertisements and white men who could "be trusted."

On April 2, Dock Crenshaw, a twenty-one-year-old black laborer from Roanoke, Alabama, agreed to take work at Samples. After one day, Crenshaw and several other young black men realized they had been grossly misled. Instead of $1 a day in wages, plus food and a place to stay, the men were being stockaded and fed prisoner's rations. Other workers told them they would never receive pay. Instead, they were being charged $2 a week for their food and shelter—a third of their supposed total wages.

Five young men, Crenshaw, Charles Williams, Pat Hill, Jim Coleman, and Ed Moody, decided to leave at the end of the workday and return home. This was a particularly galling act to the white men in charge of Samples Lumber and an overt challenge to local white authorities. The sight of five black men, most of them teenagers, strolling up a public road, having defied their white employer, justified a harsh response in the minds of almost every white in the region.

As Crenshaw and two others ambled under a bridge at the edge of the town of Goodwater that night, Franklin and a second white man from the town stepped out of the darkness and said the men were under arrest for "jumping" a board bill—or not paying for food provided to them at Samples.

The five workers were marched back to a general store in tiny Hollands where the town mayor convened what went for a misdemeanor trial. Crenshaw refused to plead guilty, but the others, pressured by the armed whites, agreed to confess. The men had eaten only once at the mill, but the mayor found that each had walked out on a $5 tab. All were given fines of about $6, plus unspecified "costs." Franklin told the justice of the peace not to tell the men the full amount they owed and that he would take care of it.

Franklin loaded the five into a wagon and carried them back to Goodwater. After several hours locked in the same small jail near the railroad tracks where John Davis and so many others had been held, Franklin, now joined by Pruitt, ordered the black men onto the next train stopping in the town. When they rolled into the Dadeville station, a wagon was waiting to transport the men to Pace's farm on the Tallapoosa River. Pace gave $25 cash to Franklin and Pruitt, $12.50 for transporting the gang, and a check on the Tallapoosa County Bank for $100.

After several days detained by Pace, the farmer's resident magistrate, James Kennedy, read a contract out loud to the men. All Charley Williams could follow was that they would have to work there for at least seven months. They resigned themselves to their fate and began working under armed guard every day, plowing, hoeing, and ditching. At night, the men were locked in a crude cell.[42]

Williams knew he was in for a hard time, but he could hardly have imagined its details. A strapping, barrel-chested farmhand, he wasn't accustomed to the servile status Pace's farm demanded. He defied directions and challenged guards, and for that he was whipped nearly every day, usually with his pants pulled to his ankles and his back bared. The instruments of punishment used to beat him were leather plow lines, trouser belts, or saplings. "Anything happened to be in the boss man's hands," Williams testified later.[43]

The younger men in the group were terrified especially by what was happening. Within a month of arriving at Pace's farm, Pat Hill and Ed Moody, both seventeen years old, tried to run away. After traveling just four miles, they were captured by Pace's son-in-law, Anderson Hardy. Kennedy, the justice of the peace employed by Pace, staged another fake trial and convicted the pair of "breaking the contract" with Pace and sentenced them to six months of hard labor for the county. Conveniently, Pace was under contract with the Tallapoosa County judge to hold all local hard-labor convicts. So Hill and Moody returned immediately to the same chain gang, now with an additional term of six months to work and explicitly classified as criminal convicts.

There was another lesson to be learned, however, and one that Pace believed the other blacks being held on the farm needed to share in as well.

The risks and futility of attempting to escape would be demonstrated for all of Pace's laborers. Hill was led nearly naked in front of a gang of black laborers working in a field, forced to bend at the waist and squat, his hands tied together behind his knees. The point of these beatings was manyfold: the most obvious was to create a specific disincentive to escape. Just as important was to show the power of whites not just to cause pain but to force a black man to bear profound humiliation, to be reduced to a state of pathetic powerlessness, to visibly see how quickly and effortlessly even the most simpleton whites could force a defiant black man to reveal emotional vulnerability and physical weakness. "My hands were fastened under my knees. I was bent over and whipped on the naked back," Hill testified stoically. "He told me to count, and I counted up to 15, and could not count any further. He whipped me about 25 licks."[44]

# VI

## SLAVERY IS NOT A CRIME

*"We shall have to kill a thousand . . . to get them back to their places."*

The spring of 1903 arrived in Alabama with a surreal, portentous fury. Farmers pushed hard to put a new cotton crop in the ground, only to see nearly every seedling killed by an inexplicable late freeze. Rain and fungus plagued the corn stands rising in countless thousands of new rows.

In the black of night on April 8, a funnel cloud descended without warning from a vertiginous sky, zigzagging north of Birmingham, shearing one-hundred-yard-wide swaths of trees, homes, and fields as it bounded madly into the earth and back to the sky across a path of eighteen miles. The horizon coruscated with astonishing arcs of lightning. By the time the wind and rain stopped, a dozen people were dead. Five days later, another storm lashed Bibb County, scraping past the old Cottingham farm, obliterating small buildings and stripping the buds beginning to swell on fruit trees. On the same day, another tornado—mysteriously pouring hail but no rain—ripped through south Alabama, killing three more.

Finally, as evening fell on April 19, an unnatural cold swept across the state as the sky opened above Goodwater and Tallapoosa County, pouring a deluge of hail and rain. Trees were stripped bare of leaves and fruit blossoms. What was left of the cotton, corn, purple-hull field peas, and early sprouts of squash and okra was beaten flat into the soil. Farmers, sharecroppers, and day laborers—free and enslaved—rushed into the fields to replant.

But by the end of April, another kind of zephyr, something just as twisted and contradictory to the new order of the white South, was lurking on the horizon. Whispered at the train stations and among black laborers on Sunday mornings was a story so unbelievable most people said it must be fable. A man who claimed to be a federal Secret Service detective was visiting black residents in Goodwater. Some had been sent by train to testify before a federal grand jury collecting evidence that white people in Tallapoosa County were still holding slaves.

By the middle of May, the rumors were rampant—and seemingly confirmed by the nearly continual presence of a burly federal agent named E. P. McAdams. Then on May 27, newspapers across the state carried an astounding press release issued from the Department of Justice in Washington, D.C.:

*Washington, May 26—At the request of the Department of Justice, the United States Secret Service has undertaken the work of investigating the charge of peonage, or holding another in servitude to work out a debt, which has been made against persons living in the vicinity of Montgomery, Ala. The punishment provided by the statute for this crime is a fine of not less than $1,000 nor more than $5,000 or imprisonment of not less than one year nor more than five.*

*One man, named Robert N. Franklin, has already been indicted for keeping a negro in servitude for at least a year. Information in the hands of [Secret Service] chief Wilkie tends to show that a regular system has been practiced for a long time between certain magistrates and persons who want negro laborers.*

*It is said the plan is to bring a poor negro before a magistrate on a flimsy charge. He is convicted and, having no money to pay a fine, the white man offers to advance him the money, provided the negro will make a labor contract with him for a length of time sufficient to reimburse him for the money and trouble he has taken to keep the negro out of jail. He is thereupon taken away and begins what is frequently a long term of cruel servitude, being frequently whipped for failure to perform work to the satisfaction of his employer.*

*An agent of the secret service who is now on the ground will make a thorough investigation of the whole alleged system and turn over to the*

*United States Attorney of that district all information he may secure*
*with a view to the prosecution of said offenders.*[1]

Unexpectedly and without explanation, a flash of hope bolted across
the dark curtain falling on black life. Most amazing was that it commenced
in Montgomery, the city that had served briefly during the early months of
the Civil War as the national capital of the Confederacy.[2] It remained the
seat of a government that since the war had eviscerated black citizenship
more completely and enthusiastically than any other.

That the federal government would initiate such an inquiry was mind-
boggling to white southerners. Investigations of any kind by federal agencies were extraordinarily unusual in an era that predated the creation of the
Federal Bureau of Investigation. Moreover, the South's long asserted right
to manage the affairs of black residents without northern interference had
finally been achieved. Nearly every southern state, including Alabama, had
completed the total disenfranchisement of African Americans by 1901. Virtually no blacks served on state juries. No blacks in the South were permitted to hold meaningful state or local political offices. There were virtually
no black sheriffs, constables, or police officers. Blacks had been wholly
shunted into their own inferior railroad cars, restrooms, restaurants, neighborhoods, and schools. All of this had been accomplished in a sudden,
unfettered grab by white supremacists that was met outside the South with
little more than quiet assent. During the thirty years since Reconstruction—despite its being a period of nearly continuous Republican control of
the White House—federal officials raised only the faintest concerns about
white abuse of black laborers. Southern leaders were astonished that such a
protest had inexplicably arisen now.

For blacks it seemed that a true friend had miraculously come to occupy
the White House, that somehow the assurances of American democracy
might actually fulfill themselves. "The South . . . is in the hands of un-
friendly white men. . . . It has been left to the Federal Government, under
that administration of President Roosevelt, to expose this iniquity . . . and
stretch out the long arm of the Nation to punish and prevent it," wrote the
black commentator Charles W. Chesnutt. "The President has endeavored
to stem the tide of prejudice, which, sweeping up from the South, has sought

to overwhelm the Negro everywhere; and he has made it clear that he regards himself as the representative of the people."[3]

This dramatic turn of events—so revolting to southern whites, so euphoric to blacks—began with the assassination of President William McKinley two years earlier in September 1901.

McKinley had represented more than any other American leader at the turn of the twentieth century the experiences of those who directly participated in the war between the North and the South and came to see that struggle as a moral crusade against slavery and for the preservation of the union. A young private when he volunteered, McKinley rose steadily to the rank of major by the end of the war on the basis of modest acts of heroism. He was the last president who had served as an officer in Abraham Lincoln's Grand Army, and millions of aging Union veterans continued to greet him affectionately as Major McKinley.

But by the fall of 1901, the veterans he marched with through the great battles of the conflict had become a geriatric generation, their luster increasingly pale against the new economic dramas playing out between fabulously rich titans of manufacturing and production such as John D. Rockefeller, Andrew Carnegie, and banker John Pierpont Morgan and the masses of laborers and immigrants streaming into the bulging metropolises of the North and Midwest.

Theodore Roosevelt came to serve as McKinley's vice president in 1900 almost accidentally. His place on McKinley's presidential ticket was engineered by old-guard Republican leaders in New York primarily to get Roosevelt, the state's unexpectedly popular new governor, out of their way. Roosevelt was barely settled into Washington when McKinley was shot by an anarchist while standing on a receiving line for public visitors at an international exhibition in Buffalo, New York. McKinley died eight days later, and Roosevelt was sworn in as president on September 14, 1901.

Roosevelt, who had been a child when the Civil War was fought, saw himself not as heir to McKinley's archaic nineteenth-century political regimes and the contradictory outcomes of Reconstruction and industrialization. Instead, he imagined his rise to the White House as a catalyst for reconciling Americans to what Roosevelt perceived as the great missed opportunities of the nation's political and economic freedoms.

Roosevelt was also at least nominally concerned about the chasm between blacks and whites, and the gap between the conditions of African Americans and the promises made to them at the end of slavery. But none of this was to Roosevelt an intractable dilemma. Just forty-two years old upon becoming president, the youngest yet in U.S. history, he believed that Americans were a people of seminally good character, reasonable thinking, and, as a body, of singular wisdom. Reminded of their fundamental principles, all white Americans would see the necessity of fairness to freed slaves and their descendants, Roosevelt thought—just as he was confident that the leaders of the new steel, coal, railroad, and banking trusts ultimately could be relied on to balance profits against the needs of all the nation's workers.

The United States was emerging as an authentic global power for the first time in its history. The country's economic and military prowess outside the national borders was greater than at any time since the declaration of the republic. The nation was in the midst of an explosion of new economic production and wealth. In the South, centers of industry were rising in Birmingham and Atlanta. Industrial combinations such as Tennessee Coal, Iron & Railroad Co. were moving to challenge northern rivals like U.S. Steel and Carnegie Steel. The landscape of the South remained defined by the abject poverty of millions of plebeian black and white farmers, but there was a sense of psychic resurgence in the region. The actual horrors and injuries of the Civil War were receding from collective memory. Nostalgia for the antebellum South and calls for reunion and reconciliation among veterans of the armies for both sides were becoming national obsessions. The literature of Joel Chandler Harris and scores of imitators—chock-ablock with white writers' stylized depictions of "Negro" dialect and the most benevolent images of slave masters and slaves imaginable—had supplanted the canon of abolitionist novels and firsthand accounts of slaves that dominated American book sales and lecture tours in the previous generation.

The long-standing excuse for southern malevolence toward blacks— that the region left prostrate by war, the ending of slavery, and the ostensible

agonies of Reconstruction couldn't help but abuse its former slaves—struck
Roosevelt and his breed of proactive Americans as tired, dull, and simply
wrong. The assertion by white southerners of a de facto right to reverse the
guarantees of voting rights and citizenship to blacks seemed to Roosevelt so
absurd that it could only be truly supported by extremists. He reckoned—
using the same logic that compelled him to challenge the abuse of immigrant and impoverished laborers in the factories and coalfields closer to his
home at Oyster Bay, New York—that a reasonable and progressive northern man such as himself could surely safeguard the fundamental needs of
southern blacks while still reassuring southern whites that they had nothing
to fear from allowing authentic citizenship for all.

Roosevelt could hardly have been more wrong in his judgment of the
political and racial realities of the South. But in addition to his instinctive,
if ultimately naive, sympathy for African Americans, Roosevelt had explicitly political motivations for befriending blacks as well. The new president
was anything but a celebrated figure within his own Republican Party.
Viewed suspiciously by Republican leaders in New York, he was despised by
leaders of the national party's archconservative big business faction, who in
the previous three decades had engineered the steady drift of Republicans
from radical abolitionist roots toward a new position as the party of unre-
strained commerce. Roosevelt needed a novel strategy if he hoped to secure
the nomination for the presidential election in 1904.

A key element of the strategy was to forge a political base among southern Republicans, almost all of whom were black. Roosevelt believed he
could cement those loyalties without stirring white hostilities by appoint-
ing "reasonable" white Democrats to many key federal positions—such as
judgeships. The plan relied on one of the oddest curiosities of the American
electoral circumstances at the beginning of the twentieth century. While
African Americans were almost wholly barred from voting in general elections—having been disenfranchised in every state in which black voters constituted statistically significant numbers—black delegations continued to
be accorded full rights at the national conventions of the Republican Party.
The result was that while African American voters had little practical impact
upon national elections, given that they were wholly unable to deliver any
electoral votes from the southern states where nearly all blacks resided,

black Republicans nonetheless remained an essential swing factor in select-ing presidential nominees for their party.

Theodore Roosevelt made this calculation long before gaining the pres-idency, and intentionally cultivated cordial relations with African American leaders he considered moderate. Chief among them was Booker T. Wash-ington, the erudite former slave who had risen to become the nation's most prominent black leader and the founder of the Tuskegee Institute in Ala-bama. The two men grew progressively more friendly during Roosevelt's months of service as vice president. In early 1901, Roosevelt accepted an invitation to speak at Tuskegee later that year, as part of a short tour of the South that was to include a brief homage to the Georgia plantation home in which his mother had been reared.

With the death of Frederick Douglass in 1895, Washington was by far the best known and most influential of black leaders in the United States— emphasizing black self-improvement, industrial education, and acquies-cence to white political power. Washington's gradualist message to African Americans was epitomized in a speech on September 18, 1895, at the Cotton States and International Exhibition in Atlanta, urging that blacks accommodate white demands for subservience while building up their own industrial skills, farms, and basic education.

To thunderous applause from southern whites, Washington said of the two races: "In all things purely social we can be as separate as the fingers, yet one as the hand in all things essential to mutual progress." The black educator, named a "commissioner" of the event, urged African Americans across Alabama to use the exposition's "Negro Building" as a showcase for black skills in mining, lumbering and farming, the very industries in which they remained most oppressed across the South.[4]

This ideal of a class of politically and legally passive but industrious African Americans deeply appealed to white economic leaders. Near the closing day of the fair in late December 1895, when Washington returned to speak on "Colored Teachers Day," the exposition program featured on its last page a drawing of the Negro Building and a caption praising its black attendants for "attractive neatness." The exhibits were "evidence of the growing skill, advancing intelligence and promotive industry of the race."[5]

Washington's Tuskegee Institute, located less than fifty miles from the farm of John Pace, in the town of Tuskegee, became celebrated among white northern philanthropists. Washington spent much of his time touring the country to raise funds for the school and attempting to quietly manipulate government officials and the political process on racial issues.

Younger black intellectuals such as Professor W. E. B. DuBois in Atlanta came to bitterly criticize Washington as too willing to accept a secondary position for African Americans. But Roosevelt perceived Washington's views as sensible, pragmatic, and clearly in keeping with his own progressive, but eminently paternalistic, beliefs. Washington's emphasis on personal self-reliance and moral and religious rectitude as the keys to individual progress corresponded to Roosevelt's vision for uplifting yeoman farmers, immigrant laborers, ranch hands, and factory workers of whatever race or region. Roosevelt was convinced that if the "common man," whether black or white, followed these principles and that government ensured that no unjust legal obstacles impeded him, then the United States could achieve immeasurable progress. All of this could happen, Roosevelt insisted, without disrupting the exponentially expanding business, industrial, and banking sectors whose fortunes had made families such as Roosevelt's richer than most Americans could begin to imagine.

Washington's approach appealed to Roosevelt, though, only because the new president was unwilling to confront the realities of southern whites' venom toward any African American seeking social or political equality. Roosevelt's father was an ardent Lincoln Republican, but his mother was born to a slaveholding family in Roswell, Georgia, not far from Atlanta. President Roosevelt was drawn to a view of the Civil War that emphasized the valor of both sides, rather than the evils of whites such as his mother's family in perpetuating slavery. Gradual change, during which no one was forced to fully acknowledge past cruelties to blacks, made sense to Roosevelt. "I am confident the South is changing," Roosevelt wrote in a postscript to a letter to Washington in 1901.[6] Roosevelt's approach to the status of African Americans, fundamentally acceding to the inferiority of African Americans and anticipating no significant full integration into U.S. society, would be the conventional wisdom shared for the next six decades by the vast majority of white Americans who considered themselves "progressive" on race.

"I so cordially sympathize," Roosevelt wrote, with Washington's "purpose of fitting the Colored man to shift for himself and establishing a healthy relation between the colored man and the White man who lives in the same states."[7] Roosevelt was thrilled with Washington's best-selling autobiography, *Up from Slavery*, when it appeared in 1901, with the message that quiet perseverance and humility—rather than anger against his slave birth—had been the keys to the author's success. Roosevelt wrote Washington: "I do not want to flatter you too much . . . [but] . . . I do not know who could take your place in the work you are doing."[8]

Washington's theories also corresponded to Roosevelt's benign but seminal racism. Principles of fair play told Roosevelt that nothing should inhibit the individuals in any group who have the ability to achieve great success. The extraordinary achievements of black men such as Washington were dramatic proof of this to Roosevelt. But at the same time, Roosevelt believed that, collectively, no one should or reasonably could deny the obvious racial superiority of whites over all others. Indeed, Roosevelt ultimately took the view that even when whites most gravely abused the world's darker-skinned races—as in the African slaving trade, the removal of native populations in the Americas, and his own brutal suppression while in the White House of the Philippine Islands—that the outcome was overwhelmingly good. "The expansion of the peoples of white, or European, blood during the past four centuries . . . has been fraught with lasting benefit to most of the peoples already dwelling in the lands over which the expansion took place," Roosevelt said in remarks to a group of white missionaries during his second term as president.[9]

But even as the southern states used similar logic to justify the elimination of black participation in general elections, the Republican Party—the party of emancipation—was not yet able to do the same. Delegations of African Americans from the southern states—even though they could cast no more than the most scant votes in the general elections—remained full-fledged and prominent players in the national conventions of the Republican Party. (Not until after 1912 would Republicans succumb and allow African Americans to be tossed from the party organizations of the South.) Roosevelt turned to Booker T. Washington to build his base among black southern Republicans.

Before the day of his inauguration was over, Roosevelt had written Washington to cancel his visit to Tuskegee and implore the black leader to visit him quickly in Washington. "I must see you as soon as possible. I want to talk over the question of possible future appointments in the south exactly on the lines of our last conversation," Roosevelt wrote.[10] Washington made immediate arrangements to see the new president.

Less than three weeks later, U.S. District Court Judge John Bruce, the longtime federal jurist who presided over much of central Alabama, died. Roosevelt and Washington were presented with a serendipitous opportunity. The judgeship in Alabama could be an early demonstration of Roosevelt's willingness to reward a progressive southern white leader with an important position—regardless of his party affiliation. The policy left the small number of white Republicans who had hung on in the South—many of whom continued to be viewed by other southerners as radical carpetbagger allies left over from the Reconstruction era—in the cold. However, Roosevelt insisted that his cross-party appointments go to Democrats who expressed opposition to lynching and support for at least minimal citizenship rights for African Americans—and most important that they had not actively supported William Jennings Bryan, the Democratic nominee for president in the 1900 election.

Washington immediately recommended to Roosevelt that he appoint as successor the state's former governor, Thomas Goode Jones,[11] the political figure about whom John W. Pace and Fletch Turner had so vigorously faced off during Alabama's political warfare a decade earlier.

On the surface, it was paradoxical that Washington became the champion of former governor Jones, a Confederate veteran who served under Thomas J. "Stonewall" Jackson and Brig. Gen. John B. Gordon, and who was present at Lee's surrender to Grant at Appomattox. He was reputed to have carried the white flag of southern surrender. Jones's successful gubernatorial bids in 1890 and 1892 were based primarily on the interests of wealthy white plantation owners—men who abused African American laborers on a greater scale than any other whites. During those campaigns he was a vocal critic of black political power. Nonetheless, Jones was also the cynically willing beneficiary of his faction's reliance on coerced or falsified votes cast in those years by thousands of blacks.

Yet Washington and Jones had been secret allies for years—even as Jones was manipulating black votes in the 1890s.[12] It is also possible that as a result of Washington's secret influence, some of the thousands of Jones votes cast by blacks and long assumed by historians to be fraudulent, were in fact legitimate.

But Washington knew that as an officer in the state militia in 1883, Jones also had called out troops to prevent a lynching. He had spoken publicly on many occasions of the importance of respecting other new rights granted to freed slaves by the amendments to the U.S. Constitution passed in the 1870s. As governor, he blocked efforts to divert funds for black schools to white ones. At the same time, Jones maintained his base of support with the state's business elite by calling out troops to suppress a major strike by newly unionized miners in the 1890s.

Over the years, Jones appeared to have moderated even further on race. More recently, he had been a delegate to the just completed 1901 Alabama constitutional convention. The document agreed to at the meeting and later ratified, which would govern Alabama for the duration of the twentieth century and into the twenty-first, finally eliminated virtually all vestiges of the electoral and civil rights given to blacks after emancipation. But Jones defied the political winds of the day, vigorously pushing for one of the few measures approved that benefited blacks, a law allowing for impeachment of any sheriff who allowed a prisoner to be seized by a lynch mob. Jones also opposed efforts to eliminate all black voting and to require that public schools for African American children be funded only with those taxes collected from blacks. Jones quietly strategized with Washington throughout the convention, consistently engaged in a tone of equals, addressing the black leader with the honorific "Dear Sir."[13]

On the day after Judge Bruce's death, and only two weeks after Roosevelt had been sworn in as president, Washington sent a letter through an aide imploring the new chief executive to name Jones as the new federal judge in Alabama. "He stood up in the constitutional convention and elsewhere for a fair election law, opposed lynching, and has been outspoken for the education of both races," Washington wrote. "He is head and shoulders above any of the other persons who I think will apply to you," Washington wrote to Roosevelt on October 2, 1901.[14]

Roosevelt took the advice and appointed Judge Jones less than a week later. The decision elicited the effect Roosevelt hoped for. Many southern whites were impressed by the president's willingness to turn to one of their "best men" for a critical federal position, despite Jones being a prominent Democrat. Newspapers in the region hailed the move.

Ten days after the appointment, the president was informed that Washington was in the capital city. He insisted that the black educator come to a private dinner at the White House with the Roosevelt family. It was a dizzying sequence of events for Washington and other African Americans who shared his belief that accommodating discrimination while incrementally working to reverse it was the best route to black freedom. Here was proof, it seemed. Regardless of the struggles still faced by the majority of slave descendants, black men of accomplishment could rise to unprecedented levels of influence.

Blacks had visited the White House before, and prior presidents had sought the advice of black men. But never had a black man appeared to be among the very most influential figures in a president's execution of so critical a task as selecting federal officials in an entire region. Yet more astonishing was that the white president who had taken his advice won accolades for the resulting decision. Black men could not *be* the leaders of whites in this regime, but they could quietly wield great influence as to who the rulers would be. Now, the president wished his African American counselor to openly sup with himself, his wife, and his children—making no effort to conceal the event or minimize its significance.

Roosevelt had no hint of the reaction that would ensue. Notwithstanding Washington's national fame and his widely known view that blacks should in most regards accept their legally inferior position in the South, word that "a Negro" had dined at the same table as the president, his wife, and his children—violating one of the most sacrosanct protocols of southern racial custom—provoked a sensational backlash.

U.S. senator Ben "Pitchfork" Tillman of South Carolina sputtered: "Now that Roosevelt has eaten with that nigger Washington, we shall have to kill a thousand niggers to get them back to their places." The *Memphis Press Scimitar* called the evening meal "the most damnable outrage which has ever been perpetrated by any citizen of the United States." The *Rich-*

*mond News* declared that Roosevelt "at one stroke and by one act has destroyed regard for him. He has put himself further from us than any man who has ever been in the White House." The governor of Georgia, Allen Candler, said, "No southerner can respect any white man who would eat with a negro."[15]

Laced throughout the vilifications was the implicit or explicit message that Roosevelt's decision to allow Washington to share his personal dining room amounted to an endorsement of sexual relations—and predations—between black men and white women. "It is simply a question of whether those who are invited to dine are fit to marry the sisters and daughters of their hosts," said Governor Miles Benjamin McSweeney of South Carolina.[16]

The opprobrium continued for months, growing more virulent with each announcement of another in the slow trickle of black appointees made by the White House. After several black officeholders and their wives attended a White House reception in early 1903, the race-baiting Mississippi politician James K. Vardaman called Roosevelt a "little, mean, coon-flavored miscegenationist." The White House, Vardaman said, was "so saturated with the odor of the nigger that the rats have taken refuge in the stable." Vardaman was elected governor of Mississippi the following year.[17]

A century later it is difficult to comprehend the degree to which most southern whites had so thoroughly adopted the rationale embodied by the *Plessy v. Ferguson* ruling less than ten years earlier—which effectively held that African Americans had no basis of legitimate complaint regarding the racial climate at the turn of the century, regardless of how overtly apparent was the disparate treatment of and opportunities for whites and blacks.

Roosevelt's overtures to blacks were not just violations of an accepted social custom, but galling because they suggested that in fact African Americans did have reason to object to their current status in the United States. White southerners by and large shared a consensus that this view was simply nonsensical. They were certain that the vast majority of blacks were entirely content and that their contentment would only increase as freedmen were pushed nearer to a legal status barely distinguishable from those of their parents in antebellum society.

The *Birmingham Ledger* newspaper—describing a state in which African Americans could no longer vote, could not hold office, could not serve on local juries, were proscribed from most higher-wage work, could arrange only the slimmest legal representation in the courts, and were subject to utterly arbitrary enforcement of the law—summed up the fantasy shared by millions of southerners: "The court of Alabama and schools of Alabama are open to negroes and every door of opportunity can be entered and above all it is easier for a negro to get rich here than anywhere else in the world."[18] That delusion would not waver in the South for at least another fifty years, until the very climax of the civil rights movement.

The *Dadeville Spot Cash*, the voice of John Pace's Tallapoosa County, enunciated this white delusion—and its offense at the inherent impudence of Roosevelt's attitudes—in a detailed fulmination in early March 1903. "Alabama has many negroes and many kinds of negroes, as little boys have many kinds of marbles. We have good negroes and bad negroes, industrious negroes and idle negroes, negroes determined to better their own condition and negroes who care no more about the future than the birds care. Alabama has negroes who have earned the respect and regard of the people who know them, and Alabama has negroes who wear the stripes of the convict."[19]

The Dadeville editor also reflected the broadly shared paranoia that any effort to change or improve the conditions of blacks amounted to an effort to seize control of society: "Alabama has negroes who own land and cattle and who are rearing their families respectably and who can go to the bank and borrow money without security. There are negroes who are teaching and many who are following honorable lines of work, and it has some who think with the president that the door of hope for them means governing white people as officials. All these we have and others."[20]

The message was clear, and shared almost universally among whites: whatever happens to black men is strictly the result of their own choices. Those choices ultimately were to submit quietly to the emerging new order or be crushed by it.

The reaction of southern leaders to Roosevelt's gesture to Washington further underscored how far southern whites could extend their ability to reconcile the obvious and extraordinary abuses of blacks occurring around them with their rhetorical insistence that African Americans were entirely free, content, and unmolested. Never before in American history had so large a portion of the populace adopted such explicitly false and calculated propaganda. Many southern whites actually came to believe claims that black schools were equally funded, black train cars were equally appointed, and that black citizens were equally defended by the courts—as preposterous as those claims obviously were.

Those who truly knew better nonetheless relished the clever fabrication of this mythology, and how it so effectively stymied the busybody friends of African Americans in the North. The most cynical thread in the mosaic of racial myth was the outrage of southern white men at Roosevelt's supposed encouragement of sexual interrelations between blacks and whites. White men openly forced black slaves into their beds for two centuries before the Civil War, and sexual access to local black women remained a running point of confrontation between white landowners and their black laborers deep into the twentieth century—a phenomenon that continued to demonstrate itself a century later with the public revelation that South Carolina senator Strom Thurmond fathered a black child with an African American family servant in 1925.

"The whole country well knows that white men of the South have come into closer relations with negroes and committed far grosser sins than that of sitting down to meat with a reputable and representative colored person," wrote William A. Sinclair, a black physician, in 1905. "And in the eyes of their fellows they suffered no disgrace."[21]

President Roosevelt was shocked by the calumnies and vitriol spewing from the South regarding his friendliness toward blacks. He moderated slightly—never inviting another black man to his dinner table again—but continued to insist that good Americans could not legitimately object to the view that law-abiding and industrious blacks should be treated with equity and full protection of the law.

Roosevelt concluded a long circuit of speeches across much of the country in the spring of 1903 with an address in Springfield, Illinois, on June 4, at the monument there to Abraham Lincoln. Arriving on a 10:15 A.M. train, Roosevelt was greeted euphorically, first by aging Union soldiers in the Lincoln-McKinley Veteran Voters' Association, then by more than five

thousand schoolchildren massed along the street leading past the state capitol and furiously waving American flags. Businesses and homes were decorated in elaborate patriotic bunting and flags. A gathering of ten thousand
impatiently awaited the president at a nearby new armory he would dedi-
cate later in the day. Also in the crowd at the Lincoln memorial were several detachments of the Illinois National Guard, including the all-black
Company H of the Eighth Regiment. "It seems to me eminently fitting that
the guard around the tomb of Lincoln should be composed of colored soldiers," Roosevelt said, citing his own service in Cuba beside black soldiers.
"A man who is good enough to shed his blood for his country is good
enough to be given a square deal afterward."[22]

The words were a modest anodyne for black Americans, given the scale
of the campaign over the previous two decades to circumscribe their constitutional protections and limit their free participation in American society.
Yet the sentence—condensed by newspaper reporters and repeated ubiquitously as a promise by Roosevelt of "a square deal for the negro"—inflamed
white southerners yet again. What most galled whites was the implication
by Roosevelt that African Americans were not already receiving as square
and fair a deal as they could possibly deserve.

In Alabama, as Secret Service agents scoured the countryside for slavery, whites recognized that Roosevelt's remarks might be more than the
pitiable window dressing of equal civil rights they had heard from McKinley and the other Republican leaders of the previous decade.

By early June 1903, Alabama was aflame. Judge Jones—only nineteen
months into his service as the new member of the federal bench—had
proven to be precisely the figure Roosevelt hoped. The slavery investigation announced in late May was spreading across the state. Prominent
white landowners in a half dozen counties had learned they were under
examination or at least allegation. Black laborers—while still acutely aware
that the investigation subjected them to a new degree of jeopardy with
angry whites—quietly expressed a level of anticipation unlike anything
since first word of the coming emancipation had arrived forty years earlier.

The inquiry began when an attorney named Erastus J. Parsons was hired
to represent a black prisoner being held in Shelby County. Local authori-

ties obstructed Parsons's efforts to find the prisoner and refused to say why he was being held. Parsons contacted the U.S. attorney in Montgomery, who in turn told Judge Jones. The first handful of frightened witnesses were brought before a grand jury sitting in Birmingham and presided over by Jones. They told the first shocking account of Pace's slaving network.[23]

In March, Judge Jones fired off a bewildered letter to Attorney General Philander C. Knox in Washington, D.C. "Some witnesses before the Grand Jury here developed the fact that in Shelby County in this District, and in Coosa County in the Middle district, a systematic scheme of depriving Negroes of their liberty, and hiring them out, has been practiced for some time," Jones wrote. "The plan is to accuse the negro of some petty offense, and then require him, in order to escape conviction, to enter into an agreement to pay his accuser so much money, and sign a contract, under the terms of which his bondsmen can hire him out until he pays a certain sum. The negro is made to believe he is a convict, and treated as such. It is said that thirty negroes were in the stockade at one time." Already, at least one witness had been seized from a train after testifying. Judge Jones ordered a deputy U.S. marshal to protect the man. He urged the attorney general to send a special investigator into the area quickly.[24]

Attorney General Knox, a shrewd lawyer from Pennsylvania who before entering government service had amassed a fortune as counsel to some of the largest U.S. corporations, was hardly an obvious ally of southern blacks. A dapper man who contravened current fashion with a clean-shaven face and sported high collars and broad French cuffs, he had no natural affinity for the South or its black inhabitants. His greatest claim to fame was as legal counsel to Andrew Carnegie's vast steelmaking enterprises. In 1901, he played a key role in the merger of Carnegie Steel with J. P. Morgan's Federal Steel Company and virtually every other major steel and iron concern in the nation. The new organization was U.S. Steel Corporation—the largest and most powerful business entity created up to that point. It immediately controlled 7 percent of the nation's gross domestic product. Four days after the merger was officially consummated, President McKinley, a close friend since his college years, named Knox attorney general. Less than six months later, McKinley was dead, and Knox was part of Theodore Roosevelt's cabinet.

In light of Roosevelt's pledge of a renewed commitment to black civil rights, Attorney General Knox could hardly ignore Judge Jones's report of slavery still being practiced forty years after Lincoln's Emancipation Proclamation. Moreover, the allegations reanimated a running legal dilemma for the Justice Department. At least some federal officials, especially native southern Republicans serving as prosecutors, judges, or in government posts in the South, were acutely aware that slavery had never truly disappeared.

The Justice Department was already on notice. Four years earlier, in 1899, the colorful federal prosecutor in Atlanta, Edward A. Angier, went so far as to mount a lone prosecution against one of Georgia's most prominent planters, William Eberhart, in Oglethorpe County, for conspiracy to hold blacks in a state of peonage—a crime defined by an obscure and never before used 1867 federal law passed to prohibit the long-standing Mexican practice of debt slavery in the new territory of New Mexico.

Relying on his brother-in-law, a justice of the peace, to convict black laborers on any charge the planter wished to use, Eberhart enslaved men and women and forced them to bind their children to him as apprentices. He routinely claimed to have loaned money to black workers and then held them on his plantation near the town of Winterville to work off the debt—often for years at a time. Before a grand jury, witnesses described Eberhart as a sadistic brute who routinely beat adults and children to the edge of death. When laborers fled to Atlanta, Eberhart sent deputy sheriffs into the city to hunt them down, beat them into submission, and drive them back to the plantation in chains.

In one count of the indictment, Eberhart was charged with enslaving a black man named Charley Calloway in January 1896 by falsely claiming he owed the planter money. When Calloway resisted, Eberhart assaulted and degraded the laborer at every imaginable physical and emotional level: witnesses said that Eberhart brutally beat Calloway's wife, Mary, and then at gunpoint forced the woman to "yield her body to the lustful embraces" of the plantation owner.

When Charley Calloway attempted to escape the farm, Eberhart had him hauled back and placed in handcuffs. Eberhart then beat him "upon the back, head, face and body" and, in an overt act of sexual humiliation, had Calloway stripped naked and chained into a bed with a sick laborer named Orange Neeley.

Later, Eberhart brandished his pistol and forced Calloway "to pinion his own beloved son, Robert Calloway, outstretched to the ground, and did make the said Charley Calloway hold his said son while the said William Eberhart did violently and unmercifully beat the said Robert Calloway with heavy sticks and other weapons" until the boy was crippled. As a final indignity, Eberhart—like the Alabama slavemasters who attempted to seize the children of freedmen in the 1860s—forced Calloway to sign contracts apprenticing his remaining children, two of whom were still nursing babies, into Eberhart's control until they turned twenty-one years old.[25]

Despite wide knowledge of Eberhart's sadism, scores of local white citizens rallied to Eberhart's defense, signing a petition that labeled the evidence against him as "the testimony of irresponsible negroes." Angier, the prosecutor, pressed on with the case, but acknowledged to his superiors in Washington that "we are the pioneers in this movement, and as this is the first time this 'peonage' section has ever been invoked." Angier saw clearly that he was attacking more than debt slavery perpetrated by a single man. He sought permission from the Department of Justice to widen his investigation into adjoining counties and warned: "In this proceeding we have attacked the most powerful combination and formidable 'Convict Ring' (as it is called) in the State.

"Every resource known and unknown to the law will be resorted to by these potent and opulent influences to break down this Bill [of indictment], as we have selected the ring-leader for the first case," Angier wrote.[26]

In the end, it took no more than another audacious argument and a compliant federal judge to collapse the case. Before a trial could be convened, Eberhart's attorneys challenged the most fundamental premise of the case—arguing that no federal statute specifically made it a crime to hold a person in slavery. The presiding judge agreed: "The indictment did not state an offense within the jurisdiction of the federal courts."[27] The case was never tried. "The judge . . . indicated that the State Court alone had jurisdiction of the matters and things embraced in these indictments," Angier wrote to Washington.[28]

Despite the horror of the allegations, no local courts took up the case. The fate of the Calloway family was never known.

Two years later, unaware of the failed peonage prosecution in Georgia, a U.S. commissioner named Fred Cubberly, living in the Florida Panhandle town of Bronson, witnessed turpentine farmer J. O. Elvington seize a black man and his wife at gunpoint, claiming they could not leave his camp deep in the malarial swamps until a $40 debt had been paid. The incident confirmed to Cubberly rumors he had heard that forced labor was rampant among the crude forest labor camps across northern Florida and adjoining areas.[29] Nearly thirty thousand men toiled in the turpentine farms under excruciating conditions to supply a booming market for pine tar, pitch, and turpentine used to caulk the seams of wooden sailing ships and waterproof their ropes and riggings.

Workers carved deep V-shaped notches into the trunks of millions of massive slash and longleaf pines towering in the still virgin forests. Small galvanized iron boxes or gutters were attached to the trees to collect the thick, milky pine gum that oozed from the wounds in winter. During spring and summer, as sap began to run, millions of gallons of pine resin oozed into the containers. Working feverishly from before dawn to the end of light, turpentine workers cut fresh notches into every tree once a week, gathered the gum and resin by hand, boiled it into vast quantities of distilled turpentine, and hauled it in hundreds of thousands of barrels out of the deep woods. When trees stopped producing gum and resin, the camp owners harvested them for lumber. As the demand for turpentine products soared, the timber companies relentlessly acquired fresh tracts of forest to drain and armies of men to perform the grueling work.

Imprisoned in stockades or cells, chained together at night or held under armed guards on horseback, the turpentine farms were bleak outposts miles from any chance of comfort or contact with the outside world. Workers were forced to buy their own food and clothes from a camp commissary and charged usurious interest rates on the salary advances used to pay for the goods—typically at least 100 percent.

A week after witnessing Elvington's seizure of two black workers, Cubberly encountered three "man hunters" at the local train station, led by Samuel M. Clyatt, a turpentine farmer from Georgia searching for several men who had run away from his camp. Clyatt and the others, including a deputy sheriff from his home county, forced two workers, Will Gordon and Mose Ridley, back to Georgia at gunpoint.

Cubberly began investigating similar complaints and making reports to the U.S. attorney in Pensacola, Florida. In the summer of 1901, the federal prosecutor there, John Eagan, passed on to the newly appointed Attorney

General Knox letters from Cubberly and a local attorney in the area alleging that "it is common practice among parties engaged in Turpentine business in the Northern District of Florida, to hold laborers . . . in a state of Involuntary Servitude."

Eagan added that he personally confirmed some of the allegations and ordered that an indictment be sought. The system of coercion he had discovered in Florida, authorized under an 1891 state law making it a crime for a worker to leave his employer after wages had been advanced, was virtually identical to that of Eberhart in Georgia and what Alabama investigators were soon to discover. "The laborers in this line of business are as a general rule colored men and are imposed on and treated outrageously by their employers," Eagan wrote. "A warrant is issued by a Justice of the Peace and placed in the hands of a constable or sheriff who proceeds to forcibly deliver laborer to the possession of the employers who made the complaint, and the employer holds him in service until his claim, including all costs and charges of the proceedings, are worked out."[30]

In November 1901, a Tallahassee federal grand jury indicted Clyatt for peonage. He stood trial five months later—despite the unexplained disappearance of Gordon and Ridley, who were never again seen after their seizure and return to Georgia. Clyatt was found guilty and sentenced to four years in the federal penitentiary.

Recognizing that the conviction could destroy the underpinning of their industry—and a critical element of the southern economy—an association of turpentine and timber companies rallied to Clyatt's defense. They hired as attorneys U.S. senator Augustus Octavius Bacon and U.S. congressman William G. Brantley, both of Georgia. In the lawyers' appeal of the conviction, they observed to the higher courts that the holding of slaves in the United States was not technically a crime. "Congress has never passed a law providing punishment for slavery or for involuntary servitude," Brantley reminded the gallery during a speech before the U.S. House of Representatives.[31]

The peonage statute, they claimed, amounted to unconstitutional federal interference into matters of state jurisdiction. It was improper to apply it to Clyatt because no formal "system of peonage" existed in the South.

As Clyatt's case languished in the Circuit Court of Appeals throughout 1902, new allegations of slavery in the turpentine camps continued to surface. Then came the letter to Attorney General Knox from Judge Jones describing a whole new manifestation of the involuntary servitude system in Alabama, potentially extending across an even larger area of the South.

Knox responded by directing the federal prosecutor in Montgomery, Warren S. Reese Jr., to investigate the allegations. "I have this day addressed a communication to each deputy marshal in this district . . . requesting them to make a special investigation of the peonage question," Reese responded enthusiastically. "If from these reports I am satisfied that attempts are being made or have been made to deprive citizens of African descent of their liberty, I will report the same in full to you and request the detail of a Secret Service Operative if I deem the same necessary."[32]

It took less than two weeks for federal marshals to report the discovery of scores of black slaves in Shelby, Coosa, and Tallapoosa counties. The grand jury in Birmingham issued indictments against nine Shelby County men near the end of April.[33]

But the original allegations made before the Birmingham grand jury were tepid compared to what other agents in the field began to learn. It was clear that not just one slavery ring existed in Alabama, but layers upon layers of them, blanketing the state. The men forced into labor in Shelby and Coosa counties were victims of only the outermost edge of a network emanating from the farms and other business interests of John Pace and his partners in Tallapoosa County. A separate operation run by the sheriff of Lowndes County in the southern section of the state—where more than 25,000 black farm laborers and sharecroppers lived—appeared to involve hundreds or thousands of slaves and dozens of local landowners. More rings operated in at least a half dozen other locations.

In some areas, local whites who were appalled by the conduct of their neighbors, or attorneys who had attempted in the past to free forced black laborers in the southern courts, volunteered tales of excruciating abuse to federal investigators. But in most locales, few whites expressed any misgivings about the forced labor going on in plain sight.

A lawyer named L. E. White, from Columbus, Georgia, a bustling town on the main train line running through Tallapoosa County, told Reese how he had traveled to Dadeville the previous summer looking for a missing young black man named Esau Williams. He tracked him down at a farm owned by Fletch Turner, where Williams and several other black men were being forced to cut wood. White bought his freedom for $25 and returned the boy to his mother.

A few weeks later, the family of Glennie "Speedy" Helms, another young black man who had been traveling with Williams, sent the lawyer back looking for their son. White found him and more than a half dozen others working at a sawmill owned by Turner near the settlement called Jackson's Gap. He had to pay $48 for Helms. But most striking to White were the execrable working conditions he found—a scene that must have been strikingly similar to the operations of the slavery-driven sawmill near the Cottingham plantation half a century earlier. "When I found this boy he was at the sawmill at work completely naked, no clothes on at all, absolutely naked," White said. "And there were some six or eight other negroes there working in the same naked condition."[34]

Reese was astonished by the evidence piling up in his office, and quickly asked for the assignment of two Secret Service agents to assist. "I never comprehended until now the extent of the present method of slavery," he wrote to Attorney General Knox,[35] asking for a meeting in Washington to plan a dramatic legal attack.

The investigation could only have occurred with a man such as Warren Reese in the role of U.S. attorney. Reese and two part-time assistants constituted the sum total of the U.S. government's regulatory and judicial reach into the portion of Alabama he served. It would be another five years before the agency that became the Federal Bureau of Investigation was created in Washington. Until then, the handful of investigators employed by the U.S. Justice Department were nearly all accountants temporarily retained from the examiners section of the Treasury Department. The reach of federal power in a place as remote as Alabama was only as strong as the capabilities and political wills of the local U.S. attorney and federal judge.

The thirty-seven-year-old Reese exemplified the new phenotype of political and racial moderate that Roosevelt believed could emerge as a new leadership class in the South—a counterpoint of reason and modernism to noxious characters like John Pace and other men who perverted judicial and political systems against blacks and the constitutional amendments that were supposed to have freed them.

Born just after the Civil War, Reese was a new husband and fast-rising attorney in the state's capital city in 1903. Handsome, with an academic air, Reese's piercing gaze at juries was softened by a long, narrow face. An eloquent speaker and a florid writer, the attorney was just mature enough to win credibility in the courtroom, just youthful enough to ignore the obvious jeopardy that would mount as he pressed an attack on slavery and some of his state's most powerful men. As allegations of slavery in his jurisdiction multiplied, Reese demonstrated a prehensile comprehension of the murky legal framework governing black labor, and a hard-nosed unwillingness to ignore the implications of the extraordinary evidence that soon poured into his office.

Despite Reese's Republican affiliation in rabidly Democratic and white supremacist Alabama, he carried the social credentials of a true son of the South. His father, W. S. Reese Sr., was a war hero who at the age of nineteen earned a commission as a Confederate colonel for gallantry during the fighting at Chickamauga Creek in Georgia. After the war, the elder Reese became an activist in Republican politics, successfully serving as mayor of Montgomery in the 1880s and running unsuccessfully for the U.S. Senate in 1896 as a Republican "fusion" candidate—attempting to attract both black and white voters. Reese's maternal grandfather, John A. Elmore, was among Alabama's most famous attorneys—an architect of the national government of the Confederacy and a key player in secessionist politics at the dawn of the Civil War.

Even Alabama's leading Democrats could muster no authentic opposition to Reese's appointment to the federal post. Dozens of endorsements poured into the White House and headquarters of the Department of Justice in 1897, including each state Supreme Court justice, local judges across Alabama, bankers, railroad executives, the president of the state senate, the speaker of the Alabama house, Governor Joseph F. Johnston, the secretary of state, U.S. senators, and every Republican member of the Alabama legislature. White Republicans in Alabama saw in Reese the profile of a potentially dynamic new base of support—a fresh antidote to the planter class that dominated Democratic politics, but one who could avoid the carpetbagger taint of the Reconstruction-era Grand Old Party. "He is a young man of promise, belongs to an old and influential family of this state—the source from which we must have recruits if we expect permanent and lasting growth for republicanism in the South," wrote one Alabama GOP leader, in a letter endorsing Reese's candidacy. He was sworn in as U.S. attorney by President McKinley in April 1897.[36]

Four years later, Roosevelt's optimism that men such as the Reeses and Judge Thomas Jones could change the course of southern thinking failed to account for the most powerful social currents surging through the region. Not incidentally, Colonel Reese and Judge Jones knew each other at least partly through their prominent roles in the years-long drive in the 1880s to erect a massive monument to Confederate war dead and veterans in Montgomery. Their participation underscored the treacherous political and social straits through which white southern moderates were forced to navigate at the turn of the century. In the first four decades after the war, southern nativity and service in the war, as Reese and Jones each claimed, were enough to meet the prerequisites for elected office and leadership—and enough to at least partly inoculate them against the charge that any white man who supported legal rights for freed slaves was a traitor to his region.

As the twentieth century neared, though, the orthodoxy of southern patriotism was mutating virulently. It was no longer enough to have *served* honorably. The South now demanded in public forums an increasingly rabid level of absolute adherence to a baroque new mythology of the honorable southerner, the contented slave, and the tragically defeated secession. The new monument in Montgomery, one of the largest such memorials anywhere in the South, was that mythology incarnate. The aging former rebel president, Jefferson Davis, personally laid its cornerstone on the grounds of the state capitol, just a short distance from the spot where he had taken the oath of office as president of the Confederacy. The completed edifice consisted of four statues representing the four branches of military service spaced around the base of an enormous column rising seventy feet above a bronze bas-relief of a battle scene.

Atop the shaft of Alabama limestone stood a ten-foot bronze statue of a soldier titled *Patriotism*. After two decades of planning and fund-raising, the monument was finally unveiled before tens of thousands of spectators in 1898. Undoubtedly, young Warren Reese Jr. was among them.

A series of orators extolled the virtuousness of the southern rebellion and the bravery and tenacity of its soldiers. Flanking the scene was a contingent of young maidens, dressed in pure white, gray caps, and crimson

sashes, each representing one of the Confederate states. Below the sculp-
ture entitled *Cavalry*, an inscription honored the horsemen of the rebellion
as "the knightliest of the knightly race."[37] As special agents scoured the
backcountry of Alabama five years later, and brought tales of horror to
Montgomery in the spring of 1903, the cynicism of the South's claim to
hold a special position among the most noble civilizations could not have
escaped Reese's acute powers of observation.

An unnamed prisoner
tied around a pickax for
punishment in a Georgia
labor camp. Photograph by
John L. Spivak, during
research for his 1932 book,
*Georgia Nigger*.

Tennessee Coal, Iron & Railroad coke ovens
at the Pratt Mines near Birmingham, Alabama.

A southern chain gang in 1898. Photograph by Carl Weis.

"Warden and his pack after capture," at Sprague Junction labor camp in Alabama.
Photograph taken sometime in the 1890s.

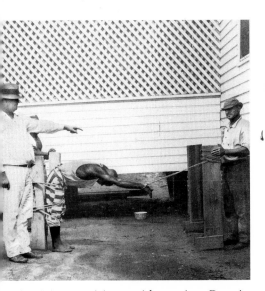

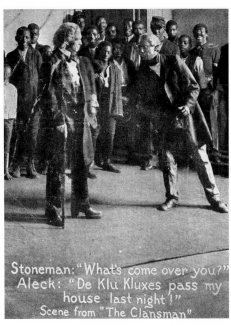

Stoneman: "What's come over you?"
Aleck: "De Klu Kluxes pass my
house last night!"
Scene from "The Clansman"

A prisoner receiving punishment in a Georgia labor camp. Photograph by John L. Spivak.

A 1905 scene from Thomas W. Dixon Jr.'s white supremacist stageplay *The Clansman*. From a postcard distributed by opponents of the drama's racist message.

Black convicts forced to work in Thomasville, Georgia, in the late 1880s. Photograph by Joseph John Kirkbride.

James Fletcher Turner.

W. D. McCurdy, baron of
Lowndes County, Alabama.

U.S. Attorney Warren S. Reese Jr.

John T. Milner.

John W. Pace.

U.S. District Court
Judge Thomas G. Jones.

An 1880s political pamphlet distributed in Georgia by opponents of the convict labor system.

Federal courthouse and post office in Montgomery, Alabama. Scene of the slavery and peonage trials of 1903. H. P. Tresslar Publisher, Montgomery, Alabama.

Abandoned convict "keep" at a lime quarry in
Lee County, Alabama. Photography by E. W. Russell, 1937.

Barracks at Slope No. 12 mine for forced laborers acquired by
Tennessee Coal, Iron & Railroad Company.

African Americans forced to help build river levees, probably in
Mississippi in the 1930s. Photographer unknown.

Convict wagons like these in Pitt County, North Carolina, 1910,
were used across the South to transport and house African Americans
compelled to work in road gangs, lumber camps, and farms.

Black prisoners at work in a rock quarry,
most likely in the early 1940s. Photographer unknown.

# VII

# THE INDICTMENTS

*"I was whipped nearly every day."*

In early May, a federal grand jury, the only province of the legal system in which African Americans could still participate in the South, was impaneled in Montgomery to take up the mounting evidence of slavery in Alabama. The jury of twenty-three, composed of twenty whites and three blacks, filed into the elegant federal post office and courthouse—with arched brick doorways and an imposing square tower at the corner of Dexter Avenue and Lawrence Street in downtown Montgomery. The foreman was Judah T. Moses, one of Montgomery's leading Jewish businessmen.[1]

Soon a steady stream of witnesses—mostly black men and women elated, bewildered, and a little shaken by the sudden interest by powerful whites in their welfare—made its way to the grand jury's chambers to tell of their entrapment back into slavery. The scene's most extraordinary paradox was that the U.S. commissioner—a federal magistrate with judicial powers one rank below Judge Jones—presiding over the testimony was a young John A. Elmore, son of one of the Confederacy's great legal architects and absolute defenders of antebellum slavery. Yet now, forty years after emancipation, he supervised an inquiry aimed at finally bringing an end to slavery in Alabama. Soon, the black members of the jury were guiding portions of the investigation with their own accounts of ongoing slavery.[2]

The first witness to make a formal statement was a white man named Jim Hoffman—without whose corroboration much of the testimony from blacks might have been dismissed. A farmer from the settlement of Camp Hill, Hoffman testified on May 8 that he had spent weeks during the previous year attempting to determine why Jim Caldwell, the son of one of his black farmhands, had been arrested. But everywhere Hoffman or a local lawyer he hired turned, they discovered that Caldwell and another young black man seized at the same time had just been resold to a different farmer or had been accused of new or different crimes.

The mayor of Goodwater, Dave White, who had fined the two African Americans, claimed to Hoffman that he couldn't recall details of the case or what had happened to Caldwell. He told Hoffman it would be a mistake for his lawyer to stir up trouble. White said to give the lawyer a message: "You had better keep out of this town. If you do not we will get after you."[3] The one practicing attorney in Goodwater told Hoffman that the town watchman, John Dunbar, had found a pistol on one of the men and a razor on the other. But Dunbar couldn't be found.

The next day, John Davis came before the jury and told of his harrowing capture by Robert Franklin. When word of the federal investigation spread across Alabama, the farmer who had purchased Davis from John Pace suddenly released him, along with other slaves. The white men hoped setting the workers free would prove they had never been held against their wills. Under questioning by Reese, Davis testified that afterward he was approached again by Franklin.

"He said, 'John?' I said, 'Sir?' He says, 'We want you for a witness . . . want you to sign a paper which won't be nothing, won't hurt you,' " Davis testified. " 'If you want to we will let you sign a little paper, do like we tell you and I will give you a pretty good suit of clothes.' I told him I did not know anything about any court."

Davis said Mayor White then intervened: "Go ahead and sign it," White said. "It is nothing to hurt you."

Davis refused. But after several days of harassment, clearly aware of the risks he faced if he refused to sign the document—apparently an affidavit in which he said his arrest was proper—Davis put his "X" on the paper. The document was never produced at court. "To keep from being bothered with them, I just went on and signed the paper," Davis said. "I did not know what the paper was for. I never read the paper. I cannot read nor write, and he did not even read it to me."[4]

•  •  •

Over the next week, federal agents presented a rush of testimony from others who had witnessed or participated in the seizure of Jim Caldwell and Herman "Joe" Patterson. It was transparent that, like John Davis and so many others, they had committed no crime. There was no gun. And carrying a razor—even if Patterson had done so—wasn't even a violation of Alabama law. The facts were that the pair passed innocently on foot through Goodwater just after dark on April 23, 1902, headed toward Birmingham to look for work. As the two approached a cotton gin on the edge of town, near the Pope House restaurant, they were confronted by the night watchman, Dunbar, and the bank clerk, J. L. Purifoy.

Dunbar told the grand jury he stopped the two because there had been burglaries in the area recently. "I discovered two slouchy negroes slipping towards town, and I suppose they were up to some devilment," he testified.[5] The watchmen approached the two young men and asked where they were going.

"To Birmingham," Caldwell said. "To work."

"You boys come on with me," Dunbar replied.[6]

The two white men shackled Caldwell's wrists and grabbed Patterson by the arms. They marched the two laborers to the lockup in Goodwater— the same place John Davis had been imprisoned. Purifoy claimed later that he had searched the two and found a razor on Patterson and a pistol in the clothing of Caldwell. The next morning, when the two men were brought before Mayor White, both were charged with carrying concealed weapons. The mayor's court docket showed that both men pleaded guilty to the charge, though Caldwell testified later he believed he had been accused of vagrancy and that neither entered a plea at all. Regardless, Mayor White declared the men guilty and fined each $10 plus court costs of $1.60.[7]

After the summary trial, Robert Franklin approached Dunbar and told him John Pace would be pleased to buy the men. The following day Dunbar asked Purifoy to accompany him to Dadeville with the two captured African Americans. Virgil Smith, a black laborer working for Purifoy at the time, warned his boss that Dunbar was in the business of selling African Americans. Purifoy was new to Goodwater, and uncertain of what his employee really meant. He had difficulty imagining that blacks were truly being bought and sold. "If they are selling Negroes," he told the black laborer, "I will go down there and see about it."

Dunbar, Purifoy, and the two black men rode to Dadeville in a horse-drawn hack. After arriving on Main Street in the town, John Pace and Fletcher Turner approached the wagon and told Caldwell and Patterson to get out. Purifoy stayed with the wagon, while Dunbar and Pace took the two black men to a nearby stable. A short while later, Turner drove away with the prisoners, still bound. Franklin had arrived in town separately to negotiate a price for the men. Pace handed over $24 in cash and scratched out a note to the president of Tallapoosa County Bank to give Franklin another $46 from his account.[8]

A little while later, Dunbar and Purifoy, back in the now empty wagon, rattled down a pitted dirt road toward Goodwater.

"What have you done with the negroes," Purifoy asked.

"Turner has got them," Dunbar replied.

Had Turner paid for the men? Purifoy questioned.

"No, nothing more than the fine and costs," Dunbar replied.

The next day, the two white men saw each other again, on the road in front of a wealthy local farmer's residence. Standing beneath the canopy of a landmark oak tree, Purifoy directly asked his friend, "John, what did you get for those negroes?"

"Nineteen dollars," Dunbar grudgingly replied.

Purifoy was alarmed that his friend had been party to the selling of men. The two continued talking for an hour. It was apparent to Purifoy that Dunbar was involved in an active traffic of African Americans.

"Do you think it's right?" Purifoy finally asked.

"Well, everybody else was doing it," Dunbar replied.[9]

The evidence of Patterson and Caldwell's capture quickly led investigators to the fate of three other black men rounded up in Goodwater a day later. This time, the night marshal rounded up Dave Johnson, Esau Williams, and Glennie Helms. All were charged with vagrancy. After a night locked in the town calaboose, they were brought before Mayor White, who refused to allow the black men to call any witnesses. White declared them guilty and fined each $6.60.[10]

None had the money to pay their fines, and the three were tied up and held until a train arrived, bound for Dadeville. After the short ride over, the young men were presented at the station to Fletch Turner, who said they could choose whether to work on his farm or Pace's. One of the most bitter incongruities of the slaving system as it persisted into the twentieth century was the participation of blacks in the holding of other African Americans— another debasement shared with antebellum slavery. Black gang leaders passed on the orders of white overseers; some blacks assisted in restraining and stripping men to be whipped by the bosses; and, as in the case of the young men seized in Goodwater that night, local black workers under the control of Pace and Turner played out a ruse to convince Johnson, Williams, and Helms to quietly go along with Turner, a man whose cruelty to blacks was widely known. "There was some colored people there told us we had better go with Mr. Turner, that we would be treated a heap better with Mr. Turner," Williams testified to the grand jurors.[11]

So the deal was completed, with just enough of a chimera that the transaction had been part of a legitimate legal process and that the black men in question had voluntarily submitted to their fates.

"Mr. Turner said he bought us all three for $50 . . . and we were to work for four months and a half a piece," testified Dave Johnson. "Mr. Dunbar sold us to him. I don't know for how much," Helms later told the grand jury. None signed contracts agreeing to the arrangement, though later such documents mysteriously appeared with "X" 's purporting to be those of the three black men. The gossamer facade of judicial process took only three days to weave. The trio had been arrested on a Thursday, tried, sentenced, and delivered to a new owner on Friday, and were at their forced labor by dawn's break on Saturday.[12]

At Turner's farm, the black laborers were put to work digging drainage, cutting wood, and cleaning up recently cleared new pasture—the most grueling sunrise-to-sunset tasks of a farm still being carved from forest. Dave Johnson was beaten on the first Saturday by Allen Turner, son of the man who had purchased the three. "I was whipped," Johnson said, "because I did not know how to ditch—laid me down flat on my stomach, one man on my head and another man to hold my legs, and whipped me across my back, my clothes were on. I was whipped with a piece of stick about as big as a broom handle. I got about 25 licks. I was whipped about every day."[13]

Helms received his first beating a day after Johnson's: "I was whipped about two days after I got there," Helms testified later. "Whipped me a long time, I could not tell how many licks. Sometimes I was whipped two or three times a day, sometimes took my clothes down and whipped me with a stick on the bare back."[14]

Esau Williams said his first corporal punishment came a week after arriving at Turner's farm. Over the following four weeks, "I was whipped nearly every day. . . . Would drop our clothes and whip us with hickory sticks," Williams recounted.[15] When guards were particularly sadistic, they attached an empty metal bullet cartridge to the end of the stick to gouge the skin with each swing of the branch.


After days of testimony by victims of the forced labor ring, the jury was greeted on May 11, 1903, by the hulking figure of John Pace. The strange weather of early spring had finally entered a long calm. Replanting was in full swing. Weeks of rain had abated, and the drying fields were teeming with workers putting in seed. Just a few weeks earlier, Pace and his son-in-law, Anderson Hardy, had been aggressively gathering more laborers, some hired as free men but most captured through the courts or their procurers scattered in the countryside.

Suddenly ordered to appear before the grand jury, Pace turned the operations over to Hardy and boarded a Central of Georgia morning train at the Dadeville depot where he had purchased hundreds of black men over the prior twenty years. The ride from Dadeville's simple train platform to the immense new red-brick Union Station in Montgomery took not much more than an hour. Completed just five years earlier, Union Station, receiving trains from six competing railroad lines, was the bustling hub of Alabama's economy—a veritable temple to the cotton-driven prosperity that the South was reestablishing for itself and that this federal investigation seemed intent on disrupting.

Well before noon, Pace was in the capital city. He walked two short blocks down Commerce Street to Dexter Street, almost certainly unaware of the irony of his passing the fountain in Court Square, where Montgomery's antebellum slave market had thrived for almost fifty years with the daily auctions of African Americans like Scip, the Cottingham slave, and the forebears of the men and women Pace held on his farm. Across the street was the federal court building. Almost exactly forty years after Lincoln's order freeing the slaves, Pace entered the grand doorway of the courthouse, the first man in Alabama to face the threat of criminal sanction for holding black slaves. Forty-two years later, the modern U.S. civil rights movement began at the same intersection when Rosa Parks boarded a bus at the Court Square stop and refused to give up her seat to a white man.[16]

In a wood-paneled private chamber inside the court building, Pace offered the grand jury a sanitized, yet nonetheless damning, version of his dealings with black laborers. It must have been unnerving for him to face a panel of "peers" that included black men, holding authority over his freedom and fate. Whatever his reaction to the African American faces gazing at him from the jury box, Pace described a plantation melodrama in which he acted not as oppressor but the rescuer of penniless blacks who preferred life on his farm to jail or a forced journey into the coal mines of Birmingham. Ignoring the first twenty years of his active trading in black laborers, Pace dated the beginnings of his dealings to April 1901, just two years earlier.

"The first man I got was Elbert Carmichael," Pace said, naming the victim in what he knew was the earliest case federal investigators had unearthed so far. Pace insisted that he asked for the proper paperwork proving that every black man sold to him was a legitimate convict serving a judge's sentence, but that he took the word of constables such as Robert Franklin and John Dunbar who sometimes said the documents had been lost. "They claimed they did not have time to make the papers out before they caught the train," Pace said of his arrangement in 1902 to acquire a young African American boy named W. S. Thompson.[17]

In the cases of Joe Patterson and Jim Caldwell, Pace testified that he "notified the white people that these boys" were under his control and that their freedom could be purchased by reimbursing the $70 he paid for them. A few days later, G. B. Walker, the attorney, arrived to obtain their release. Pace told the jury he was outraged to learn that the supposed court fees on the men had totaled only $22.50 and that they had been improperly placed on his farm. "I did not want to hold the negroes under those terms, and I demanded my money back," Pace testified.

As for John Davis, Pace said the black man freely admitted shirking a

$40 bill at Robert Franklin's dry goods store. He said Davis volunteered to work off the debt and a $35 fine under guard at the convict farm. Pace claimed to have sent $4 to Davis's wife at one point during the year that he held him, but admitted that he recouped nearly all of his expenditures at the end of the twelve-month contract by selling Davis to another white farmer for $50. He offered no explanation for how he had the power to sell Davis, even after all his alleged debts were paid.

Pace explained that Joe Patterson was kept under guard an extra half year to pay a $25 doctor's bill for treatment after Patterson's fingers were cut while working on the farm. Yet more time was added, Pace explained, as penalty after Patterson attempted to escape and used another white land-owner's boat to cross the Coosa River during his flight. The owner of the boat and Pace's foreman, Todd Berry, recaptured Patterson two days later, after trailing him with bloodhounds. Dragged back to the Pace farm, the justice of the peace, James Kennedy, held another sham trial and sentenced Patterson to an additional six months of labor. Pace said other charges could have been brought as well, but he chose not to. "I felt kindly towards the boy and I wanted the matter dropped," Pace said.[18]

The next day, Fletcher Turner arrived in Montgomery and made the same walk to the courthouse to appear before the panel of jurors. His account was even more blatantly self-serving. Turner agreed to take on Esau Williams, Dave Johnson, and Glennie Helms only as a favor to another black laborer who asked him to help the imprisoned three youngsters, he testified. There had never been any violence against anyone on his farm.

"They have three negroes down yonder," Turner quoted the other black laborer as saying. "And I know a brother of one of the boys, and the boy knows me, and wants me to come around and see if you want to make a trade with him."

When Turner arrived at the train station, he said he found the three black workers "tied in the buggy with a rope." Other white men, including John Pace, had gathered to inspect them, a common occurrence when word went out of black men for hire or purchase.

Turner said the three blacks looked worthless: "I wanted negroes but no such things as them cigarette dudes," he said, using a common epithet for independent black men. "I asked what is the cost of them negroes anyhow? Where were they tried, and what did they try them for?" Deputy Dunbar answered that they could be had for $17.50 each.

Turner repeated to the jury his dialogue with the young black men in the buggy:

" 'Hello nigger, how much is your cost?' One of them commenced crying and said, 'Boss, if you will take me I will work for you two years,' " Turner claimed. "I said, 'You are nothing but cigarette dudes and I would not have you.' "

Turner described how he nonetheless began bargaining with Grogan, the marshal from Goodwater who had arrested the three. Grogan insisted that Turner would have to pay $53 and take all three men.

"I won't pay any such amount," Turner said he replied.

"What will you give?" Grogan said.

"Forty dollars," Turner answered.

"Make it forty-five," Grogan shot back.

"No," said Turner.

Finally, Grogan relented. "Give me the money."

Turner walked into a nearby business, asked for a blank check, and wrote it out to Dunbar for $40, against an account at the Tallapoosa County Bank.

Turner told the jury he was incensed when he later learned that each of the three blacks had only been fined $5 or $6 when arrested. Turner claimed he told the young men they could leave after four months of work instead of a year. He said the workers were "perfectly satisfied," though he admitted that Speedy Helms—the "best negro of the bunch"—tried to run away. He was recaptured and returned to the farm for a reward by a policeman in Opelika.[19]

Three days later, George Cosby took the stand. Like Pace and Turner, he told the grand jury he was flabbergasted by the allegations against him by various African Americans. Cosby said he'd had nothing to do with slavery, forced labor, or peonage. He said he'd been a consistent friend to blacks, paying their debts and providing work out of kindness and good intentions. His version of events was that he paid a $10 debt to Pace on behalf of "a darkey" named Elbert Carmichael in January or February 1901. Afterward, he "allowed" Carmichael to live on his farm.

Carmichael was "a mighty good negro, a might good hand . . . a preacher," Cosby said. He freely left the farm to return to his home in another county. Cosby couldn't remember helping arrest and hold on a bond a man named Jasper Kennedy. A black woman named Matt Smith "never worked a day for me in her life," Cosby said, reporting that after he paid a $3.45 fine for Smith, she disappeared to her father's. As for Lum Johnson, a black worker Cosby paid fines for on two occasions, "that negro is working for me now. He is free. I never whipped him." The same went for Will Gettings, "a free hand . . . working for $7 month." John Bentley, another black man on the farm, "came along the road the other day and I hired him," Cosby said. Bentley feared he was about to be accused of stealing some fence wire in another town, and wanted Cosby to shelter him. Cosby said he agreed to do so for $9 a month, but insisted that Bentley remained free at all times.

"Those three negroes are all that I have. I don't lock them up at night. I have no hounds, I keep a rabbit dog. I don't go armed about my place," Cosby said. "Those negroes are absolutely free."[20]


On the same day that Cosby testified, a federal marshal escorted into the courthouse James M. Kennedy, the jack-of-all-trades justice of the peace and sawmill manager who worked for John Pace. He told the jury that in the previous eight years he had tried some workers who ended up working for Pace, but Kennedy was evasive about exactly how many. The handwritten docket book, in which the records of the arrests and trials would have been maintained, had been lost a little more than a year earlier, Kennedy testified. His new docket book contained entries relating only to a dozen black workers—the exact same workers, remarkably, whom federal agents had interviewed in the previous few weeks.

Kennedy confidently worked through the cases of each African American, crisply pointing out how the proper procedures had been followed, appropriate charges alleged, and necessary affidavits signed in every instance. He was confident even about his handling of the case of Joe Patterson, who one week earlier told jurors the harrowing story of his attempted escape from Pace's farm after being repeatedly beaten. Patterson was tracked by dogs for miles, deep into the woods. Trapped on the bank of the Tallapoosa River, he jumped in a small boat tied nearby and paddled across the water. But Patterson was soon captured by a posse of "man-hunters" on horseback, yelping dogs, and guards from Pace's farm. Wet and exhausted, Patterson was beaten with fists, boots, and sticks. Then the white men dragged him before Kennedy for a new trial.

Those events were barely two months old when Kennedy testified. He told the jury in dispassionate detail that the proceedings against Patterson were handled entirely within the technicalities of Alabama law. Patterson was ordered to work out his original contract with Pace and an additional six months for attempting to break the first contract he was coerced into. When that year of labor was finished Patterson would be held for a third six-month period, Kennedy ruled, for "removing a boat from its moorings."

"Note," Kennedy reminded jurors, lifting an index finger into the air. "In none of these cases that I have spoken about did I ever receive one cent of costs, nor was I paid in any other way by Mr. Pace or anybody else for trying these cases."[21]


The testimony of the white men in the slavery ring was crisply consistent: all of the black men and women held to forced labor were properly convicted of crimes; they freely agreed to be leased as laborers; and they were never physically abused. But outside the courtroom, the men at the center of the investigation hardly behaved as if they were innocent. They began a campaign of witness tampering and intimidation.

Worried that he would be charged, Mayor White in Goodwater boarded a train in early May to Columbus, Georgia, to warn John G. Dunbar, the marshal who had assisted in seizing so many black men, about the investigation. "White did not want to be indicted," Dunbar later testified.[22]

G. B. Walker, the lawyer who had helped bring attention to the slaving operations and set free Caldwell and Patterson, got an ominous letter from his cousin in Tallapoosa County. "Those people there were his fellow townsmen and his friends, and asked me not to stir up anything," Walker recalled the letter saying. "He said . . . for his sake not to do anything against these parties."[23]

Mat Davis—the brother of John Davis—was seized from a train, locked in the Goodwater jail, and threatened by the brother of Robert Franklin.

The white man warned Davis's father that he would "shoot you as sure as hell" if the older man interfered. Released several days later, Mat began hiding in the woods at night.[24]

Despite the efforts to frighten the growing number of accusers, the accounts of kidnappings and violence were making an impression on the jury in Montgomery. Even Alabama newspaper editors, embarrassed by national reports about the investigation, excoriated the accused slave dealers. The ringleaders were growing nervous. Kennedy began to wonder if he should tell the truth.

After giving testimony on May 15, Kennedy, George Cosby, and one of the other guards from Pace's farm shared a wagon for a wet ride back to Tallapoosa County. A steady drizzle pelted the men as the mule strained to drag the hack down a pitted, red-mud road. Deep in the bush, the wagon broke down. The men were forced to walk through the cold springtime muck. Cosby was frantic at the delay. He said he needed "to be at home and get niggers out of the way so that no papers could be served on them from the United States court," Kennedy later testified. Cosby hired a horse at the first settlement the men reached and raced ahead. Kennedy and the guard trudged on in the rain, certain Cosby intended to murder witnesses.

A week later, the three men nervously sat down to a meal together. Cosby had lost his nerve and killed no one. But suddenly he reached into his shirt pocket and pulled out a package of morphine. Kennedy tried to wrestle it away from him. "It will come to this," Cosby shouted. "I am going to be convicted, and before I will be convicted I will destroy myself. It is a heap better than to go to the penitentiary and disgrace my family."[25]

At the same time, Pace and Turner hastily began freeing forced laborers on their farms and at the quarry. Some disappeared entirely, their fates unknown. Other blacks were warned by the white men—or through other black employees—not to cooperate with the federal investigation. Indeed, of the dozens of black workers being held against their will when Kennedy conducted the 1900 census, almost none could be located by federal agents three years later.

On May 23, a few days after Kennedy wrestled the morphine away from Cosby, Secret Service Agent McAdams stepped off the first morning train to arrive in Goodwater. McAdams walked in the bright sunlight to

Robert Franklin's mercantile store, pushed open the glass-plated door, and informed the constable that the grand jury had handed up an indictment for holding black workers in peonage. Franklin, and five others whom McAdams wouldn't identify, were named in the indictment. By nightfall, Franklin sat in a cell at the Montgomery County jail.

Kennedy's anxiety was growing. He had participated in dozens of bogus trials, though he had never reaped the financial rewards of Pace, Turner, and the Cosbys. He was certain the government—and perhaps his employers—would eventually try to pin the slave trade on him. Kennedy told one of the Secret Service agents in Tallapoosa County he was willing to testify again—this time telling the truth.

A week after Franklin's arrest, Kennedy went back to Montgomery and stunned the grand jury. He admitted trying scores of black laborers to force them to work for Pace, Turner, and Cosby. He could recall at least thirty cases in which he didn't make any record of the proceedings or report a verdict to the county judge, as he was required to do by law. It was clear from Kennedy's testimony that the traffic in African Americans hadn't been limited to men. The white landowners sought out nearly half a dozen black women as well, Kennedy said, with the clear implication that they were seized for sexual services. "There were many others, but I can't remember their names now," Kennedy said.

He claimed to have initially used his authority as a justice of the peace properly, but that eventually the white landowners he worked for demanded that he convict any black laborer they desired. "They would send one there and have an affidavit made," Kennedy said. The black man would be arrested, fined, and sent to whichever farmer had arranged the arrest.

"The agreement was there was no record to be kept," Kennedy testified. Nearly every case, he said, "was a trumped up affair."[26]

Other white men, fearful of the mounting evidence, began breaking their silence about the truth of the slave farms. Wilburn Haralson, a young farmer living near the Pace plantation, testified that the Cosbys compelled him to swear out false charges against several black men whose sentences to work for them were about to expire. "I was afraid not to do it, I was afraid of those folks," Haralson testified. "I was afraid they would get me in some scrape, swear some lie on me, and get me into it, and I had a wife and children."

A black woman named Mattie Turner was held on the farm indefinitely, falsely accused of prostitution, Haralson swore. The implication was clear that Turner was held for the sexual exploitation of the farm. He knew of at least one slave worker who had been murdered by a relative of the Cosbys. Haralson said few African Americans ever escaped. George and Burancas Cosby patrolled their farms with guns and used specially trained blood-hounds to track any who tried to take flight. "They had nigger dogs," he said. "There were two dogs at George Cosby's and two dogs at Burancas Cosby's house."[27]

On May 28, U.S. Deputy Marshal A. B. Colquitt hauled Francis M. Pruitt, the constable and livery stable keeper in Goodwater, to Montgomery to hear his indictment read aloud. A total of six indictments were handed up against Pruitt and two justices of the peace, outlining for the first time publicly how Pace's slaving network operated.[28]

The indictment charged Pruitt with "forcibly seizing the body of Ed Moody, a negro," in Coosa County and selling him on April 3, 1903, to Pace, who had held him against his will since then. At the courthouse on the day of his indictment, Pruitt claimed he had never seen Moody and didn't know Pace. Appointed to his position as a constable by former Alabama governor William Jelks, Pruitt stoutly defended his county, claiming that Coosa citizens are "as good as any in the State." The town of Goodwater was an "especially law-abiding community," he added. Without qualms, Pruitt told a newspaper reporter that as a constable he had "frequently" arrested African Americans who then were fined by a local magistrate and "paid out" by local white farmers. But he insisted this was entirely within the law. The *Montgomery Advertiser* reported that his claim had "an honest ring."

The following day, Pace returned to Montgomery. This time, he was accompanied from Dadeville by U.S. marshal A. B. Colquitt. The men arrived at Union Station at dusk and headed directly to the courtroom of Judge Jones. Pace was informed he had been named in eight indictments as the buyer of black men seized by local constables. Reese recounted key evidence gathered against Pace—maintaining that one Negro woman had been killed on his farm, that men and women had been forced to work nude for lack of clothing, and that the laborers were mercilessly beaten.

Pace brought with him to the courtroom a bond posted by William Gray, the Dadeville banker who at Pace's direction had paid out the cash used to purchase most of the enslaved black workers.[29] When the bond turned out to be insufficient, Jones allowed Pace to travel back home with the marshal in tow to make new arrangements to avoid jail. Pace expressed his appreciation and retired to a Montgomery hotel to await the next morning's train to Tallapoosa County.

Outside the courthouse that night, Pace insisted to a newspaper reporter that he was innocent of any wrongdoing, even as he conceded without hesitation that he had purchased men from Coosa County officials and worked them on his farm. He said the African Americans were put into the prison maintained on his property, where they and the convicts were watched over by hired guards and hound dogs trained to track men.

He described buying John Davis from Robert Franklin for $70, but said Davis begged to be left at the farm. Pace said he explained to Davis that he would be held with the county convicts and treated the same. Davis readily agreed, and Pace drew up a contract under which he agreed to work sixteen months to pay off his fine.

Pace was unapologetic, but denied that he had acquired or held a large number of black laborers. He had purchased no more than five in the previous year, he said, all of them as favors to the black workers themselves. They were never treated brutally, and it was "always understood," he said, that the men would be freed if relatives or friends reimbursed him for the costs of bailing out and holding the laborers.[30]

Next to make the trip to Montgomery were George Cosby, his nephew Burancas, and James H. Todd, one of the strongmen used as an enforcer on the Pace farm. The men arrived in the state capital near daylight on June 10, having spent the night on a Western Railroad train stranded between Opelika and Montgomery. Accompanying them were Deputy Marshals Hiram Gibson and A. B. Colquitt, who had arrested them on Tuesday.

The defendants wouldn't talk to reporters on the day of their court appearance. Todd had been an overseer for Pace for more than fifteen years. Burancas Cosby, a twenty-three-year-old "wide in stock, build and ruddy face," worked for his uncle George. The younger Cosby claimed that at least two of the blacks named in the indictment were "unknown to him." By nightfall, all had returned to Dadeville by train.

As word of the arrests raced across Alabama and the rest of the country, an epic legal and political confrontation began to take shape. J. Thomas Heflin—the stirring white supremacist orator who proclaimed to the constitutional convention two years earlier that God put "negroes" on the earth to serve white men—was the Alabama secretary of state by 1903. Almost immediately, Heflin began circulating word that he would aid the indicted white men, perhaps even representing them in the courtroom. He would have none of the spineless apologia for new slavery that southern journalists and some politicians first offered. He embraced it as a return to the natural order of man.

A few southerners stepped forward to genuinely condemn the new slavery system—but very few. One was Joseph C. Manning, the postmaster of Alexander City in Tallapoosa County. A fiery populist, he had fought in the 1890s to hold on to a coalition of black and white voters in Alabama, and after the turn of the century railed against the growing national consensus that blacks should be excluded from all political activity—even within the Republican Party. "What has become of the ringing declaration of Abraham Lincoln that 'The nation cannot endure half slave and half free,' " he wrote to an Ohio newspaper.[31] He denounced the de facto annulment of the Fifteenth Amendment and condemned Republican leaders for their crass willingness "to acquiesce in slavery for the south and stand for human liberty in the north."

Later, Manning wrote to the *New York Evening Post*, lashing out at the abuses of blacks he had witnessed and the men in his county alleged to have held slaves. "It is today under the law in Alabama, a crime for a farm laborer (black) to quit his employer. He may be denied his pay, he may be half fed, he may be beaten with a buggy trace but if he 'fails to keep his contract' then he is a criminal," Manning insisted. "There are black belt planters who do starve, mistreat, abuse and beat men, and force them to break their contract in order to get them arraigned before some demon in white skin, but with a heart as black as hell itself; and another year of servitude is attached by a chain more galling than that of chattel slavery to the ankle of the black man. The case of Patterson is only one in thousands, yes, in ten thousand. . . .

"The Mayor of this town of Goodwater . . . would be complimented in his own estimation no higher than to have it written that any negro is no more worthy of human sympathy or political consideration than is any mule, and of less kind treatment than a good dog," Manning continued. "Here is the truth about the South that some men of the North would 'let alone.' Here is the South that should be permitted to adopt its own course in settling the race problem!"[32]

Goodwater Mayor Dave White fired back in defense of his town, claiming that no black man or woman had ever been abused in his court. "Unjust punishment of negroes is absolutely repulsive to me and that no negro is imposed on when it is in my power to prevent it," he wrote.

> *I defy any person to prove that any negro or white man has ever been convicted in my court that was not guilty or that didn't have a fair trial, or that received illegal or cruel punishment after they had been convicted. And I am certain that I can truthfully state no negro has ever been worked in slavery in the town of Goodwater since the day when slavery was abolished in the sixties. It is a fact that numerous negroes have been tried and convicted in Goodwater for stealing and have received a small fine and a light punishment, when a white man under the same circumstances would have been much more severely dealt with as a great allowance is always made for the negro owing to his standing in life.[33]*

Editors of the state's most prominent daily, the *Montgomery Advertiser*, were apoplectic that Manning, an Alabama native, had uttered such heresy in the northern press. It called Manning "rattle-brained" and, reaching back to an archaic term for any creature that turned against family doctrine and patriarchy, a "nest fouler."

The newspaper labeled his description of widespread slavery an "outrageous exaggeration." The *Advertiser* also railed at Roosevelt's promise at Lincoln's tomb of a "square deal" for African Americans, and any assertion

that the peonage cases were part of a larger movement in the South to disenfranchise black men and reassert white dominance.

Peonage was no worse than the treatment of workers in the factories,
mines, and sweatshops of the North, the newspaper maintained.[34] "These
cases of 'new slavery' have nothing to do with the adoption of the new Constitution in Alabama. If there is any difference, the mass of white people are
more kindly disposed toward the negro now than before their disfranchise-
ment. These peonage cases are simply a few here and there. There have not
been tens of thousands of such cases. We doubt extremely whether there
have been even hundreds of them in all the State in the past twenty years."[35]

Nearly every Alabama leader contended the events in Tallapoosa
County constituted a small anomaly, easily stamped out by making examples of a few offenders. "Deputy U.S. Marshall Colquitt seems to have
taken up with this county," wrote the Dadeville *Spot Cash*. "In fact three or
four men of this community have been escorting him to Montgomery
where he placed them under bond, charged with Peonage—that new word
lately sprung on us which means the enslaving of a freeman against his will,
as we understand it. This is a pretty bad state of affairs in Alabama, but not
so bad as the northern papers would make it. These conditions will be thoroughly investigated and we hope every guilty party will be punished so that
the evil will be stopped and the blot on our state and county removed."[36]


Underscoring southerners' sense that it was hypocritical for their region to
be targeted for its racial misdeeds, residents in Belleville, Illinois, went on a
rampage a day after the Dadeville editorial appeared. A black schoolteacher
named David Wyatt and the town's white school superintendent had argued
over the renewal of Wyatt's teaching certificate. An altercation ensued. The
superintendent was shot, but not seriously harmed. Wyatt was arrested and
taken to jail. By nightfall, at least two thousand whites were gathered in the
town—including many women and children encouraged to attend the spectacle. A phalanx of two hundred men attacked the steel doors at the rear of
the jail with sledgehammers, pounding it with thousands of hammer blows.
The city's police did not voluntarily hand the prisoner over to the crowd,
but also gave no meaningful resistance. Wyatt, an educated and imposing
man—standing six feet three inches tall—waited in his cell on the second

floor of the jail, enveloped in the cacophony of the hammers pounding out his death beat. After half an hour, the doors splintered open. Wyatt was seized from his cell and his head immediately smashed.

Dragged into the street, the mob surged around him, kicking and stomping his body until it was matted in blood and dirt. A rope was secured to his neck and tossed to two men who had climbed a telegraph pole. Hoisted just a few feet off the ground, Wyatt's body whipped back and forth as members of the crowd gouged, stabbed, and sliced his torso, legs, and arms with knives. Others in the mob gathered pickets from nearby fences and roadside signs to build a crude pyre beneath his dangling corpse. Still more went for gasoline and benzene. Soon Wyatt's body was engulfed in flame. By the time the earliest churchgoers left their homes on Sunday, June 7, the grotesque form of Wyatt's carbonized remains lay amid a heap of ashes and smoldering wood on the street.

"The mob knew that the negro's victim was alive and had a fair chance to recover," a correspondent for the *New York Herald* dutifully noted. "The excuse given is that the lawless element among the negroes has been doing all sorts of deviltry, and that it was determined to teach the negroes a wholesome lesson."[37]

Wyatt's lynching was unremarkable in many regards. His was the thirtieth African American lynched in 1903. There would be at least fifty-five more before the year ended. Yet few developments caused as much delight to leading southern whites than a gruesome racial atrocity committed in the North. Such incidents proved, in their reckoning, that northerners were just as inclined to crimes against African Americans as their southern cousins, and that the end result of greater racial equality like that in the North was simply more brazen criminality and chaos caused by blacks. Many white southerners were further gratified when less than two weeks later a mob in Wilmington, Delaware, seized a black man named George White from his jail cell. White, accused of rape and murder, was tied to a stake, forced to confess the crimes, then shot repeatedly and finally burned.

The *Advertiser* could hardly restrain its glee.

*In the North the negro is an alien, an exostosis on the body politic, as it were. They do not understand him and cannot do so. They talk sympathetically and humidly of his wrongs and his rights, shed some tears over his alleged cruel fate in the South, and then, if he aspires to be a laborer in the hive of industry, they turn on him and drive him out with curses and revilings. If he resists or falls back on the sacred laws of self-deference and self-preservation, he is either shot down or lynched. They love him— at a safe distance.*

*With us here in the South it is different. We received the negro by inheritance. He came to us through the generations of slavery. Emancipation left him stranded on the shores of a new world, for which he had no preparation and no fitness. The Southern people, remembering the negro of the olden time, when he was the faithful servant, the willing worker and the protector of the family of his master—with all this in their minds our people have borne with him, have helped him and have tried to fit him for some of the duties of citizenship. We recognize in him a part of our population a necessary worker on the farm, in the shop and in the home, but not in any way an equal.*

*And for all this because the negroes have come down to us from the good days of old; because they are at home with us, and must perhaps forever be in some degree our wards, we owe them justice, fair treatment, and protection in all their civil rights. Now that they have practically lost the right of suffrage, we more than ever owe them our watch care and should throw over and around them the shield of law and justice. The fact that they are lynched in the North, or driven out like dangerous wild beasts is no reason that our people should do the same. Let us not follow the evil example set by those Pharisees who preach what they do not practice and who condemn in others the deeds which they practice among themselves. In short, let us steadfastly refuse to follow the evil examples set by our brethren of the North and the West.*[38]

South Carolina senator Ben Tillman summed up the sentiment more succinctly to a northern audience: "I see you are learning how to kill and burn 'niggers.' That's right. Let the good work go on. Keep it up. You are getting some sense."[39]

Roosevelt had to be astonished. Only a day before Wyatt's murder in Belleville, he had been in the same state, visiting Springfield, barely a hundred miles away, praising black soldiers and promising his "square deal" for African Americans. At the same time, the Justice Department was telling him that slaves were still being held down south. There was nothing the president could do about Wyatt's death; murder was clearly outside the jurisdiction of federal officials. But surely slavery, of all things, was different. He told Attorney General Knox he was personally concerned about the Alabama allegations and asked for a full report. Roosevelt was assured that "vigorous and uncompromising prosecutions" were under way.[40]

In Montgomery, U.S. Attorney Reese was growing more troubled by the scale of the crimes coming to light in the grand jury room. On June 10, he sent an alarmed report to Attorney General Knox. "The conditions of the 'black belt' in this district are more deplorable as the investigations of this grand jury proceed. It is now being revealed that hundreds of negroes are held in peonage and involuntary servitude of the most vicious character," Reese wrote. "Men and women are arrested on the flimsiest charges . . . they are brutally whipped, worked and locked up without let or hindrance. The tortures inflicted are severe and sometimes result in total disability or death. Some counties in this district are honey combed with these slave trade practices."[41] Worried that his report might sound like hyperbole—and recognizing the potentially explosive reaction to the case that was bound to soon develop locally—Reese asked for an urgent meeting with officials in Washington.

The stoutly bourgeois Knox, hardly two months removed from his lavish Pittsburgh law offices and now ensconced in the presidential cabinet, was perplexed by Reese's letter. He had to take it seriously. President Roosevelt had expressed concern, and the inquiry grew from charges first lodged by a federal judge—one of Roosevelt's earliest appointees. Reverberations were still rippling across the country from the president's "square deal" speech less than a week earlier.

But Knox couldn't avoid a measure of incredulity. How could so dramatic a state of affairs come to pass, without challenge, in twentieth-century America, even in uncivilized reaches so far from his rarefied world? Moreover, the prosecutor in Montgomery was entirely unknown to Knox, who knew that among the scores of U.S. attorneys named in provincial centers around the nation, many were less-than-extraordinary political operators— holding their positions purely as patronage to local presidential allies or financial backers. Two days later, on the last workday of the week, Knox told an aide to telegraph Reese for a more complete report on the details of the investigation. For the moment, he ignored Reese's request for a personal audience.

The telegraph from Washington arrived at the drafty offices of the U.S. attorney above the Montgomery post office as Friday's work hours came to a close. Reese no doubt shared it with the two other lawyers who assisted him in government cases, Julius Sternfeld and James K. Judkins, and the office secretary—his cousin Mildred Elmore. Sitting near the transomed door to the hallway, she managed his correspondence and appointments and attended to the two modern luxuries of the office—a single Remington typewriter and one telephone.[42]

Reese knew he faced the most consequential matter of the five years since his first appointment to office. In the balance of the report requested by the attorney general hung all of the family prestige and political support—perhaps even all of the aspirations of eventual Republican power in his state—that had been so dramatically reflected in the flood of supportive letters that paved the way for his selection by President McKinley.

The heavy humid heat of early summer in Alabama was already seeping into the hallways of the post office building. Fixed at his desk that afternoon, he perspired as the temperature approached 90 degrees, sunlight shafting through the wide sash of rippled glass in his window. Past the arched doorways opening from the dark interior of the federal building onto crowded Dexter Street, Reese could have seen and heard the noisy throngs of pedestrians crowding the cobblestone street on either side of the clanging electric trolley line running through the heart of Montgomery. Lines of carriages and horsemen pushed slowly through the crowd. Open wagons pulled by mules driven by muddy black teamsters waited to cross from side streets littered with manure and the debris of commerce.

Four blocks to the east, just beyond the field of view from Reese's window perch, the domed Alabama state capitol peered regally across a city that had become, more than any other, a royal capital of the New South—

collecting the tribute of both the region's reengineered cotton empire and its smoke-belching new industrial expansion.

The trolley line ran in an asymmetric loop the length of Dexter Street, then passed out of his view by the old slave auction fountain in Court Square across from the Exchange Hotel. Here, buyers from textile makers and cotton exporters encamped from hundreds and thousands of miles away to bid and contract for delivery six months later of millions of dollars' worth of cotton from plants only just beginning to peek from the deep black soil of the South's richest cotton region.

If Reese climbed into the five-story-high tower rising atop the post office, he could have followed the line as it threaded through the crowds, drays, buckboards, and early automobiles chugging down Commerce Street toward Union Station. The streetcars crossed Bibb, Coosa, and Tallapoosa streets, as they rolled past the long row of cotton warehouses that, by early fall, would be packed with the bulk of southern Alabama's economic output. The cotton compress on the same street packed billions of pounds of lint into five-hundred-pound bales ready to be loaded on railcars or the perpetual line of steamboats waiting a few hundred yards beyond, at the edge of the Alabama River. On the docks there, scores of black men stacked cotton bales atop loads of pig iron taken in Birmingham the day before from the furnaces of Sloss-Sheffield and Tennessee Coal, Iron & Railroad.

Montgomery luxuriated in the wealth of this surge of cotton—still unmolested by the scourge of the boll weevil and other new insects and diseases that would ravage the crop beginning in a little more than a decade—and the rich new windfall pouring into the state capital from the sale of convicts into the coal and ore mines in Birmingham.

Cotton, steel, and timber were by far the state's largest sources of wealth and livelihood. Alabama produced more than 1.1 million bales of the white lint in 1900—surpassing the pre–Civil War output for the first time and almost tripling the state's production during the first years following the war.[43] Vast tracts of forest were under the saw. Yet mineral production and the iron and steel industry surpassed all other economic activity. In 1905, the state's mines, anchored by the slave camps near Birmingham, generated nearly twelve million tons of coal and almost four million tons of iron ore—

making Alabama one of the foremost producers of iron, steel, and coal in the world.

Early in the testimony before the grand jury in May of 1903, Warren Reese shared the conventional assumption that the stories of John Pace's abuses in Tallapoosa County were anachronistic relics—isolated redneck antics, certain to be the subject of scorn once exposed. But by the beginning of June, Reese realized how significantly the new slavery underpinned Alabama's cotton, timber, and steel paradise. He knew he was on the verge of an attack on its heart. He could not know how the fight would end, or whether he would survive it.

At noon on June 10, the grand jury filed into the courtroom to report seventeen additional indictments. Then, foreman Judah T. Moses, a wealthy seller of real estate and insurance, gave Judge Jones a written request for advice on the constitutionality of the Alabama statute making it a crime for a worker to break a farm labor contract—which was punishable by a fine of up to $50 or six months of hard labor.

In the note, the jury asked whether the act violated the Thirteenth and Fourteenth amendments of the Constitution. Judge Jones replied that he had devoted "much thought" to this question and would give them an answer later. One juror also inquired whether a justice of the peace who gave a sentence in excess of his authority was guilty of peonage. The judge said that the justice of the peace would not be guilty if the sentence had simply been an honest mistake, but that if the official "acted in bad faith or corruptly" he would be guilty of causing the person to be held in peonage. No judicial proceedings, regardless of how lawful they appear on their face, would be a defense, the judge noted, if they were "a cloak or a fraud to cover up the illegal design to cause persons to be held in peonage."[44]

Five days later, on June 15, Judge Jones issued a formal charge to the grand jury, answering their inquiries and directing how they should interpret the federal peonage statute as their deliberations continued. Jones began with a long discourse on the origins of the peonage statute after the acquisition of

New Mexico by the United States, and then laid out how the new labor system of Alabama appeared to violate that law.

Jones explained that any man who induces a laborer to sign a contract agreeing to be held under guard and unable to leave until a debt is paid was guilty of peonage. A citizen or law enforcement officer who tricked a laborer into believing he could avoid criminal prosecution or a sentence to hard labor only by signing such a contract was guilty of peonage, the judge explained. Anyone who falsely accused a person of a crime in order to compel him or her to sign such a contract or conspired to obtain the labor of a worker through such false charges, Jones wrote, was guilty of violating the pre-emancipation slave kidnapping act, which forbade "carrying away any other person, with the intent that such other person be sold into involuntary servitude."

Jones also declared Alabama's labor contract law—which bound hundreds of thousands of black workers to white landowners—unconstitutional. Any person held against his will under this statute, Jones ruled, should be released on habeas corpus—the ancient legal principle used to win the release of the falsely imprisoned.[45]

Southern whites immediately recognized the implications of the ruling, and the reaction was furious. "Judge Jones' . . . opinion, if sustained by the highest court, is far reaching and with disastrous consequences to the labor system of the South," wrote the *Prattville Progress*, a newspaper in the heart of a slave-riddled county. "There must be a revolution in the labor system."[46]

The residents of counties across eastern Alabama were baffled by Judge Jones's interpretation of the law. Tens of thousands of black workers were at labor in Alabama under contracts signed when a white man "confessed judgment" for an arrested black man—paying his "fines" before any prosecution commenced and receiving in return a signed contract for labor.

These arrangements sounded precisely like the ones described by Judge Jones as illegal. Hundreds of farmers were at risk of arrest. Thousands more African American laborers were being forced to work in mines and timber camps under similar contracts signed between county governments and the state of Alabama itself. Some local attorneys asked if farmers who worked convicts for debts were guilty of peonage, wasn't the state of

Alabama equally guilty in its handling of convict leases?[47] It occurred to virtually no one in Alabama that this was precisely the point. The vast majority of black laborers leased from the law enforcement system were being held illegally.

Even Judge Jones failed to comprehend the full ramifications of his opinion. Like many well-intentioned but still fundamentally racist whites, he naively believed that the system engineered by Pace in Tallapoosa County was an isolated instance of abuse. He accepted the common convention of the time that African Americans were less intelligent and more inclined to criminal behavior than whites. He presumed that the vast majority of blacks arrested in the South were in fact guilty of their crimes, and merited severe punishment. What made him more "progressive" than other whites, and where he differed from most white southerners, was that he believed blacks could not be brutalized in their punishment, and that the concept of impartial treatment of all citizens by the courts had to be upheld.

Rank-and-file southerners, especially in rural sections with large black populations, had no such illusions. They knew Judge Jones had set a standard by which thousands of white men were guilty of slave dealing, that hundreds of state and county officials were in jeopardy, and that the whole financial structure of governments and local economies was at risk. A correspondent to the *Birmingham Age-Herald* reported that "more than 100 men" in the area of Coosa and Tallapoosa counties—just two of Alabama's nearly seventy counties—were at risk of arrest in the federal investigation. "The people of East Alabama are very much wrought up. . . . They have been working criminals for twenty years, and the majority of such men do not know they are violating the law," the writer said.

Inundated with bewildered queries, Judge Jones began to realize the breadth of coerced labor in his state. He hadn't intended to set off panic. To quell anxieties, Jones quietly summoned a reporter for the Associated Press and explained that white men could avoid breaking the law if their contracts with blacks were approved by a local judge and signed in court.[48] Surely local judges could never condone slavery, Jones reasoned.

While Judge Jones tried to soothe Alabama's worries, Warren Reese asked Sternfeld, the assistant who had listened to much of the testimony brought to the grand jury, to collect for the attorney general the most egregious allegations that had surfaced so far in witness statements and reports from U.S. marshals in the countryside. As Mildred Elmore rattled the Remington's keys, they dictated what became an eight-page report to Washington.

"There have been flagrant abuses and violations . . . on the part of wealthy and influential men," Reese began. "These violations have not been confined to one or two periodical and independent instances, but it has developed into a miserable business and custom to catch up ignorant and helpless negro men and women upon the flimsiest and the most baseless charges and carry them before a justice of the peace who is usually a paid hireling of these wealthy dealers. . . .

> The victim is found guilty and a fine is assessed which, in the beginning cannot be paid by the victim, and then it is that one of these slave dealers steps up, pretends to be the friend of the negro . . . telling him he will pay him out if he will sign a contract to work for him on his farm . . .

> . . . the negro readily agrees rather than go to the mines, as he is informed he will have to do, his fine is paid, the contract is signed, and the negro is taken to the farm or mine or mill or quarry of the employer. . . .

> Placed into a condition of involuntary servitude, he is locked up at nights in a cell, worked under guards during the day from 3 o'clock in the morning until 7 or 8 o'clock at night, whipped in a most cruel manner, is insufficiently fed or poorly clad—in fact the evidence in nearly all of the cases investigated reveals that the negro men are worked nearly naked, while the women are worked in an equally disgraceful manner.

> Brutal things have transpired and sometimes death has resulted from the infliction of corporal punishment. . . .

> When the time of a good working negro is nearing an end, he is re-arrested upon some trumped up charge and again carried before some bribed justice and resentenced to an additional time. In this way negroes have been known to have worked on these places in this situation for years and years. They can get no word to friends nor is word allowed to

reach them from the outside world. . . . They are held in abject slavery without any knowledge of what goes on in the outside world.

If they run away the dogs are placed upon their track, and they are invariably retaken and subjected to more cruel treatment. . . .

The indictments so far found are based upon some twenty-five negro men and women who have been the subjects of these violations. These are some of the most severe instances, but it has been discovered there are hundreds of other cases.[49]

Reese and Sternfeld detailed the physical abuses they had discovered and the extraordinary obstacles to their investigation. In Tallapoosa County, the grand jury had already issued indictments against Pace, Fletch Turner, and the Cosbys. Also charged were the enforcers and procurers of the system, including Robert Franklin, Grogan, Pruitt, and Dunbar, all constables. The jury had indicted the three justices of the peace most flagrantly involved—James M. Kennedy, Jesse L. London, and W. D. Cosby. Another eight men who had worked as whipping guards for Pace and the other buyers were also under charge, including Turner's son, Allen, and Pace's son-in-law, Anderson Hardy.

Beyond Tallapoosa County, Reese reported, the grand jury was also investigating conditions in Lowndes County—a hundred miles away and deep in the plantation country of the Black Belt, with more than 35,000 black farmhands and sharecroppers working cotton on the land of white men. "This county is really the center where it is charged these practices are more freely indulged than anywhere else. This county, it is claimed, is honeycombed with slavery."[50]

The slaving practiced in Lowndes County was orchestrated by the sheriff himself, J. W. Dixon. In one case described by Reese, Dixon chased down a black worker named Dillard Freeman, who had left his plantation without permission to visit a sick brother a few miles away. Tracked to his mother's home, Freeman was beaten by Dixon with a pistol, tied with a rope around the neck, and forced to run behind a mule for more than five miles, while the sheriff followed on horseback, "whipping him whenever he would lag behind."

Once back at the plantation, Reese wrote, Dixon began whipping Free-man with a wide piece of rubber belt attached to a wooden handle. "Four men were required to hold him off the ground while Mr. Dixon himself administered the punishment. When Mr. Dixon became tired, another man was made to do the whipping. In this way, the boy was whipped nigh until death. He cannot tell how many licks he was hit, nor can he tell how long this happened." After the whipping, Freeman was chained to the floor near the beds of Dixon and his overseer.

In the grand jury room, Freeman revealed his back, Reese said, show-ing "one mass of scars from his thighs to his neck."

Yet already the prospects of pursuing a conviction against the slavers of Lowndes County and the other plantation regions where hundreds of thousands more black farmworkers lived were being challenged, Reese advised the attorney general. Dillard Freeman was threatened with death if he testified to the grand jury. A member of the Dixon family had followed him to the courthouse in Montgomery on the day of his first appearance. "It was impossible to get anything out of him because of his fear of death."

When a black grand juror who lived in Lowndes County went home after a week of hearing witnesses, Sheriff Dixon and his four brothers rode up to his house at midnight on horseback and demanded to know what was being said to the grand jury—testimony that is dictated to be secret under the U.S. Constitution. They told the juror to remember that "he had to live in Lowndes county, and if he did not stand up for his own people he knew what to expect," Reese wrote.

The Dixons are "dangerous men," Reese continued. "They are said to have killed several men. It is believed that witnesses who come here and who expect to return to Lowndes county are practically compelled to per-jure their souls because they fear their lives."[51]

As the letter to Knox continued, Reese outlined how the new slavery was far larger than one or two places, and involved far more than scattered pockets of involuntary servitude, confusion about the law, or unintended violations. His timbre rising as the report continued, Reese said that he was receiving daily letters from other Black Belt locations—Wilcox, Sumter, Chambers, and Coffee counties. "Unquestionably, there are hundreds of these people in this district who are held in abject slavery," Reese related.

The prosecutor continued that Judge Jones had just ruled that Alabama's contract labor law—a statute shared in some form by every southern state and effectively criminalizing any black worker who left the employment of a white farmer without permission—was unconstitutional. The implications of the ruling were just dawning on Reese. He realized the black men and women of the South had never been truly set free.

Judge Jones's ruling, Reese wrote, "in effect, amounts to an actual and not a theoretical emancipation of the negro, and it is now necessary that this office make an effort to rescue these people from their condition by and through habeas corpus proceedings."

Reese recognized that his investigation could eventually require thousands of court filings. He asked the attorney general to assign a Secret Service agent to assist with the investigations and to create a new special assistant U.S. attorney to move from county to county in Alabama instituting legal challenges to free enslaved blacks. "Unless the government will take steps to bring these habeas corpus proceedings . . . they will not be much benefited by these investigations."[52]

As Mildred typed out the last lines of the report, the telephone rang. Western Union told the secretary a bicycle delivery boy was pedaling toward them with an urgent message. When the telegram arrived, Reese read that the attorney general wished him to personally deliver his report to Washington. President Roosevelt had been briefed on the investigations and directed that a legal attack be fully pressed.[53] Reese called Western Union and dictated a reply. Mildred hastily retyped the last page of Reese's report: "I have just received your wire . . . I will report to you at ten o'clock morning of seventeenth."[54]

Reese rushed to Washington, where he outlined for the attorney general the details of the investigation and his belief that much more than scattered peonage was at stake. Knox was cautious, but given the president's specific interest in the cases, the expectations raised by his speech at Lincoln's tomb, and a chorus of cries from northern publications, he could not move slowly. "The new slave-driving in Alabama has pricked the conscience of the nation," proclaimed *The Nation* on June 11.[55]

After the meeting, the attorney general authorized what amounted to the most sweeping federal investigation into the working conditions of southern blacks since the Civil War. He directed U.S. attorneys in Montgomery, Birmingham, Mobile, and in the southern sections of Georgia to begin inquiries in their districts, including the densely populated Black Belt, and other areas where more than a million impoverished African Americans lived. Across Alabama and Georgia, the prosecutors sent deputy federal marshals into the countryside with orders to bring back any evidence of ongoing slavery.

Not since the first years of Reconstruction had law enforcement officials of any kind expressed interest in the legal protections of blacks. Suddenly a squad of Secret Service agents led by an indefatigable detective named Henry C. Dickey, as well as every federal marshal across a three-hundred-mile-wide swath of the South, was quietly, if often reluctantly, quizzing African American pastors, sharecroppers, and farmhands about the treatment of black laborers by many of the most prominent white landowners in the South.

By late June, sixty-three indictments had been returned by the Montgomery grand jury, and locals expected as many as twenty more white men to be arrested. The government was holding nearly thirty black witnesses in a closely guarded boardinghouse in a black neighborhood of Montgomery. Not all came from Tallapoosa or Coosa counties. And many witnesses were reported to have appeared at the federal courthouse from counties other than those originally targeted in the investigation.

The ten white men from Coosa and Tallapoosa counties who had been indicted up to that point were summoned to appear in court on June 22. Pace, Fletcher, and many of the others arrived by an evening train the previous day. Monday morning they filed into Judge Jones's courtroom for a grueling, hours-long hearing. Soon, the corridors of the federal building were clogged with lawyers in dark, vested suits and the curious wandering in from the streets and the stone steps of the courthouse. Throughout the morning, U.S. Attorney Reese came in and out of the courtroom, consulting repeatedly with the battery of prominent lawyers representing John Pace.

Montgomery buzzed with speculation. Word rippled through the onlookers that all charges against Kennedy would be dropped once he testified in open court. By now Kennedy was a pariah among his longtime friends. His confessions to the grand jury, implicating at least a dozen other white men, had been widely reported. Meanwhile, word was spreading of letters sent the previous day to every Montgomery newspaper by Fletcher Turner, insisting that all accusations against him were false—most especially testimony that women had been murdered at the Turner farm. He specifically denied the claim that Sarah Oliver had been brutally beaten to death at his place during the previous winter. Then came the day's most sensational story: Pace planned to plead guilty to the charges—and then challenge the validity of the anti-peonage statute to a higher court.[56]

The court formally convened at noon, with U.S. Marshal L. J. Bryan calling the names of men to form petit juries to hear the evidence in the cases. A large crowd of spectators jammed the courtroom, craning their necks to catch a glimpse across the gallery of the Tallapoosa farmers. Pace, Fletcher Turner and his son, the three Cosbys, and other defendants sat together on a bench near the front of the room. At the bar were the half dozen members of their defense team. The old guard of Alabama was rallying to the men. Among the lawyers was Thomas L. Bulger—son of the Tallapoosa County Confederate war hero, and D. H. Riddle, the Goodwater attorney who had actually participated in some of the fake trials held by his mayor.

Later, the lawyers announced the defense of the Turners had been joined by Gen. George P. Harrison, a flint-eyed lawyer with a jet black beard in the imperial style of the day. He too was a widely remembered former Confederate commander, best known for his central role as a newly appointed colonel in the bloody repulse of the Union army's most famous black regiment, the 54th Massachusetts Infantry, during the gruesome battle for Fort Wagner in July 1863.

Judge Jones ordered that the trial of Pace, the Cosbys, and John Kennedy—the newly cooperating witness—begin one week later on charges of peonage and related crimes. Fletcher Turner and his son, Allen, would stand trial beginning July 6. A few days later, the trial of Robert Franklin and Francis Pruitt would begin, followed within a week by Jesse Berry and James Todd, two of the enforcers who helped violently hold slaves on the farms, quarry, and sawmills.

After forming two juries and giving them instructions from the bench, Judge Jones turned to the crowd, warning that any person who entered the court with a weapon would be "sent to the penitentiary" for contempt of court.

Before the day ended, Reese announced that additional indictments had been issued against J. Wilburn Haralson, of Dadeville, and John G. Dunbar, the former city marshal of Goodwater then serving as marshal in Columbus, Georgia. New charges were also announced against the Turners, for holding a black woman named Camilla Hammond. In total, the grand jury had issued ninety-nine indictments against a total of fifteen defendants. Pace alone faced twenty-two counts.

Lawyers for the defendants urged Judge Jones to delay the trial to give the farmers time to harvest their fields and to study the "peculiar" and unfamiliar charges they faced. Reese said the farmers had created the situation for themselves and that black witnesses were being held in Montgomery to protect them from intimidation before trial. "The government is not at liberty to give in detail the instances of this kind," Reese said. "But it can be said that intimidation both of witnesses and grand jurors have been going on in connection with these peonage cases."

Judge Jones concluded that a speedy trial would not burden the defendants unfairly, and made clear that he feared efforts to frighten the witnesses. "The court has nothing to conceal, gentlemen," Judge Jones said. "In a great many of these cases intimidation has been practiced. A witness has been taken from a train. I need not say more. These cases must be tried as early as possible consistent with proper opportunity to make defense."

It was clear that black witnesses were in danger. For days, Reese had been gathering African Americans critical to the trial in Montgomery, housing thirty of them under federal guard in "negro boardinghouses." At one point in the proceedings, Secret Service agent Capt. Henry C. Dickey arrested two black schoolteachers who went to the boardinghouse posing as detectives sent by Judge Jones. They quizzed the black workers about what they were telling government agents, apparently to report back to Pace and the other whites.

Before any of the trials began, federal officials learned that Tallapoosa County had appointed a deputy marshal specifically "to keep an espionage on the negro witnesses of the government," reported Montgomery newspapers.[57]

Until the day of the arraignments, most of Alabama's political elite and the white general public had imagined that the slavery investigation was entirely the handiwork of the White House and its representative in Montgomery, U.S. Attorney Reese. Judge Jones's directions to the grand jury a week earlier were startling, but his confusing equivocation after denouncing involuntary servitude left open the question of where Jones's true allegiances rested. Across the South, newspapers and politicians still banked on the fact that he would uphold a well-honed ritual of southern posturing in high-profile court cases involving blacks: factitiously expressing the importance of legal rights for African Americans while simultaneously ensuring no harm to a white defendant and aggressively curtailing redress to the black victim.

"It turns out that the main mover in Alabama to break up what is called the peonage system, whereby convicts are held to labor indefinitely by white men, who pay their penal fines and contract their labor in return, is Judge Thomas G. Jones, ex-governor of the state," wrote the *Atlanta Constitution*. "If there is anything criminal in the system, that criminality should be exposed and punished properly, and whatever of false hue and cry there is on the affair should be exposed."[58]

The *Montgomery Advertiser* continued to proclaim mock surprise at the discovery of forced labor in Alabama: "The character of offense was peculiar and unknown in this country since the emancipation of the negroes. It was practically and to all intents the enslavement of men for a period of time in violation of State and Federal law. There has been much brutality charged and a great deal of testimony given . . . few of . . . the people of Alabama . . . ever dreamed of such things as seem to have existed."[59]

As the first trial neared, however, it was clear that Judge Jones was deviating from the script. He appeared to be serious. The *Advertiser*, alarmed that a southern leader would join with a Republican president from New York to attack southern whites who resubjugated blacks, poured forth with what had become the ascendant view of turn-of-the-century white southerners. "A sentiment that is now practically unanimous throughout the Southern States . . . is that we, the white men of the South, propose to settle racial questions in our own way and in our own time. And we will do it in the way best for both races," the newspaper editorialized.

*Several millions of ex-slaves, suddenly exalted to citizenship, was the heritage we received from the Federal government. As if the mere fact of their presence in changed conditions was not serious enough, they were*

*endowed with all the political rights that any citizen of the Union pos-*
*sessed, and for which they were neither prepared nor fitted. And then,*
*to add to the bitterness of our degradation, and the hopelessness of the*
*problem, our country was overrun with adventurers from the North,*
*some of them good and well meaning men, but others as unprincipled*
*scoundrels as ever scuttled a ship or robbed a safe. It was these and their*
*kind who made the condition of the Southern people unbearable and*
*revolt inevitable.*

*Forgiveness is a Christian virtue and forgetfulness is often a relief,*
*but some of us will never forgive nor forget the damnable and brutal*
*excesses that were committed all over the South by negroes and their*
*white allies, many of whom were federal officials, against whose acts our*
*people were practically powerless. And one of the worst features of this*
*saturnalia was that the ballot in the hands of ex-slaves was in almost*
*every instance, both from their own ignorance and at the instigation of*
*their carpet-bag allies, used to despoil, degrade and humiliate the real*
*citizens of the almost helpless South.*

The *Advertiser* asserted that southern whites made a choice for which
they should be applauded—declining to resume armed rebellion against the
federal government and instead only stripping African Americans of the
right to vote and most other legal rights. That northerners would complain
about this—and that some southerners agreed—was infuriating.

*What do we see? All over the North we find public speakers and newspa-*
*pers assailing our methods and our people and in every way, as words can*
*do, inciting the colored people to resist, fomenting discord between the*
*races and in many cases maligning and vilifying the Southern people for*
*their course.*

*Our people do resent the interference of Northern people in a mat-*
*ter with which they have no real concern, and we intend to continue*
*resenting it. What is more, we intend to settle this race question in our*
*own way and if the result is to have the country "rent again into factions*
*hating each other" . . . we shall not feel that we of the South are the*
*offending party. We do not hate the North, but we will settle the race*
*question.*[60]

Even in the North, there was consternation about the trials beginning in Alabama, and stirring up issues that northern whites increasingly agreed should be left to southern whites to handle. The *Chicago Tribune* opined that relations between the South and North had deteriorated to their worst state in more than a decade and pointed to the current message of former President Grover Cleveland and other leading northerners: "The South—the white and the black South—should be let alone to settle their problems in their own way," Cleveland said.

Edgar Gardner Murphy, a moderate white Montgomery resident, insisted in letters to northern newspapers that the Tallapoosa peonage cases did not indicate a massive level of continued black enslavement. In a letter to the *New York Evening Post*, Murphy wrote:

> *The sentiment of the whole state has been unanimously insistent upon a thorough investigation of the charges and upon the rigorous punishment of the guilty. . . . An ignorant and lowly people settled in isolated regions where local courts and local constabularies are often inefficient and sometimes corrupt are always in danger of becoming the prey of brutality and greed. If it is hard for the best sentiment of New York to protect effectively the poor immigrants of her great port from the avarice of thieves and "loan sharks," and it is difficult for your city to protect some of its young girls from the degrading barter of the "cadet."*

He argued that the peonage cases weren't the result of leaving the South alone to deal with race issues. Instead, the new rise of slavery was caused by "a persistent policy of intrusive censure and of political threatenings." He said the North placed undue "pressure upon Southern life, putting the South ever on the defensive and partly neutralizing the forces of self-criticism and of local responsibility. Whatever evils may now exist at the South have not resulted from the policy of letting the South alone."[61]

But as each defendant stood perspiring before Judge Jones in the increasingly crowded courtroom, wearing his best black church suit, bolo tie, and clutching his hat, it became clear that whatever the judge's southern pedigree nothing would be sacrosanct in this proceeding.

# VIII

## A SUMMER OF TRIALS, 1903

*"The master treated the slave unmercifully."*

Negotiations over Pace's plea to the charges against him continued for days. His attorneys initially believed that Judge Jones—like any other white southern judge—would feel compelled by tradition and public pressure to acknowledge the untested status of the peonage statute and offer a symbolic punishment to Pace in exchange for a guilty plea. But Judge Jones showed no sign of doing so. Reese, the prosecutor, was insistent that Pace be meaningfully punished. Pace's lawyers were certain, regardless of the public brouhaha in the preceding weeks, that no Alabama jury would actually convict a white man on such charges. They urged him to wait for trial.

Meanwhile, the city was ablaze with anxiety. In the early evening of the day following Pace's arraignment, a former U.S. marshal named Charles E. Taylor confronted Deputy U.S. Marshal Byron Trammel on the sidewalk beneath the white-columned portico of the elegant Exchange Hotel, where many of the attorneys and others involved with the peonage cases were staying. Trammel was assisting Reese in the investigation.

The two men had long disliked each other, according to mutual acquaintances, and there was no record of the words exchanged when they faced off outside the front doors of the hotel. But within minutes, Taylor drew a pistol. Trammel responded in kind. Shots were fired. Taylor was soon dead.

Stanley W. Finch, another Department of Justice investigator in Montgomery, was certain the shoot-out was brought on by the peonage cases. He wrote to his Washington bosses that federal agents in Alabama—feeling increasingly more like the interloping Freedmen's Bureau agents who scattered across the South thirty years earlier—were encountering unprecedented hostility wherever they went.

"The country throughout this district wherever [peonage] exists is pretty thoroughly aroused," Finch wrote. "The fact that a Secret Service agent is engaged on these cases is well known and many have the impression that a number of secret service agents are scouring the country. . . . Any one traveling through the country engaged in an investigation on behalf of the government is liable to be mistaken for one of these detectives. In some localities the sentiment has reached such a pitch that it is considered unsafe for anyone known as or suspected as being a government detective to travel."

Nonetheless, Finch reported that involuntary servitude was indeed widespread across the state. He succinctly summed up the economics of the new slavery. "It is by no means confined to a few isolated communities. I have also been again and again informed by these persons that this peonage system is more cruel and inhuman than the slavery of antebellum days, since then the master conserved the life and health of the slave for business reasons just as he did that of his horse or mule, but now the master treated the slave unmercifully and with the sole object of getting the greatest possible amount of labor out of him. Moreover a peon costs but a few dollars while a slave used to cost several hundred."[1]

Pace, agitated at the attention his case drew, appeared alone early in the morning two days later at the offices of U.S. Attorney Reese. He said he wished to plead guilty to all eleven counts of peonage and obviate the need for trial. Pace's supporters spread word that he had approached Reese against the advice of his own lawyers. In reality, the gesture was a calculated gambit to shift the focus of the prosecution to other defendants—while preserving Pace's challenges to the constitutionality of the indictment.

Reese refused to accept the plea unless Pace was represented by his attorney. At noon, after rounding up one of Pace's lawyers—the others had already departed for Dadeville—court was called into session, and the peonage counts read aloud. Pace pleaded guilty to each one, though only after his attorney filed "demurrers" to the indictments—objections in modern legal parlance—arguing that the federal peonage statute didn't apply to the acts alleged in the indictments.

The federal government had no jurisdiction over the use of forced labor in Tallapoosa County, the lawyers argued, regardless of whether individuals had been held in slavery. Judge Jones, acknowledging Pace's right to challenge the applicability of the peonage law to a higher federal court, overruled the objections and ordered Pace to stand for sentencing.

Asked if he had anything to say, Pace—in stark contradiction to his initial claims to the press—said he was guilty of the seizure of eleven African Americans, including John Davis, Rita Scott, Jim Caldwell, and another laborer named Owen Green. Yet Pace denied that his capture and enslavement of workers violated any United States laws.

Green had also raised his shirt to show the grand jury his injuries during earlier testimony. "They whipped scars on me," Green said as he revealed the marks on his skin. "They laid me up for a week and a half one time. One of the scars on me is where Mr. Tom Blassingale struck me on the head. He struck me with a stick . . . and knocked me senseless. . . . Mr. Jim Kennedy choked me and jumped on my head. After I was stamped, the blood came up from my lungs. . . . I bled a good deal from my lungs."[2]

In the case of Green, Pace lured the farmhand by approaching him in a saloon in Dadeville, offering to hire him for $4 per month, help his father pay off the mortgage on a $16 horse, and allow him to come and go freely from the farm. But once a contract had been signed, Green was placed in the lockup on Pace's farm for nearly two years. "I was made to do farming, locked up at nights and whipped," Green testified. "Mr. Jim Kennedy whipped me five times in one day. Mr. Bob Smith also whipped me. He whipped me four times. Mr. Bill Brown whipped me." Later, Pace sold Green to George Cosby.

In the courtroom, Reese stood and, playing out a carefully choreographed arrangement with Judge Jones and Pace's lawyer, made one act of deference to the defendant—who appeared in court looking far older than his forty-nine years.[3] Reese pointed out Pace's "diseased" condition and asked that the defendant be allowed to sit for the rest of the proceeding.

Judge Jones agreed and then sentenced Pace to five years in the federal

penitentiary in Atlanta on each charge. Taking into account Pace's infir-
mity, the judge ruled that the sentences would be served concurrently. The
charges that Pace had conspired with others in the seizure and enslavement
of blacks were postponed until after the court of appeals ruled on Pace's
challenge. Accepting assertions that Pace was in dire health, Jones also
allowed him to post a $5,000 bond and remain free pending the outcome of
those legal machinations. William Gray, the Dadeville banker, reappeared
at the bar, along with co-defendant Fletch Turner, to sign the bond for
Pace. He was released from custody.

Pace appeared visibly relieved, though the stiff sentence sent a wave of
anxiety through the other defendants—who realized Pace was now likely to
be called to testify against them and that Judge Jones would hand down
similar penalties to others convicted.

The *Advertiser*, like most local whites, remained certain that Pace would
never actually be imprisoned, regardless of whether the guilty pleas were
affirmed by the court of appeals. "He is in an almost helpless physical condition. He suffers from a bone disease which has affected his feet, and he
walks with great effort. It is said that he will be able to produce a surgeon's
certificate showing he is in a terrible physical condition."

Reese was elated with the guilty plea. But a growing chorus of politicians,
journalists, and southern commentators—the same voices that originally
applauded the investigation as proof that southerners could be relied on to
clean up slavery—hailed Pace's admission that the continuing slavery was
limited to a pocket of miscreants in one county. They loudly proclaimed
there was no need to pursue any further charges or allegations.

Reese knew better. The publicity around Pace's arraignment and plea
triggered a wave of new allegations, some even more grim than any yet
heard by the grand jury. Moreover, Attorney General Knox's earlier order
of investigations into peonage and involuntary servitude across Alabama,
Georgia, and northern Florida was detecting dozens of other cases. U.S.
District Court judge Emory Speer in Macon, Georgia, was presiding over
his own proceedings stemming from a multilayered slave trading conspiracy in the southern half of that state.

Three white men—William Shy, Arthur Clawson, and Robert Turner—

pleaded guilty there to capturing a black man they claimed owed them money, whipping him, and forcing him into labor. Judge Speer—behaving more like Alabama had initially expected of Judge Jones—fined the men $1,000 each but then immediately suspended the punishments.

Apparently unaware of the earlier peonage allegations in his state, Speer made the extraordinary assumption that the three men before him were the only whites to reenslave a black man since the Civil War. "In view of the fact that this is the first crime of the kind which ever has occurred in Georgia," Speer told the defendants, "and because of the frank confession of the young men, sentence is imposed, in order to convince the public that the purpose of the court is to warn and deter others from like crime. During good behavior, fine is suspended upon payment of $100 each." Given the "problems of the times," Speer maintained harsh measures would be counterproductive. "I deemed it for every reason best to deal very leniently with the prisoners," Speer wrote to the attorney general.[4]

Reese was concerned that too many in the South viewed the new slavery cases just as Judge Speer appeared to, as an anomaly. To prove the broad scope of involuntary servitude in his jurisdiction, Reese planned to aggressively broaden his investigation. Just two days after Pace's guilty plea, the prosecutor sent federal marshals back to Coosa County to arrest Laray Grogan, one of the Goodwater watchguards who had been so busy in the town's trade in black labor.

Grogan was accused of arresting an African American woman named Emma Pearson on a bogus charge of vagrancy and then selling her to Eliza Turner, the brother of Fletch Turner, who managed the family's limestone quarry in Calcis. After arriving in Montgomery, Grogan told a local reporter that he had done nothing wrong and further that the peonage cases had made the blacks of Coosa and Tallapoosa counties "unbearably impertinent." His bond was immediately posted by two wealthy Goodwater businessmen, and Grogan was released.

The same day, J. Wilburn Haralson was arrested in Columbus, Georgia, where he worked in a cotton mill, and brought by a Saturday morning train to Montgomery. Known as the Cosby family's "affidavit man," Haralson routinely wrote out and swore to any fictitious charge George Cosby told him to lodge as a ruse for seizing blacks. He was placed in the county jail to await trial on five counts of peonage.[5]

Despite the continuing stream of new charges and the opening of the Cosby trial a few days away, Reese worried that public support for his campaign was wavering. Newspapers across the South were growing more belligerent in tone as Reese and a few other prosecutors continued investigations. Alabama's most popular political figure, Secretary of State J. Thomas Heflin, was also growing louder in his denunciations of the cases.

Three days before the Cosby trial was set to begin, Reese conducted a formal interview with the *Montgomery Advertiser*. He said that while the charges against the Cosby men were technically termed peonage, the case was in fact about slavery—the overt buying and selling of humans, and holding them in a condition of coerced forced labor. "These indictments are for . . . kidnapping and taking and carrying away any person with intent to place him in a condition of slavery, and holding and returning him to a condition of peonage," Reese said.

He also made it clear that the cases were aimed not just at cleaning up an isolated nest of slavery hanging on in one area of Alabama. The prosecution was an attack on widespread practices of involuntary servitude across the state. The Tallapoosa cases were the high-profile criminal thrust of the effort, but just as important was Judge Jones ruling that the Alabama contract labor law was invalid. "The contract labor law which has just been declared unconstitutional . . . was passed for the protection of landlords in the cotton growing belt.

"It is a matter of common knowledge that under this statute, the laborer or renter has not been guilty of any criminal act in thus leaving or abandoning the premises," Reese said. "He has simply breached a contract which creates the relation of debtor and creditor. Under this statute the creditor commands the debtor on peril of hard labor not to work at his accustomed vocation for any one else during the term of that contract." Reese blamed the nearly unchecked and unaccountable power wielded by justices of the peace in rural areas.[6]

The following morning, the Cosbys appeared on the second floor of the federal building accompanied by Dadeville lawyer Thomas L. Bulger, son of the Confederate hero at Gettysburg. But the first train from Tallapoosa County, packed with spectators and key witnesses, had been delayed. Finally, at 1 P.M., the court convened with a crowded gallery of white spectators. White witnesses milled in the corridor. For their safety, the African Americans who would testify, explained Reese, would be produced only as they were called to the stand.

Reese announced to the gallery that the government would first prosecute case No. 4218, in which the Cosbys, Pace, J. W. Haralson, and James Kennedy were charged with conspiring to sell Pike Swanson into labor on the Cosby farm. Swanson had testified previously to the grand jury that he was held on the Cosby plantation until just before the peonage investigation began. A farmhand from Macon County, he said he went to the Cosby farm the previous July and freely signed a contract to work for $2 a month. But once Swanson began work, the Cosbys refused to pay him. Instead, he was arrested, then arrested a second time, on bogus affidavits by Haralson accusing him of disorderly conduct and fighting. Swanson was put through a sham trial by Kennedy, the justice of the peace. Then Cosby pretended to pay Swanson's fines in return for holding the worker at least fourteen more months.

Swanson testified he was never paid for any work on the Cosby plantation and was held under guard seven days a week, and locked in at night. Two weeks before the Cosbys were indicted, the white men freed Swanson, who then fled to his home county. A week before the trial, Burancas Cosby claimed never to have seen Pike Swanson.

After Reese announced that Swanson's capture would be the first case, Judge Jones granted a one-day delay to give the defense lawyers time to prepare. But early that afternoon, George Cosby sent word that he and the other members of his family wished to avoid the trial, as Pace had done. G. R. Shaffer, of Dadeville, one of the men who made bond for the Cosbys, urged them to plead guilty and had gathered scores of signatures in Tallapoosa County on a petition asking for clemency.

At 5 P.M., Shaffer called the judge from his Adams Street home back to court chambers, where they met with Cosby's lawyers. Judge Jones refused to promise clemency. But in return for guilty pleas from two of the men, Jones and Reese agreed to accept the attorneys' arguments that the statute of limitations had passed on the crimes alleged against W. D. Cosby—the man who had been ready to take morphine a few weeks earlier. His case was dismissed.

With shafts of summer sun cutting sharp diagonals through the court-room windows, George Cosby and his nephew Burancas stood before the bench, heads bowed, eyes downcast. They quietly pleaded guilty to forty-five counts of peonage and conspiracy to hold blacks in slavery.

The two insisted they had no idea that their actions were against the law. They vigorously protested allegations by the U.S. attorney that they treated the forced laborers cruelly. They implored the court to recognize the hardship on their families that would come from imprisonment.

"The excuse that you did not know that you were violating the laws of the United States can have no legal weight, since every man is conclusively presumed to know the law," Judge Jones responded. "It is not entitled to a particle of moral weight in these cases, because you are bound to know that what you did was a violation of the laws of God and of the State regardless of any law of the United States. Helpless and defenseless people who are guilty of no crime have been brought into court and by collusion with jus-tices of the peace, who prostituted the authority of God and of this State in the administration of justice have been deprived of their liberty, fined and forced to work and in some instances cruelly beaten.

"You have violated not only the laws of your country but that great law of honor and justice, which bids the powerful and strong not to oppress the down-trodden."[7]

Judge Jones sentenced each of the men to one year and a day in the fed-eral penitentiary in Atlanta.

Reese was jubilant. The swift guilty pleas seemed to prove both the extent of involuntary servitude and the power of the federal sword to stop it. The clear implication was that he was at the beginning of a massive cam-paign to root out slavery once and for all. The trial of Fletch Turner was next on the docket, and would be followed by many more. Agents contin-ued to probe Lowndes County and other areas where evidence of even more widespread slavery was rampant. Reese began advocating to the De-partment of Justice that his assistant, Julius Sternfeld, be named a special prosecutor solely to oversee the expanding investigation. "These cases jus-tify the contention of the government that peonage and involuntary servi-tude has been practiced in Alabama in no small degree," he quickly wrote the attorney general. "These practices are indulged in many other counties in the district and our effort shall be made in the direction of putting an end to them."[8]

But more practical men than Reese could better see what the future held. White leaders were rallying across the South, emboldened by men such as Secretary of State Heflin, who was crisscrossing Alabama denouncing Reese's investigation and castigating any white man who did not agree. At the same time, black preachers and African Americans who had established some sliver of financial security grew fearful of the rising temperature around them. They had learned through bloody experience the dangers of challenging the status quo of white domination, and also that in the inflexible rituals of southern racial interaction men such as themselves were expected to prostrate themselves before whites as proof that they too gave no credence to the inquiries demanded by President Roosevelt and Judge Jones.

Shortly after the Cosby sentencing, Edward M. Adams, a Secret Service agent stationed in Montgomery, wrote to Washington headquarters in hopes of softening any disappointment that might come if no jury convictions were won in any of the slavery cases. He was particularly concerned that another agent assigned to the cases not be tainted by any such failure. "He has secured evidence in a number of cases that ought to bring convictions, yet, knowing public sentiment as I do, I fear, unless compromise verdicts can be secured, that no convictions will result," Adams wrote. "The iniquity of peonage will always remain in this country in practice, to eradicate it is an interminable work. The sentiment against the infliction of punishment to offenders finds its strongest exponent in Secretary of State Heflin, an orator of no mean ability, and he is going about the state like a roaring lion. I merely write this, to say, that whatever the result in the trial of the cases in this court, the failure to convict and punish offenders, cannot be charged to our service."

Adams included with his letter a newspaper clipping reporting that petitions signed by hundreds of blacks in Tallapoosa and Coosa counties had been presented to Judge Jones asking for clemency for the Cosbys. "These cases have caused a bitter feeling between the two races," the article said with profound understatement, "and that the petitioners believe that the peonage system is broken up, and further says that the Cosbys are good citizens of the community."[9]

. . .

Indeed, whatever initial contrition white southerners expressed at the first revelations of slavery was evaporating as it became clear that Judge Jones and Reese had no plans to stop after a few symbolic guilty pleas. Facing the dock of the courtroom, Fletch Turner and his son, Allen, were ready to embrace the most brazen defense of the new slavery yet offered.

On July 4, attorneys for the father and son filed demurrers, challenging the peonage charges against them. Their fundamental objection was constructed upon a startling argument. The Turners' lawyers conceded that their clients indeed had engaged in a form of slavery, but that involuntary servitude wasn't peonage and therefore wasn't illegal.

"Unlawfully and knowingly holding a person forcibly and against his will and requiring such person to labor for the holder to work out a debt claimed by the holder to be due him . . . does not constitute holding such person to a condition of peonage under the laws of the United States," they wrote.[10]

Moreover, the Turners' lawyers argued that no system of peonage existed in Alabama at all, making the statute forbidding it irrelevant, and charges based on the law impossible. They added that since peonage was defined as forced labor in repayment of a debt, the Turners couldn't be convicted of peonage if, as the government contended, the debts owed to them by black workers were bogus.

Ignoring the claims of extreme abuse and homicide committed on the Turner farm, the attorneys argued that the men's behavior might constitute a form of slavery but that no federal statute made slavery a crime. Cases of slavery would have to be brought in a state court by local officials under Alabama's law against false imprisonment, the lawyers argued. No acknowledgment was made that in a local court, the prosecutor would be a white man elected in all-white elections, the jury guaranteed to be all-white, the judges likely involved in the slaving conspiracy, the buyers of men almost certainly prominent local figures, black attorneys barred from appearing, and black witnesses treated as unreliable by nature. In the four decades since emancipation, no one could recall any such criminal charges ever being brought in a southern court. No one imagined that ever changing.

Astonishingly, the lawyers were on some level correct. The Civil Rights

Act of 1866, passed in the wake of the war to formalize the ending of slavery, simply declared all persons born in the United States to be full-fledged citizens with the right to vote regardless of race or previous "condition of slavery or involuntary servitude." But it did not clearly state that the *holding* of slaves was a crime, and the disparate treatment of former slaves was made only a misdemeanor, carrying a maximum penalty of one year in jail. Later statutes in the 1870s made segregated accommodations, schools, and anti-black-voting measures illegal, but actually weakened the minimum penalty for violations. In 1883, the U.S. Supreme Court declared even those laws unconstitutional, ruling that the Thirteenth and Fourteenth amendments—approved in 1868 to abolish slavery and establish black citizenship—didn't authorize Congress to pass such enforcement laws. Following the growing national sentiment that race matters be left alone, Congress did nothing to fill the vacuum—leaving a constitutional limbo in which slavery as a legal concept was prohibited by the Constitution, but no statute made an act of enslavement explicitly illegal.

It didn't matter to the Turners' lawyers that little of their defense claims matched their earlier sworn statements when first questioned by a federal agent and a special U.S. commissioner two months earlier. Turner had scoffed at the suggestion that his past handling of black laborers was legally or morally suspect. He offered elaborate explanations for why he imprisoned a series of blacks the federal officer identified. In the case of Joe Strickland, the white farmer conceded that the laborer didn't appear anywhere in the records of the local courts but was nonetheless a criminal prisoner. He claimed Strickland's records were in a different jurisdiction, and that the Goodwater deputy sheriff, Grogan, brought two black men to the Tallapoosa County jail in July 1901 and asked Turner if he wished to "buy" one of them out of jail. Turner claimed he entered into a formal labor contract with the worker, who had been tried for "riding a train," and that the local probate judge said it was unnecessary for the court to authorize the arrangement.[11]

"If you behave yourself," Turner claimed to have told Strickland, "I will let you off in five months." Turner demurred that he "had just commenced in the convict business" and didn't understand the ins and outs of the rules. In kindness, he had paid a doctor, Turner claimed, to treat Strickland's syphilis—and then kept him at work an extra six months simply to cover the costs. By the time of the trial, Strickland was working in the coal mines near Birmingham, he added.

On July 7, Glennie Helms became the first victim of the Tallapoosa cases to testify publicly. Moving to the witness chair just after 5 P.M., Helms sat calmly and confidently before the courtroom filled with white spectators. Neatly dressed and his head cleanly shaven, Helms said he was eighteen at the time of his capture and was attempting to travel from Calcis—where he had worked for a week in the lime quarry owned by Turner's family— back to his home in Columbus, Georgia. As Helms and two companions passed on foot through Goodwater on April 15, 1902, they were seized by the town marshal, charged with vagrancy, immediately convicted by the mayor, and then sold at the Dadeville depot to Fletcher Turner.[12] Turner was apparently unaware that the three had been working for his family's quarry and put them to work digging ditches on his farm.

Under questioning from Reese, Helms told the twelve white jurors how he was brutally beaten on his arrival at Turner's farm. Reese, regal in a high, stiffened collar and checkered cravat, asked whether either of the Turners or their employees whipped him again during the four months he was held on the farm. Helms testified he was beaten nearly every day by Turner's son, Allen, or another armed guard. After about a month of work, he escaped— only to be captured by the sheriff of another county and returned to the farm. As punishment for fleeing, he said Allen Turner whipped him severely with a thick stick.

The cross-examination that followed must have been one of the most extraordinary encounters ever in a southern courtroom. In the witness chair sat an eighteen-year-old black boy in the simple attire of an indigent farmhand, largely illiterate and almost certainly the child of parents born in antebellum slavery. Standing before him—challenging his account of re-enslavement—was the aristocratic form of U.S. representative Ariosto Appling Wiley, prominent congressman and one of the city's most notable attorneys.

Unfazed by the disjuncture of the scene, Helms hewed to his story—as unswervingly as a skilled plow hand cutting neat furrows across a field. Unable to budge the verisimilitude of the young man's descriptions of his capture and beatings, Representative Wiley obsessed on what he called contradictory details in the testimony. Was the buggy in which Helms and the others were transported to the farm owned by a livery stable or some-one else? he hammered. Finally, the lawyer portrayed Helms as a "shiftless negro" enjoying his moment in the spotlight at the expense of the federal government.

"Who's been taking care of you since you came here?" Wiley asked sharply.

"Captain Dickey," replied Helms, referring to the Secret Service agent who had guarded the black witnesses housed in a boardinghouse since May.

Night was falling, and the court recessed for the evening. Outside the federal building, Fletcher Turner, soaked from the heat of the courtroom, fumed to local reporters about published allegations that his son had bru-tally killed a black woman named Cornelia Hammock.[13] He insisted that the woman died of disease and offered to have her body exhumed to prove it.

The next day, a series of witnesses called by the government corrobo-rated Helms's account. Dave Johnson, one of the other blacks captured with him in Goodwater, the night watchman John G. Dunbar, town mayor Dave White, and others confirmed how the three African Americans were seized and sold.

The Turner defense aggressively attacked each witness. After the testi-mony of the white attorney who bought Helms's freedom after finding him being worked naked at the Turner sawmill, Colonel Wiley launched a with-ering cross-examination—insinuating that the lawyer, L. E. White, was so friendly to Helms's family and other black workers that he couldn't be trusted. Wiley didn't use the specific words, but his message to the jury was that White was a "nigger lover"—a man operating outside the racial rituals of the South. The questions became so sharp that Judge Jones recessed the proceedings and reprimanded Wiley for the calumnies against White. "The witness must not be sneered at or insulted," Jones said.

The strategy was designed not to prove that Helms hadn't been cap-tured and sold—since the Turners admitted those facts—but to mock the black witnesses and discredit any white men who corroborated them. It was a time-proven and honored southern lawyerly ruse. In the rare instance that a black man or woman received a day in court, attorneys simply ridiculed the very idea of a black man being treated respectfully and anyone who appeared willing to do so. Triggering an almost tribal form of group soli-darity, the tactic usually triggered juries of white men to guffaw at the comedy of a black man under oath. If the jury concluded that the government's case was built on the testimony of worthless African Americans and unreliable whites, Colonel Wiley was confident of an acquittal. He knew Alabama was tired of the peonage cases. And he wanted to remind the jurors that to do otherwise would subject them to their own ridicule as "lovers" of blacks.

On the trial's third day, the defense presented a stream of witnesses testifying to the Turners' excellent character and care of black convicts they leased from local governments. For weeks leading up to the trial, court observers and journalists speculated that Secretary of State J. Thomas Heflin, Alabama's most flamboyant white supremacist, might represent the Turners in court in a show of support for the men.

Just before noon, as the defense prepared to close its case, Heflin was called as a witness. In previous weeks, there had been no indication that the men knew each other. But taking the stand, Heflin swore that he had known Fletcher Turner for "several years" and that Turner had always been a man of good character. The message to the jury—that the white orthodoxy of the South was behind the defendants, not the opponents of slavery—was clear.

The next morning, the gallery was jammed with observers, including a large crowd of African Americans. As eight hours of closing arguments by four separate attorneys ground through the day, the stifling courtroom became a throng of perspiring men, aflutter with dozens of handheld fans.

The final defense argument was explicit—whatever the facts of the case, every white man must acquit Fletcher Turner as a message to the rest of the United States. "Forever put at rest the agitated minds of our Northern friends, and brand the newspaper criticisms and caricatures which have appeared in the northern journals as a falsification and a slander upon the fair name of Alabama," fumed attorney Bulger. "I have great faith in the sons and grandsons of the heroes of forty years ago, who followed Lee and Jackson for four long years through blood and fire, even from Sumter's battered walls to the famous apple tree, who went to the battlefields of Virginia and poured out their blood like water in defense of our Southern homes."[14]

Colonel Wiley followed with an unrepentant message that while "good negroes" deserved the care of the courts and the affection of white southerners, other blacks did not. "Shiftless vagabonds" take the money of farms and violate contracts, just as Glennie Helms had done, Wiley said. "If they were to be protected in this sort of thing the farmers of this country would be ruined," he concluded.

After a two-hour break to cool the courtroom, Reese returned with the government's final argument. Lacing his closing with references to the Bible and a passage in Exodus denouncing those who traffic in slaves, he scored members of the gallery who sneered when blacks were referred to in court as "American citizens." Reese argued that Turner deserved no mercy. "He bought the negroes just like one of you would buy a horse or a cow," Reese told the jury. "Can this man come here and ask you for mercy after that?"

After 5 P.M., Judge Jones began an emotional two-hour charge to the jury. Offering a detailed history of the peonage statute and the laws of labor in the United States, he reviewed the evidence presented and then explicitly urged the jurors to put aside the appeals to Civil War loyalties and white racial allegiance offered by Turner's lawyers. Jones, visibly aroused, left little doubt as to the verdict the jury should reach. "If you believe from all the evidence that Turner bought this darky, took him to his place, forced him to stay there, when he wanted to go away, and worked him as a convict under guard to liquidate the debt paid for him, then he is guilty," Jones said.[15]

Representative Wiley and Colonel Bulger shifted nervously as the judge all but instructed the jury to convict their clients. In truth there was also little doubt what would happen. Within hours of beginning deliberations that night, word spread through the courthouse that the jury was deadlocked—with eight men voting for acquittal and four to convict.

Notified of the split the following morning, an exasperated Judge Jones called the jury back into the courtroom. His confidence that southern white men could be counted on to police themselves was badly shaken. "If you do not return a verdict of guilty you will perjure yourselves in the sight of God and dishonor yourselves in the eyes of men," Jones told the jurors. Representative Wiley rose to object, but the judge ordered him silent and told the jurors they would not be excused until a verdict was reached. "The court does feel impelled under an earnest and solemn sense of duty as to the verdict you ought to render in this case, to appeal to your manhood, your sense of justice, and your oaths, not to declare that a jury in the Capital of Alabama would not enforce the law of the United States because it happened that a negro is the victim of the violated law and the defendant is a white man."[16]

When the jury resumed deliberations, the vote shifted to seven men for conviction and five for acquittal. But among those five, there was no possibility of change. On July 13, the jury reported that they were impossibly deadlocked. Judge Jones, barely concealing his scorn, declared a mistrial and set the Turners free.

"God forbid that the time will ever come in this country when you are helpless and distressed and have been the victim of oppression when you will be denied that protection of the law to which you appeal and to which every law-abiding human being is entitled among all civilized people," Jones told the jury. Reese vowed to bring the Turners back to trial before another jury.[17]

That would not be needed. On the following Monday, Fletcher Turner surprised Montgomery when he returned to the federal building and took a seat with his attorney at the front of the gallery. When Judge Jones convened court to begin selection of jurors for the peonage trial of Robert Franklin, one of Turner's lawyers, N. M. Lackey, rose to speak. Turner was ready to plead guilty to a charge of peonage in order to avoid further prosecution on any other charges and in return for the dismissal of the counts against his son. "My client did not realize that he was violating the law. He did not know that he was doing anything that was not justified by law," Lackey explained. "If any cruelty was practiced it was done without the consent of my client. In this affair my client was mistaken."[18]

Judge Jones insisted that the facts proved Turner engaged in true slavery. "He purchased their liberty and services," the judge remonstrated, as Turner stood emotionless before the bench. But Judge Jones was no naive young Republican prosecutor. Even as he lectured the unrepentant farmer still driving slaves forty years after emancipation, Jones knew hardly any jury in America, most certainly not one in Alabama, could be relied on in 1903 to convict the man before him. A new trial would accomplish nothing. He accepted the plea of guilty, levied a fine of $1,000, and the case was closed.

# IX

# A RIVER OF ANGER

*The South Is "an armed camp."*

In the three months since Reese began his slavery investigation, the guilt of every defendant called to court had in one manner or another been established. He'd won the personal attention and support of the U.S. attorney general and of President Roosevelt himself. Indeed, a new position had just been created in his office to oversee an even more expansive attack on slavery. Reese believed history, and the power of the nation, were with him. Even rabidly anti-black, white supremacist politicians and newspapers such as the *Montgomery Advertiser* initially reacted with embarrassment to the peonage charges that so suddenly burst into the public eye.

In truth, the mistrial in the case of Fletcher Turner marked an ominous reversal. Resentment to the exposure of the new slavery was growing. Other voices, defiant and rancorous, began to rise.

On the Saturday before Turner's surprise guilty plea, Alabama secretary of state Heflin spoke to an annual reunion of Confederate veterans in the town of Luverne, issuing a ringing endorsement of how men such as Pace and Turner had nobly returned black workers to their proper position as slaves and attacking Reese and Judge Jones as willing to sacrifice the honor of southern whites in return for advancement under President Roosevelt. They were nest foulers and "nigger lovers," cried supporters of the accused. Heflin and his allies said any man who did not defy them deserved all the contempt of the white South.

Reese and Heflin traded charges through the newspapers—the U.S. attorney asserting that Heflin deceitfully mischaracterized the facts of the case; Heflin, annealing his coarse racism in the language of the U.S. Constitution, retorted that Judge Jones was usurping the American ideals of trials by jury.[1]

While the Turner trial was under way, a frenzied mob in Scottsboro, Alabama, gunned down the town sheriff in front of his family as he refused to turn over a black teenager who had allegedly "attempted criminal assault" on a nineteen-year-old white girl. Once the sheriff was dead, the black man was seized from his cell and hanged from a telegraph pole that night.

Midway through the trial, a lawyer in Dothan, Alabama, telegraphed Reese to report that a client, Enoch Patterson, was being held in peonage by the town's chief of police. Obviously, no local system of justice was available to defend Patterson. "I have no redress here for his wrongs," the lawyer wrote. "I know of no way to get justice for him but to submit the matter to you."[2] Similar charges flowed into his office, so numerous and substantial that Reese—already frenzied with the duties of the trial and other indictments—could barely manage to send acknowledgments of the information, much less open investigations.

In Georgia, allegations surfaced in the court of Judge Emory Speer, in the cotton-dense version of that state's Black Belt, that the family of state representative Edward McRee, one of the most prominent in the state, was operating a slave plantation even more expansive and brutal than anything alleged in Tallapoosa County.

Across the nation, the spring and summer of 1903 marked a venomous turn in relations between blacks and whites. A pall was descending on black America, like nothing experienced since the darkest hours of antebellum slavery. If anything, the poisoned atmosphere and accelerating disintegration of the structure of civil society more resembled to blacks a time two centuries earlier, when white slave traders and their corrupted indigenous allies descended without explanation upon the villages of West Africa to plunder the native population. For at least the next four decades, especially on the backcountry roads and rural rail lines of Louisiana, Mississippi, Alabama, Georgia, South Carolina, and Florida, no black person living outside the explicit protection of whites could again feel fully secure.

The plummeting position of black Americans was driven by the con-

vergence of transforming currents in American life. In the years of abolitionist fervor before and after the Civil War, northern whites who pushed
for full citizenship for black freedmen operated under naive assumptions.
Many believed that once schools and wages were extended to liberated
slaves, they could be quickly and fully assimilated into U.S. society. In the
span of half a generation, they imagined the nation's eleven million African
Americans learning to read and write and becoming dark-skinned versions
of the yeoman white farmers fanning across the western prairies.

Human slaves had been freed many times before—from the Israelites,
to the Romans, to Africans in the vast British Empire as recently as 1834.
But no society in human history had attempted to instantly transform a vast
and entrenched slave class into immediate full and equal citizenship. The
cost of educating freed slaves and their children came to seem unbearably
enormous, even to their purported friends. Their expectations of compensation radically altered the economics of southern agriculture. And even
among the most ardent abolitionists, few white Americans in any region
were truly prepared to accept black men and women, with their seemingly
inexplicable dialects, mannerisms, and supposedly narrow skills, as true
social equals.

Moreover, Charles Darwin's still new theory of evolution was threading
through American culture with unintended sinister repercussions. Before
the publication of Darwin's landmark *On the Origin of Species* in 1859, virtually all Americans viewed the presumed higher and lower racial order of
whites, blacks, and native Indian tribes as mandated by God. But the nearly
ubiquitous acceptance of Christianity by American blacks—at the active
encouragement of whites—also clearly established the essential humanity
of slaves. Christianity said slaves—despite their legal categorization as
chattel—and their owners were indisputably members of the same race.
Regardless of the violence used by whites against slaves, there was a loose
consensus, even in the South, that whites and blacks were linked in their
humanity and that God demanded some measure of moral consideration
and compassion for all. Northern opposition to slavery before the Civil
War was deeply rooted in this religious precept.

But swirling concepts of evolution upended those traditions. Dehu-
manizing interpretations of the racial order were unleashed—driven and
defined not just by skin color but by ever more refined concepts of blood. A

new conceit of multiple, distinct human species emerged. The Indian wars of the 1870s solidified a growing sense of genetically propelled white superiority and of raw violence as an appropriate method of protecting white political supremacy and racial purity. Thousands of Civil War soldiers who had been introduced to battle in a morally complex war of racial liberation were later immersed on the Great Plains in the simple absolutism of the pure, racially motivated violence that would haunt the twentieth century.

Popular American culture embraced the western conflicts as proof of white superiority—spawning hundreds of novels and short stories that extolled the extermination of Indian populations as the inexorable march of white progress and eminent domain. William "Buffalo Bill" Cody's Wild West Show became a pageant of white supremacist rhetoric, drawing tens of millions of American and European spectators in the 1880s and 1890s.

A whole new genre of fiction extolling the antebellum South and an idealized view of slavery became immensely popular. Joel Chandler Harris's books filled with stories of contented slaves and kindly masters—first serialized in the *Atlanta Constitution*—sold in enormous volumes in the North. The most sensational book in all regions of the country remained *The Leopard's Spots*, a southern romance by a former preacher named Thomas Dixon Jr.

Published in New York by Doubleday, Page & Co. the previous year, the novel was built around the quest of Confederate colonel Charles Gaston to attain love and glory as he swept away black political participation in Reconstruction-era North Carolina. Underscoring his repudiation of past depictions of cruel antebellum slavery, Dixon co-opted for his characters many of the names of the infamous Simon Legree and other key figures in Harriet Beecher Stowe's prewar abolitionist bible, *Uncle Tom's Cabin*. Yet in Dixon's rendering, the brutal southern slave masters were kindly; former slaves risen to power in Reconstruction were a gruesome plague upon whites and themselves. Late in the novel, Gaston gives his own blood for a transfusion to a girl raped by a black man. After her death, a relief from a life marked as despoiled, the father refuses to have his daughter placed in a grave dug by a black man. Confederate veterans at the funeral rally to dig a new one.

In the novel, a black man accused of the crime is tied to a pine tree, doused with oil, and burned to death. Dixon writes of Gaston pondering how "the insolence of a class of young negro men was becoming more and more intolerable."[3] Gaston "was fast being overwhelmed with the conviction that sooner or later we must squarely face the fact that two such races, counting millions in numbers, can not live together under a democracy. . . . Amalgamation simply meant Africanisation. The big nostrils, flat nose, massive jaw, protruding lip and kinky hair will register their animal marks over the proudest intellect and the rarest beauty of any other race. The rule that had no exception was that one drop of Negro blood makes a negro." The book's initial printing of fifteen thousand was immediately consumed. Soon more than a million copies had been purchased. Dixon instantly became one of the most widely read writers of the first decades of the century.

Another best-selling novelist of the romanticized South, Thomas Nelson Page, became one of the country's most influential voices on race relations. Asserting that blacks constituted the vast majority of rapists and criminals in the United States, and that the overwhelming preponderance of blacks remained "ignorant" and "immoral," Page warned that the continued coexistence of the races was likely impossible. "After 40 years in which money and care have been given unstintedly to uplift them . . . the Negro race has not advanced at all," Page declared. Blacks are "a vast sluggish mass of uncooled lava over a section of the country, burying some sections and affecting the whole. It is apparently harmless, but beneath its surface smolder fires which may at any time burst forth unexpectedly and spread desolation."[4]

Few white Americans expressed disagreement. Southern whites cheered news in April 1903 that the New York public school system ordered the removal from its reading lists of *Uncle Tom's Cabin*. Echoing Dixon, New York public school libraries superintendent Cland G. Leland said Stowe's depiction of antebellum slavery "does not belong to today but to an unhappy period of our country's history, the memory of which it is not well to revive in our children."[5]

White Americans across the country were adopting a dramatically revised version of the racial strife of the nineteenth century—a mythology in which the Civil War had sufficiently ameliorated the injuries of slavery to blacks and that during the ensuing decades southern whites heaped assistance and opportunity upon former slaves to no avail. The new version of events declared that African Americans—being fundamentally inferior and incorrigible—were in the new century a burden on the nation rather than victims of its past.[6]

A widely disseminated treatise on blacks published in 1901 concluded that cohabitation in the same society by whites and free blacks would forever be cursed by the immutably brutish aspects of African character. "The chief and overpowering element in his makeup is an imperious sexual impulse which, aroused at the slightest incentive, sweeps aside all restraints in the pursuit of physical gratification."[7]

The *Montgomery Advertiser* reported with obvious satisfaction on a declaration of thanks issued by the "colored people of Richmond" to a white education conference for all that it had done for African Americans. While inviting attendees of the meeting to attend First African Baptist Church while in the city, the declaration assured whites, "The negroes of Richmond have always been able to live in peace and harmony with the white race. The same kindly feeling which coursed in the veins of the 'mammy' and body servant of bygone days exists today."[8] White southerners clung to any fragment of such obeisance as demonstration that their racial conduct was a corrective measure aimed at bringing African Americans back to their natural posture toward whites—not an eruption of supremacist venality.

A young white chambermaid at the English Hotel in Indianapolis, Indiana, named Louise Hadley, became a brief cause célèbre in May 1903, hailed in the North and the South, after she refused to make up a bed that had been occupied by Booker T. Washington. After being fired from her job, Hadley issued a public statement: "For a white girl to clean up the rooms occupied by a negro . . . is a disgrace," she wrote. "I have always felt that the negro was not far above the brute." Committees formed in Georgia, Alabama, and Texas raised several thousand dollars in contributions to Hadley. "We admire this young woman's discrimination and think she took exactly the right action," beamed the *Dadeville Spot Cash.*[9]

When Boston leaders publicly discussed a proposal to transport large numbers of southern blacks to New England's declining farm regions, southerners sputtered with skepticism. "We could well spare a few thousand 'crap shooters' and banjo pickers from the South," one Alabama letter writer responded on the pages of the *Advertiser.* "The only negroes who will probably agree to go will be those with whom it would be a mercy not only for the whites, but the negro of the South, to part," said the *Chattanooga Times*. "Since the mulatto Crispus Attucks led the phlegmatic Bostonians in their revolt against the British troops, dark skins have been popular up there," sneered the *Montgomery Advertiser*. "Such a movement might be good for the South. It would probably rid our section of a good many negroes who are worse than useless here. . . . It would give those far-sighted philanthropists a chance to learn by actual contact and experience something of the race problem about which they prate so much." The *Advertiser* editorialized on the need for African Americans to be "fixed" through hard labor.[10]

In the barely veiled racist invective of the day, the *Columbus* (Georgia) *Enquirer-Sun* said it doubted the movement would amount to anything until watermelon season was over.[11]

The popular sentiments used to justify the violence appeared to correspond with the work of a generation of American physicians and scientists—in the North and the South—who busily translated or mistranslated the elementary evolutionary principles outlined by Darwin into crude explanations for why blacks should be returned to a "mild form of slavery," as one delegate to a Virginia constitutional convention phrased it. At a meeting of the state medical association in Georgia, one physician presented a paper that purported to document the close similarities between a long list of black features—skin, mouth, lips, chin, hair, nose, nostrils, ears, and navel—and those of the horse, cow, dog, and other barnyard animals. From that claimed evidence, Dr. E. C. Ferguson extrapolated that the "negro is monkey-like; has no sympathy for his fellow-man; has no regard for the truth, and when the truth would answer his purpose the best, he will lie. He is without gratitude or appreciation of anything done for him; is a natural born thief,—will steal anything, no matter how worthless. He has no morals. Turpitude is his ideal of all that pertains to life. His progeny are not provided for at home and are allowed to roam at large without restraint, and seek subsistence as best they can, growing up like any animal."[12]

The new science of anthropology embraced the notion that quantifiable characteristics of whites, blacks, and Indians—such as brain size—demonstrated the clear physical and intellectual superiority of whites. In May 1903, as Warren Reese's Alabama investigation got under way, the *Atlantic Monthly* magazine published a long tract titled "The Mulatto Factor," written by an erudite planter in Greenville, Mississippi, Alfred H. Stone, arguing that the presence of mixed-race blacks—with superior intelligence and leadership skills derived from traces of white blood—was the cause of current race turmoil.

New exhibits on primitive peoples made the American Museum of Natural History in New York City a scientific temple to the inevitability of white dominion over nonwhite races. The institution was emerging as a hotbed of the embryonic concepts of eugenics and "racial hygiene" that would eventually lead to unimaginable violence later in the twentieth century.

The St. Louis World's Fair in 1904 featured an exhibit of live pygmies, transported from the Belgian Congo—then reaching a gruesome apogee of colonial slavery under King Leopold strikingly similar to that emerging in the U.S. South. After the fair, one of the pygmies, Ota Benga, appeared briefly as an exhibit at the Museum of Natural History, before transferring to the monkey house at the Bronx Zoological Park—initially sharing a cage with an orangutan named Bohong. After several years as a freak curiosity in the United States, Benga killed himself in 1916.[13]

The same year that Benga appeared at Central Park West, the Carnegie Institution funded the establishment of the Station for Experimental Evolution at Cold Spring Harbor, New York. The center eventually became the Eugenics Records Office and the leading scientific advocate of notions of racial superiority and inferiority. With broad support from the federal government, prominent jurists, and scientists at major universities, researchers there pursued a decades-long, but scientifically flawed, project to collect data on the inherited characteristics of Americans. (For the next four decades, the work of the Eugenics Records Office and its leaders was the backbone of a highly successful campaign to promote sterilization for "feebleminded" and other ostensibly inferior genetic stock, strict laws against racial intermarriage, and stringent limits on the immigration of Jews and southern Europeans to the United States.)

Amid that swelling wave of public sentiment, shared by the simplest and most advanced white Americans, the moral implications of the Civil War faltered. More than thirty-five years had passed since the end of the conflict, long enough that the grief and anger associated with individual deaths and disasters had muted. Aging Union veterans of the Civil War were declining as a national voting bloc. In place of the war's fading emotional resonance, a cult of reunion and reconciliation among whites in all regions arose, embraced by leaders of all national parties who had grown weary of the "bloody shirt"—a euphemism for demagogic political tactics designed to stir regional emotions.

There was a palpable sense that northerners were no longer willing to risk renewed violence to enforce a thinly supported victor's justice on the South. All demands for southern acquiescence to guilt for the war were dissolving. A generation of post–Civil War southerners—like Pace, McRee, and their contemporaries—were approaching middle age. They were anxious to redeem their fathers who fought and died in southern regiments and the skill of the officers who led them from the tarnish of defeat, the scandal of treason, and the perceived amorality of slavery. Southerners—and growing numbers of northern whites—gravitated to a new interpretation of the rebellion, one that abandoned any depiction of the war as a defeated insurrection and instead permitted open reverence for southern "qualities" of battlefield ferocity and social chivalry, and for specific acts of Confederate heroism to be incorporated into collective American history.

Georgia's federal judge Emory Speer, overseeing the new slavery cases emerging in southern Georgia, summed up the new conventional history in his 1903 commencement speech to graduates of Atlanta's Emory University. Taking the life of Robert E. Lee as his topic, Judge Speer called for an explicit rehabilitation of the once disgraced Confederate military commander. America, he said, "can no longer afford to question the military and personal honor of Lee and his noble compatriots. America, with all her acknowledged power, cannot fail to appropriate that warlike renown, which gleamed on the bayonets and blazed in the serried volleys of the soldiers of the South."[14]

The South had nothing to be ashamed of anymore. The myth that the war had been fought over regional patriotism rather than slavery became rooted in American identity. Even slavery itself came to be remembered not as one of the basal crimes of American society, but as a nearly benign anachronism. White Americans arrived at a contradictory but firm view that slavery was a relic of the past that had rightfully expired, but that coerced servitude and behavior was nonetheless the appropriate role in national life for blacks. Whites in the North and the South could be on the same side in this perverse recasting of the war's narrative. That new consensus unleashed typhonic waves across black life.

The blithe testimony of an elderly black man to a Georgia legislative commission inquiring into financial improprieties in that state's convict leasing system illustrated the gratuitous cynicism that steeped the lives of African Americans. In June 1901, the man, named Ephraim Gaither, was being held in a work camp for men arrested and convicted of minor offenses at an isolated location about fifty miles north of Atlanta. Gaither had been arrested on a dubious charge of carrying a concealed weapon. After conviction, he was sold along with 105 other men to a timber-cutting operation controlled by one of Atlanta's most prominent businessmen, Joel Hurt. That month, a sixteen-year-old boy arrived in the camp to serve three months of hard labor for an unspecified misdemeanor he had allegedly committed.

"He was around the yard sorter playing and he started walking off and got to trotting a little bit, playing around there and got behind a pine tree," Gaither recounted calmly, in testimony to the committee of Georgia elected officials. "There was a young fellow, one of the bosses, up in a pine tree and he had his gun and shot at the little negro and shot this side of his face off," Gaither said as he pointed to the left side of his face.

> *The fellow runs off to the woods about thirty or forty yards and the guards follow him. Then Charley Goodson, he goes and gets the dog and puts on the trail of him and they start off, the dogs are barking the way the negro went off. Directly they came back and I heard one of the guards say that negro he done and goes across the mountain and we can't get him. That is when they come back with the dogs and everything was quiet. That was on Thursday, Thursday evening. They let that negro stay there lying in the woods from Thursday to Thursday and it gets to stinking so bad we couldn't stand it hardly; and we complained about the smell. That day we noticed a bitch, a hound bitch it was going across by the edge of the woods with something in its mouth and we looked and seed that it was the arm of that poor negro that they had killed down there in the woods. The dog had torn the arm off of him and was dragging it down through the edge of the woods with the fingers dragging on the ground. The Bosses took John Williams and two or three others, I don't*

*remember the names now and made him a pine box and went down there*
*and buried him.*

Members of the committee responded by grilling Gaither about why
he came to the state capitol that day to testify and whether a black man's
word could be trusted. "Did any white men see that?" asked one state representative, about the events described by Gaither. Another quizzed Gaither
as to whether any white man in Atlanta could vouch for him. Finally he was
asked: "You were a bad negro?"

Gaither responded: "No boss, I was no bad negro. They thought I
was." No queries were made as to the identities of the boy killed, the camp
boss who shot him, or why myriad state regulations governing the treatment of prisoners at the time or the handling of a convict's death were
never fulfilled.[15] The homicide Gaither described was never investigated.

The harvest of that river of animosity was palpable for thousands of African
Americans. A venomous contempt for black life was not just tolerated but
increasingly celebrated. On Tybee Island off the coast of Georgia, guards
drove a squad of black men arrested by the local sheriff into the surf to
bathe. Few could swim. Weighed down by balls and chains, four were swept
into the sea. The body of misdemeanant Charles Walker surfaced a day
later on the edge of nearby Screven Island.[16]

When a black man in Henderson, North Carolina, refused to give up
his reserved seat in a local theater to a white patron in April 1903, he was
forcibly ejected. When he resisted being removed, the black man was shot
dead by a policeman.[17] White southerners applauded broadly.

A white mob seized an African Methodist Episcopal minister in Lees-
burg, Georgia, named Rev. W. W. Williams that spring after he began to
emerge among local blacks in the farm community as an influential leader.
White men owned nearly all the area's land and were accustomed to the
same conjugal rights with black women on their farms as had existed during antebellum slavery. Rev. Williams began preaching that black women
should resist the sexual advances of the dominant white men of the community, wrote Rev. J. E. Sistrunk, in an account of the attack sent to the
Department of Justice. "The mob . . . went upon him without warning and

taken him out of the parson aide [parsonage] . . . and strip[p]ed him naked and one sat upon his h[e]ad and each by turns with a buggy whip, whipped him until his back was raw from head to foot and after whipping him they told him that they whipped him because he was controlling colored women."[18]

Southerners particularly reveled at gruesome scenes of racial violence that occurred outside their region, affirming the hypocrisy of those Yankee critics who still criticized racial conditions in the former Confederacy. For weeks, carnage continued between blacks and whites in Joplin, Missouri, and Wilmington, Delaware. In April, a thirty-year-old black man named Thomas Gilyard was lynched in Joplin, followed by the reported expulsion of every black in the city.[19] In May, newspapers closely followed a "race war" in Louisville, Kentucky.[20]

Accounts of mortal clashes between whites and blacks, and the raging mobs that often followed such incidents, littered the pages of newspapers in the first years of the century. "Race War in Mississippi," the *Advertiser* screamed in May 1903, after blacks and whites near the town of Laurel battled over several days, leaving at least one white farmer and "several negroes" dead. "The enraged white men of the community are still in the saddle searching for the negro who instigated the trouble," the paper reported with dramatic thrill.[21]

The same month, whites in Indianapolis, Indiana, began meeting to formulate a plan for removing African Americans from the city. Independence Day 1903 stirred extraordinary black and white hostility. In the tiny South Carolina town of Norway, a white farmer's son severely beat four black workers. In retaliation, the father, a one-armed Confederate veteran, was gunned down at his dinner table with a shotgun blast through a window. Local whites seized a black man in retaliation and lynched him. In response, more than two hundred armed blacks surrounded the town on July 4, threatening to burn it to the ground. The state's governor dispatched the South Carolina militia to counterattack.[22]

In Evansville, Indiana, crowds of blacks and whites battled on July 5 over the fate of a black man accused of killing a white police officer. Whites successfully broke into the city jail, but were driven back by armed blacks. Police charged in to disperse the crowds and spirit away the accused man.

On the same day, a mob of six hundred whites went in search of a black woman in Peoria, Illinois, who was accused of having beaten a white boy. After discovering that the woman already was in jail, the crowd attacked her home, dismantling it to the foundation and throwing all her furniture and belongings into the Illinois River. In Thomasville, Georgia, a street argument between a black man and his wife accelerated into a running gunfight between a white posse and crowds of African Americans.[23]

*The New York Times* opined in mid-July 1903 that "respectable negroes" should ban the city's bad ones. "There are in New York thousands of utterly worthless negro desperadoes," the *Times* wrote, "gamblers when they have money and thieves when they have none, moral lepers and more dangerous than wild animals." The newspaper followed up later in the month with hysterical coverage of racial disturbances in the city. "Negroes Attack Police" blared a headline over an account of a fight that broke out on West 62nd Street after an Irish policeman shoved a "disrespectful" black man on a sidewalk.[24]

Infuriated by the setbacks suffered by blacks in all regions of the country, W. E. B. DuBois, the rising young sociologist—the first African American Ph.D. graduated by Harvard—wrote that the South "is simply an armed camp for intimidating black folk." The emancipation act that had ended the Civil War had transmogrified into "a race feud," he said. "Not a single Southern legislature stood ready to admit a Negro under any conditions, to the polls; not a single Southern legislature believed free Negro labor was possible without a system of restrictions that took all its freedoms away; there was scarcely a white man in the South who did not honestly regard Emancipation as a crime, and its practical nullification as a duty."[25]

# X

# THE DISAPPROBATION OF GOD

*"It is a very rare thing that a negro escapes."*

Warren Reese refused to believe the white South was irredeemably lost. He insisted, despite the mushrooming resistance to his work, that justice still could be served in Alabama.

Judge Jones remained embarrassed and distressed at the mistrial in the case of Fletcher Turner. He had been convinced that twelve white men in Montgomery could put aside racial animosity long enough to see the obvious guilt of a man such as Turner—even if the jurors did so only to preserve the honor of their home state. At the conclusion of the brief trial of Robert Franklin during the week after Turner's guilty plea, Jones once again signaled to the jury the defendant's guilt as he assailed Alabama's system of lower courts. "The counsel of defendant spoke of the negro as a 'so-called citizen,' " Jones told the court incredulously. "A man is a citizen whether he can vote or not, and nobody loves a Government that would not protect him." He decried Alabama's provincial sheriffs and judges who "have reestablished slavery for debt in this state."[1]

Much to the relief of Jones and Reese, the jury agreed. Franklin was convicted of a single count of peonage. Finally, a southern jury had been willing to honestly adjudge the actions of a white man, finding obvious involuntary servitude to be what it truly was: slavery.

Reese was privately adamant that his office would soon bring another volley of slavery charges from elsewhere in the state. But Jones was ready to declare victory. The enormous public pressure in Montgomery to end the probe was wearing on him. Jones declared publicly that the "peonage ring was nearly all broken up." Alabama had been taught its lesson, Judge Jones hoped, and further consternation was unnecessary. Franklin, the constable who had so brazenly seized John Davis, was ordered to pay $1,000. Word spread quickly among the attorneys representing other defendants that the court would deal just as leniently with those awaiting trial.

Within a few days, John Pace's son-in-law, Anderson Hardy, and guard James H. Todd pleaded guilty to five counts of peonage. Judge Jones fined each man $1,000. They were taken back to the Dadeville city jail, to remain there until the penalty was paid.[2] But both men ignored the fines and were soon set free. Before the summer term of court was over, another half dozen men pleaded guilty and received from Jones symbolic fines. When court reconvened in the fall of 1903, the rest of the defendants did the same. Every major figure admitted guilt. That was enough for Jones.

Anxious to show that Tallapoosa County was no longer a center of antebellum criminality and repair its reputation, a local grand jury was impaneled in Dadeville to examine questions of slavery and peonage in early August. Two weeks later, in a final report, the panel of local men concluded that John Pace had been responsible for virtually all of the peonage in the area. It remonstrated Pace for having "kept East Wilson, a negro woman who is serving a twelve months sentence for larceny at his farm, out of the way, so that the Sheriff could not serve on her a subpoena to appear before this Grand Jury. . . .

"We suspect that he has kept other witnesses out of the way so that they could not be served," the report continued. "It is our opinion, that John W. Pace and his convict farm are more responsible, by far, than all others in our county for the abuse of ignorant and helpless people, which is the crime known as peonage in the Federal Court. This evil is practiced by very few in our County, to the detriment of all, should be discontinued in our County forever."[3]

Meanwhile, local residents were rallying around the Cosby family. George and Burancas had begun their sentences in the Atlanta federal prison. A growing number of whites complained that it was unfair for the two men to be imprisoned when every other participant in the slaving scheme received symbolic punishment. More than three thousand names were affixed to a petition seeking a pardon from President Roosevelt. Soon, even Judge Jones supported the Cosby plea for clemency,[4] directly urging the president to free the two men. On September 16, 1903, he did so. Almost as if the testimony of kidnappings, murders, whippings, and enslavement had never been heard, the Cosbys returned to their Red Ridge Road farm.

John Pace, the leader of the slavery ring, quietly restarted his trade in black labor. As 1903 closed, the Alabama Board of Inspectors of Convicts—the state entity charged with overseeing the state's penal systems—was chagrined to discover that the county commissioners of Tallapoosa County had renewed Pace's contract to lease all county convicts.[5]

As much as Judge Jones—and the more brazen apologists for slavery across the South—had hoped the Alabama cases represented the end of the affair, difficult realities continued to intrude. The fall of 1903 brought new indictments in Louisiana for holding slaves, but residents were so outraged that the marshal investigating the cases had to flee the state for his safety. Newspapers across the North published accounts of additional involuntary servitude in Louisiana, Texas, Tennessee, and Mississippi.[6]

The U.S. attorney in Mobile, Alabama, who had initiated his own inquiries into slavery in the southern part of the state, reported "credible reports" of peonage across his territory and in multiple counties. But investigating the allegations and questioning terrified witnesses was proving difficult. "Many of them are unwilling to communicate anything . . . unless assured that it would be confidential," wrote M. D. Wickersham to his superiors at the Department of Justice. "Persons manifested such terror when requested to disclose what they knew that it is doubtful if they can be persuaded to give any valuable testimony either in the grand jury room or before the court."[7]

As in so many other places, the federal marshals in the field discovered that the official systems of leasing black convicts to private companies and individuals had become indistinguishable from the casual slavery flourishing on private farms. If the former was legal, few southerners—white or black—understood why the latter would not be. "So many illiterate persons have confounded the harsh, and at many times cruel, execution of the convict laws of the state with the practice of peonage that it has been very difficult to make them understand the line that distinguishes the one from the other," Wickersham wrote.

In late November, a grand jury in Macon began hearing testimony that Georgia state representative Edward McRee, his brothers Frank and William, two former sheriffs, and other members of some of the most powerful families in south Georgia were operating a vast slave-driven enterprise at their 22,000-acre Kinderlou plantation near the Florida state line.

The McRee brothers' farm was a plantation and industrial center that dwarfed that of John Pace—operating on a scale no antebellum slave owner could have comprehended. Edward McRee became a powerful elected official serving in the state legislature. By 1900, the four siblings who inherited the enterprise from their empire-building father, a noted Confederate officer named George McRee, each lived in a lavish mansion within a square mile of the center of the plantation. Between them a bustling village—called Kinderlou in honor of the Aunt Lou who raised the four brothers from childhood after the death of their mother—thrived with farm laborers, tradesmen, and several small stores. Consuming the bulk of an entire county, the farm—basking in the subtropical warmth of the Gulf Coast—included thousands of acres of lushly fertile sandy loam under till at any given time. On a private spur of the Atlantic Coast Line Railroad thrust into the center of the plantation, dozens of boxcars waited at all times for the hundreds of thousands of bushels of tomatoes, watermelons, cantaloupes, corn, tobacco, and cotton. The McRees owned their own cotton gins, compresses to make bales, and warehouses to store enormous quantities of lint. A five-horsepower steam engine ground the plantation's sugarcane to make syrup. Five eighty-foot-long barns were built to cure tobacco. Cuban workers were imported to work the plantation's cigar factory.

Thousands more acres of dense pine and hardwood fed a ceaselessly turning sawmill, planing mill, and dry kiln. A factory on the plantation produced thousands of pallets, wooden crates, and baskets for shipping agricultural produce. Deep in the forests, McRee turpentine camps collected rosin for their naval stores distillery. Three to four trains stopped daily, beginning with one at 3:30 A.M. to pick up dozens of three-foot-high barrels of milk produced in the Kinderlou dairy.[8]

The backbone of the plantation was small armies of farmhands and hundreds of mules, who were awakened by the first bell at 4 A.M. each day and remained in the fields or factories until dark. From "can't see to can't see," as the laborers called it.

Initially, the McRees hired only free black labor, but beginning in the 1890s, they routinely leased a hundred or more convicts from the state of Georgia to perform the grueling work of clearing lands, removing stumps, ditching fields, and constructing roads. Other prisoners hoed, plowed, and weeded the crops. Over fifteen years, thousands of men and women were forced to the plantation and held in stockades under the watch of armed guards. After the turn of the century, the brothers began to arrange for more forced laborers through the sheriffs of nearby counties—fueling what eventually grew into a sprawling traffic in humans across the southwestern section of Georgia.

"So I was carried back to the Captain's," said a black laborer in 1904, telling of his imprisonment on what was almost certainly the McRee plantation. "That night he made me strip off my clothing down to my waist, had me tied to a tree in his backyard, ordered his foreman to gave me thirty lashes with a buggy whip across my bare back, and stood by until it was done."

The worker vividly described to a passing journalist how the farm descended from a place of free employment in the late nineteenth century to one of abject slavery by the first years of the twentieth century. The unidentified man was born in the last years before the Civil War, and then hired out at age ten to the father of the McRee brothers, a man he knew simply as "Captain." While a teenager, the black man attempted to leave Kinderlou and work at another plantation. Before sundown on the day of his departure, one of the McRees and "some kind of law officer" tracked him down. The new employer apologized to McRee for hiring the young worker, saying he would never have done so if he had known "this nigger was bound out to you."

Soon afterward, one of the Captain's sons, likely Edward McRee, took over the farm and convinced the free laborers to put their mark on what was ostensibly a contract to work on the plantation for up to ten years, in exchange for pay, a cabin, and some supplies. Then McRee began building a stockade, with a long hallway down the center and rows of crude stalls—each with two bunk beds and mattresses—on each side. "One bright day in April . . . about forty able-bodied negroes, bound in iron chains, and some of them handcuffed were brought," the laborer recounted. Word came that any African American, whether free or convict, who attempted to leave the farm would be tracked down with hounds and forced back. The contracts they had signed contained the same language that John Pace forced men to accept, allowing the McRees to hold the workers against their will and beat them if they were disobedient. "We had sold ourselves into slavery—and what could we do about it?" the black man asked. "The white folks had all the courts, all the guns, all the hounds, all the railroads, all the telegraph wires, all the newspapers, all the money, and nearly all the land."

When his labor contract finally expired after a decade, the laborer was told he was free to leave Kinderlou, so long as he could pay his accumulated debt at the plantation commissary of $165. Unable to do so, the man was compelled to sign a new contract promising to work on the farm until the debt was paid, but now as a convict. He and several others were moved from their crude cabin into the filthy stockades. The men slept each night in the same clothes they wore in the fields, on rotting mattresses infested with pests. Many were chained to their beds. Food was crude and minimal. Punishment for the disobedient was to be strapped onto a log lying on their backs, while a guard spanked their bare feet with a plank of wood. When the slave was freed, if he could not return to work on his blistered feet, he was strapped to the log again, this time facedown, and lashed with a leather whip. Women prisoners were held across a barrel and whipped on their bare bottoms.[9]

As the Alabama peonage prosecutions were getting under way in Montgomery, newspapers in Georgia published accusations of extreme cruelty at Kinderlou. Embarrassed by the publicity, state prison officials withdrew their convicts still held on the McRee farm. The assistant U.S. attorney in Macon asked the Department of Justice to send him the detective who had cracked the case against John Pace. Agent Henry Dickey arrived by train and began inquiring how Kinderlou plantation came to hold dozens of African Americans against their will. He soon discovered that the McRees had arrangements with sheriffs and other officers in at least six Georgia counties to seize blacks and sell them into labor—all outside the regular processes of the criminal courts. When the McRees learned a federal investigation was under way, they hastily freed all of the remaining workers being held involuntarily on Kinderlou. At least forty fled immediately.[10]

James Robinson, the fourteen-year-old boy whose sister, Carrie Kinsey, had written President Roosevelt begging for his intercession after James was captured and sold, was likely one of those allowed to flee in the summer of 1903. Kinderlou was the farm where Robinson was being held "in chanes" when Kinsey wrote the White House, though officials at the Department of Justice never connected that her plea related to a farm then under investigation by their agents.[11]

In November 1903, a grand jury handed up a sweeping indictment against Edward McRee and his two brothers. The men were charged with thirteen specific counts of holding African American men and women. Several of those enslaved had never been charged or tried in any fashion. Several public officials were indicted for conspiring to buy and sell blacks arrested on trivial or fabricated charges in nearby Ware County and then turning them over to the McRees.

A day later, Edward McRee and his brothers appeared in a Savannah courtroom. McRee assured Judge Speer that while his family had held many African Americans in the four decades since slavery's abolition, they never intended to enslave anyone or break the law. "Though we are probably technically guilty we did not know it," McRee told the court. "This custom has been [in] existence ever since the war. . . . We never knew that we were doing anything wrong."

He insisted that no black workers were ever beaten or brutalized—in part because no worker had ever refused to perform their assigned duties. Hounds were never used to track runaways because no one had ever wished to leave, he claimed.[12]

Whatever had happened at Kinderlou, Judge Speer was of like mind with his counterpart in Montgomery. He was certain that symbolic punishments like the ones he handed down to smaller-scale farmers earlier that summer—designed to demonstrate the illegality of slavery but not inflame the anger of local whites—were the best remedy. The McRees were allowed to plead guilty and accept a token fine of $1,000.

Sheriff Thomas J. McClellan and another man who helped in the capture and sale of African Americans to Kinderlou fought the charges against them, arguing as the Turners had in Alabama that no law specifically made slavery a federal crime. A member of the U.S. Congress submitted a legal brief in support of their arguments. Prominent state officials sat at the defendants' table during a hearing on the challenge to their charges. Across Georgia, operators of lumber camps—where thousands of other men were being held under similarly dubious circumstances—watched the proceedings closely. After reviewing the arguments, Judge Speer cited the words of U.S. Supreme Court justice Samuel Miller in the *Slaughter-House Cases*, a landmark decision in 1873 establishing the distinction between federal and state civil rights. "Undoubtedly, while negro slavery alone was in the mind of the Congress which passed the 13th Article, it forbids any other kind of slavery, now or hereafter."[13]

Speer overruled the defendants' challenges to the case. But once again, in return for a guilty plea, the judge agreed to impose a symbolic fine of $500. In the end, the only person jailed in connection with nearly a half century of post–Civil War slavery on the McRee plantation was a black man named George P. Hart. For his role in selling a teenage girl to Frank McRee for $25, Hart spent thirty days in jail.[14]


Back in Alabama, Warren Reese urged the Roosevelt administration to mount an even more vigorous attack on slaveholders. His office reported to Attorney General Knox in November that Julius Sternfeld, the special assistant U.S. attorney assigned to the slavery investigations, was pursuing more than forty cases in Coffee, Geneva, Covington, Barbour, Dale, Pike, Houston, and Crenshaw counties—all in the heavily black plantation areas of southern Alabama. "The conditions in some of these counties are deplorable, negroes are taken out at night time, stripped and whipped in a most fiendish manner until the blood comes from them," Sternfeld wrote to Washington. "Negro farm hands and mill workers have been unmercifully whipped, two negro churches destroyed by fire, the house of one negro being shot into and a negro woman's house was riddled with shot, and while fleeing with her baby in her arms she and the baby were shot."

He vowed to fulfill "the desire of President Roosevelt and the Honorable Attorney General to eradicate peonage and involuntary servitude . . . and the real emancipation of hundreds of poor, helpless creatures."[15]

Complaints of slavery streamed continually into the Department of Justice offices in Washington, into the White House, and into federal law enforcement offices across Alabama and the South. Most were allegations made by the rare quietly outraged attorney or local Republican-appointed postmaster who, as representatives of the party of Lincoln, still felt some lingering political obligation to African Americans or still harbored hopes that blacks could again become critical voters for the GOP. The rare first-hand accounts of blacks held in slavery, many of them plaintive pleas furtively scratched out in nearly indecipherable hands, were themselves testaments to the utter isolation and economic desperation of millions of rural blacks.

In November 1903, Rev. L. R. Farmer, pastor of a black Baptist church in Morganton, North Carolina, a verdant small town in the rolling foothills of the Appalachian Mountains, was on the verge of despair. Farmer sent a dolorous letter to the Department of Justice. His daughter had been stolen by white men and was being held in slavery on a farm in Georgia.

"i have a little girl that has been kidnapped from me . . . and i cant get her out," Farmer wrote. "i want ask you is it law for people to whip (col) people and keep them and not allow them to leave without a pass."[16]

Farmer had exhausted every remedy available to a black man trapped in the isolation of the turn-of-the-century American South. He had contacted local authorities about his daughter's abduction, even going so far as to attempt to serve on her captors a writ of habeas corpus. All his efforts were ignored.

"The people in Ga wont do any thing with him and if the negroes tell any thing they will beat them to death and they are afraid to testifie against" the man holding his daughter and many others, Farmer wrote. If any African Americans did talk of what was happening, whites would "cary them write back and beat them to death," he wrote. "some of them has beened killed trying to get away from their and i got a little girl there," Farmer implored. A postscript on the back of his letter was a telling indication of the desperation and shattered confidence he shared with millions of blacks. Farmer pleaded for a swift answer from the government. He enclosed a stamp for the return answer.

On November 20, after the letter's arrival at the new headquarters of the Department of Justice, an aide to the attorney general assigned a file number to Farmer's letter, 3098-1902. The following day, a terse, typewritten response was mailed on behalf of the attorney general. It concisely acknowledged receipt of the letter and then issued a directive to Rev. Farmer:

*If you wish this Department to take any action to have your daughter released, and the guilty parties prosecuted, you should furnish me with the names of the parties holding your daughter in bondage, the particular place, and the names of witnesses by whom the facts can be proved.*

*Respectfully,*
*Attorney General*

No reply from Farmer to the attorney general was filed. No further action was recorded by the Department of Justice.[17]

The tone of communications between officials in Washington and federal prosecutors around the South was beginning to drift. Investigators and U.S. attorneys such as Reese believed that as they uncovered more and more instances of ongoing slavery and reported these horrors back to Washington, top federal officials would grow proportionally more alarmed— allocating more urgency and resources to defeat them. In fact, President Roosevelt and his administration were growing weary of what increasingly appeared to be a moral crusade without a clearly attainable resolution—a quagmire of unintended consequences. At first imperceptibly, then more clearly, as the allegations of slavery grew more voluminous, caution and inertia overtook the White House in equal proportions.

The violence of the white South grew yet more indignant. In December 1903, as federal agents prowled adjoining areas of the Alabama countryside, a backwater town in Wilcox County, called Pine Apple, was the scene of a singularly remarkable episode of racial carnage.

Deep in Alabama's Black Belt region, Pine Apple embodied the new paradigm of the rural, post-Reconstruction cotton economy.

Situated on a critical railroad connecting to Selma and the key Gulf Coast port of Pensacola, Florida, Pine Apple boasted a handsome collection of genteel homes and an impressive array of enterprises centered on the train station and its wide-planked loading docks. An imposing bank building was the center of commerce for the area's landed white gentry, whose children attended a distinguished private school called Moore Academy. Its founder and first principal in the 1880s, John Trotwood Moore, went on to modest literary renown in the South. Scattered around the bank stood a red livery stable, a few dry goods stores with wide windows facing the muddy streets, hitching rails tied with mules, and a water trough served by a pump. Outside the stores, an assortment of horse- and mule-drawn gigs, wagons, and canvas-topped buggies stood at the wait. Near the station, warehouses, a cotton gin, and a compress were surrounded by bales upon bales of the just completed harvest. Smoke belched from the gin as the teeth of its machinery threshed through the last cotton of the season, separating fiber and seed. In the compress, thousands of wagons of white lint were pressed into bales for shipment. Between the big houses and the town's center, wood-frame cottages were wedged onto newly delineated lots. Along the pitted roads fanning out into the denuded countryside, small clusters of log cabins, rough hewn from nearby forest and chinked with sticky red clay, housed black families bound to the land owned by whites.

Dozens of plantations radiated across the flat landscape from the Louisville & Nashville Railway line cutting due south on a perpendicular through Pine Apple and across the Black Belt. More than 35,000 people—the great majority of them black farm laborers at work on land owned by whites—lived here. Unprecedented numbers of white families made wealthy by the turn-of-the-century cotton boom had emerged as a new class of manor-born aristocrats—consolidating land, intermarrying, and vying for prestige in the resurgent southern planter elite. Their towns were strung along the railroad lines through plantation country like antique pearls of white-columned antebellum nostalgia. The harvest season had been a euphoric one, the most bountiful in five years, exceeding 11 million bales of cotton in the South.[18] Across Pine Apple wisps of white fiber—the detritus of the massive harvest—clung to tree branches, windowsills, and clumps of grass.

No family in Pine Apple was more prominent among the nouveaux riches than the Meltons. As the end of 1903 approached, the family anxiously prepared for a crowning wedding—the union of the most glamorous young couple in the adjoining counties and of two great new families. Lovely Leila Melton, the twenty-two-year-old daughter of William and Clara Melton, was set to marry Claud Swink, a year her senior and a promising young planter in Dallas County. The Melton clan had long been governed by three brothers—William, Evander, and John—whose expansive families controlled thousands of acres of property near Pine Apple. Swink was the only child of a similarly successful cotton barony, large and prosperous enough that the settlement at the crossroads nearest the family plantation had come to be known as Swinkville.

The union of the two young people was momentous as well as a distraction for family members still grieving the death of the family patriarch, Leila's father, William Melton. More than four years after he succumbed on July 4, 1900, the legacy of the fifty-four-year-old plantation master still loomed over Pine Apple, his brothers, Clara, and his eleven grown children. Even in death, he would be present for Leila's wedding, gazing out from an alabaster monument on a pedestal above his grave on the hilltop across the road from the church.

Melton intended to be remembered in precise detail. His statuary captured in crisp relief the distinct planter's regalia: a neat fedora on his brow and a long overcoat reaching past his knees, a trim bow tie above the vest, a heavy watch chain across a protruding midriff, an intricately decorated walking stick in his right hand, a bulging Masonic ring on his left—totemic emblems of the wealth and power he had extended over the family's cotton empire.

Leila's wedding also was similarly designed as an expression of the family's extraordinary position in southern life. The ceremony could not have been more removed from the spare affair in which the ex-slaves of the Cottingham plantation set Henry and Mary on their way a generation earlier. As the December 29 date approached, the sanctuary of Pine Apple's Friendship Baptist Church was decorated in an opulent display of wealth. Arches of smilax and pink and white chrysanthemums were erected before the altar. Above the center arch, a stuffed dove held loops of white tulle. Along the aisle, pillars held a candle for each year of the bride's age.

Leila's mother busily completed the stitching and embroidery on a stunning gown of white peau de cygne silk and duchess lace ordered from France. The bride's second-eldest brother, Henry, was to give her away in an elaborate ceremony of eighteen attendants, including male and female cousins, two nieces as flower girls, nephews as ring bearers, and Leila's brother nearest in age, Tom, as the best man. Unbeknownst to her daughter—or the groom-to-be—Clara Melton planned to give the couple an extraordinary gift: $1,250 in gold with which to begin their life together.[19]

The lavish plans belied the cold brutality on which the wealth of the Melton clan rested. However burnished was the Meltons' new patina of sophistication, the family was infamous in the area for brutal subjection of black workers and intimidation of neighbors, whether white or black. The three Melton brothers for years had relied on the local constable to help violently coerce blacks to work on their farms. Another white farmer, J. R. Adams, incensed at the Meltons' contumacious terrorization of local African Americans, including his own workers, wrote the attorney general to urge that the family be investigated for involuntary servitude.[20]

"In all probability there is no other section of state in which the crime of peonage is so common as here," Adams wrote. "The Meltons and their connections are the worst offenders. They have held negroes in peonage for years. It is a very rare thing that a negro escapes from there. . . . It is next to impossible for a negro who has 'contracted' with one of this gang to ever get away."

Adams said two years earlier one of Melton's men killed a black worker who attempted to escape from the farm. "A poor little negro girl who is kept at [the constable's] house occasionally runs away and begs other negroes to let her stay with them to keep [him] from beating her," Adams continued. "The negroes are so intimidated that they refuse to shelter her. . . . It is very hard to get evidence out of the negroes, for this gang keeps it impressed upon them that they will be killed if they give evidence."[21] The local U.S. magistrate near Pine Apple agreed, writing the U.S. attorney that among the fearful black population near the town, there was virtually no possibility of convincing witnesses to testify.[22]

Late in the afternoon on Christmas Eve, just four days before the wedding ceremony, Evander Melton, the bride's seventeen-year-old cousin and a likely groomsman in the wedding, appeared in an alleyway near the Pine Apple train station. Evander, the second son of John and namesake of his imposing uncle, was a fat and pugnacious boy known in town simply as "Pig." The group of young black men throwing craps in the alleyway must have known nothing good could come when Pig Melton, drunk and belligerent, pushed his way into the game.

They had few options. Meltons did as they wished among black people.

Besides, the young blacks were caught up in the jovial ebullience of the Christmas season—which for southern African Americans represented far more than a religious holiday. Christmas marked the end of the long and difficult cotton harvest—a straining process that in some years extended from September all the way to yuletide—and the only payday of the year for most southern blacks. After the final cotton was in, tenants and share-croppers—all those blacks who had some illusion of independence—came to the white planter on whose land they lived and asked for "settlement." Apparently, landowners tallied the cost of seed, supplies, rent, and every other purchase taken on interest from their plantation stores since the pre-vious Christmas, subtracted the total from the value of each family's share of the cotton they grew, and then paid out the difference in cash.

The reality was endemic fraud. Landowners, acutely aware that any worker fully clear of his debts might then attempt to relocate to a friendlier or more generous white property holder, routinely exaggerated costs and interest so that virtually no sharecroppers could ever fully extinguish their obligations. Instead, African Americans typically left the transaction with a small cash "bonus" or loan to use for a few weeks of merriment before work for the new cotton season would begin again.

The young black men in Pine Apple were quickly burning through their Christmas windfall—consuming liquor and trading what little cash they retained with the dice bouncing across the chilly soil.

Soon, the dice turned against the Melton teenager. He grew angry and loud. His losses mounting, a quarrel ensued. Unexpectedly, a pistol shot crackled in the crowd, from an unknown gun. More shots may have been fired in response. Whatever the case, Melton fell to the ground, bleeding profusely. In the pandemonium that followed, the black gamblers fled the scene—rushing to reach the sanctuary of cabins deep in the forests or scrambling madly to escape the county before nightfall. Arthur Stuart—a thirty-one-year-old black farmworker whose wife, two-year-old son, and infant daughter waited for him on rented land at the edge of town—wasn't fast enough.

No one knew who fired the shot that hit young Melton—who was taken to his family's house for a doctor to attend the wound. But Stuart was black and nearby. He was instantly identified as an accomplice. That he was still in the town at all when the sheriff came was the strongest evidence

of his innocence. Any black man aware that he was within miles of a shooting of a Melton would have fled for his life.


There was little doubt what would happen next. Word spread on Christmas
Eve that Pig Melton was recuperating at home and would survive his injury.
Yet the Meltons vowed a lesson was still to be taught. Late on Christmas
night, after the day's church services in praise of the birth of Jesus, family
dinners, and singing of carols had been finished, a small group of white men
led by fifty-one-year-old Evander M. Melton assembled at the center of
Pine Apple. At 4 A.M., the mob easily broke into the jail—the constable was
assisting them—and beat Stuart senseless in his cell. In short order, the men
doused his body with kerosene and set it afire.

Hoots and cheers arose from the unpaved street outside as the lynchers
rushed out the doors of the jail. But soon more than Stuart was burning.
Flames quickly filled the first floor of the building. Orange and red swells
pushed through the windows and flashed up the sides of the jail. Then
briefly the scene was silent except for the loud roar of fire and the groans of
the building as its skeleton collapsed into an embering heap.

The murder of Arthur Stuart and even the destruction of the jail would
have been an almost routine affair except for what followed. A sudden gust
of wind whipped through the town. A shower of burning embers—thousands of missiles of fire—poured into the sky and then scattered across Pine
Apple. The wispy blanket of cotton dusting the town ignited unpredictably.
A burst of flames appeared on the porch roof of the farm feed store adjacent
to the jail. The roof of cedar shake shingles was a mass of fire within minutes. Whipped by the gusting winds, the flames leapt next to a wagon repair
shop, the inferno now rippling across the sky like a zephyr turned red and
gold. It blew onto the town bank, the post office, and then beyond to
houses and eight stores clustered at the center of town. Most devastating,
the flames reached the great mounds of cotton bales stored in and around
the warehouses of the gin and compress—turning the cubes of burlap-
wrapped white cotton into roaring blocks of fire. Within minutes of Stuart's
last cries in his cell, the entire commercial district of Pine Apple was a mass
of raging heat and blaze.[23] Where just hours before the sounds of "Joy to

the World" sung from the square-note hymnals of the Baptist church had wafted down the muddy streets, now only the crackling of coals and flames and the glow of an ashen town penetrated the night.

Blacks in Pine Apple—and across the country—couldn't help but savor the apocalyptic consequences of the white mob's rampage. After three hundred years of Christian teaching that it was some curse or providential intent that placed Africans in slavery and the purgatory that followed it, the fire could only be seen as the Almighty's sign that it was the white man earning his vengeance now. The flames were "reinforced by God's disapprobation," one black preacher said. Booker T. Washington wrote to a northern ally: "The white people are now in quite a state of indignation. . . . One wonders if the same indignation would have been shown if the property of the white people had not been burned."[24]

Whatever anger surged from other whites whose homes and businesses had been destroyed, the Meltons still had a wedding to complete. Four days after the conflagration, the Baptist church, far enough from town to be spared from the fire, was filled for Leila's nuptials.

The Meltons were never prosecuted, either for the murder of Arthur Stuart or for the enslavement of so many black workers who created their wealth. No peonage cases were ever brought in the area. Adams, the white informant, was so fearful for his life that he burned all letters from the U.S. attorney investigating the incident. The perpetrators of the lynching escaped punishment. Local African Americans did take bitter solace in a final turn that seemed to affirm God's contempt for what the white family had done: three weeks after the wedding, on January 26, young Pig Melton, fevered from an infection of his wound, died. He was interred a few steps from his Uncle William's precipice—near, but just outside, his imposing elder's stony line of sight.

Every day that passed after the immolation of Arthur Stuart without response by the federal government was further ratification that the African Americans of the South had been returned to the white men who sought to control them. Almost exactly a year later, as if a demonstration that no one should interpret the catastrophe as evidence of any change in the state of black-white relations in the town, two more black men from Pine Apple, brothers Edward and William Plowly, were accused of murdering a white man and then hanged by a mob.

Indeed, where federal investigators initially stirred near panic among slaveholding farmers when they first arrived in Alabama, Georgia, and Florida, the impotence of the investigations was becoming richly obvious. Even when men were brought to trial for the most egregious offenses, they hardly risked conviction. Even if found guilty, they were in no real jeopardy of meaningful penalties. Just as the federal Freedmen's Bureau agents sent into remote southern towns had learned immediately after the Civil War, the new representatives of northern justice brought more risk upon themselves than to any person still holding slaves.

Indeed it was open season on Secret Service investigators. A government auditor sent to check the books of Reese's office in February 1904 found that two deputy marshals employed in the investigation had been hiding out at their homes in rural Alabama when they were supposed to have been pursuing slavery cases in the most hostile areas of the state, Lowndes and Dallas counties—the Swink family home territory. "The reason for this was that the persons living in said counties had sent word to the District Attorney and his assistants to the effect that, if they had regard for their personal safety, they would not attempt to prosecute the peonage people in said counties," wrote the examiner.[25]

Reese insisted the inquiries must proceed. He wrote to Washington a month later urgently asking for additional help from Secret Service agents to protect witnesses who testified against five whites in Pike County. The holders of slaves fought back violently, he said, burning the sawmill of one white landowner willing to speak against the defendants, setting black churches afire, and intimidating large numbers of African American workers who were fleeing the area. "The lumber mills were shut down and the farming interests paralyzed," Reese wrote.[26] Department of Justice officials waited nearly two weeks to reply, and then indicated that no agents were available at the time.

Reese continued to draw indictments from grand juries in the Black Belt, but often with little result. Charges against one Alex D. Stephens in early 1904 alleged that Stephens sold a black worker named William Brown to a white man in Coffee County named Samuel W. Tyson in July 1902.[27]

Attorneys in the state by now knew the drill for responding to such actions. Tyson pleaded guilty and was then pardoned. Charges against Stephens and two others involved in related seizures and sales of black slaves were dismissed.

Even as the federal investigations seemed to weaken from the interior, external opposition to the campaign against slavery mounted. A mass meeting of sawmill and turpentine camp owners in Tifton, Georgia, convened in April 1904 to plot strategy and collect funds for a legal defense of the involuntary servitude used by virtually every member of the group. "Every turpentine operator and saw mill man, as well as every one employing labor in this section, feels that they are affected," wrote a newspaperman who attended the meeting.[28]

Nearly a year had passed since John Pace—the primary target of Reese's initial investigation—pleaded guilty to holding debt slaves. His sentence of fifty-five years—with five to serve—remained suspended. There had been no activity in his appeal of the constitutionality of the statute under which he pleaded guilty, and Pace had made no effort to obtain a presidential pardon for his crimes like the one the Cosbys had obtained. He remained free on a $5,000 bond signed by his partner in the slaving enterprise, Fletcher Turner, and his banker, William Gray.[29]

By now, even Reese had begun to doubt whether the laws on the U.S. books were actually sufficient to prohibit the holding of slaves. In legal filings, Pace's lawyers freely conceded that the farmer admitted "unlawfully and knowingly holding a person forcibly and against his will and requiring such person to labor." But this did not technically fit the definition of peonage, they argued, saying the arcane statute could only be prosecuted in locations where a formal system of peonage had once existed—as in New Mexico.

Reese believed they might be legally correct. "I very much fear," he wrote to Washington, that Pace's conviction would be overturned on that argument.[30] Since there was no other U.S. law making it a crime to hold slaves, Pace would forever go free.

Attorney General Knox resigned in June 1904 to accept an appointment to the U.S. Senate. His successor, William Moody, a former congressman from Massachusetts and then secretary of the navy, pressed for the existing cases of involuntary servitude violations to be fully pursued. But it was obvious that Reese's enthusiasm for a sweeping assault on new slavery did not arouse him.

In December of 1904, Attorney General Moody made one last major federal gesture in the campaign against peonage, personally arguing to the U.S. Supreme Court that the conviction of Samuel M. Clyatt for having two black men seized and enslaved more than three years earlier should be upheld. Clyatt's slow-moving appeal—using the same argument as Pace and his fellow defendants that the anti-peonage statute couldn't be applied, had finally reached the highest court in the land. Three months later, the court surprised Reese and other government lawyers across the country. Clyatt won a new trial on minute technical grounds. But the court upheld the validity of the anti-peonage statute.[31]

The practical import of the ruling was to sustain the fundamental illegality of involuntary servitude and of the federal judicial system's one limited weapon for attacking it. But at the same time, the opinion by Justice David Brewer also affirmed that the South's growing practice of using hyper-technical interpretations of U.S. law to thwart the rights of black men on a wide range of issues—from segregated schools and housing to voter registration and government aid for the poor—would be abided by the federal courts.

Days later, in Savannah, Georgia, Judge Speer, emboldened by the section of the Supreme Court ruling declaring peonage abhorrent, ordered from his bench that Georgia's vast system of charging African Americans in the lower courts of towns and sentencing them to hard-labor chain gangs was illegal. Speer ordered the freedom of Henry Jamison, a black man arrested on a charge of drunk and disorderly conduct and then sentenced to spend 210 days chained into a work crew repairing roads in Macon. The judge found that local courts had no power to order such penalties for petty and largely undefined crimes such as vagrancy, drunkenness, or throwing trash in the street. "Enforced labor on a local chain-gang, imposed for an offense not amounting to crime, is involuntary servitude and peonage, in the light of the decision of the United States Supreme Court, no matter what the state law or the municipal ordinances on the subject may be," Speer wrote. "Let but this crime continue, we will all be slaves. We will be slaves to our

prejudices, slaves in that like slaves we tolerate the violation of the constitution and the law which we are sworn to support; slaves because we slav-
ishly fail or refuse to perform a lofty civic duty."[32]

Speer's ruling rippled across the southern landscape. Here was a legal
rationale far more sweeping than anything previously articulated by any
jurist involved in the involuntary servitude cases. Under the logic of Judge
Speer, thousands—perhaps tens of thousands—of African Americans being
held against their will to work off fines levied for trivial, alleged misdemeanors should be freed.

Back in Montgomery, Reese recognized the import of the decision
instantly. Just a few weeks earlier, he had convinced another grand jury to
hand up sixteen additional indictments on peonage charges against men
in another section of Alabama. But Reese could see the ineffectual nature
of the scattershot prosecutions. There were clearly thousands of African
Americans being coerced into labor, and contrary to Judge Jones's original
hopes, convictions in a few high-profile cases weren't causing other whites
to abandon the practice. Reese knew a broader and more sustained attack
was the only hope. In Speer's ruling, Reese saw a basis for challenging the
root of the South's forced labor blight—the system of selling convicts followed by the state of Alabama, nearly all of its counties, and at least a half
dozen other southern states.

Then came an astounding revelation, a discovery that must have been the
most dispiriting setback yet in the two years since Reese made his vow to
root out slavery for President Roosevelt. The U.S. attorney learned that
John Pace, his original nemesis in Tallapoosa County, continued to hold
African Americans in involuntary servitude. "There are two boys ages fifteen and sixteen respectively who are now illegally restrained of their liberty on the farm," Reese wrote to his superiors. The teenagers were almost
certainly Luke and Henry Tinsley, one of the pairs of brothers James M.
Kennedy had enumerated on the Pace farm during the census five years
earlier.

Like many other blacks overlooked by investigators and grand jurors
during the probe of Pace's operation, the Tinsleys were never discovered
during the federal inquiry. Now Reese learned the children had been ille-

gally held by Pace since 1897—eight years earlier—and were still working off a court bond paid on behalf of their mother. Reese doubted whether he could bring a peonage charge based on the sketchy facts surrounding the pair. He knew without doubt it would be useless to seek charges against Pace in a local court. Based on Judge Speer's ruling, the vehicle for freeing the boys would be to seek a writ of habeas corpus—forcing Pace to demonstrate his authority to hold the two boys against their will. The maneuver wouldn't stop with Pace, Reese believed. "There are, in my judgment, hundreds of negroes that can be freed this way, if I be given this authority," he wrote to his superiors.

Attorney General Moody was unmoved. Undoubtedly, the administration was not going to authorize Reese to begin challenging hundreds or thousands of whites about the status of their black workers. "If you have good reason to believe that Pace is holding minors to involuntary servitude, without the consent of the parents . . . you should have warrant issued," came the reply. "The habeas corpus proceedings should not be instituted."[33] A few days later, Pace, having heard that Reese was preparing another prosecution, released the two boys to their mother.[34]

But Tallapoosa County was quickly reverting to its former ways. A woman who signed her name only as Susanna wrote Judge Jones in mid-1905, describing another slaving operation already under way a few miles from Pace's farm on the Tallapoosa River. "I whish to enform you that theare is one J. D. Hugens and son holden Negroes here in peonage at thear terpen tine Still 10 miles South of Dadeville. . . . Please send your detective heare at once."[35] No one was sent.

Reese was convinced that his prosecutions had proved the perverse nexus of debt slavery and the organized convict leasing system that flourished around him. He made one last thrust to destroy it. Writing to Attorney General Moody in March 1905, Reese pleaded again for permission to file habeas corpus petitions on behalf of thousands of Alabama convicts then forced to work in mines owned by Tennessee Coal, Iron & Railroad Co., other companies, and on private farms like John Pace's.

"I am perfectly willing for one to shoulder this responsibility and commence these proceedings . . . though in doing this I appreciate fully what this means," Reese wrote. "I am willing to jeopardize . . . my relationship with all the nine congressmen and the two Senators from this District, the local Bar, the Bench and the people of the city of Montgomery, where I was born and raised," the attorney continued.

"I desire to know . . . in case I commence this crusade, so to speak, that I will have not only your support, but in time to come if these very men who have always supported me politically should turn upon me, because I have instituted these prosecutions and done my duty, that you will protect me from such attacks."[36]

Reese knew that white leaders across Alabama were conspiring to have him replaced when his term as U.S. attorney expired at the end of 1905. He wrote Booker T. Washington a few weeks earlier asking the black leader to send a discreet letter to President Roosevelt endorsing Reese's work.[37]

Attorney General Moody would have none of it. He ordered that the young district attorney take no action until the Supreme Court ruled on an appeal of Judge Speer's decision striking down Georgia's misdemeanor convict system.[38]

As Reese was pressing to use the federal courts to free the thousands of slaves held in Alabama mines—and set a precedent that might have freed ten thousand or more in other states—the writer Thomas Dixon released in 1905 the follow-up to his spectacular novel *The Leopard's Spots*. The new book, an even more overt paean to the Ku Klux Klan violence that swept away black political participation in the 1860s and 1870s, was titled *The Clansman*. It sold in vast quantities in 1905 at the price of $1.50 and became perhaps the first true blockbuster in modern U.S. publishing. Its success—commercially and as revisionist history—was so complete that, in an irony of immeasurable proportion, newspaper announcements for the volume featured a letter from Abraham Lincoln's son Robert praising it as "a work that cannot be laid down."[39]

The author quickly fashioned the storylines of his two racist novels into a stage play to tour the United States. The production featured a cast of exquisitely attractive young white actresses, white actors in blackface playing lecherous emancipated slaves hungry to assault white women and cowering and buffoonish black elected officials, gallant former Confederate officers, and a fully outfitted contingent of white-robed Klansmen who rode across the stage mounted on horseback. The show opened in Norfolk,

Virginia, in August 1905 at the Academy of Music, and an epic, record-breaking run of performances followed in theater halls across the South, Midwest, and Northeast.

It played to packed crowds everywhere, drawing in a period of ten months "more people . . . than any other attraction . . . in the theatrical history of United States theater," wrote one newspaper critic.[40] Not surprisingly, a new generation of southern white leaders absorbed its account of Reconstruction and the fury of its white actors as absolute fact. Audiences roared approval almost everywhere else too—including standing-room-only audiences in New York City. In Atlanta, the city's most prominent debutantes held "box" parties for their friends in the expensive reserved seats of the Grand Opera House when the play arrived in the city. Mrs. Dixon, the author's wife, was feted by the finest ladies of Atlanta.[41]

After the first performance on a chilly late October night, Dixon addressed an adoring crowd—revealing from the stage that his father had been a Ku Klux Klan member when the night riders waged a campaign of violence on black political leaders during Reconstruction. Georgia governor Joseph M. Terrell watched approvingly from a special box. Later that night, Dixon was honored at a lush private dinner at the Aragon Hotel hosted by the Kappa Alpha Order, a fraternal order founded at the University of Virginia in tribute to the life of Robert E. Lee. Raising their glasses in a series of toasts to the guest of honor and his long membership in the fraternity were many of the most prestigious white men of the city—the leadership elite who would govern and sculpt the South's leading city for the next fifty years—including Hugh Dorsey, a young attorney who a decade later inflated evidence to prosecute Jewish businessman Leo Frank for the rape and killing of a young woman that he did not commit.[42] After his conviction, Frank was murdered in an infamous lynching by an anti-Semitic mob, led by the city's leading political and business leaders. Elevated by his role in the Frank case, Dorsey went on to become governor of Georgia.

Scattered voices of concern were raised against the brazenly inflammatory racial rhetoric of the production, and in some cities gangs of white men—adrenaline raised by the play's stirring call to defend their delicate women from the lusts of black brutes—subsequently attacked random African Americans in their cities. A committee of northern activists attempted to encourage protests when the production arrived in new cities with specially printed postcards showing a scene from the play and urging a boycott.[43] Most notably, Dixon's own brother, the Reverend A. C. Dixon, called the stage play "rotten and slimy."[44] Here and there moderate leaders complained that the production painted an exaggerated portrait of black and white antagonisms. The pastor of the Baptist Tabernacle in Atlanta decried the performance as a "disgrace to southern manhood and womanhood" and the heroic portrayal of the Ku Klux Klan as fraudulent.[45]

In an interview before one performance in the South, Dixon said that "the North" was beginning to see the urgency in repressing African Americans. "It is only within the past 12 months that I have seen big buck negroes parading up and down Broadway with white girls hanging on their arms." When some members of an audience hissed the show in Columbia, South Carolina, Dixon mounted the stage to defend himself against critics. Stirring the crowd to his side, he declared: "God ordained the southern white man to teach the lessons of Aryan supremacy."[46]

# XI

# SLAVERY AFFIRMED

*"Cheap cotton depends on cheap niggers."*

Some African American leaders still held out hope that at least northern whites could be turned back from the rising venality of white Americans. Instead of embracing the accommodationist philosophy of Booker T. Washington, a generation of younger black intellectuals led by W. E. B. DuBois insisted that it was whites who needed to adapt to full black citizenship. Born in Massachusetts and schooled first in Germany, then in Harvard, DuBois had been since 1897 a groundbreaking professor of sociology at Atlanta University, one of the most prestigious majority-black institutions in the country. A stream of his articles, novels, and nonfiction assessments of the progress of African Americans, including *The Souls of Black Folk*, published in 1903, were scathing incisions into the state of race relations in the United States. Later, after the formation of the National Association for the Advancement of Colored People in 1909, DuBois would emerge as its most central early figure.

The arrival of DuBois in Atlanta had put him deep in the heart of the new system of southern slavery. As part of his university duties, DuBois directed a series of extraordinary statistical and sociological surveys of the rural South, and black people within it, between 1898 and 1904. The last of them, "Negro Farmer," became a bedrock demonstration of the new science of sociology and a rigidly empiricist approach toward quantitative analysis in the study of social forces. Two years later, the U.S. commissioner of labor, whose office had funded the previous studies, agreed to back a new DuBois project, this time focused specifically on the state of black share-croppers in the South.[1]

Choosing as his venue Lowndes County, Alabama, DuBois's project injected one of the most extraordinary American intellects of the era into a place as backward and forbidding as any on the continent. Named after a nineteenth-century U.S. congressman from South Carolina, William Lowndes, who prior to the Civil War strenuously advocated the extension of slavery into new U.S. territories, the county sat at the center of the Black Belt.

At the beginning of the Civil War, more than nineteen thousand enslaved blacks—the twelfth-largest population of slaves in one place in the country—lived on 1,100 farms in Lowndes County, nearly five hundred of which exceeded one thousand acres in size. The war obliterated the hope of Congressman Lowndes and others to expand slavery. But despite Lowndes having the largest proportion of blacks to whites of any Alabama county, the war seemed to have had little effect on the question of whether slavery would continue there. By 1900, even as the white population dwindled further, the landholders who remained reforged an almost impenetrable juris-diction into which no outside authority could extend its reach. By then, more than thirty thousand blacks worked the rich flat cotton fields, no longer called slaves but living under an absolute power of whites nearly indistinguishable from the forced labor of a half century earlier. Black land ownership in the county was inconsequential. Where it existed on paper, the appearance of independence was a chimera behind which local whites continued to violently control when and where blacks lived and worked, and how their harvests were sold. Most offensive to blacks, white men in Lowndes County continued to exercise their slavery-era presumption that they were entitled to the sexual companionship of virtually any African American woman residing on their property.

During the grand jury investigation of peonage that led to the trials of 1903, Warren Reese concluded that Lowndes County was the fountain-head of Alabama's new slave labor. W. D. McCurdy, one of the original operators of the most notorious convict slave mines near Birmingham, also kept dozens of black workers imprisoned on his home plantation in Lowndes County. It was here that federal investigators working for Reese had reported—until being run out of the county at gunpoint—that the sheriff, J. W. Dixon, was an active participant in a violently enforced convict slave system that held hundreds or thousands of black laborers. The Smith family—whose deadly convict farm had become the symbol of convict leasing's most lethal manifestations in the nineteenth century—was one of the county's most prominent landholders. But Reese could bring no charges in Lowndes County because no blacks forced into slavery were willing to risk the lives of family members or their own by testifying to the grand jury in Montgomery. Even a black grand juror from Lowndes County participated in the inquiry only under protest—for fear he would be killed upon his return home.

But the failure of the federal investigation to reach Lowndes County didn't indicate there had been less slavery than federal agents initially claimed. Indeed, there was vastly more. In the summer of 1906, W. E. B. DuBois and a team of more than a dozen researchers, including sociologists Monroe Work, Richard R. Wright, and others of the most extraordinary young black minds of the new century, arrived at the Calhoun School. Founded in 1892 by a wealthy white northern socialite, the institution operated largely on the industrial education principles of Booker T. Washington. But the Calhoun School was distinct in one regard among the many institutions for blacks established near the end of the nineteenth century—often naively and ill-fated—by wealthy benefactors. Going beyond training black children in basic academics and advanced vocational skills such as bricklaying and carpentry, the school's founder, a well-bred Connecticut spinster named Charlotte Thorn, actually moved to Lowndes County and eventually promoted a land ownership experiment for blacks in the heart of what was likely the single most repressive white-power regime in the South. Over time, land companies established by the school purchased a total of more than four thousand acres of cotton land, encouraged local blacks to operate the farms on a quasi-communal basis, and ultimately resold smaller tracts of land to African Americans.[2]

DuBois, whose differences with Booker T. Washington had not advanced to the complete rupture that eventually pitted the men against each other as committed enemies, was attracted to the Calhoun School as a preserve in which idealistic and educated whites and blacks could interact freely. He also delighted in the effrontery the school presented to the white dominance that surrounded it.

DuBois went to Lowndes County in hopes of capturing an unassailable, empirically proven portrait of the penury and exploitation that African Americans there—and by extension most of the South—were forced to endure. With funding from the federal Bureau of Labor, the DuBois team fanned across the countryside carrying ten thousand copies of question-naires containing a battery of piercing questions regarding land ownership, labor control, family life, education, sexual mores, morality, political activ-ity, and other aspects of black life. By late fall in 1906, more than 21,000 of the county's black farmers had been interviewed through a cabin-to-cabin canvass, with researchers scrupulously recording the answers and compil-ing tables of the responses back at the school. Separately, two white inves-tigators provided by the federal government conducted an even more discreet inquiry into the political operations and sexual morality of Lowndes County whites. To cross-reference the individual interviews, white re-searchers examined and analyzed prodigious volumes of Lowndes County mortgages, liens, arrests, incarcerations, and proceedings of local justices of the peace—all of the key instruments of government used by whites to contain and control blacks throughout the South. DuBois used the legal record and personal accounts to create detailed maps and tables of the county, showing between 1850 and 1906 the evolution of economic, social, and political power and a chronological movement of land ownership among blacks and whites.[3]

No social study on such a scale of research and ambition had ever been undertaken in the United States, certainly not one focused on black life and even more so never one attempted in the environment of overt physical danger that existed in Lowndes County.

Local whites were already openly hostile toward the existence of the Calhoun School and its implicit challenge to the neo-slavery that sur-rounded it. DuBois wrote later that researchers met "with the greeting of . . . shotguns in certain parts of the county."[4] He told U.S. commis-sioner of labor Charles P. Neill that two investigators "were shot at and run out of one corner of the county."[5]

Yet DuBois and others believed the enormity of the data and the impregnability of a federally authorized analysis conducted under the most rigorous scientific methodology presented an opportunity to smash the racial myopia and growing indifference to conditions in the South of the majority of American whites. DuBois later called the project his "best sociological work."[6] By the end of 1906, the report had been completed, written by hand, and delivered to the Bureau of Labor for publication.

The growing ubiquity for all African Americans of the dangers DuBois and his colleagues encountered in Lowndes County was underscored on September 22, 1906, when the team learned that a mob of as many as ten thousand whites was on the rampage in Atlanta. DuBois rushed aboard a train to return to his wife, Nina, and daughter, Yolande, who had remained in their quarters at South Hall on the campus of Atlanta University, where DuBois was a professor. He sat in vigil on the steps of the building with a shotgun. But white attackers never arrived.

By the time the riot ended, hundreds of African Americans, by virtually all accounts, had been attacked on the streets of the city. Atlanta had never completely cooled since the performances of *The Clansman* ten months earlier. Tensions—driven by rumors of black ambitions for political power and open race baiting by candidates running for governor—had mounted over the months.

In the weeks just before the riot, the fall of 1906, Atlanta was whipped into a fury by weeks of exaggerated and fabricated accounts published in the *Atlanta Constitution* and other local newspapers of blacks allegedly raping and insulting white women. A second visit to Atlanta by the touring *Clansman* production was being arranged—this time featuring in the cast two cousins of Jefferson Davis, the late president of the Confederacy. Two days after the production began its new tour on September 20, with packed performances in Charleston, South Carolina, a crowd of whites—delirious with racial animosity—gathered in downtown Atlanta.[7]

Heeding an anonymous public call to revive a new Ku Klux Klan, a group of men gathered to discuss how to respond to the alleged series of sexual assaults against white women. Almost none of the alleged attacks were ever proven. But by late afternoon, the city's competitive newspapers were rolling off extra editions to report even newer dubious claims of black men attacking young women. Just before midnight, the crowd began marauding indiscriminately through the city. For five days, vigilantes, police officers, and soldiers grabbed and beat African Americans, seizing them off sidewalks and streetcars. They broke into businesses where blacks were employed and crashed into homes in African American neighborhoods, spilling blood everywhere they went. In some areas, blacks stood their ground, fighting back with guns and fists—spurring even more anger and a rationale for police and militia to join on the side of white rioters. In the end, the mobs were believed to have killed at least two dozen African Americans. Fewer than a half dozen whites died.[8]

Three weeks after the riot in September 1906, a former U.S. congressman from Georgia, William H. Fleming, raised a rare voice against rising racial animosity. "How many causes have recently been cooperating in that line from the theater, the press and the stump to familiarize us with the disrespect for law and to arouse hate and contempt by the whites against the blacks?" Representative Fleming asked. "Chief among offenders stands a former preacher, Rev. Thomas Dixon, with his Clansman."[9]

In Washington, federal officials who previously had shown such assiduous interest in the research by DuBois—and the possibility it would document the widespread slavery of the South—suddenly faltered. Tabulations that had appeared acceptable months earlier now looked questionable to Commissioner Neill. He signaled that publication of the report would no longer be immediate. Nearly a year after completion, it remained under review, when a new commissioner replaced Neill. After reading the report, W. W. Hangar, the new head of the agency, wrote taciturnly to DuBois: "It would be extremely unwise to make any use whatsoever of the material which was gathered."[10] A year later, after months of pushing for publication of his research, or at the very least that the document be returned, DuBois was informed that the study's conclusions "touched on political matters." It could not be sent to him because "it had been destroyed."[11]

Nothing of what might have been a seminal study of black life survived—with one exception. Three years later, DuBois penned his first novel—*The Quest for the Silver Fleece*—a richly descriptive portrayal of African Americans struggling against the strictures tightening against them in the North and South. The heart of the novel was a narrative drawn from what DuBois and his researchers had witnessed during their dangerous summer in Lowndes County. Substituting new names for the Calhoun School, the McCurdys, and other great white landholding families, DuBois rendered the social order of what he called Tooms County in sharp, but unexaggerated, relief. The baronic family whose patriarch, Colonel Cresswell, had been the county's largest slaveholder before emancipation still controlled in the twentieth century fifty thousand acres of prime cotton land and uncounted black families who lived upon it in the novel's account.

In the portrait etched by DuBois, Colonel Cresswell lived in a sprawling mansion far from town, surrounded by endless numbers of broken cabins inhabited by terrified and uneducated "tenants." Cresswell was intent on crushing any semblance of movement toward economic or political independence among those blacks. "Cheap cotton depends on cheap niggers," he exclaimed. No manner of shared interests between blacks and whites could ever be contemplated. "We've got whips, chain-gangs, and—mobs if need be. . . . It's the Negro . . . we've got to beat to his knees."

In the county described by DuBois, black sharecroppers lived or died on the whim of the white men still called "master" by most. They begged the white men for their broken-down log cabins, for food and cloth to make clothes. Maturing black girls complied with their initiation into sexual activity when Colonel Cresswell's son demanded it, because "he was our master."

The Cresswells and other whites "bought" and sold sharecroppers at will—substituting the sale of their alleged debts for rent and supplies as a proxy for the sale of humans themselves. Able black men and their families routinely "sold" for $250 in this Lowndes County. Black families who resisted their sale to other whites were subject to brutal violence and the confiscation or burning of their homes and possessions. Once under a labor contract to any white man, blacks knew they would almost certainly never be free of it. Disputes over the value of the cotton they raised were settled by local officials controlled by the white farmers. Any man who fought back against overseers beating workers in the field risked gruesome punishments and sale into the convict leasing system.

Robbed of her crop, DuBois's central character, Zora, knows she has no recourse: "What should she do? She never thought of appeal to courts, for Colonel Cresswell was Justice of the Peace and his son was bailiff. Why had they stolen from her? She knew. She was now penniless, and in a sense helpless. She was now a peon bound to a master's bidding." She knew that signing a contract to work for the Cresswells "would mean slavery, jail, or hounded running away."

While hunger and the physical abuse of overseers haunted every day, it was jail, the chain gang, or any other contact with the judicial system that loomed as the greatest constant jeopardies to blacks. Starved and manacled squads of black men prowled the town square and the roads between plantations, hustled along by gun- and whip-toting guards—a scene hardly changed from the traveling slave salesmen of a half century earlier. At the slightest provocation, Cresswell threatened this ignominious horror to any uncooperative or insolent blacks. The result of any accusation by a white man would, almost without exception, be court-sanctioned ownership. Once hauled before a judge, any African American could be purchased by Colonel Cresswell or another white. One passage of DuBois's novel described the routine courthouse scene:

> *"What's this nigger charged with?" demanded the Judge when the first black boy was brought up before him.*
> *"Breaking his labor contract."*
> *"Any witnesses?"*
> *"I have the contract here," announced the sheriff. "He refuses to work."*
> *"A year, or one hundred dollars."*
> *Colonel Cresswell paid his fine, and took him in charge.*[12]

In October 1905, the U.S. Supreme Court overturned Judge Speer's order against Georgia's county convict leasing system,[13] finding that the federal courts had no jurisdiction to dismantle the system of obtaining and selling prisoners so vividly described by DuBois. In January 1906, Warren Reese gave up the modest office in the Montgomery federal building from which he had waged his quixotic war on slavery. The White House named a new district attorney for central Alabama.

Three months later, in April 1906, John W. Pace was pardoned for his crimes by President Roosevelt.[14] The following year, Fletcher Turner was elected to represent Tallapoosa County in the Alabama House of Representatives.

# XII

## NEW SOUTH RISING

*"This great corporation."*

For three years, Americans had received periodic reports on the slavery of Tallapoosa County. The county, with its exotic Choctaw Indian name meaning "pulverized rock," and the image of John Pace, a brutish farmer from the backcountry, became the only enduring symbol of the peonage cases—even as hundreds and then thousands of other incidents emerged in parts of Alabama, Georgia, Florida, Mississippi, and Louisiana. Darkness was crowding black life in America in an ever more sinister way.

Lost in the Alabama peonage inquiry was how the case began—with the report to Judge Jones of a miscarriage of justice in the adjacent Shelby County. Whatever misdeeds had occurred there—especially the fact that Fletcher Turner's family operated a slave-driven quarry within the county—had been almost entirely forgotten. The town of Columbiana—a provincial county seat urgently hoping to embody the incipient gleam of the new century—escaped excoriation. One town nearer to Birmingham than Dadeville, bustling with prosperity, new residents, and a vague sense of Rooseveltian modernity, Columbiana was swelling with new wealth. Old one-man, one-mule mines of the nineteenth century—little more than crude horizontal pits dug into hillsides outside the town—were fast disappearing, replaced by giant brick edifices of factories like the Siluria Cotton Mill, where white men and women could earn wages in regular hourly increments. They worked defined shifts, rather than the meteorological clock of sunup to sundown that had governed farm life since the days of the first settlers. Keystone Lime Co. supplied trainloads of the caustic essential ingredient for iron to the county's biggest employer, the antebellum Shelby Iron Works, and to the ravenous new furnaces coming into blast on the fringes of Birmingham.

The bounding economic progress promised far more for whites than blacks, but African Americans could not resist the entrancing allure of new prosperity. Shelby County was now home to growing numbers of the black members of the Cottingham clan. Brierfield, the old Confederate munitions foundry where Green Cottenham and his family had sheltered during the 1890s, couldn't survive against the new millennium's technology of coal, iron, and steel production. The foundry town had been a refuge for the family in the storm of the late nineteenth century. Sheltered by the foundry's need for a steady supply of black workers, some of the Cottenhams avoided for a time the resubjugation of African Americans occurring on millions of southern farms. A succession of black men linked back to the Cottingham farm—Scip, the patriarchal slave who now spelled his name Cottinham, his sons, Elbert and Henry, his grandsons, and others—worked in the wilting orbits of fire surrounding the furnaces. Mary and the other wives and older daughters kept house and washed or cooked for laborers. The foundry work was grueling, but for a little longer Brierfield afforded these African Americans a way station of modest freedom and a residue of authentic independence that was fast disappearing for most rural blacks. Relatively remote from any large population of whites, the six hundred African Americans there could avoid the implicit risk of mingling with whites on the roadways into the county seat or accidental conflicts on the back roads of the countryside. The whites of the furnace town needed them. Rev. Starr's old Methodist church still stood—giving Brierfield's black families their own forum for leadership and worship. In a crude, over-crowded school for black children, Green and his two older sisters learned to read and write.

What irony that the maker of cannons for Lee's armies and armor for the Confederacy's warships became a place of refuge for freed slaves. But Brierfield, with its redolent sense of post-emancipation freedom, was vanishing. By 1910 only twenty-nine people remained. Mary, Green, and the girls, Ada and Marietta, followed the path of the South's evolving economics, moving to Montevallo, a little town perched on a new coal mine in Shelby County just south of Birmingham. Soon, Mary was working—washing and cleaning for a white man. Columbiana was a short freight car ride away. Whatever remained to harbor Green and his siblings would quickly dissolve before the torrent of trouble pouring across their world.

Late in the summer of the great 1903 peonage trials in Montgomery, Green turned eighteen years old.[1] Ada was twenty-one and Marietta nineteen. Green and his sisters and cousins had experienced none of the emancipation exhilaration that their parents and grandparents remembered from the end of the war. Theirs had been a life of perplexing contradiction, of an ostensible but most often unrealized freedom, of supposed political and economic independence from whites but in truth, even in Brierfield, ultimately a complete dependence on the authority and protection of whites—or simply the security of isolation. The sisters would stay with their mother at least until marriage. But Green was nearly a man now, tall, lean, and muscular like his father, sharpened by the paucity of food, hardened by the incessant labor demanded of his life. The freedom of approaching male adulthood—even in the circumscribed South—was an inescapable allure.

Green soon ventured deep into the sphere of white men, though they must have remained a mystery to him. He had to know all the stories of his father and aunts and uncles who had lived with the white Cottinghams on the farm by the river. But those were ancient tales from before his birth. In his iron-town childhood and young adult years, there had never been familial bonds with any white people, especially not the old Cottingham master and his acknowledged offspring.

Green's uncle, Abraham Cottingham, the once spirited Republican, having journeyed farther from the country crossroads where the freed slaves congregated after emancipation from old man Cottingham's farm than any others, made his home in Shelby County. Abraham's sons, Jimmy—known as "Cap"—and Frank, were nearly two decades older than Green, and had already tasted the bittersweet paradox of black life at the dawn of the twentieth century. They had never been slaves. They had voted in elections. Now they had seen all vestiges of legal citizenship stripped away. Cap, Frank, and

Abraham cast ballots for the last time in 1901, the final election in which blacks were permitted meaningful participation in Alabama. Green would never experience that act.

Cap Cottingham's ouster from the voting rolls was punctuated a few months later by his arrest, during a visit back in Bibb County, on a misdemeanor charge. He was quickly sold into the bondage of a white farmer named O. T. Grimes. On February 18, 1902, Cap and another prisoner named Henry Johnson successfully fled the farm and escaped.[2]

In the fall of 1903, as Warren Reese prepared for the last peonage trial in Montgomery, Cap was arrested again, this time by a Shelby County deputy. The charge was for violating the Alabama statute forbidding any person from carrying a concealed weapon. The records of Cap's arrest signal that he was picked up as part of a general roundup in Columbiana to fill an order for black labor from Tennessee Coal, Iron & Railroad Co. Cap, a muscular six-foot-tall thirty-five-year-old with skin as deeply black as his great-grandfather Scipio's, was arrested along with another African American named Monroe Wallace. Both were charged with carrying concealed weapons on October 2, 1903, and sentenced to four months and twenty days of hard labor to pay their fines and fees to the sheriff and court. By the end of the month, the two were joined in the jail by seven other blacks arrested for climbing aboard an empty freight car, another for gambling, and one more for an alleged petty theft.

Six weeks later, on November 21, the county's convict labor agent, W. J. Farley, emptied the jail and delivered its contents to Tennessee Coal, Iron & Railroad. Cap Cottingham was turned over for $9 a month.[3] He survived his winter in the Pratt Mines and returned to Columbiana the following year. The creep of darkness paused, but it would not last.


As the new century bloomed, the civic confidence of the editor of the gray-typed *Shelby County Sentinel* was so great that he ordered a photographer to document the landmarks of the burgeoning town and penned a twenty-page paean to its economic prospects and fine citizenry. It was natural, and more than a little self-interested, for editor J. A. MacKnight to do so, given that on the side he was also the town's leading real estate man.

"The town is beautifully situated, on a plateau which is splendidly drained," MacKnight gushed. "There is so little sickness that the doctors are nearly all poor men and their number is few."[4]

Hyperbole yes, but there was good reason to be enthused. The county was in the sweetest bend of a rising economic curve. More land was under farm production than at any point since the arrival of white squatters a century before. In each harvest since the turn of the century, Shelby's cotton gins and compresses pumped out more than ten thousand bales—totaling in excess of five million pounds of handpicked fiber. The only hint of new coming boll weevil debacle that a decade hence would sweep in to ravage the fields were fearful exclamations from farmers in far-away Texas. The town population, more than two thousand already, was growing at a heady rate. Two railroads, the Southern Rail Line and the Louisville & Nashville, converged at the freight terminal at the end of Depot Street. A cotton gin, grist mill, and warehouses crowded the edge of the commercial district, and plans were being finalized for that most tantalizing of new luxuries, an electric light plant.

Columbiana was brimming with fin-de-siècle optimism. Working furiously to bring a measure of refinement and civic improvement, still coarse towns across the South were laying the building blocks on which twentieth-century American prosperity would rise. The community's most respected leaders championed effulgent campaigns to bring the first paved streets, public schools, and shared utility systems—all social advancements carefully engineered to transform their town but that would also exclude from its benefits nearly all African Americans.[5]

(There was proof to Columbiana of the town's rising sophistication in Henry Walthall, the son of the sheriff and himself chief deputy at the Shelby County jail a few years earlier. In the 1890s, he helped his father capture and sell black prisoners full-time and taught theater on the side. In the summers, he produced Shakespeare with a local cast until finally joining a traveling theater company. Removed to the nascent Hollywood, Walthall starred a decade later as the Colonel in *The Birth of a Nation*, D. W. Griffith's 1915 blockbuster film based on the Dixon blockbuster, white supremacist stage show, *The Clansman*. The film was the first moving picture ever shown at the White House. President Woodrow Wilson, a southerner and an open racist, was said to have praised the film.)

At the monumental cost of $250,000, Shelby County erected a new courthouse that without exaggeration could be described only as extraordinary. Replacing an unadorned brick edifice scuffed and scarred with more than a half century of unceremonious use, the new building was a temple to citizen governance and, even more so, to the county's rising expectations for itself.

At the grand entrance on Main Street, four columns soared fifty feet to an ornate Greek Revival portico. Encircling the roofline on every side, a carved parapet railing framed cupolas of hammered brass leaf on each wing of the building. At the center of the roof rose an immense octagonal clock tower, looming magnificently above the town. In the low sun of early evening, the building's chiseled west facade, constructed of thousands of tons of yellow limestone quarried from the ridges above the nearby Coosa River, glowed luminescently. The shadow falling to east and south was nearly large enough to blot out the rest of the town's jumble of humble red-brick stores and whitewashed houses. The building was the community's flag plunged into the earth of the new century, a clear portent of the ambitions of those who led it. A new future was coming, to be built and shaped in the manner of its new makers.

The architect of this bold new vision, if not of the courthouse itself, was Judge A. P. Longshore. A lawyer, a devout Baptist, and a fervent populist, he commanded a nearly mesmerized local following. How else that a county still licking its wounds from the Civil War would agree to borrow a fortune to build the grandest courthouse in the South? To Longshore, a rate of 6 percent per annum on county bonds was simply the wage to be paid for a different future. Already, he dressed and looked in the manner of the new century rather than the last. Above a mustache twisted at each end and a tiny tufted goatee on the point of his chin, Judge Longshore looked ahead, only ahead.

From atop the courthouse, Columbiana's other highest spire was clearly visible at the opposite diagonal of town. With angular Victorian sternness, it descended sharply into a square tower of stacked bricks and then three stories down to the iron-barred door of the Shelby County jail. A dozen dank cells on the other side of the building were heated by coal grates and illuminated by shafts of sunlight coming between the bars on every window. As new prisoners passed Sheriff J. H. Fulton's house next door and approached the front entrance on West Sterrett Street, one odd window at the top of the jail's tower could not escape their notice. Almost as tall as a man, circular at the top and rectangular at the bottom, the opening in the shape of a giant keyhole gave view into the county's hanging chamber. There, men condemned to die would arrive on steps from the second-floor cellblock and then twist at the end of a rope, safe from any last efforts to escape their fate, but with justice still plainly on view.[6]

In the newspaper editor's assessment of Columbiana in 1907, Mac-Knight included just one photograph containing a black face. Standing, expressionless, with each arm draped on the shoulders of a young white child in her care, the woman was identified only as "Black Mammy on Duty." On the whole, MacKnight reported that "the negro population is not excessive, and is orderly and law-abiding. They have their own churches and schools, and many of them own their homes. The ease with which a livelihood is made here renders them independent, and it is not easy to secure either male or female help from among them."[7]

Indeed, obtaining African Americans was crucial and sometimes difficult, as any traveler arriving in Shelby County during the first decade of the century would have seen long before the train pulled up to the weathered wooden platform in Columbiana. The rails into and out of town were surrounded by endless vistas of cotton and its production.

While the twentieth century brought wonders of technological advancement in the realm of early automobiles, faster trains, and electric illumination, every square foot of cotton field was being tended in a way little different from how Scipio had done it on the Cottingham place in 1840. It took hands. Millions of them had to be available to plow and seed, and millions more to hoe and pick. That meant African Americans. Strong, dependent, docile black men. The leaders of Shelby County and thousands of other southern towns and counties were intent on assuring that they could be found.

The great crusade against involuntary servitude—and especially Judge Jones's famous charge to the grand jury and the Supreme Court's ruling against Georgia's Judge Speer—achieved an unexpected result for those in the South most reliant on black backs. Instead of ending the new regimes of forced labor, Judge Jones's denunciations and the subsequent legal rulings became guideposts for a reorganization of the contemporary traffic in black men. Indeed, the further the court opinions decrying peonage echoed across the southern landscape, the more hollow they became.

The Supreme Court's renunciation of Speer's attempt to outlaw the misdemeanor convict leasing system was so complete that the opinion was not even written, but issued summarily and orally. Among the thousands of words of Judge Jones's famous direction to the federal jury on the definitions of legal and illegal labor practices, a single sentence ultimately rose to greatest prominence. Jones advised that persons convicted of misdemeanors whose sureties "confessed judgment" for them and worked them against their will could avoid violating the peonage statue by following a simple procedure. The laborers must be convicted in an authentic court—not by any bumpkin justice of the peace. The judgment and penalty had to be written down and recorded with the local courts. And the contract between the defendant and the person paying the fine—in which the defendant agreed to work for a certain amount of time to pay off the penalty—had to be signed "in open court with written approval of the judge."

The implication was clear. There would be no risk of another energetic U.S. attorney arresting white farmers for peonage so long as they, and local judges, were sufficiently hygienic in the records they maintained.

The old southern window dressing of legal rights for African Americans won the day again. There was no evidence of the decline anticipated by Reese and Jones in the number of African Americans being held by private individuals as a result of ostensible court fines. If anything, the number of black men "confessing judgment" swelled, now plainly and unabashedly acknowledged in open court. Moreover, undaunted by Judge Jones's ruling against the state's laws forbidding black men from leaving the employment of one white man without permission to work for another, the Alabama legislature passed a new but essentially identical "false pretenses" statute. Once held under a labor contract, black men who attempted to leave their employers faced criminal prosecution for doing so. If they had entered into the contract to avoid an earlier prosecution, the departure would exponentially increase the time they could be held as slaves.

In Shelby County, the number of African Americans "confessing judgment" in open court ballooned.[8] Between November 1890 and August 1906, the dank county jail admitted 1,327 prisoners, facing a total of more

than 1,500 charges. Physical descriptions were recorded only intermit-
tently, but during the periods when notations of race were made, more than
90 percent of those arrested were black. A few were women.

A fortunate group of 326 prisoners—generally whites and black men
with some modicum of means—were able to scrape together enough cash
to post a bond and obtain freedom until a later trial date. Most then simply
forfeited their bonds and remained free.

Among the 1,001 prisoners left behind, acquittals were infrequent.
Fewer than 250 defendants won their freedom, by virtue of a not guilty verdict or some other discharge during the sixteen years. All but a handful of
the other 750 were ordered to pay nominal fines coupled with huge fees. A
total of 124 of those new convicts, fewer than 17 percent, were able to pay
their judgments.

Ben Holt, convicted of vagrancy on August 29, 1906, was ordered to
pay the county a fine of $1. The costs of his arrest and prosecution, how-
ever, totaled $76.28. Instead of paying, he confessed judgment with a white
farmer named James Wharton, who paid the fine and fees and in return
owned Holt for a minimum of two hundred days.[9]

Of the remaining six hundred men, convicted of petty crimes and
unable to pay what the courts demanded of them, almost five hundred were
bartered into forced labor. More than two dozen convicts were leased to
other industrial concerns, eight each to the Sloss mines and Alabama Manufacturing Co. Eight more were acquired by two sawmill companies, Walter Brothers, in Sprague, Alabama, and Henderson-Boyd Lumber Co., in
Richburg, Alabama.[10]

Among the leadership circles of a place such as Shelby County, the
casual acquisition of blacks through the now carefully choreographed ritual
at the courthouse became a routine perk of modest influence.

Arrested for petit larceny in May of 1905, Jim Goodson was fined $25.
To avoid being sent to the mines with other county convicts, he agreed to
sign a contract for labor with Robert E. Bowden to work 236 days "in his
rock quarry." Bowden bridged two groups common in southern towns—as
both an important local entrepreneur and a savvy political intimate of the
most powerful town leaders. His thriving quarry, Keystone Lime Co., was
a busy competitor to the Turner lime quarry not far away in Calcis. Bowden's much larger enterprise produced 1,500 barrels of quicklime a day, in

fifteen kilns. Deriving lime from the massive formations of limestone undergirding all of Shelby County before the advent of the steam shovel required armies of men engaged in the crudest form of manual labor. Hardly any person would choose such work freely. Convicts were ideal.

For a quarter of a century, Bowden benefited handsomely from the availability of strong black men at the Shelby County jail. Between 1905 and 1913, he took possession of at least eighteen people arrested in the county, after each confessed judgment in open court—just as required by Judge Jones's order.

Nearly all of the essential local enterprises in Shelby County enjoyed at least periodic use of entrapped African Americans. Shelby Iron Works, the area's largest employer and biggest commercial taxpayer, continued to acquire black men by confessing judgment for their sentences before Judge Longshore—continuing a nearly uninterrupted use of slaves and other forced black labor from the early 1860s to the end of the first decade of the twentieth century.

Even Sheriff Fulton periodically acquired blacks through the court for his personal use. Fulton paid fines and costs totaling $58 on a man named John Mack in October 1907, and in return took control of him for six months. One of his favored deputies, W. J. Finney, arrested—and then purchased—four different black men between 1905 and 1913.[11]

Later that year, Peter Minor, faced with a $126 fine for carrying a concealed weapon, agreed to become a sharecropper for W. W. Wallace, the popular mayor of Columbiana and secretary of the Democratic County Committee. Minor agreed to give up half of anything he produced on land provided by the mayor.[12]

But the largest portion of the men arrested in Shelby County, nearly 250, were sold immediately, for periods of up to a year, to Tennessee Coal, Iron & Railroad Co. About one hundred others were sentenced to "hard labor for the county" and then almost certainly transferred to the same place.

Alabama's slave system had evolved into a forced labor agricultural and industrial enterprise unparalleled in the long history of slaves in the United States. During 1906, the state sold nearly two thousand black men to twenty different buyers. Nearly half were bought by the two biggest mining companies, Tennessee Coal & Iron and Sloss-Sheffield. The McCurdy brothers of Lowndes County bought dozens. Hundreds more went to timber camps and sawmill companies.

In addition to the prisoners auctioned off by the state, nearly seventy individual local governments, like Shelby County, parceled thousands more laborers to a hundred or more other buyers.[13] These prisoners lived in such misery that even some political figures in Alabama acknowledged the shamefulness of the system. In a 1904 report to acting governor Russell Cunningham, the state's top prison official, J. M. Carmichael, reported that Sloss-Sheffield had been "required to move its prison" at the Flat Top mine to a new location "because of the death rate at the prison formerly occupied by them." Carmichael added that he found: "Hundreds and hundreds of persons are taken before the inferior courts of the country, tried and sentenced to hard labor for the county, who would never be arrested except for the matter of fees involved. This is a condition inexcusable, not to say shameful."[14]

"The County Convict System is worse than ever," wrote Shirley Bragg, president of the Board of Inspectors of Convicts, in 1906. "The demand for labor and fees has become so great that most of them now go to the mines where many of them are unfit for such labor, consequently it is not long before they pass from this earth. . . . If the state wishes to kill its convicts it should do it directly and not indirectly."[15]

Bragg was no softhearted interloper in southern affairs. He was a son of a great and once slaveholding Lowndes County plantation family—one whose property had been destroyed, according to family lore, because of their connection to a famous Confederate general during the same raid by Union general Wilson that also freed the Cottingham slaves in 1865.

Yet Bragg, a child during the Civil War, was nauseated by the degradation he witnessed in oversight of the state penal system. "I am more convinced that the ideas of humanity and civilization would be better carried out if the torch were applied to every jail in Alabama. It would be more humane and far better to stake the prisoner out with a ring around his neck like a wild animal than to confine him in places that we call jails, that are reeking with filth and disease and alive with vermin of all kinds," Bragg continued. He called the prison mines, where at last sixty-four miners had died of disease, accidents, or unrecorded causes in the previous two years, "nurseries of death."[16]

Sloss-Sheffield, the successor to John Milner's horrifying Coalburg and Newcastle mines of the 1880s, had long excelled at the exploitation of this county convict system. The old Coalburg mine—scene of more than twenty years of continuous slave labor—was nearly exhausted. To exploit the remaining coal in the area, new managers at Sloss-Sheffield were building a new two-thousand-foot-deep mine nearby, named for Flat Top Mountain, and an adjoining complex of two hundred coke ovens. Work was hastened after a new round of criticism when thirty-two prisoners died at Coalburg of pneumonia, tuberculosis, and other sickness in just the first three months of the year.[17] In September 1902, the company relocated its nearly two hundred state prisoners and nearly a thousand more men purchased from county governments to the vast new Flat Top mine.

But the Pratt Mines complex, so long in production and now so large and intricate that not even the owners could keep up with the locations of all its shafts and underground tangents, outrivaled all other buyers of black men. Spurred by technological advances, Tennessee Coal, Iron & Railroad Co. finally conquered inherent chemical flaws that limited the use of iron ore from its mines and mastered production of steel at a commercially viable cost—the first success at rolling steel in the South. "This great corporation has probably done more toward the industrial development of the South than any other agency," enthused the *Birmingham Age-Herald*.[18]

By the mid-1890s, more than six thousand men toiled in the Pratt Mines, performing dozens of tasks—digging coal, engineering trains, building ovens, loading and unloading cars, washing coal, charging ovens, operating furnaces—the free workers each earning from $1 to $3 per day.[19] About a quarter of the workers were seized through the judicial system, including 504 at Prison No. 2 in June 1900 and another 400 at Prison No. 1.

The number of free laborers surged past ten thousand, as the company's thirty coal mines—including the fourteen on the outskirts of Birmingham—generated nineteen thousand tons a day in 1900. To provide the most critical raw materials in iron and steel production, TCI—as Tennessee Coal, Iron & Railroad was commonly known—operated 3,722 coke ovens and four quarries producing one hundred railroad cars of limestone and dolomite every day. Twenty blast furnaces smelted 3,550 tons of pig iron each day. More than two dozen furnaces generated 830,000 tons of iron and steel, shipped to thirty-five states and eight foreign countries. TCI owned in excess of 400,000 acres of mineral lands.[20]

W. F. Tyler, purchasing agent for TCI's prison mines and fourteen company stores, stocked food, clothing, furniture, and tools to supply ten thousand miners and their families—including provisions for more than one thousand prisoners. "Quote us your lowest price on say 3,000 yards 10 oz wool convict stripes," he wrote to a fabric maker in Columbus, Georgia, in 1899.[21] The company issued pay in its own coinage and paper scrip, emblazoned with the Tennessee Coal, Iron & Railroad Co. name and the promise "Good At All Stores"—the company's stores. By 1900, the enterprises collected $2 million a year in revenue.

Responding to booming demand, TCI invested heavily in its Pratt Mines complex and dozens of other sites across the seemingly boundless coalfields surrounding Birmingham. It spent $7.4 million to open new shafts, refit old mines, and streamline equipment to extract coal from ever deeper in the earth and speed the tasks of sorting, cleaning, and shipping coal to market. The company's operations teemed with more than twelve thousand miners, guards, construction, and the endless clang, steam, and whistles of locomotives and coal cars.

A thriving, permanent town called Pratt City sprang up nearby, with a bustling commercial district, bars, brothels, streetcars, churches, and an overwhelmingly black population. Six miles to the west, another town, Ensley, grew around the company's mushrooming pig iron plant and six open-hearth blast furnaces, each topped with a looming red smokestack perpetually billowing with cinders and toxins. The plants created thousands of the types of skilled jobs that only whites could seek to obtain, and soon more than ten thousand residents crowded into Ensley's houses and hastily erected tenements. TCI's production of train rails and other steel surged to more than four hundred thousand tons annually in the first years of the century.

Scattered everywhere were bulging stacks of rough-cut timber and posts used to shore up the walls and ceilings of mine shafts. Smoke, belching from coke ovens, train engines, and houses, never cleared. The skies were cast with a constant gray haze. In dry weather, a thick black residue of coal coated every flat surface, windowpane, branch, and leaf—insinuating itself under doors and into cupboards of TCI mining camps, inescapable for an army of men and their families. More than a dozen separate major mines near Pratt City soon produced nearly three million tons of coal a year.

Where each shaft disappeared underground, enormous hoist houses contained the elaborate mechanisms—as big as train engines—used to lower coal cars containing miners into the shaft at the beginning of each day and to withdraw them sixteen or eighteen hours later filled with coal. Past the hoist house sat the coal washer—where each day's bituminous produce was washed and any slate or stone accidentally added to the mix removed. Then rose the tipples—massive timbered structures in the design of the huge railroad bridges spanning the great gorges in the West. Trams loaded with cleaned coal were pulled to the end of the tipple and the contents dumped into much larger railroad cars waiting on a track below. From there the coal was rolled to Tennessee Coal, Iron & Railroad's thousands of stone ovens—to be baked into coke.

Dozens of the beehive-shaped coke ovens sat a few hundred feet east of the prison built at the mine called Slope No. 12. Further on, fanning out from the base of the hill was a rowdy community surrounding Slope No. 12 and nine other coal shafts operated by free men. Thousands of miners and their family members were packed into shacks, tenements, and company houses nearby. A private rail line passed through the nearly denuded landscape, connecting the mines, tipples, and furnaces owned by the company. One spur of track reached a mile-long row of another two hundred ovens, visibly pulsating the darkness with their heat. Beyond them, stretched along a fouled stream called Black Creek, was "Smokey Row," an encampment of rough-sawn company houses occupied by free African American miners, many of whom had survived their time in the prison shaft and then stayed on in the town to dig coal for pay.

Tennessee Coal, Iron & Railroad Co. had always been reluctant for politicians, the public, or the region's embryonic unions to realize how lucrative its army of forced laborers had proven to be. Company officials publicly complained about the shiftless and uninspired work of prison laborers and black workers in general. They accused sheriffs of palming off sick and dying men to the mines.

But in fact, the economic value of the slaves scooped up by labor agents across Alabama was enormous. In August 1903, just as Judge Jones was issuing his peonage ruling that, counter to its intention, ratified and codified the process of enslaving young black men, Erskine Ramsey, the longtime chief of the Tennessee's company operations, was privately gloating at the profitability of relying on slaves. "The operation of the convict mines has been very remunerative," Ramsey wrote in a letter to Henry Clay Frick, the notorious Pittsburgh industrialist.[22] After building his own coke and coal company in the 1880s and 1890s, with forty thousand acres of coalfields and twelve thousand coke ovens, Frick became partners with Andrew Carnegie, eventually taking over management of Carnegie Steel Company.

Frick was most well known as the man who during the 1892 Homestead incident ordered a small army of company detectives to make war on workers striking at a Carnegie plant on the Monongahela River in Pennsylvania. A dozen people died. Eventually, the state governor sent in eight thousand militiamen to end the fighting. The strike—and organizing union—were crushed. In 1901, Frick guided Carnegie Steel into the merger that created U.S. Steel. Two years later, Frick was one of the wealthiest individuals in the United States, if not the world, and continued to invest periodically in other industrial enterprises.

Ramsey had known Frick his entire adult life—literally growing up as a mechanic in a Frick coal mine supervised by his father. Later, Ramsey was a prodigy executive in the Frick company, becoming its youngest-ever mine manager. An uncanny engineer and inventor, he moved to Alabama in 1887 to become chief mine engineer for Tennessee Coal, Iron & Railroad. In 1903, Ramsey, who recently had been pushed out of his role as the top official at TCI, was quietly scheming to create a new coal conglomerate in Birmingham. Eventually he would establish Pratt Consolidated Coal Company, which grew to rival the Pratt Mines in size and scope. (The two operations shared the name of Alabama's first frontier industrialist, Daniel Pratt, after whom Alabama's biggest coalfield was named. But the two enterprises were completely independent of each other.)

Ramsey wrote Frick to test his interest in investing in the new projects. Publicly, Ramsey decried the inhumanity of forced labor systems in the mines, but in his letter to Frick the engineer combined a recitation of his last successes at Tennessee Coal, Iron & Railroad, unveiled attacks on the new management, and provided a report on how effectively forced laborers could be managed.

Ramsey wrote that just before leaving the company, he opened a new mine, Slope No. 10, at the Pratt Mines complex. Transferring convicts taken from the company's first slave mine, No. 1, the new prison was successfully obtaining the "cheapest coal ever produced by the Company"—at a cost of 50 cents a ton. Powered by access to an extraordinarily inexpensive and indefensible source of labor, the company reached a record output of 3.4 million tons of coal in 1900 and continued averaging three million or more tons a year into the next decade. The racial nature of the system was obvious. Of the nearly one thousand convicts in the two mines, no more than seventy were white.[23] Without forced laborers, Ramsey's startling successes would have been impossible.

A year after Ramsey's letter to Frick, white miners launched their most ambitious strike ever against Tennessee Coal, Iron & Railroad, seeking acknowledgment of their new union as a collective bargaining entity. Readying for battle, the company shut down their least efficient furnaces, and most significantly, converted two more mines from free workers to forced laborers.[24]

The strike collapsed within twelve months. Explaining the company's rationale for crushing the union, Don Bacon, the president of Tennessee Coal, Iron & Railroad told *The Wall Street Journal:* "Conditions forced upon the management . . . had become intolerable. The authority over your property . . . had to be restored and maintained, or all hope of permanent, successful competition . . . would have to be abandoned."[25]

Slavery, and the ability to obliterate free labor afforded by coerced workers, was seminal to the company's success. It continued to aggressively seek more and more compulsory workers—from the state of Alabama, from any city or county, from any source that would sell them. Sometime between 1903 and 1907, TCI acquired from the family of Fletcher Turner—partner in John Pace's brutal forced labor operation—the limestone quarry at Calcis, where so many men seized off the back roads had been forced into slavery.[26] The Turner family, quietly back in the trade of black men after Fletcher Turner's pardon, continued to operate the quarry for Tennessee Coal, Iron & Railroad.

•  •  •

Nearly a thousand miles—and seemingly a half century in time—removed from the frightening Turner quarry, a historic series of capital events was unfolding in the fall of 1907. A syndicate of Wall Street investors, backed by brokerage firm Moore & Schley, bought a majority stake in the shares of Tennessee Coal, Iron & Railroad. Armed with new financing from the syndicate, the company launched a major expansion of steelmaking capacity. Its output of iron ingots increased to 400,000 tons in 1906. The following year, it won an order for 157,000 tons of steel rails for the Union Pacific and Southern Pacific railroads—a direct challenge to the hegemony of U.S. Steel Corporation, the great conglomerate of the North.[27]

But economic turmoil around the world was rattling the network of trusts that had come to dominate Wall Street. These highly speculative banks and financiers paid exorbitant interest rates, maintained lower cash reserves, invested heavily in risky schemes, and backed investors seeking to monopolize key commodities. The future of the great trusts was also in growing doubt due to a push by President Roosevelt to punish John Rockefeller's Standard Oil. A wide-ranging criminal indictment of Standard Oil, alleging illegal pricing practices, rattled the market. In late October, the failure of two prominent stock speculators in a bid to take over United Copper Company led to the bankruptcy of two Wall Street brokerages, a bank, and another mining company. As word spread of the failed scheme and its effect on other prominent bankers, panic set into the markets. Suddenly, multiple trust banks were under threat, and dozens of stock brokerages appeared poised to disintegrate.

To stave off a complete collapse of the New York Stock Exchange and the national depression that might follow, J. P. Morgan, patriarch of the gilded Morgan Bank and architect of the 1901 merger that had created U.S. Steel, began propping up ailing trust banks and investment houses with infusions of his own cash and from other bankers working with him. On October 28, Morgan and two other bankers agreed to loan $30 million to the city of New York, to prevent a failure of the local government.

Five days later, still battling to hold Wall Street together, Morgan concluded that he needed to simultaneously rescue three desperately threatened investment houses, Trust Company of America, Lincoln Trust, and

Moore & Schley, the brokerage that had backed the takeover the previous year of Tennessee Coal, Iron & Railroad Co. The firm's shares of TCI had been placed as collateral for $25 million in loans that Moore & Schley could not pay off. It would soon be forced to liquidate the stake—the beginnings of a sell-off that Morgan believed might wreck Wall Street.

Morgan proposed that U.S. Steel prevent the dumping of Moore & Schley's stock by buying the stake for a fraction of its value. In return, the presidents of the great Wall Street trusts had to agree to provide $25 million to help bail out the other banks. Henry Clay Frick, still a major owner of U.S. Steel, recognized the potentially vast value of obtaining Tennessee Coal, Iron & Railroad's mineral holdings and of eliminating it as a competitor. The chief executive of U.S. Steel, a former Illinois judge named Elbert H. Gary closely allied with Morgan, agreed to the purchase only on the condition that the White House first give a promise not to attack the deal as a violation of new anti-monopoly laws.

After an all-night negotiation in Morgan's offices beginning Saturday, November 2, the terms of the deal were hammered out. Judge Gary and Frick sped for Washington at midnight in a special single Pullman car. Interrupting the president's breakfast, they laid out the details of the transaction to Roosevelt and Secretary of State Elihu Root, emphasizing the potential for a national economic disaster if the stock markets weren't reassured.

Within twenty minutes, the president, freshly returned from a Louisiana bear-hunting trip, agreed to support the buyout—one of the biggest financial transactions in the history of American capitalism to that date. Roosevelt wired Attorney General Charles J. Bonaparte that the federal government would not oppose the merger. Judge Gary called Morgan at his offices. Word of the deal spread through Wall Street as the stock exchange opened on Monday morning. The panic subsided. U.S. Steel took control of Tennessee Coal, Iron & Railroad for $45 million—a minuscule fraction of the estimated $1 billion value of its Pratt Mines and other assets in Alabama.[28]

That TCI was the largest customer of the Alabama slavery system Roosevelt had once championed the destruction of was not discussed at the White House breakfast. Three weeks later, U.S. Steel's newly installed president of its Alabama property, thirty-eight-year-old George G. Crawford, signed a new lease to acquire four hundred prisoners from the state of Alabama for use in the company's No. 10 and No. 3 mines.

Crawford agreed to pay $42 per month for the strongest laborers and agreed to pay $10 for the weakest. The contract made clear that as soon as the company's newest prison mine, a deep shaft called Slope No. 12, was ready, as many prisoners as possible would be shifted there.[29]

# PART THREE

■ ■ ■

## THE FINAL CHAPTER
## OF AMERICAN SLAVERY

# XIII

## THE ARREST OF
## GREEN COTTENHAM

### *A War of Atrocities*

Green Cottenham huddled behind the worn, whitewashed walls of the train depot in Columbiana. It was a clear, brisk Thursday—sunny and crisp before noon, the temperature easing toward the 70s by early afternoon. Green walked to the train station to play dice, or to find a day's labor, or for some other claimed reason that in truth was no different from any other. The train station was simply where he went almost every day, where nearly all young black men found themselves.

The freight docks of the station in Columbiana, and in every other county seat on the Southern Railway line between Birmingham and Eufaula, a lush cotton center deep in southern Alabama, were the hub of life for African American men in the South in 1908. Open freight cars, easily boarded as trains eased out of towns like Columbiana or when they slowed to cross rickety bridges and tight curves, were the only mechanized means of movement for the armies of destitute blacks searching or waiting for work in the first years of the century—especially those like Green who had uncoupled themselves from the traditional black life of serfdom in a cotton patch. The tracks themselves, removed from the view of most whites, were the safest paths for walking from town to town as well. Either way, a man on the rails or the trains was violating Alabama law by entering the property of a railroad company. But the appeal of motion and movement, of opportunity, that the tracks and trains represented was too much for a young man like Green to resist.

That spring, there were hardly any jobs for cash to be had for a black man, unless he was willing to take up a cotton hoe or venture into the giant lumber camps on the rail lines thrusting into the swampy jungle forests below the Florida state line, or across the Georgia border. Railroad companies claimed to pay $2 a day for a strong hand who could handle an axe, cutting trees or shaping rail ties. But the railroad camps sat at the ends of long spurs cut into near-virgin forests, with no roads or other means of exit except via the trains that brought more fresh backs every day. Once a man arrived, there was no departing unless the camp boss allowed it. And there was no knowing whether the Southern Railway or any other company would keep its word to pay the amount it promised, or even to feed men or keep them out of the rain and swamps. Guards with shotguns and dogs patrolled the perimeters of the worksites. The captains of the camps kept long leather straps, affixed to thick wooden handles, to beat men who tried to flee. County sheriffs developed an uncanny eye for spotting any fleeing African Americans who made it through the woods to a farm or town, and received rewards for hauling them back in chains.

That was the work available to an independent black man like Green: free labor camps that functioned like prisons, cotton tenancy that equated to serfdom, or prison mines filled with slaves. The alternatives, reserved for African Americans who crossed a white man or the law, were even more grim. Still, the freight depots were a magnet of excitement. There was always in some corner a simple game of dice being played for pennies or tobacco. Now and again, the freight agent or some farmer in town with a wagon would pay a man a nickel or a quarter to help move a trolley of crates from an open freight car. In picking season, white men would come to the station every day looking for extra hands in the cotton fields, apprising on sight—by the look of their hands or the smell of liquor on their breath—whether an African American boy or man was worth paying for a week's work in his fields, or whether they belonged to the new class of independent blacks that whites saw as the scourge of their lives and towns.

Regardless of their conclusions, every African American was a *nigger* in a white man's eyes. So the term for those African American men deemed specifically worthless for their defiant attitudes was "cigarette dudes." These were men cocky by comparison to their peers; they had learned some reading and writing, and sometimes worked and sometimes slouched on street corners. Sometimes cigarettes sat akilter on their lips. There was likely a bottle of moonshine or a pistol in a pocket somewhere among each throng of young men gawking from their poses against the board and batten walls of the freight station. Instead of threadbare overalls, the uniform of all blacks and poor country whites for as long as anyone could remember, these men might wear trousers and jackets, even neckties. They stood by the dozens in the studio of a black photographer in Columbiana, cigarette dudes lounging with their arms draped around black girls in their best Sunday dresses, glaring at the lens. On their faces an air of defiant confidence, visages of the men they knew they should have been allowed to be. Among a population of 8.5 million blacks in the southern states, crushed into subservience in the forty years since the Civil War, these men were the last refuges of resistance as the twentieth century dawned.

According to almost every white, these cigarette dudes were the source of every trouble in the South. These were the blacks never to be hired, never to be befriended—to be denied embrocation of any kind. To be rid of them forever, by whatever means could accomplish that goal, was something nearly every white man in the South, most certainly in Columbiana, had openly called for and worked toward for at least three decades.

This was the snare waiting for Green Cottenham at the Columbiana railroad station on March 30, 1908. On the prior day, a Wednesday, the sheriff's chief deputy, a scrawny white man named Newton Eddings, grabbed Monroe Dolphus, a black man about Green's age, as he stood in the train yard of the depot. The deputy seized Cottenham the following day and tossed him into the same fetid cell where Dolphus had spent the night. There was uncertainty about what charges against the men should be entered into the prison registry at the jail.

Initially, Eddings claimed that the crime committed by Dolphus was taking a 25 cent tin of fish from the lunch pail of a Southern Railway worker. Cottenham was charged with riding a freight train without a ticket. There was no tangible evidence that either man had committed any infraction at all.

Taken before Judge Longshore the following day, Cottenham and Dolphus each denied the charges. Eddings was unable to produce any evidence or witnesses to convict them. But sticking to the cynical script followed thousands of times in the South, Judge Longshore chose not the release the men anyway. Instead, he declared them guilty of "vagrancy," that catchall offense to which any black man was vulnerable at almost any time.[1]

Longshore sentenced both Dolphus and Cottenham to three months of hard labor for Tennessee Coal, Iron & Railroad. Under its standing contract with Shelby County, the company would pay the county $12 per month for each man as long as he worked in their mines.[2] The two prisoners were also ordered to pay fees to the sheriff, judge, and other local officials totaling $31.85 for Dolphus, $38.40 for Cottenham—extraordinary sums for an unemployed black man. Unable to pay those costs, Dolphus was ordered to work an extra two months and twenty days at the mines to cover the fees. Cottenham would have to spend an additional three months and six days.[3]

A day later, Eddings arrived at the county jail with his shiny, six-inch-barreled Colt .38 pistol in a holster dangling against his thigh. A simple metal badge pinned to his coat read "Deputy Sheriff." He carried thick round manacles connected with three tight steel links. A trace of chains was draped over his shoulder. Eddings barked for Cottenham and the nine other men in the Shelby County cells to get up. It was time to go to "Pratts."

The jail sat at the corner of South Main and Mildred streets, almost directly across from the spare old county courthouse that the town fathers had just abandoned for their ostentatious new structure three blocks to the north.

Green had never felt irons before that day.[4] As Deputy Eddings clapped a shackle on his left ankle, Green must have been surprised how quickly his skin began to bruise, how heavily the rings of iron clung to the ground between himself and Monroe Dolphus. Then there was the startling sharp cold of the steel when Eddings slipped a metal collar around his neck.

Eddings locked the clasp on Green and did the same to "Mun," as the men called Dolphus, and then to each of the other eight prisoners in the lockup that morning. Earley Bolling, House Pearson, and four others had been arrested at the train station too and convicted for hopping a ride on an empty freight car without permission. Henry Witherspoon was found guilty of petit larceny—a crime applied to the theft of any object worth more than $10. John Jones, arrested as he played dice inside a circle of other black men squatted in the dirt on the edges of the railroad yard, was convicted of gambling. Once all ten were chained together, Eddings told them to start walking back to the railway station. They trudged out the scuffed rear door of the jailhouse and around the corner, passing by the back porch of Sheriff Fulton's wood-frame house next door and on toward Main Street.

All in the ragged group were still in the street clothes they had worn at the time of their arrest. But now the men were smeared with the filth of the jail's grimy, wet interior. Most had been there for several weeks, waiting for the monthly delivery to Tennessee Coal, Iron & Railroad. Several walked shakily, taken aback by the bright sunlight and unbalanced by subsistence on the sheriff's meager rations and the partial sleep of nights on remnants of putrid bedding.[5] As they passed the sheriff's home, the men crossed the shadow of the jail, looming above them, higher than all the surrounding structures, the face of the massive tower interrupted only by the keyhole window in the hanging chamber.[6] On a Saturday morning three months later, the sheriff would release the trapdoor of the scaffold there, and Tom Patterson, a thirty-eight-year-old black man convicted of murder, would twist to his death at the end of the rope.

At the station, Eddings took Green and the other prisoners to the far end of the platform to wait for the early morning train. They rode the one-hour journey in the baggage car. Outside the Birmingham depot, Eddings piled the shackled men into an open, horse-drawn wagon he had telegraphed ahead to hire. Two mules slowly pulled Green and the others away from the city's bustling center, then through the tempestuous streets of Pratt City, past a haphazard cemetery bulging with dead prisoners' remains near Smokey Row, and finally up the long hill rising from the saloons and whorehouses past the Catholic church to Tennessee Coal, Iron & Railroad's newly completed wooden stockade at Slope No. 12.

It was a familiar journey for Eddings, and one he didn't mind. He had delivered more than sixty men to the Pratt Mines in the previous twelve months, nearly all of them black men he had himself rounded up and testi-

fied against to obtain conviction. As chief deputy, Eddings made consider-
ably less than the high sheriff, but the business of arresting blacks and getting them to the Pratt Mines was a good one for a scantly educated man
from deep in the countryside. He'd come to Columbiana to get away from
the drudgery of the isolated farm road where his father and older brother
lorded over his childhood, while the mother who gave birth to him midway
through the Civil War grew progressively demented. By the time Eddings
reached manhood, she was fully insane.[7]

Sometimes it seemed the whole South was insane in 1908. Vast numbers
of freed slaves and their offspring like Green had abandoned their former
owners' lands and scattered across the rural landscape, demanding wages and,
almost as ridiculously to whites such as Eddings's father, insisting on written
contracts to be paid for their labor—despite that only the rarest among blacks
could write their own names, much less read the words on the page. Still,
blacks insisted upon it, and whites initially acquiesced, knowing that cotton
could not be grown and picked without black labor. Stranger still, until just
barely a decade earlier, in the counties to the south of Eddings's boyhood
home, where slaves had outnumbered whites before the war, tens of thousands of African Americans continued to cast ballots in every election. Only
the sustained war of atrocities against African Americans in every section had
finally forced them to fully submit to Alabama's new constitution and its provisions banning them from the vote and any aspects of legal equality. Still, a
perverse cloud hung over the state of white and black coexistence.

The New South, with its rising great cities of Birmingham and Atlanta,
railroads and factories, was by contrast a utopia compared to the civil battlefields of the countryside. Like thousands of other young southern whites
and crowds of young blacks, Deputy Eddings fled the scarred rural landscape for a semblance of civilization and opportunity. Now, at the age of
forty-two, he was fully a town man, moving on the edge of the circle of
leaders who were shaping Columbiana into a model of what prosperous
Alabama wished to be in the young twentieth century. He enjoyed the
monthly trips, or sometimes more often if the mines needed more men, to
deliver African Americans to Pratt City. He ignored the prisoners' pleas to
let them escape and their promises to bring him cash from a father or uncle
if he would set them free.

When girlfriends or mothers of young black men came begging at the jailhouse, he couldn't help but be tempted. The carnal pleasures of taking a black girl when you pleased had been a privilege of rich white men for so long in the South. Now simple men like Eddings could do the same—telling girls to come around to the jailer's room for an hour of compulsory sexual performance in exchange for a favor to their man inside. It was hardly even furtive. Guards did the same at hundreds of jails. At the lumber camps in southern Alabama, women seeking the freedom of their men were simply arrested when they arrived, chained into their cells, and kept to serve the physical desires of the men running the camps. The slave camps and mines produced scores of babies—nearly all of them with white fathers.[8]

There was no risk of penalty to any white law enforcement officer who chose to force himself on a black woman who presented herself in the vulnerable circumstances of a jail. To all whites, these were by definition worthless women—even more worthless than other black females. Even many African Americans, terrified of losing further respect or security among whites, looked askance at any black who became associated with prisoners and debt slavery. These women were friendless and abandoned even among their own. And the laws of the South were interpreted explicitly to ensure that the rape or coercion of a black woman by a white man would almost never be prosecuted as a crime.

Indeed, South Carolina governor Cole Blease, citing his belief in the animalistic inability of blacks to control themselves, routinely pardoned the killers of black men, especially in the case of African Americans committing violence against African Americans. "This is the case of one negro killing another—the old familiar song—'Hot supper; liquor; dead negro,'" the governor wrote in one explanation of a pardon. As for sexual assaults of black women, Governor Blease asserted it was the nature of every African American woman to want sex at any opportunity. "Adultery seems to be their most favorite pastime," he said. "I have . . . very serious doubt as to whether the crime of rape can be committed upon a negro."[9]

On each trip to Pratt, Tennessee Coal, Iron & Railroad Co. paid Eddings a fee for every African American, in addition to his expenses for train fares, meals, wagon rental from the livery, and, occasionally, lodging in the city when Eddings couldn't make the last train back to Columbiana.

Arresting, convicting, and transporting these prisoners was Eddings's primary livelihood. His and Sheriff Fulton's entire compensation came from an assortment of fees charged for every action taken by the office and paid into the Shelby County Fine and Forfeiture Fund. The courts collected fees for serving subpoenas, foreclosing on delinquent loans, arresting and testifying against criminal defendants—tacking the charges onto the fines levied against nearly every person brought before the county or circuit judge. Eddings and the sheriff—along with the court clerk, the town solicitor, jury members, witnesses, and nearly any other white person who played a part in the seizure and conviction of each prisoner—were awarded fees by the judge and received warrants to exchange for the money as the prisoner's labor paid down his fines. Since that typically took months, or years, the sheriff and others accumulated court-issued scrip for the money—IOUs of a sort. Over time, they cashed the redeemable warrants as money accumulated in the county coffers.

The remuneration was often lucrative. Sheriff Fulton, a smooth-shaven man partial to bow ties, was already balding when he was first elected at age thirty-one in 1906. He defeated the former chief deputy by just seven votes—and even then only by packing the ballot box with votes cast by dead men. (Fulton was thrown out of office by a judge two years later for the fraud, but never pursued criminally.) During the November before Green Cottenham was arrested, Fulton cashed out a stack of scrip stemming from sixty-five different cases in the prior year, and collected a total of $373.50— equivalent to about $7,000 a century later.

More lucrative still, Sheriff Fulton, like all his counterparts in Alabama, also was allowed to keep whatever excess remained from the state's monthly "feeding" payments received for food provided to prisoners in the jail. Since nearly all the arrests in the county were of black men who were soon shipped to Pratt Mines, they required little more than cornmeal mush and pork fat, which Sheriff Fulton's wife could prepare. Unlike the occasional white man thrown into the jail, the black prisoners, nearly all of them itinerants with no local families or white landowners to speak for them, could neither say nor do anything about the scant provisions.

Deputy Eddings arrived at the Pratt Mines complex and continued up the hill, past the coke ovens, to the new Slope No. 12 mine at Booker City, a black neighborhood bought up by Tennessee Coal, Iron & Railroad when a thick mineral vein was identified there a year earlier. He delivered Cottenham, Dolphus, and the others to the prison captain. What the company's mine boss and guards did with Cottenham, or any of the hundreds of other black men they purchased, was entirely up to them.

Even as a child of two former slaves, versed in the old people's stories of whips and dogs and weeks spent with feet blistered and fingers bleeding from picking cotton, Green had never conjured anything so foreign as what he witnessed on the surface and in the catacombs beneath Pratt City.

For five days after arriving at Slope No. 12, Green Cottenham had not seen the rising dawn or the setting sun. It was not as if he were a "farm Negro," panging to be on the land and in the sun like so many of the others around him. It was not as if he had never before been in the company of brutish or crude men. And it was not as if he had never before been compelled to spend his days in grueling labor. But however contemptuous he might have been of the whining country boys shivering and sniveling at the shouts of the crew boss, and however boldly he may have challenged any man to touch him, Green could not have been prepared for his fate befallen here.

Green spent every day but one in a vast labyrinth of black rock tunnels, shared only by dozens of dirty mules and squadrons of desperate men, all slick with sweat and coated in pulverized coal. The absence of sunlight, vegetation, or any prospect for the touch of a not venal human hand had to tear at his soul.

Long before sunrise each morning, two white men swung open the doors from the entryway at the center of the wooden prison barrack and pushed into the rancid wooden cavern where Green and two hundred other black men, chained to one another, lay wrapped in coarse blankets. Running the fifty-foot length of the room, a continual series of bunk beds dangling on pipes attached to the ceiling were piled with bodies. Where there was no space on a surface, men draped themselves in suspended contortions across canvas hammocks stretched between the bunks on either side of a narrow aisle down the center. A single potbellied stove, long gone cold, stood at the center of the room.

On Saturday, April 11, 1908, the sudden opening of the doorway ushered in a blast of crisp spring air, cutting with swift relief through the musty wet stink of the men, still sheathed in the black detritus of the mine waiting for them outside. As the guards moved toward the opposite end of the room, releasing the men's irons from chains looped through their beds and barking for reluctant prisoners to wake, the men responded in an awkward, collective undulation. As each awakened and moved, a succession of pairs of legs and irons slid wearily toward the keys held in the hands of the guard, each time pulling the legs of the next man toward the guard as well, and then the next, and the next, all of them spilling gradually off the bunks in a long, groggy metallic jangle.

Once on their feet and refastened to their chains, Green and the column of prisoners filed out through a front stoop, down the wooden steps, and into a plain kitchen. Each man stuffed a biscuit and a cut of cold bacon into his mouth and shuffled out the door. At the point of shotguns, they tramped into the deep darkness, across the bare yard, past the pen of bloodhounds trained to track "Negro scent," past the barrel across which men were stretched naked almost nightly to be whipped with a leather strap, out the mammoth gate of the stockade, and up to the orifice where they would enter the earth.

There, high on the ridge above Pratt City, Green for a moment would have glimpsed the luminescence of the industrial spectacle throbbing atop the geological wonder of the coal and iron ore discovered beneath the hills of northern Alabama. There had been nothing more than one prosperous farm in this valley forty years earlier, but now in 1908 a city of nearly 150,000 people was consuming the land. The acrid smell of coal smoke never dissipated. On the farthest horizon glowed the Sloss Furnaces, where Col. James W. Sloss, the man more responsible than any other for the sensational economic boom of what was called "the Magic City," had presided over a conflagration of fire, machines, and molten iron unlike anything ever before seen in the South. In the valley between the high smokestacks of the furnaces and the hilltop perch of Slope No. 12, the lights of new office buildings and churches glimmered at the commercial center of Birmingham.

One can only imagine what filled Green's mind as he walked toward the manway to Slope No. 12 in the darkness that Saturday morning. Farther than he had ever been in his twenty-two years from the two counties—Bibb and Shelby—where his family, first as slaves, then as freedmen, lived for four generations, blinking through the darkness and the grit in his eyes, he must have studied the molded letters in the concrete archway above the portal spelling the name of the company that for all intents and purposes owned him then as much as old Elisha Cottingham had owned his father and grandfather. Perhaps he mouthed the words—Tennessee Coal, Iron & Railroad Co.—and then craned his neck to glimpse behind him the clinking column of slaves, the glow of the city, and, beyond, a last flash of stars and predawn sky.

# XIV

# ANATOMY OF A SLAVE MINE

*"Degraded to a plane lower than the brutes."*

By all accounts, Slope No. 12 was the finest prison ever built in Alabama. The two-story wood-frame dormitory, constructed in the shape of a giant T, stood at the center of the fenced compound where Green Cottenham was deposited by Deputy Eddings. From the front door, atop ten steps beneath a small portico, the prison extended outward in three wings. The six "sleeping rooms" were each large enough to accommodate up to sixty men sleeping in close quarters on the odd swinging bunk beds. One room was reserved for whites only. A contained walkway connected the building to a kitchen immediately to the rear.

Inside, prisoners young and old, hardened and innocent, mingled whenever they were not chained apart. On Sundays, the one day of rest, card and dice games continued unceasingly. "They will gamble the buttons off their clothes," an inmate told one visitor. Sexual abuse was rampant, in the darkness of the prison and the isolation of the mine shaft. "Sodomy is prevalent among these massed men," wrote journalist Shelby Harrison in 1912, after a visit to Pratt No. 12. "The older men pick out the young ones to make advances to. It is commonly said in some of the camps that every prisoner has his 'gal-boy.' "[1]

Across a field of grass cropped close by goats wandering inside the compound stood the officers' quarters, a simple but spacious two-level house with a veranda and rocking chairs flanking three sides. Nearby was a mess hall for the guards. A pressurized water spigot—a luxury—stood beside the front porch. A tin cup and towel hung permanently on a nail, where officers stopped for a drink or to wash on the way inside at mealtimes.

At the opposite corner of the enclosure stood a storehouse, where prisoners fortunate enough to have any money could buy from their keepers tobacco or extra rations on Sundays. Nearby was a small hospital building where the sick could be segregated. When the mine opened in early 1908, with a workforce made up totally of forced laborers, state officials declared the prison the "best in the state."

For more than a decade, Tennessee Coal, Iron & Railroad—irritated by criticism that its mines and furnaces were inferior to those of competitors in the North and that its miners, free and forced, worked at perpetual risk to their lives—had invested heavily in dramatic technological improvements and fresh underground exploration. The new prison cost $54,570— a substantial sum.

The company installed thousands of additional coke ovens, added miles of new railroad track, and developed a breakthrough technique for forging steel train rails—a first for any company in the South. On the outskirts of Birmingham, at the edge of Red Mountain, the company built a new complex of deep-shaft iron ore mines. Tennessee Coal, Iron & Railroad also was abandoning its old system of dragging coal to the surface in carts pulled by mules and installing steam-powered systems using cables to pull enormously greater tonnage of coal from the shafts.[2]

With U.S. Steel's acquisition of Tennessee Coal, Iron & Railroad in November 1907, the pace of new construction and advancements in the mines accelerated rapidly. But with the company's progress also came destruction. On the surface, the toxic effluent of the digging was pumped into wooden flues that poured into vast, fouled moonscapes of dead forest. Nearby, steam shovels clawed scars fifty feet deep and hundreds of feet wide into the landscape to lay bare ore, limestone, and other minerals. Near every mine—especially those in long operation—gargantuan mounds of slag, the worthless rock drawn out with the coal, loomed ever larger on the horizon.[3]

The shafts closest to the center of Pratt City—some of them in production for more than two decades—were depleting. Most had already been repeatedly extended, first hundreds of feet below the surface and then for

thousands of feet horizontally, following the thick deposits of coal threading from the Pratt seam. The longer the mine shaft grew, the slower and
more expensive it became to remove coal from the mine—prompting the
company to install new shafts to the surface closer to the most active areas
of mining.

Even the construction of the model new prison carried an ironic
human cost. In 1902, leaders of the Colored Methodist Episcopal Church
bought ten acres in a new residential development designed by a white investor as a refuge for prosperous African Americans on the outskirts of Birmingham. The place was called Booker City—after Booker T. Washington.
The African American church opened a small and struggling high school
for black children, similar to the Calhoun School in Lowndes County, on
an elevated point three miles from the center of the Pratt Mines complex.

Five years later, Tennessee Coal, Iron & Railroad recognized that the
acreage owned by the black school would be an ideal location for a new
mine. In return for thirty acres of property in another location and $30,000,
the church sold the property on which the Slope No. 12 prison would soon
be built. A year later, the Methodists opened a new four-year institution for
African Americans, named Miles Memorial College, in honor of a former
slave who became a famous church bishop after the Civil War.[4]

At the same time, Tennessee Coal, Iron & Railroad built Slope No. 12
and its prison compound. Connecting the mine and prison to the company's coke ovens and industrial infrastructure was a new railroad spur
snaking along a ridge rising from Pratt City's old convict cemetery to the
site of the then empty Booker City High School.

The black Methodists there had struggled to keep their school operating and
its desks and teaching positions filled. There was no such difficulty with the
prison that succeeded it. Under the lease U.S. Steel quickly signed with the
state of Alabama, the company could shift four hundred convicts from two
other Pratt Mines to No. 12. U.S. Steel also obtained leases on hundreds
more county prisoners. Under a contract with Jefferson County, the company paid the local government nearly $60,000—equal to about $1.1 million
a century later—to acquire every prisoner arrested during 1908.[5]

Similar standing agreements were in place with twenty other Alabama counties, setting the prices for each laborer between $9 per month for Choctaw County and $28.50 for prisoners captured in the state capital of Montgomery.[6] New leases entered into by U.S. Steel after it bought TCI were supposed to guarantee a steady stream of convicts until at least the end of 1912.[7]

The supply of forced labor became even more critical as tensions mounted between the coal-mining companies of Birmingham and the local United Mine Workers organization—which had aggressively organized more than ten thousand free miners in Alabama. Convicts—who had no choice but to continue digging coal under whatever circumstances the company demanded—were crucial to maintaining operations during a strike or other labor interruption.

Through the spring and summer of 1908, the number of men purchased for use in Slope No. 12 steadily climbed—by August reaching nearly six hundred prisoners taken from county sheriffs and just under four hundred from the state.[8] Of the sixty men delivered by Deputy Eddings in the twelve months before Cottenham's arrest, nearly half were charged with "jumping"—or riding a freight train without a ticket. Eddings's jail registry said George Roberson was sent on a conviction for "assault with a stick." Another black man, Lou William, was sold to Slope No. 12 for adultery. John Jones had been sold for gambling.[9]


All his life, Green had heard of Tennessee Coal, Iron & Railroad. Every African American in Alabama had been told stories about the vast prison mines at Pratt City. For a generation it loomed over the lives of black people, a mysterious hell in living earth buried beneath a licentious mining boomtown. Men sent there for three months or six months instead disappeared for a year, or forever. The few men who straggled back to their homeplaces told of a whole city of mines, where shafts crisscrossed the subterranean world like a crazy quilt of streets with hundreds of underground "rooms," sometimes nearly intersecting with the shafts of other mines. Other mines named Flat Top, Coalburg, and Banner, owned by different companies, cut from nearby camps into the fabulous seam of bituminous coal coursing, four feet thick in some places, through the low ridges of northern Alabama.

Like Pratt City, the mines at Flat Top and Coalburg were packed with black men forced underground at gunpoint. The others filled each day with white men paid by the hour who despised the black convicts, partly out of the habit of despising African Americans but more now for the crippling damage their presence did to the free miners' pleas for better wages and working conditions.

Sometimes the convicts laughed at how the free miners so hated them, as if black laborers chained to their beds had *chosen* to be there. It was another sign that most white people seemed to be simply crazy when it came to the lives of black people. No sane man who had ever visited Flat Top, with its two thousand desperate black prisoners, or the slopes at Pratt City, filled with 1,500 emaciated African American laborers, black whipping guards, and the white captains who wielded the lash as mercilessly as any of the old slave masters, could believe such a thing.


Shortly after Slope No. 12 opened in 1907, arrangements were made for a series of celebratory photographs for the company. At the storehouse, convicts stand in bright white uniforms. The grassy yard is pristine and dotted with newly planted banana trees ready to unfurl their long, wide leaves. The fence around the compound is hidden in trees. But behind the barred windows, Slope No. 12 and the other prison shafts at Pratt were beginning a hellish headlong descent in the chaotic aftermath of U.S. Steel's abrupt takeover.

In February, three months after the merger, a wave of pneumonia and tuberculosis swept through the prison miners, killing nine. In March, six more convicts died of tuberculosis, including Roberson, the Shelby County man convicted of "assault with a stick."

Nearly all the men thrown into Slope No. 12 shared the same difficult background of deep poverty and the circumscribed opportunities of their Black Belt origins. They came in hues every man of the Black Belt could describe—deep dark like country night, gingercake, the high yellow of mulattoes, the sharp features of red bone. They were farmhands mostly. Baptists and African Methodists. Nearly all were the children or grandchildren of slaves. Most knew the families who had once owned their kin. They all knew no black man would ever see justice in the prisons of white men.

Yet in the bowels of Slope No. 12, there was little more kinship of skin than that. When Green arrived, nearly a thousand laborers toiled in the same grueling rhythm. Transported deep into the shaft on the same narrow gauge trams that would be used to carry out the coal they mined from the soft bituminous seam, each man carried a pick, a shovel with a short handle, a sledgehammer, and two iron or wooden wedges.

Once deep in the mine, the convicts were parceled in pairs into narrow "rooms" carved at right angles from the sides of the main shaft under the seam of coal. Many of the rooms were more like long tunnels—some as tall as four feet but many barely two feet high and two feet wide. The circumscribed chambers extended more than twenty-five feet from the main shaft, forcing Green and other miners to slide on their stomachs a distance five or more times the length of their bodies. The cavities were illuminated by flickering lanterns hooked on leather straps around their heads. Shaped like a small teapot, a lantern held a reservoir of oil, with a wick running through the snout to the flame.

Crouched or lying in the claustrophobic space, with no light other than the feeble flame of his oil or carbide headlamp, Green slung his steel pick in constricted sidelong arcs, shattering the worthless stone and rock below the coal. He drove wedges into the coal to separate sections weighing a half ton or more. After enough slams of the sledge, the huge slabs of coal cracked free, sometimes unexpectedly for inexperienced convicts, landing in thunderous crashes inches from the prostrate miners. When men worked entirely beneath the coal seam, they installed wooden supports called sprags to prevent an unexpected collapse. Sometimes only blasting powder—wrapped in newspaper to make simple cartridges and placed in holes drilled at the edge of the seam—could separate the coal from surrounding rock. Lighting a cartridge with a crude fuse, the miners hurried out of the room and back into the shaft seconds before the ceiling of coal collapsed with the explosion. Many men were caught by the falling coal and killed or maimed.

Once broken free, the coal was hammered into fifty- and hundred-pound pieces and loaded into the train cars. Once a day, another prisoner came by with a bucket containing portions of crude food.

Here there was little of the field hand or rail bed singing that Green had heard among country blacks back in Bibb County, no community of shared perseverance. There was only the furious scramble to crack and pry and stack and sort the rock and coal, and watch other stone-faced men moving in the shadowy dark.

Each day, Green spent nearly every waking hour stretched in a room off the main shaft. Once the coal was freed and broken up, he loaded coal furiously as a boss, another black convict, snarled that he would feel the whip if Green mixed rock with the coal in the wagons to be pulled from the mine sixteen hours later. After six days in Slope No. 12, Green had only to return to the mine once more before Sunday, the one day of rest and of daylight. After that, there would be twenty-four more Sundays before his time in the mine was scheduled to end.

If the worst of a day in Slope No. 12 had been only the physically wracking intensity of the labor, then this sentence, even if meted out by a crude sheriff for the flimsiest alleged infraction against the law, might have been bearable. But there was far worse. Green and Mun were fortunate that they were strapping, grown men, at the peak of their physical strengths. They were fortunate too that their stay with the sheriff had lasted only three days, not long enough for the starvation rations to weaken them materially.

The prison mine in some respects was an improvement over the Shelby County jail. The men were fed semiregularly. A doctor lived in the simple "hospital" across the yard—a big advance over earlier medical care at Pratt Mines, which consisted of a crude one-room shed, with barn doors, a dirt floor, and one window for light.[10]

Conditions at the Pratt Mines had improved since the deadly epidemics of disease that regularly occurred in the 1880s and 1890s—but only marginally. Inside the shafts, deadly gases accumulated in unventilated sections, work continued even as water, seeping from the walls and fouled with the miners' waste and excrement, accumulated in the shafts. Intestinal disorders, malaria, pneumonia, and respiratory problems dogged the men. Endless contact with coal dust led to black lung disease, a miserable and certain slow death.

Hardly a week passed that accidents didn't take men's fingers, hands, toes, or worse. Often the cause was a careless swing of a pick. But almost as frequently men were crushed by coal falling before they expected, or pinned by railroad cars that derailed. After electric trolleys and lights were installed in some areas, many a miner died from "touching a live wire," according to state inspectors.

Younger and smaller men—and the dozens of pubescent boys forced into the shafts—on their first days in the mines faced a terrible initiation. Argued over—often violently—by the convicts with bitter months and years of time in the mine behind them, the boys were pushed into corners of the pitch black mine rooms, beaten into submission with the handles of the pickaxes or rough leather belts worn by the men, and raped daily and nightly. Disagreements over ownership of the sodomized "gal-boys" or other infractions of the prisoners' code erupted into bizarre violence. Men made huge by their years of labor and hardened by their fates attacked each other in the constricted spaces with axes, knives, rocks, and bare hands. Homicides were a constant occurrence.

The ranks of those condemned to the mines were so broadly uneducated and illiterate—even by the elementary standards of 1908—that hardly any eyewitness accounts were recorded of the nightmarish episodes beneath the surface. The shame of witnessing—or being a participant in—such acts further stifled acknowledgment of the rapes and violence that accompanied them. But virtually every surviving account of life in the slave mines referred in at least muted tones to these spectacles of sexual abuse. One white man wrote after his release how "men, degraded to a plane lower than the brutes, are guilty of the unmentionable crimes referred to by the Apostle Paul in his letter to the Romans." He cited the verse: "The men, leaving the natural use of the woman, burned in their lusts one toward another, men with men, working that which is unseemly."[11]

As shocking as the sodomy were the official punishments of the mines and convict labor camps administered under the sanction of government authority. At the end of the day, whatever had happened deep in the earth, each man was held to account for the coal he collected while in the shaft. Healthy prisoners such as Green and Mun were required to produce eight tons each day. Any man who came up short of his assigned "task" was subject to the whip—held over a barrel by two other black men with his shirt removed and his pants pushed to his knees as the white mine superintendent or the designated whipping boss lashed him with a thick, four-inch-wide strap of leather. On some days, as many as two or three dozen men felt the bite of forty or fifty strokes. Those who chronically failed to meet task were beaten every day, often in the morning as well to remind them of the fate that awaited failure that night.

A convict named Alvaran Snow Allen published a simple religious leaflet near the turn of the century titled "The Story of a Lie," recounting the misdeeds of his life and how they led him to become "Convict No. 2939" in an unspecified labor prison. In excruciating detail, he recounted the methods, lexicons, and apparatuses of prisoner punishment used throughout the southern prison labor system. "Come-a-longs" were steel bracelets snapped onto the wrists and fastened by a chain to a small metal crossbar. Turning the crossbar instantly twisted a man's arms into a knot, forcing him to his knees. In a punishment known simply as "the chains," a prisoner was placed in handcuffs attached to the ends of a thirty-inch-long steel bar, which was then hoisted with a pulley until the man hung clear of the floor, to be left suspended "from 50 minutes to two hours."[12] A variation on this torment was known in some camps as the "alakazan degree," in which the victim's ankles were cuffed behind his back and then his feet "drawn upward and backward until his whole body is stretched taut in the shape of a bow" and then tied to his wrists. Once pinioned, the most unfortunate prisoners were then placed in a closed and darkened box called a "crib" and left there in suffering. "The intense agony inflicted by this method of torture is indescribable; every muscle throbs with pain," wrote one prisoner after his release.[13]

"Little shackles" were egg-shaped pieces of iron riveted onto ankle rings on prisoners in rural work camps to make their feet too heavy to run. "Whipping straps" weighed two to seven pounds for routine beatings. "Shackles and chains" was a three-foot section of chain with an ankle cuff at one end and a two-inch ring at the other end. Once the cuff was riveted to a prisoner's leg, the chain was wrapped around the leg during working hours, and then unspooled at day's end to be attached to the one long chain holding all convicts in a particular sleeping area.

Famous to prison mines and camps in Alabama, Georgia, and Florida was the "pick shackle," which Allen described as a sharpened pick head riveted upside down to a prisoner's ankle—making it utterly impossible to run or even walk normally—and typically left there for the duration of a convict's sentence.[14] Worn for months or years at a time, the twenty- to thirty-pound picks rubbing against bare skin caused abrasions that led to pus-filled lesions and infections prisoners called "shackle poison." Littered through the records of convict camps are amputations of feet and lower legs as a result of blood poisoning from the injuries.

By far the most torturous and widely used punishment was the "water cure," a medieval cruciation whose many variations rendered the strongest and most defiant of men utterly compliant. In its most moderate form, the water cure was simply forcing a man to stand naked under a shower of cold water until he convulsed with cold. More often, prisoners described being stripped of their clothing and tied to a post or chair. A water line—often a high-pressure fire hose—was turned on the naked prisoner, pounding his skin with intense pressure and filling his mouth and nose with torrents of water until he became convinced he was about to drown.

In the Alabama prison mines where Green Cottenham was now an inmate, the preferred form of the water cure was simply to lift a man off his feet and plunge him headfirst into a barrel, with his arms tied or held use-less to his sides. Guards or prisoners working under the supervision of one held the man's furiously kicking feet to keep the barrel upright until his thrashing subsided—usually two to three minutes after being plunged into the liquid. Then the prisoner was hauled, gasping, out of the bucket, given a few seconds of air, then plunged down again. Repeated again and again, virtually no prisoner could avoid being turned into a shivering, begging wretch.[15]

For the hundreds of men who could not endure the physical abuse or the grinding labor, or who were killed by guards and other prisoners, death brought a final brief journey into the earth. At dead center of the sprawling Pratt Mines complex, facing Smokey Row, sat an unkempt 1,300-acre tri-angle of land, hemmed on two sides by tracks to the three nearest shafts. Here and there, heaps of coal slag and rocky debris jutted from the ground, amid a helter-skelter pattern of shrubby trees. Littered randomly among the debris and a web of muddy footpaths were hundreds of graves—many already slumping slightly into the earth and overgrown with weeds, many others still mounded high from recent burials.

Just outside the fence at Slope No. 12, another burial field held the men who died in the newest shaft. In the big cemetery at the bottom of the hill, a few graves bore simple stones with the names of free blacks permitted by TCI to be buried on company land. The rest—and all the burials outside the new prison at the top of the slope—were the hastily filled graves of mine prisoners from families too poor or forgotten to retrieve the bodies of their dead.[16]

A few days after Cottenham arrived at Slope No. 12 in April 1908, the president of U.S. Steel, W. E. Corey, and a contingent of other top executives from the Pittsburgh headquarters made their first visit to inspect the new Alabama properties. There was great applause in Birmingham for the men whose purchase had saved Tennessee Coal, Iron & Railroad Co. from financial ruin. But the enthusiasm of the city's leaders was tempered by the quiet recognition that the South's greatest industrial concern had come under the control of men in Pennsylvania. Whatever ambition there had been for Alabama's iron and steel industry to eclipse its rivals in the North was lost. Already, there were rumors that the new owners were uneasy about the conditions of the prison mine and the brutality inflicted on African Americans there. For the time being though, little would change. Four more convicts died before the end of the month. Five more in May. Another four in June and four more in July.[17] The burial field at Slope No. 12 quickly began to fill.

By midsummer, U.S. Steel and other mine owners in Birmingham were moving toward a bitter climax in their struggle with the United Mine Workers. Seven thousand free miners were on strike—this time joined by five hundred free black miners, many of whom had been brought in as strikebreakers during earlier labor unrest and had never been welcomed by a union run by white men. Now hundreds of miners swarmed the entryways of the mines, harassing any workers who entered and threatening to break free convicts as they moved from the mines to their prison. The homes in Pratt City of some leading company officials, as well as miners who continued to work, were dynamited in the night.

Coal company officials petitioned the state to break up the strike with militiamen and hired armed deputies, importing sixty "Texas sharpshooters" to help defend the mines. To keep operating, Tennessee Coal, Iron & Railroad and Sloss-Sheffield pushed Cottenham and other convict laborers—who had no choice but to continue working—to excruciating limits. They soon resurrected the long-abandoned and notorious practice of hiring black work gangs through white foremen—often farm owners with large groups of African American tenants under their control. In a practice reminiscent of the Confederate government's inducements to slave owners to work mines during the Civil War, white foremen brought in workers from the countryside and directly supervised them in the mines. The white "owner" collected all their wages and paid his black subjects a fraction of the pay of real miners.[18] Trains loaded with black farmworkers from the Black Belt pulled into Birmingham each day—to the hoots and threats of strikers. All the while, company labor agents prowled the countryside for more convicts, encouraging local sheriffs to arrest and sell as many more men as possible.

The specter of black and white miners unified against the coal companies was terrifying to the elite of Birmingham—and across the South. Mine owners responded with an aggressive campaign to divide the union along racial lines. A prominent African American union leader, William Millin, was taken from jail and lynched with the aid of two white deputy sheriffs. A week later, another union miner was hanged from a tree—again by a deputy sheriff—after being accused of dynamiting a company miner's house. Governor Braxton Comer issued orders preparing the state militia to mobilize and banning strikers from congregating outside mine entrances.[19]

In the midst of the crisis, on August 2, Cottenham could not return to his place in the mine. Green had survived five months at Slope No. 12. But he had become a shadow of the man arrested behind the train station in Columbiana. A doctor diagnosed Cottenham as having syphilis. If the doctor's assessment was correct, Cottenham almost certainly was already infected at the time of his arrest in Shelby County. Even in the bacterium's most aggressive form in a nineteenth-century medical regime without knowledge of penicillin, syphilis took at least two years to reach Green's mortally ill condition. In the unsanitary circumstances of the prison mine, the symptoms of syphilis were exacerbated and sometimes confused with other maladies. Already, the organism that causes syphilis—a bacterium called *Treponema pallidum*—had infected his central nervous system. The dorsal columns of Cottenham's spinal cord already were hardening or developing lesions—triggering excruciating stabbing pains in his legs, rectum, and upper extremities.

Even for the most fortunate patients, there was no cure for syphilis in 1908. Doctors gave those who could afford it doses of mercury in the belief it fought the progress of the bacteria. Otherwise, good food and clean surroundings were the only prescription for extending the vigor of the patient. Cottenham had neither. His symptoms progressed rapidly. Temporary blindness. A lack of sensation in his feet. Searing pains. Soon, his doctor diagnosed asitia—a loathing of all food—and locomotor ataxia, the archaic term for syphilis of the spinal cord.[20]

Green began to lose his ability to maintain balance, and then to control the movement of his legs. First, he would have walked only with a stick to stand on, then only with a cane in each hand—struggling to keep his feet from flying uncontrollably to his sides, front, or rear—slapping his feet back to the floor as he struggled to contain the movement of each step. His stomach convulsed agonizingly at the sight or swallowing of food, vomiting almost anything he attempted to ingest.

Cottenham might have lived for weeks or months in such a state—declining steadily toward a state of complete paralysis. But in his gravely weakened condition, Green was even more vulnerable to tuberculosis—the endemic respiratory disease cycling through the prisoners of Slope No. 12. Transmitted through impure water supplies, infected food, close contact with other victims, unsanitary surroundings, and a host of other means common to a prison mine, tuberculosis was the world's leading killer. Triggering vomiting, night sweats, and chills, it attacked the outer lining of victims' lungs, so sapping them of strength and color that the "consumption"—its common name at the time—was sometimes mistaken for vampirism.

However or whenever Green became infected, he was spiraling toward death by the time he entered the prison hospital on the first Saturday of August. Wracked with convulsive pains, starved by his own disgust for food, fevered and unable to control the movement of his limbs, friendless and lost to the other descendants of old Scipio, Green Cottenham died thirteen days later.

On August, 15, 1908, his body was placed in a crude pine box and carried by other convicts out the gate of Slope No. 12. A little more than a hundred yards down the hill, alongside the track following a long creek bed, past the last pockmarks of shallow sinking graves dug earlier that year, the men rested the simple casket on the ground and began digging among the trash and debris of the burial field. In the distance, the belching chimneys of the Ensley furnaces blackened the western horizon. No record was made of precisely where Cottenham's twisted remains, riddled with tubercular infection, were buried. The company couldn't even clearly remember his name. The doctor for Tennessee Coal, Iron & Railroad Co. logged the event only as the death of "Green Cunningham."

# XV

## EVERYWHERE WAS DEATH

*"Negro Quietly Swung Up by an Armed Mob . . . All is quiet."*

On the night before Green Cottenham's death at Slope No. 12, a mob of twelve thousand white people rampaged in Springfield, Illinois, the birthplace of Abraham Lincoln and site of Theodore Roosevelt's "square deal for the Negro" promise five years earlier.

A month earlier, on July 4, Springfield police thwarted the killing of a black man accused of murdering a local white businessman. On July 12, passengers on a Central of Georgia train passing Round Oak, Georgia, watched out their windows as a crowd seized and hanged a black man for pulling a knife during a brawl with a local white. Two days later, in Middleton, Tennessee, a mob of one hundred hanged Hugh Jones for allegedly making an advance on a seventeen-year-old white girl.[1] Less than twenty-four hours after that, an elderly black man was shot to death in Beaumont, Texas, after a gang of marauding whites mistook him for a younger African American accused of hitting a thirteen-year-old white girl. The mob was setting two black-owned businesses afire when the victim passed, but paused long enough to kill the man.[2]

The next week, news of a notably sordid lynching in Dallas, Texas, flashed across national newswires: after an eighteen-year-old African American named Tad Smith was accused of raping a white woman, a crowd of one thousand whites tied him to a stake in the ground, surrounded him with kerosene-soaked wood, and cheered as they watched him burn to death.[3]

A week later, only a detachment of Georgia state militia in the town of Ocilla was able to prevent the lynching of four randomly seized African Americans taken by a mob after a white woman claimed an unidentified black man entered her hotel room. The next day, a mob in Pensacola, Florida, attacked the jail where Leander Shaw was being held for an alleged sexual assault and knifing of a white woman. The sheriff and two deputies resisted a crowd that grew to one thousand, shooting and killing at least two of the white men attacking the jail. Sometime after midnight, the crowd overwhelmed police, took Shaw from his cell, dragged him two blocks with a noose on his neck, hanged him from a light pole in the center of the city's park, and then began firing on his corpse. "2,000 bullets completely riddled his body," wrote a correspondent for the *Atlanta Constitution*. On the same night, in Lyons, Georgia, a white crowd tore through a brick jail wall to reach and kill a black man accused of assault on a local white girl.[4]

Two days later, about one hundred white men broke into the Russell-ville, Kentucky, jail and seized a black farmer accused of killing his white landlord; they took three other African Americans from the jail as well, and hanged all four from a tree on a country road. A note attached to one body read: "Let this be a warning to you niggers to let white people alone."[5]

Back in Springfield, a white woman falsely claimed rape on August 14, after her secret sexual affair with a local black man was discovered. The mob that raged that Friday night killed at least seven black people, destroyed much of the African American section of the town, and issued proclamations that no blacks should return to the city. Calm was restored only after the arrival of four thousand soldiers.[6]


Two weeks later, a delegation of prominent Birmingham citizens visited leaders of the striking miners still encamped in tents outside the Alabama mines and issued an explicit threat. The owners of Tennessee Coal, Iron & Railroad, Sloss-Sheffield, and Pratt Consolidated Coal—the three biggest companies and each a major buyer of forced black laborers—made clear they would do anything necessary to crush the strike. Unless the strike ended, Birmingham would "make Springfield, Illinois look like six cents," according to a newspaper reporter who shadowed the visit.[7]

Alabama governor Braxton Comer issued a statement insisting no such madness would be necessary to destroy the biracial labor activists of Birmingham. Telling union leaders that he and other white officials were "outraged at the attempts to establish social equality between black and white miners," he demanded that the strike end. He added that he would not tolerate "eight or nine thousand idle niggars in the State of Alabama."[8] When the walkout continued, Governor Comer called the unrest a threat to white supremacy and dispatched the militia on August 26 to cut down the tents of strikers and break up their camps.

Facing armed military units and out of money, the strike collapsed on September 1. Free miners returned to their company housing and reentered the forbidding shafts. Tennessee Coal, Iron & Railroad redistributed its prisoners back into multiple shafts at the Pratt Mines.


Tensions hardly eased. Death in U.S. Steel's slave mines continued its march—two men in September; six more in October. Early in November, Birmingham buzzed with word of the latest southern lynching. A black man named Henry Leidy was accused by a fifteen-year-old girl in Biloxi, Mississippi, of sexual assault. Quickly taken from the town jail, he was hanged from a tree overlooking picturesque Back Bay on the Gulf of Mexico. "Negro Quietly Swung Up by an Armed Mob . . . All is quiet here tonight," wrote the *Birmingham Age-Herald* on its front page.[9]

Less than a week later, black convicts working alongside free miners in the Pratt No. 3 mine grew desperate enough to attempt an impossibly irrational escape plan. As the day shift of workers was leaving on November 16 to return to the prison stockade, about fifty African American prisoners couldn't be accounted for. Extra guards were called, but the missing miners didn't reappear. A new crew of sixty men descended into the shaft to keep operations under way.

Long past nightfall, a guard spotted smoke and then a burst of flames coming from timbers supporting the manway, the tunnel used by miners to enter and leave the shaft. Within minutes, the passageway was filled with flames. Guards quickly discovered forty of the missing miners waiting near another mine entrance with dynamite—planning to blow open an iron gate during the chaos and make their escape.

Eight other conspirators, who had set the diversionary fire, became trapped in the burning manway when one section of the tunnel's roof collapsed as the conflagration incinerated support timbers. Engulfed in the flames, the miners were "roasted and suffocated," according to a newspaperman on the scene.[10] The Board of Inspectors of Convicts recorded the deaths due to "asphyxiation." The fire burned for days. But within a week, convicts were back in the tunnels of No. 3, digging coal again. By the end of 1908, the first full year of U.S. Steel's ownership of the Pratt Mines, nearly sixty of the company's forced laborers had died.[11]

Everywhere in the slave mines of Birmingham was death. Hardly any week passed when one or more dead black corpses weren't dragged up from inside the earth, heaped atop the mounds of coal in the railcars, or found dead in the simple infirmaries of a prison. Often no one knew or would say how a man died. The coroner of Jefferson County—a dour man named B. L. Brasher—made almost continual visits to examine the dead or investigate the causes of their demise.[12]

On July 20, 1909, Brasher went to examine the body of Joe Hinson, sentenced to a life term for murder and sold into Pratt's No. 11 mine. Hinson had encouraged the story that his sentence was for chopping off the head of a man in the town in East Lake after an argument over Hinson's dog. A brutish record like that—whether true or not—could save a convict from other prisoners, but not from the mine itself. Charles Jones, another "prisner at Prat mines #11," as Brasher scrawled the notation, watched as Hinson loaded his coal car deep in the shaft and then slipped in the confined quarters. As he fell, his hand touched a live electric line. He died instantly from electrocution.

On March 12, 1910, Harrison Grant, a slight eighteen-year-old boy from Lowndes County with dark brown skin and a small scar atop his head, was digging alone in a room off the main shaft of Pratt No. 12—seven months into a term of one year and one day for burglary. Grant had no formal education. His parents, three brothers, and a sister lived in Montgomery.

As he hammered a wedge into shale beneath the coal seam, the entire

wall of rock suddenly collapsed, crushing him. There was little in the obliterated mass of his body with which to identify him. The coroner noted that
he "wore shoe and hat #8."

Matt Dunn, an illiterate twenty-six-year-old black farmer from Pickens
County with missing teeth and only five feet three inches tall, was crushed
on April 22, 1910, in the No. 12 mine, trapped between a mining car and a
"rib" of the mine—slang for the columns of rock and coal left as supports
for the roof of underground chambers and shafts.[13]

The next day, inmates Will Burck and Will Williams began fighting in
the same shaft. Burck, a common laborer arrested in Russell County for
burglary, was gored first in one side and then through the head with a mining pick. Archey Hargrove, a black man from Hale County, was found dead
in No. 2 mine on July 3, 1910.

Sometimes death came in plainly obvious ways. Eugene Phillips, a
twenty-five-year-old black prisoner with a "ginger-cake complexion," being
held at the No. 12 prison for two years on a charge of forgery, died July 16,
1910. "I found deceased came to his death from a lick in the left side with a
mining pick, at the hands of Clifford Reese," wrote Brasher. The two men
had fought for reasons no witness could recall. It ended with the shaft of pick
imbedded in Phillips, a farm boy from Chilton County. W. M. Hicks died at
the same mine on July 28 for reasons unknown. Frank Alexander was
stabbed to death on August 25, by a convict defending himself from Alexander. Gus Miles was crushed by falling rock in another Pratt mine on September 24.

On the first day of October, miners at the No. 3 prison in Ensley
entered a dormant section of the mine and found submerged in the rancid
backwater the rotting body of Will Lindsay. A forty-one-year-old black
man, he had been sold by Shelby County sheriff Fulton to Tennessee Coal,
Iron & Railroad in November 1908. Lindsay was reported escaped the following July. Guards assumed he slipped out of the prison. His remains
proved he'd disappeared into the black labyrinth of the forgotten section of
the dig. "This negro has never been heard of since his escape and is quite
possible that in trying to make his escape he got lost in abandoned part of
mines and died from starvation and bad air," the coroner wrote.

Just before Thanksgiving, a sixteen-year-old black farmhand from Barbour County, serving 729 days leased to the mines for an unrecorded theft,

was killed by an accidental explosion of dynamite in the Banner Mine. Also dead was twenty-seven-year-old John Tate and a free white worker named Fred Woodman.

Four days later, on December 5, the desiccated remains of Joe L. Thomas, another black man who had attempted to escape the Pratt No. 2 prison, was found lost in the fearsome place miners gave an almost ethereal name: the "gob." Inside the great maze of tunnels and rooms abandoned beneath the earth, often filled with escaping methane gas and the toxic runoff of active shafts, the gob was an utterly lightless, nearly impenetrable maze of tunnels and unventilated gas. "Deceased came to his death from exposure, as he had been in 'gob' of mine for two or three weeks, trying to escape," the coroner wrote.

On January 21, 1911, Walter Cratick's skull was split with a mining pick by another convict at the Banner Mine. A county convict arrested in Jefferson County for petit larceny barely a month before his death, Cratick was a twenty-seven-year-old farmhand from Barbour County, with a limp from a broken hip, one tooth missing from his upper and lower jaws, and a long scar on his left side. Just 145 pounds and a little over five feet, his term was six months. The coroner ruled his death a justifiable homicide.

On January 31, 1911, Dink Tucker was found dead "for unknown reasons" at Pratt Slope No. 12. Nearing the end of his one-year sentence to the mine, Tucker left behind a wife and two young boys in Chambers County.

Cassie McNally died from falling rock at the Pratt No. 2 mine on February 28, 1911. Essex Knox was found dead at the same shaft on April 6. "I found deceased came to his death by being mashed to death in the #2 prison by falling rock," wrote the company physician.

By the spring of 1911, the coroner was making more and more trips to the rising new competitor to U.S. Steel's Pratt Mines. One of Birmingham's most admired coal mining engineers and executives, Erskine Ramsey, organized the Pratt Consolidated Coal Company in 1904—quietly merging several small companies and acquiring 98,000 acres of coalfields in Alabama.

A lifetime bachelor more comfortable with machines and metal than men and women, Ramsey was intent on eclipsing his former employer by building the most aggressive and profitable industrial concern of the South. Pratt Consolidated had by 1911 opened nine new drift mines on previously undeveloped coalfields twenty miles north of the Pratt Mines. The company's showcase was the Banner Mine, a deep shaft featuring the first installation of electric lights, cutting tools, and hauling equipment—some of it invented by Ramsey himself—and the largest prison compound in the state, surrounded by a fifteen-foot-high wooden stockade.[14] Ramsey sought to obtain as many convict workers as the sheriffs of Alabama would sell.

On April 8, 1911, two black convicts at the Banner Mine died from inhaling afterdamp—the noxious combination of carbon monoxide, nitrogen, and other gases left behind when methane vapor ignites in a mine. One week later, near dawn on a rainy Saturday morning, just after the day shift of convicts reached their positions inside Banner, an ignition of blasting powder triggered a massive detonation. A handful of men nearest the initial blast died instantly; the ventilation fan that pushed fresh air deep into the shaft was blown out of position by the force of the explosion. The sudden flash of fire consumed much of the oxygen in the tunnels. Into the chemical vacuum created by the absence of oxygen poured what miners called, with terror, "black damp"—a suffocating mixture of nitrogen and carbon dioxide. About a dozen men still near the 1,700-foot chute leading into the shaft escaped to safety. The rest—113 black prisoners, the vast majority of them being held for trivial misdemeanors, ten white prisoners, and five free miners—were killed by the gases.

A quickly impaneled coroner's jury certified that the company was "using all reasonable means for the prevention of accidents" and was not culpable in the deaths. Most of the bodies of the dead were quickly dumped in a long trench dug by other prisoners in the mine's convict cemetery just outside the stockade.[15] Within two weeks, the Banner Mine was in operation again, with a fresh contingent of black prisoners.

Alabama's other slave mines never slowed production in the aftermath of the disaster. Cleve Watts died at Prison No. 12 on May 22, 1911, "struck in the head with a mining pick." Less than a month later, June 20, 1911, Lee Lawson was killed in the same mine in a rock fall. On July 29, Frank Miller was shot to death by two guards as he tried to escape No. 12.

A week later, Jim Minor died in a pickaxe fight at Sloss-Sheffield's Flat Top mine. Ed Jerring was crushed by "being jammed between two cars" in TCI's No. 12 mine on September 29, 1911. Jackson Wheeler died from "an electric shock" at the company's No. 2 prison on October 3, 1911. Henry Carter was killed at Slope No. 12 prison the same day, "from falling rock."[16]

The gruesome fates of all those men ricocheted across the landscape of black life, depositing as they spread new layers of tragedy atop the deep residue of trauma left by thousands of prior horrors from inside and outside the South's forced labor camps. Together, these events formed the foundation of a collective recognition among African Americans of their precarious vulnerability in American society. In the early years after Reconstruction, such news traveled like a telegraph, flashing from one outraged bearer of the word to another. Preachers decried the crimes against innocent men from their pulpits. Before the final ouster of blacks from virtually all southern elections, African American voters cast ballots against those who abided the system, in rare cases forcing a local official out of office—as blacks once did to a sheriff in Chattanooga, Tennessee, after he permitted the lynching of a man from his jail.[17] There were isolated cases when black prisoners collectively refused to work in protest of brutal punishments meted out—and of convicts physically attacking their overseers.

But such resistance was almost invariably crushed with the sheer force of guns, mob violence, and economic isolation. By the end of the first decade of the twentieth century, word of each new outrage moved osmotically, absorbed often without explicit note into the shared experience of a black society in which nearly all realistic hope of authentic independence had been shattered. The new slavery of Alabama achieved its zenith. Three massive industrial concerns—U.S. Steel's Tennessee Coal, Iron & Railroad unit, Sloss-Sheffield, and now Pratt Consolidated—competed mercilessly for forced laborers. Other industrial concerns stood ready to step in if any major player receded. The system arrived at a cynical optimum of economic harmony, knitting together the interests of capitalists, white farmers, local sheriffs and judges, and advocates of the most cruel white supremacy—all joined and served by an unrelenting pyramid of intimidation.

The companies, producing nearly fifteen million tons of coal annually by 1910, held more than three thousand black men against their will in Alabama's mines at all times—creating a bulwark against labor unrest and an enormous economic subsidization to their most critical cost of production. Hundreds more African Americans worked in southern Alabama timber and turpentine camps operated by Henderson Lumber Company, Horse Shoe Lumber Company, McPhaul Turpentine Company, a textile factory in Prattville, and other businesses. Hundreds more—no one kept count—were parceled out by local sheriffs to farmers and businessmen scattered around the state.

The reality of incarceration in the slave mines became so ubiquitously understood for African American men that landlords and local sheriffs— equipped with almost unchecked powers of arrest and conviction and enormous personal financial interest in providing labor to the mines and other enterprises—could make almost any demand upon any black man. More often than any other, that demand was that they remain on the land of specific white farmers, living lives of supposedly voluntary serfdom or as prisoners sentenced to that fate under the system of "confessions" ratified by Judge Jones in 1903. Across the Black Belt of Alabama, more than ninety thousand African American families lived in the darkness of that oppression with only rare protest.

In Barbour County, 170 miles from Birmingham, deep in the cotton country of southern Alabama, the shadow was cast in the shape of two brothers, William M. and Robert B. Teal. In 1911, when a term-limit law forced William to give up his job as sheriff, Robert was elected to the job instead. William became his chief deputy. "The brothers just swapped places," according to the local newspaper, the *Clayton Record*.[18]

Because it controlled the county's convict leasing franchise, the sheriff's office was a plum asset. Over one ten-year period, Barbour County sent 691 men to the coal mines, primarily those operated by Sloss-Sheffield and Tennessee Coal, Iron & Railroad.[19]

The *Record* took little note, among its weekly coverage of cotton prices, buggy accidents, and lost mules, of the disappearance of so many local black men. It enthusiastically covered the lynchings of African Americans, occurring with regularity in nearby towns and across the South. It labeled as "niggers" those African Americans who gathered in Georgia for a celebration on the anniversary of the Emancipation Proclamation. Northern whites who lent support to well-known African Americans such as Booker T. Washington were "negrophilists."

On Confederate Memorial Day that April, the keynote speaker, standing atop a platform festooned with the battle colors of the Confederacy, received "deafening" applause, according to a reporter, as he told the crowd nearly five decades after the legal end of slavery that the forced labor of blacks had been completely constitutional and never violated "divine or moral law." A local white girl gave a reading of Uncle Remus stories. Organizers plied the crowd for donations to help erect a memorial on the town square to southern veterans of the Civil War.[20]

Prospects for any black man who crossed Sheriff Teal and his brother were grim. The jail itself was cramped and unsanitary, and had been formally condemned by state inspectors.[21] What went for justice for African American defendants was swift. After one trial of "a negro charged with violating prohibition" in 1911, a local judge in Eufaula, the more prosperous cotton trading town twenty miles to the east, explicitly instructed the jurors to convict the man. When the jury unexpectedly acquitted instead, Judge M. Sollie threatened to have the jurors arrested for contempt of court.[22]

Once convicted, African Americans were routinely sent to the coal mines near Birmingham for offenses as slight as selling a bottle of moonshine. Most months, the Teals arrested fewer than twenty men. Then suddenly dozens of minor offenders were rounded up over a few days' time and charged with vagrancy, alcohol violations, and other minor offenses. Nearly all were quickly sentenced to hard labor and shipped out within ten days to fill a gap in men at the coal mines.[23]

On any given day in the summer of 1912, the county jail near the town square in Clayton held from ten to two dozen men, awaiting the arrival of circuit judges who rotated through the area's towns. A man named Edwin Collins was charged with eavesdropping. Another black man, Josia Marcia, was being held for allegedly having had sexual relations with a white woman. Louis Denham had been arrested for vagrancy. Housed with them were Ad Rumph, Henry Demas, Jackson Daniels, and Peter Ford, four African American men accused in the murder of a sharecropper named George Blue. Demas, seventeen years old, and his wife were boarders in the house of Rumph, another young black farmer, on property near the remote farming community of Mt. Andrew. Demas could read and write, but had no formal schooling. Rumph, nineteen years old and illiterate, was married to a woman named Fredie.[24]

Blue had been killed the prior spring by "a party of negroes," according to the *Record*. As often happened after black homicides of that era, a large number of African Americans were charged in the case. Indeed, on the same weekend that Blue was killed, seven African Americans—including thirty-two-year-old farmhand Will Miller—were charged in the death of another black man in Eufaula. Miller spent the summer in the Barbour County jail as well.[25]

Whatever evidence was presented against the various defendants was later lost, along with any record of their trials or whether the men had access to attorneys. By fall, though, all had been convicted and sentenced to varying terms of hard labor. Each of the accused murderers received between twenty years and life. Collins received six months' hard labor; Denham got five months. No sentence was recorded for Marcia.

Emaciated and marked, the men's bodies told their own story. Miller was logged into state records as having "one good tooth on top," "shot through top of right shoulder," "badly burnt on back left leg." Demas stood five feet nine inches tall but weighed just 150 pounds. Scars were scattered across his frame—the biggest a six-inch gash stretching from above his left eye down the side of his face.[26]

In Henry County, the adjoining county to Barbour, Martin Danzy was a thirty-three-year-old sharecropper and a husband of nine years. He was arrested with another local black man in connection with a third man's death, though no records of the precise charge survived. On October 21, 1915, Danzy was sentenced to a term of twenty-five years at hard labor. The man arrested with him, Bud L. Clark, was sentenced to twenty years.[27]

Danzy was promptly sold to Henderson Land & Lumber Co., which put him to work in a turpentine harvesting camp near Tuscaloosa. Clark lasted just over two months at labor before pneumonia killed him. Danzy contracted pneumonia as well. Five months after his conviction, he too was dead.

Among the prisoners from Barbour County, Collins and Denham survived their terms of labor. Miller lived only a few months, until he died the following April in a Pratt Consolidated mine, at the hands of another convict. In November 1916, Rumph died of tuberculosis in a state prison hospital. Demas died the following month of pneumonia, at the Banner Mine.

Daniels was killed July 27, 1917, while attempting to escape the Sloss mine at Flat Top.[28]

Years later, the authorized biography of Elbert H. Gary, the founding chairman of U.S. Steel, who ran the corporation from 1901 to 1927, quoted Gary as saying he was outraged when he learned that the mines he acquired in Alabama in 1907 were using slave labor. He said he ordered the executive just installed as president of Tennessee Coal, Iron & Railroad, George G. Crawford, to halt the practice immediately. Gary, namesake of the U.S. Steel–designed city of Gary, Indiana, was widely regarded among U.S. executives at the time as the national leader on progressive labor practices and business ethics. "Think of that!" Gary was quoted as saying. "I, an Abolitionist from childhood, at the head of a concern working negroes in a chain gang, with a state representative punishing them at the whipping post! Tear up that contract . . . I won't stand for it."[29]

Perhaps Gary believed he had in fact ended U.S. Steel's slaving practices. Alabama was far from Pittsburgh. But deep in the bowels of U.S. Steel's newly acquired mines, slaves remained at work. This new southern unit of the company held contracts guaranteeing thousands of forced workers from the state of Alabama for at least four more years. The reality of the southern economic situation was that even under the mandate of the most prominent and modern new corporate executive of the era, U.S. Steel was unwilling to simply cease the practice of slavery at its new subsidiary.

Shortly after U.S. Steel acquired Tennessee Coal, Iron & Railroad, rumors circulated in Alabama that the northern owners were unenthusiastic about the convict system. In later testimony during an investigation into corruption in the state's convict leasing department, U.S. Steel executives said Judge Gary had indeed directed them to abandon convict leasing "as soon as possible" after the merger.

"Judge Gary said whether the hire of convicts was a good thing or a bad thing that he didn't care to be connected with the penal system of the State of Alabama," testified Walker Percy, a lawyer for Tennessee Coal, Iron & Railroad.[30]

But in correspondence between company executives and state officials,

U.S. Steel made clear that despite the chairman's discomfort with the system, it realized the benefits of a captive workforce, particularly in thwarting efforts to unionize local labor. It was in no rush to give up the prisoners under its control.

In a letter to the state Board of Inspectors of Convicts in 1911, the president of TCI was unequivocal: "The chief inducement for the hiring of convicts was the certainty of a supply of coal for our manufacturing operations in the contingency of labor troubles."[31]

Instead of quickly ending its reliance on forced labor, as Judge Gary later claimed, U.S. Steel made modest improvements, primarily by raising health standards at the No. 12 mine. At the same time, it publicly praised Tennessee Coal, Iron & Railroad's past record of "humane and considerate treatment" of prisoners,[32] and entered into new agreements to acquire more convicts from county sheriffs. In 1911, the number of deaths at U.S. Steel prison mines fell to eighteen.

But when Alabama officials began cutting the number of men supplied to U.S. Steel in the middle of that year—four years after Gary claimed he had ordered an end to slaving in his mines—the company protested forcefully. The company's general superintendent, Edward H. Coxe, wrote convict bureau president James Oakley to complain, "asking him for 30 or 40 more men." When the number of prisoners dwindled below three hundred later that summer, Coxe paid a personal visit to Oakley to demand more forced laborers.[33]

As the end of Tennessee Coal, Iron & Railroad's agreement with the state was approaching, the company told Alabama officials it wanted to begin negotiations to extend the contract for at least one more year. The state responded that it intended to lease all the convicts to the Banner Mine—ostensibly because Erskine Ramsey's company would pay more for them.

"I wish to enter a very vigorous protest against this action, as it is manifestly unfair to us to take the men from us," responded Coxe in a September 25, 1911, letter to the official in charge of convicts. "We are paying the State a great big price for these convicts, and it is certainly a hardship on us to deplete our organization."[34]

State officials, some of whom were receiving secret payments to help Ramsey's company, were unswayed. On January 1, 1912, the last remaining two hundred state convicts held at the Pratt Mines were marched out under guard and turned over to their new overseers to help replenish the ranks of forced laborers at the Banner Mine, decimated by the disaster less than a year earlier.

On December 13, 1912, a roaming labor agent for U.S. Steel sent out to hustle up as many workers as possible made a last stop at the Shelby County jail. Deputy Eddings no longer made regular deliveries to Birmingham. With all state prisoners in the Banner Mine, other companies sent out their own agents to local sheriffs to collect convicts and haul them back to the shafts. The man from Tennessee Coal, Iron & Railroad paid $103.50 to acquire one last lot of men. George Morris, William Garland, John Archie, J. W. Walls, and John H. Huntley had all been arrested together on the crime that had supplied thousands of laborers to the company: "train riding."

There must have been some amazement that day in that all of the men purchased were white. It was likely the only instance in the company's thirty-year relationship with Shelby County sheriffs in which a shipment of men included no blacks. It would have been no surprise though that for the "crime" which thousands of African Americans were sent to the mines for months or years—and hundreds of whom died for it—these five white men received sentences of just ten days' labor.[35]

# XVI

## ATLANTA,
## THE SOUTH'S FINEST CITY

*"I will murder you if you don't do that work."*

During the same scorching southern summer that Green Cottenham and so many others died deep in the Alabama coal mines—or at the ends of ropes in places from Texas to Illinois—a litany of horrors from the slave camps of Georgia was spilling into public view in Atlanta.

Beginning late in July 1908, a commission established by the Georgia legislature convened a series of remarkable hearings into the operations of the state's convict leasing system. Meeting early every day and late into the night to escape the city's excruciating heat, the panel called more than 120 witnesses over the course of three weeks to give testimony in the state capitol's regal Room No. 16.

The architects of the investigation—primarily state senator Thomas Felder—launched the inquiry in hopes of proving corruption in the management of Georgia's extensive system of buying and selling prisoners. It would prove that. But as the long line of witnesses perspired beneath the chamber's whirling ceiling fans, they learned of crimes far greater than graft and payoffs.

Across Georgia, fourteen separate camps held men sold by the state; at another sixteen locations men charged in county and city courts were held in slavery—including more than 430 at Durham Coal mines; more than 350 at Egypt, in the plantation belt of south Georgia; nearly 200 at Chattahoochee Brick Company on the outskirts of Atlanta; and scores more at a coal mine near Lookout Mountain. In total, at least 3,464 men and 130 women lived in explicit forced labor in Georgia.[1]

Yet so many men had been sold, under so many separate arrangements with work camps, factories, and timber operations scattered across the state, that no one in Georgia government could say where any particular man might have ended up, or the true total of African Americans being held against their will. Complicating any effort to track the fates of these forced laborers, the new slavery of Georgia had metamorphed into a full-blown system of human trafficking.

Felder's committee learned that at least six hundred slave workers, nearly all of them African American, had been resold to other buyers after being leased from the state for convictions on minor offenses.[2] Witness after witness—ranging from former guards to legislators to freed slaves— offered nauseating accounts of the system's brutalities. Wraithlike men infected with tuberculosis were left to die on the floor of a storage shed at a farm near Milledgeville. Laborers who attempted escape from the Muscogee Brick Company were welded into ankle shackles with three-inch-long spikes turned inward—to make it impossibly painful to run again. Guards everywhere were routinely drunk and physically abusive. In almost every camp, forced laborers lived and slept for months in the same tattered clothing. They bedded each night on fragments of bed linens clotted with dirt and filth.

One legislator told of a black man at Lookout Mountain Coal and Coke Company in the mountains of north Georgia whose arm was broken in a rock fall inside the mine. Months later he was working again, but with a disjointed arm, distended in a grotesque misalignment, where the bones healed together in an unnatural shape. At a camp in Floyd County, black women riddled with venereal diseases worked on a roadway chained to one another. Everywhere, prisoners worked, ate, and slept almost continually shackled. Legislators who visited the Pinson & Allen lumber and turpentine camp in Miller County were so revolted by the trash and insect-riddled food given to prisoners, they had to leave without completing the tour.[3]

In late July, a circumspect fourteen-year-old black boy with a clenched hand gave his name as Daniel Long. What followed was a plain-spoken description of his sentence served a year earlier in a turpentine camp after being accused of stealing a watch chain.

Senator Felder asked him if he'd been whipped.

"Yes sir," Long responded. "Say I wasn't working good enough."

Felder asked how severely and how often.

"Hit me 75 licks. . . . Some times twice a day," Long answered.[4]

Asked what was the matter with his hand, Long said the camp whipping boss beat it with a leather strap after Long said he was getting cramps from his work. After that, the boy could never open his hand again. Finally the chairman of the commission asked Long to take off his shirt and let the panel see his back. To gasps of horror in the audience and grimaces on the faces of the committee, the slight young man doffed his shirt and turned to reveal a back grossly swollen and scarred with stripes from the turpentine camp beatings. Scars and marks covered the trunk of the teenager. One foot was still seriously infected where a whipping had literally removed a piece of skin.

Long's mother moved into the witness chair and told the committee how she was notified after his last beating that Daniel was soon to die. The boy had been convicted of petty theft in Marietta, just north of Atlanta, but was sold and resold by traders in black labor until he arrived at the turpentine camp hundreds of miles to the south. She borrowed money to travel to the camp in south Georgia—walking for miles on country roads in search of him. By the time she found the camp, her son had been sold again, along with a crew of healthy prisoners, to a nearby farm. She asked the whipping boss where to go to find her son.

"I don't know anything about the goddam black son of a bitch, I beat hell out of him," Mrs. Long quoted the man saying. "He told me if I went down that road . . . he would kill me and throw me in the river. He said he had killed lots of goddamn negroes and throwed them in the river."

She went anyway and found Daniel barely alive, lying in a bunk with his clothes stuck to his scabs and oozing skin. The new owner of the lease on her son allowed her to take him home. Only after three months of recuperation did a doctor conclude Daniel would survive.[5]

As the inquiry progressed, what began as revelations of brutish behavior by uncouth men in distant labor camps slowly became instead an unsettling portrait of some of Atlanta's, and Georgia's, most prominent families—many of whom appeared to be direct beneficiaries of the most sordid revelations in Room 16. The committee learned that the killing of the young black boy described by Ephraim Gaither—whose account of the decomposed body being dragged through the woods by dogs sickened the gallery—occurred in a camp owned by Joel Hurt, one of Atlanta's most esteemed businessmen, and run by his adult son, George.

Other witnesses recounted the fate of a sixteen-year-old white boy named Abe Wynne, who was sold into the Durham Coal and Coke Company mine after being caught two years earlier stealing two tins of potted ham. The company, owned by former Atlanta mayor James W. English, operated a dangerous shaft in north Georgia. Some sections of the mine were filled with more than waist-deep water, which seeped out through the slate surrounding the coal. Pumps were inadequate to remove the water. Not enough timbers were provided for miners to brace the tunnels, leading to routine and often deadly cave-ins. Even when material was provided, miners often skipped the safety steps for fear of being punished if they ran out of time to dig their required daily allotment, or "task," of coal.

"Many times the men wouldn't take time to do it because they knew that they could not timber the walls and finish their tasks, and it meant a whipping if they did not finish them," testified R. A. Keith, a former prisoner allowed to work as a clerk at the mine office.

Every morning, slave laborers at the Durham mines were forced to gather in the yard of the camp to receive a breakfast of corn bread and a piece of raw meat and to watch whippings of any worker who failed to make task the prior day. "I have seen them punish the convicts severely for not finishing their tasks and have seen them work until ten and eleven o'clock at night to finish their tasks and then be whipped for working overtime," Keith said.

Asked to describe the instruments used by the camp whipping boss, Keith said convicts were beaten with a thick strap of leather attached to a handle. "You take a strip of heavy harness leather about as wide as my three fingers or a little bit wider and about two and a half feet long. It would weigh somewhere in the neighborhood of . . . three and a half pounds," Keith testified. "Some times they would wet the leather by spitting on it and rubbing it on the sand; that was when they wanted to bring the blood. It would hurt a great deal worse to flog them with it than with the dry strap. . . . The sand will take the skin off."[6]

In the yard where the whippings took place, the warden also kept a herd of between forty and fifty hogs. The aggressive animals—made fearless of the docile prisoners—crowded in on the emaciated men to grab scraps of bread or other food that fell to the ground. One evening, Abe Wynne was allowed to brew a pot of coffee on an open fire in the yard. Since arriving at the mine as a fourteen-year-old, his once stout, six-foot frame withered to just 160 pounds. When a hog began nosing against him for food, he splashed a cup of hot coffee on the pig to drive it away.

Word quickly spread to the warden that Wynne had abused one of his hogs. As punishment, witnesses testified that Wynne was forced to strip naked, held stretched across a barrel by two other prisoners, and then whipped with a leather strap sixty-nine times. "The whipping was more than he could stand," Keith said.

A few days later, Wynne's older brother, Will, visited what was called the mine hospital. He told the commission his brother was lying on a filthy bed, still wearing his convict stripes with no underclothes and coated in the dust of the mine. "I saw that the boy could only live a short time and it grieved me," testified Will Wynne. "About all I asked him was if he was prepared to die." Delirious and unable to tell his brother what happened, Wynne died a week later. The boy's family was told he'd contracted "galloping" tuberculosis and succumbed suddenly.[7]

James W. English, the owner of Durham Coal and Coke, was a luminary of the Atlanta elite and a man hardly anyone in the city rising from the Civil War's ashes would have associated with so cruel a killing as Abe Wynne's. But by 1908, English—despite having never owned antebellum slaves—was a man whose great personal wealth was inextricably tied to the enslavement of thousands of men.

Born in 1837 near New Orleans and orphaned as a teenager, he apprenticed himself to a carriage maker and then served notably as a young man in the Confederate army, rising to become a captain in a prominent Georgia brigade. Serving in a forward position near Appomattox, he received the first written surrender demand from Ulysses S. Grant to Robert E. Lee. After the South's defeat, he went to Atlanta, to establish himself in the business and politics of the bustling new capital of southern commerce. He was elected to the city council partly on the renown of his war service, and later served on the Atlanta school board and as the city's police commissioner. He led a drive to make Atlanta the state capital of Georgia, cementing its foundation as an economic center, and in 1880 he was elected mayor.[8]

Presiding from a regal home a few blocks from the center of the city, English, a portly man with a thick shock of white hair and a matching mustache, fostered a collection of enterprises that grew as Atlanta emerged from its Civil War ruin. The base of his wealth was the Chattahoochee Brick Company, a business perfectly consonant in the 1870s and 1880s with the needs of a booming metropolis recovering from Union general William Tecumseh Sherman's firing of the city a decade earlier.

As a police official and as mayor, English saw the rich potential of using black forced laborers in his enterprises. Chattahoochee Brick relied on slave workers from its inception in 1878, and by the early 1890s more than 150 prisoners were employed in the wilting heat of its fires. The company held another 150 forced laborers at a sawmill in Richwood, Georgia, three hundred slaves at its Durham mines in Walker County, and several dozen more at English's Iron Belt Railroad and Mining Company. By 1897, English's enterprises controlled 1,206 of Georgia's 2,881 convict laborers, engaged in brick making, cutting cross ties, lumbering, railroad construction, and turpentining.

During his tenure as mayor of Atlanta, English launched the Georgia Pacific Railroad, eventually tying Atlanta to the coalfields of Alabama and then on to the cotton nub of Greenville, Mississippi. While building that rail line in 1883, English illegally bought hundreds of convicts—and the coal mine they worked in—from Alabama's leading slave driver, John T. Milner.

English parlayed his industrial wealth to become one of the South's most important financiers as well. In 1896, he founded Atlanta's Fourth National Bank and became its first president. Early in the next century, after a series of mergers, it became First National Bank of Atlanta, one of the largest financial institutions in the South.[9]

Before the legislative commission in 1908, former employees of Chattahoochee Brick testified that the factory on the outskirts of Atlanta was a place of even greater physical coercion and indignity than the coal mine where Abe Wynne was killed. By the first years of the twentieth century, English had turned over daily management of the business to his son, Harry, who later would take over operations and build a landmark home on Atlanta's elegant Paces Ferry Road, directly across from the governor's mansion.

English strenuously denied to the committee that any "act of cruelty" had ever been "committed upon a convict" under the control of himself or any member of his family. He insisted that he and his son were essentially absentee owners of the brick factory, having little to do with its daily operations. "I have not been there in over three years," English maintained. His son visited no more than once or twice a month, he said—despite company records showing close family management.

The former mayor claimed he ordered the superintendent of operations to make certain workers "were well fed, well shod, well clothed, and well cared for. . . .

"If a warden in charge of those convicts ever committed an act of cruelty to them," English said indignantly, "and it had come to my knowledge, I would have had him indicted and prosecuted." Yet his testimony affirmed how Chattahoochee Brick—like so many southern industries in which the new slavery flourished—forced laborers to their absolute physical limits to extract modern levels of production from archaic manufacturing techniques of a distant era. The plant used a brick-making process little changed from seventeenth-century Europe. Nearly two hundred men sold by the state of Georgia, the local county, and the city of Atlanta—virtually all of them black—labored at the complex of buildings, giant ovens, and smokestacks nine miles from the city and a short distance from the Chattahoochee River. Thousands of acres of cotton and vegetable fields owned by the company surrounded the plant.

Gangs of prisoners sold from the pestilential city stockade on Bryan Street dug wet clay with shovels and picks in nearby riverbank pits for transport back to the plant. There, a squad of men pushed clay that had been cured in the open air into tens of thousands of rectangular molds. Once dried, the bricks were carried at a double-time pace by two dozen laborers running back and forth—under almost continual lashing by

English's overseer, Capt. James T. Casey—to move the bricks to one of nearly a dozen huge coal-fired kilns, also called "clamps." At each kiln, one worker stood atop a barrel, in the withering heat radiating from the fires, furiously tossing the bricks into the top of the ten-foot-high oven.

After being baked for a week or more, the fully hardened bricks were loaded, still hot, in groups of eight or ten onto crude wooden pallets tied to the necks and backs of young black men. The laborers ran—also carrying two more hot bricks in each hand—across the yard and up a narrow plank to train cars waiting on an adjacent railroad spur and stacked the new bricks for delivery. Witnesses testified that guards holding long horse whips struck any worker who slowed to a walk or paused. By the end of every day, 200,000 or more new bricks were loaded on the railcars.

English obviously had grown rich in his years in Atlanta, but few people realized quite how lucrative the slave labor business became. The prisoners of the brickyard produced nearly 33 million bricks in twelve months ending in May 1907, generating sales of $239,402—or roughly $5.2 million today. Of that, the English family pocketed the equivalent of nearly $1.9 million in profit—an almost unimaginable sum at the time.[10]

A string of witnesses told the legislative committee that prisoners at the plant were forced to work under unbearable circumstances, fed rotting and rancid food, housed in barracks rife with insects, driven with whips into the hottest and most intolerable areas of the plant, and continually required to work at a constant run in the heat of the ovens. The plant was so hot that guards didn't carry guns for fear their cartridges might spontaneously detonate. One former guard told the committee that two hundred to three hundred floggings were administered each month. "They were whipping all the time. It would be hard to tell how many whippings they did a day," testified Arthur W. Moore, a white ex-employee of the company. Another former guard said Captain Casey was a "barbarous" whipping boss who beat fifteen to twenty convicts each day, often until they begged and screamed. "You can hear that any time you go out there. When you get within a quarter of a mile you will hear them," testified Ed Strickland.[11]

A rare former convict who was white testified that after a black prisoner named Peter Harris said he couldn't work due to a grossly infected hand, the camp doctor carved off the affected skin tissue with a surgeon's knife and then ordered him back to work. Instead, Harris, his hand mangled and bleeding, collapsed after the procedure. The camp boss ordered him dragged into the brickyard.

"They taken the old negro out and told him to take his britches down, he took them down and they made him get on his all fours," testified the former prisoner, J. A. Cochran. "I could see that he was a mighty sick man to be whipped. He hit him twenty-five licks."

When Harris couldn't stand up after the whipping, he was thrown "in the wagon like they would a dead hog," continued Cochran, and taken to a nearby field. Still unable to get on his feet, another guard named Redman came over and began shouting. "Get up from there and get to work. If you ain't dead I will make you dead if you don't go to work," Redman said. "Get up from there you damn negro. I know what's the matter with you, you damn negro, you want to run away." Harris never stood. He died lying between the rows of cotton.[12]

Another black laborer drew the wrath of Captain Casey when he said he couldn't complete his assigned task of tossing 100,000 bricks to the top of a kiln. Sweating so profusely in the heat that the barrel beneath and the ground all around were drenched, the man said he was about to collapse. "God damn your soul," shouted Captain Casey, according to witnesses. "I will murder you if you don't do that work."

Then the overseer told the man to climb down, whipped him with a leather belt attached to a wooden handle, and ordered him back to work. Incensed at the pace the brick thrower was working, Casey ordered two other black laborers to hold him across a barrel and began whipping again. Lash upon lash fell across his back and buttocks. Finally the unnamed man was released. "The negro staggered off to one side and fell across a lumber pile there, and laid there for a while," testified one witness. Soon he was dead. The camp doctor declared the cause of death to have been drinking too much water before going to work at the kiln.[13]

On Sundays, white men came to the Chattahoochee brickyard to buy, sell, and trade black men as they had livestock and, a generation earlier, slaves on the block. "They had them stood up in a row and walked around them and judged of them like you would a mule," Cochran said. "They would look at a man in the row and say, 'Trot him around and let me see him move.' They would come to one fellow and they say 'there is a god damn good one.' . . . They would make such remarks as, 'There is a man worth two hundred and fifty dollars. There is one worth two hundred.' "

A similar picture emerged in the investigation around slave camps and coal mines owned by Joel Hurt, the rich Atlanta real estate developer and investor most remembered in Atlanta as the visionary behind the city's earliest and most elegant subdivisions. Virtually every white person of any social significance lived in one or the other of Hurt's signature developments—the High Victorian Inman Park or Druid Hills, an area of wide promenades and lush parks designed at his behest by the firm of Frederick Law Olmsted. Hurt was also the founder of Atlanta's Trust Company Bank—the city's other preeminent financial institution, the streetcar operator that became Georgia's first electric power company, and an early investor in concerns that would become some of the most iconic companies in the South. His namesake building near the Five Points business center dominated the early Atlanta skyline at seventeen stories—making it one of the tallest structures of the early twentieth century.

In 1895, Hurt bought a group of bankrupt forced labor mines and furnaces on Lookout Mountain, near the Tennessee state line. The mines were previously owned by former Georgia governor Joseph E. Brown, who enthusiastically led the secessionist movement in Georgia prior to 1861, governed the state during the Civil War years, and afterward remained a staunch defender of antebellum slavery.

The most powerful politician in Georgia from the 1860s until his death in 1894, Brown, still contemptuous of the Emancipation Proclamation, filled his mines with scores of black men forced into the shafts against their will. A legislative committee visiting the sites the same year Hurt bought them said the prisoners were "in the very worst condition . . . actually being starved and have not sufficient clothing . . . treated with great cruelty." Of particular note to the visiting officials was that the mine claimed to have replaced whipping with the water cure torture—in which water was poured into the nostrils and lungs of prisoners—because it allowed miners to "go to work right away" after punishment.[14]

Called to testify before the commission at the Georgia capitol in 1908, Hurt lounged in the witness chair, relaxed and unapologetic for any aspect of the sprawling business he'd taken over from Brown and aggressively expanded through the traffic of forced black laborers.

After acquiring Brown's mines, Hurt ramped up production, in part to fulfill contracts to sell coal to Tennessee Coal, Iron & Railroad in Birmingham—which couldn't get enough fuel and ore from its own slave mines to keep furnaces burning at full operation. Hurt already had 125 convicts in his largest slave mine. He bought one of English's mines to acquire fifty men held there, and then set out to obtain even more forced laborers from other work camps around the state.

Hurt's gentle appearance in the witness chair—wavy black hair slicked to his scalp and a soft shaven face that defied the day's convention for thick mustaches—was an almost obscene contrast to the account of slave trading he quietly offered the committee.

Needing more laborers in 1904, Hurt, who identified his profession as "capitalist," said he turned to a man who was "trading in" the sale and resale of leases on convicts. Soon, he was put in touch with J. W. Callahan, who held thirty-nine black and two white men on a turpentine farm in the deep woods of south Georgia. Hurt wrote him on Christmas Eve asking if the men could be purchased. "If you will name the lowest price at which you are willing to dispose of them, we may be able to come to an agreement," Hurt wrote. "In making a price, state whether the men are average able-bodied; how many of them are white, if any; whether any of them are maimed or crippled, or in any way disabled. . . . Yours very truly, Joel Hurt."[15]

Over the next week, amid the yuletide and New Year celebrations, Hurt and Callahan furiously traded letters and telegrams negotiating an arrangement for fifty black men. Callahan first demanded an up-front fee of $200 per worker—or a total of $10,000—followed by monthly payments totaling $200 a year for each man. The price of slave labor had changed little in fifty years.

Hurt counteroffered an $8,000 up-front fee, and urgently wired his thirty-one-year-old son, George, managing the company's iron furnace on Lookout Mountain, that the men had been obtained. Before the deal could be consummated, though, Callahan was contacted by another bidder. On January 6, 1905, he sold the men to the competitor in an all-cash transaction.[16] An infuriated Hurt continued to wheel and deal in the byzantine web of Georgia's slave traffic—threatening lawsuits against Callahan when he failed to deliver laborers on time and giving cash to state wardens who demanded payoffs to facilitate the movement of laborers from one location to another. "We will hold you for all damages which we may sustain if you fail or refuse to deliver the convicts," Hurt wrote Callahan in early 1905.[17]

The refined Atlanta businessman was nonchalant when the legislators asked about execrable descriptions of his camps, blaming any excesses on lax guards and wardens who—despite the payoffs made by his companies—he said refused to work the prisoners hard enough.

"They would stand up and let a convict run away from them and be afraid to shoot at him, and the only way to get a warden that was any account was to pay him extra money," Hurt testified. "When a convict starts to escape he ought to shoot, he ought to stop him or run him down and catch him."[18]

Another witness before the commission—former chief warden Jake Moore—testified that no prison guard could ever "do enough whipping for Mr. Hurt."

"He wanted men whipped for singing and laughing," Moore told the panel.[19]

When the commission called Hurt's son George to testify, the younger Hurt said convicts in his coal mines had been punished too little—not too much. Asked to cite an occasion when a warden refused to punish a prisoner who should have been, Hurt said: "That would be like numbering the sands of the seashore."[20]

"Do you remember what you wanted them whipped for?" responded a commissioner.

"For the lack of work," the younger Hurt replied.

"What was the task you required of them?"

"From two to six tons," said Hurt.

Asked why men had been forced to work in the mines into the night, violating prison rules that convicts should labor only from sunup to sundown, Hurt mocked the question: "Yes sir, but they are under the ground and it's rather hard for the warden to tell exactly when the sun is up or down."

Hurt was also sarcastically dismissive of charges that arose from the death of a black convict named Liddell, explaining that the man died not because of a whipping he received but because of "the bursting of a blood vessel while the convict was struggling *against* a whipping."

Hurt said Liddell was a huge man, weighing nearly three hundred pounds, who refused to enter the mines. A guard chained Liddell to a tree in the same yard where the boy named Wynne had been beaten to death, and forced him to sit for hours exposed to the bright sun. Later, the guard ordered Liddell to lie down for a whipping. When he refused, four men held Liddell while the guard whipped him with a leather strap. Liddell began "growing purple under the eyes," and later died, Hurt testified. He added that the blood vessel most likely burst because "the man was guilty of committing masturbation to such an extent that his mind had become affected."

Hurt said he witnessed another occasion when the warden was struggling to deal with a "powerful negro . . . who had been insubordinate ever since" arriving at the mine. To force the prisoner to begin digging, a guard told another black convict, named Jim Blevens, to attack him. The two African American men, both forced against their wills into the coal mine camp, now stood in the prison yard facing each other like gladiators, holding mining picks in their hands. The face-off lasted only seconds. The "insubordinate" man lunged forward, swinging his pick wildly. The smaller man stepped aside to dodge the attack and then swung his own tool in a high downward arc. The long blade of the pick descended onto the other man's head—piercing his jaw, throat, and chest. The wounded prisoner fell to the ground, Hurt testified, and Blevens "then put his foot on the negro's head and pulled his pick out." The injured man died from the wound.[21]

As the legislative inquiry progressed into August 1908, the sordid stories of illness and mayhem—coupled with even more voluminous accounts of corruption and payoffs—stirred an outpouring of public condemnation. Atlanta's leading pastor, Dr. James W. Lee, sermonized at Trinity Church that the convict leasing system was a "disgrace" to the state. His and other churches passed resolutions calling on the legislature to abolish the practice entirely.[22]

A technologically more advanced competitor in the brick-making business—a young engineer named B. Mifflin Hood—began advertising "Non-Convict Bricks" in the *Atlanta Constitution*. The city council—which previously bought millions of the former mayor's hard red rectangles to pave hundreds of blocks of sidewalks—voted to bar the purchase of any goods made by convicts.

Finally a crowd of more than two thousand people gathered for a mass meeting in Atlanta's Grand Opera House—the same forum where *The Clansman* had drawn sell-out crowds two years earlier. Presided over by the state's sitting governor, Hoke Smith, the gathering listened to a series of speeches condemning the lease system and then voted overwhelmingly to support a call for its abolition. Similar public meetings in the town of Rome and elsewhere across Georgia on the same day produced the same result. Newspaper editorials chimed in agreement—though most said the prisoners should be taken out of private hands and put to work improving the state's desperately inferior roads.[23]

Spurred by the public outcry, Governor Smith called a special session of the state legislature, which authorized a public referendum on the fate of the system. In October 1908, Georgia's nearly all-white electorate voted by a two-to-one margin to abolish the system as of March 1909. Without slave labor, business collapsed at Chattahoochee Brick. Production fell by nearly 50 percent in the next year. Sales—of nineteen million bricks—dropped to less than half of 1907. Total profit dwindled to less than $13,000.[24]

The apparent demise of Georgia's system of leasing prisoners seemed a harbinger of a new day—especially coming just two years after Atlanta's bloody race riot. Social progressives applauded the abolition of state-sponsored forced labor as a sign of racial moderation. Several states had already taken the momentous step before Georgia. Tennessee eliminated the sale of men into its coal mines in 1893. South Carolina moved to end the state government's direct involvement in selling prisoners by the turn of the century. Louisiana banned the leasing of state prisoners in 1901—spurred by a political rivalry between the biggest buyer of men in the state and elected leaders in control of the state capitol. Mississippi's uncouth governor James Vardaman successfully pushed for stopping the lease in 1907, primarily to punish the rich cotton planter class that were his primary political enemies.[25] Within another five years, Arkansas and Texas had abandoned the system as well. In Arkansas, the outgoing governor, a longtime opponent of the practice, pardoned in his last days in office hundreds of the prisoners held by the state—making leasing moot.

But the harsher reality of the South was that the new post–Civil War slavery was evolving—not disappearing. North Carolina banned leasing just before World War I and then revived it afterward. In Florida and Alabama—where the state-sanctioned practice of buying and selling slaves was just reaching its most evolved and highly organized form—convict leasing remained immune at every level to the ostensible "reforms" that swept other states. Most of the "abolitions" were motivated either by political imperatives or simply by the changing economic and technological circumstances of the South. As African Americans across the region were ground into political and economic penury, the difference in the costs of legally enslaved and free, but impoverished, labor narrowed dramatically. The cost of buying prisoners from state governments had risen substantially—while the cost of "free labor" available from hundreds of thousands of essentially indentured black laborers working on southern farms was flat or declining.

Moreover, while thousands of state prisoners in Georgia, the Carolinas, and other states were no longer leased to private corporations, they were being forced into an "improved" method of coercing labor and intimidating African Americans—the chain gang. Throughout the South, peonage and the leasing of prisoners by county sheriffs—long the most terrible aspect of the practices—continued unabated.

Alabama's system of selling black men through its courts and prison laws continued for more than fifteen years after U.S. Steel took its last shipment of convicts. Shelby County and most local governments continued a prosperous trade in African American forced laborers, though in the new and more orderly fashion mandated by Judge Jones. The confessions of judgment coerced upon thousands of African Americans for trivial or unprovable offenses were now carefully recorded in court files.


In Washington, D.C., there was little evidence that forced labor was abating. The offices of the attorney general and the White House continued to receive a stream of allegations of peonage and involuntary servitude as elaborate and extreme as those that had occurred on the farm of John Pace.

A deputy U.S. marshal in Roanoke, Alabama, reported in the spring of 1906 that a white man named Silas Lacy was operating a railroad construction camp as terrifying as those of three decades earlier. Dozens of slaves were arrested on fabricated charges, held against their will, starved, and subjected to daily lashings and tracking dogs. At least three workers had been murdered by the owners.[26]

Notified of the findings, the U.S. attorney general authorized sending a federal detective in to perform a larger investigation. On May 7, 1906, the agent wrote Warren Reese's successor in Montgomery, Erastus J. Parsons, describing the sweep of involuntary servitude and the perversion of the local courts to sustain it in the southeastern counties of Alabama. The deputy said Lacy was holding throngs of black men under the cruelest conditions, he wrote. One "negro boy" who attempted to flee Lacy was recaptured, whipped, and left for dead. Another black man, Josie Frank, was "held by force and kept in a state of fear." Two other black men, Curly Johnson and Carry Hatton, were "arrested on a bogus charge" and held in involuntary service to pay a fraudulent fine. "There are dozens of other similar cases," the deputy wrote. At another camp nearby, a white man named Henry Lee chased down two fleeing black workers with dogs, "captured them and carried them back to his camp chained together." Just west of the Tallapoosa River, a partnership called Mason & Brother routinely "had negroes arrested on bogus warrants, in order to get them, making them work out the cost of the arrests," wrote the marshal.[27]

"Many of these parties are cruelly treated and chased by dogs whenever they attempt to make escape," Parsons wrote to his superiors in Washington. But even Parsons feared that a prosecution of the slaveholders would fail. "The trouble in getting convictions has been that the defendants, after being arraigned before a Commissioner, somehow succeeded in driving away the witnesses," he wrote. "The negroes employed about these railroad camps are gathered from the large cities throughout the south. They are invariably given nicknames upon reaching the camps and after making their escape . . . it seems utterly impossible to get any trace of them whatever."[28]

Parsons also knew that regardless of how gravely blacks were abused, cases brought against whites for holding slaves were almost certainly doomed in Alabama. No matter how strong the evidence, he became reluctant to seek charges. He passed on to Alabama officials the report he received from a Secret Service agent on the Lacy case. "I have requested the authorities of the State of Alabama to investigate," the prosecutor added.[29] It was ignored.


An atmosphere of intimidation suffused the areas where involuntary servitude remained rampant. A black man named D. P. Johnson spirited a letter to the Department of Justice in the late winter of 1907 through a veterinarian near Banks, Alabama, claiming he was being forced to work on a county road gang to pay off debts in connection with "a contract which he forced me to sign." The white claiming the debt had already seized Johnson's farm, but insisted on receiving more. "He sent me here to work out the fine and cost of the court and the sum of money he claims to advance me. Please investigate case for I am deprived of my liberty without due process of law." Johnson said he had been denied the opportunity to bring witnesses before the jury that convicted him. A federal agent visiting the Pike County convict camp, Johnson wrote, "will find condition unparalleled in our free country." The letter was filed without follow-up.[30]

In the fall of 1907, Parsons dolefully reported to the Department of Justice an account of what happened to Ed Bettis, a black man in Lowndes County who had the temerity to testify against Jim Payne, the white farmer holding him as a slave. Payne was arrested by a federal marshal on the basis of Bettis's statements, but the charges were dropped at a preliminary hearing. Avoiding prosecution, however, was not sufficient for Payne, who after the court hearing paid a local deputy sheriff named Underwood to seize the black man and drag him to a county jail in the provincial town of Hayneville. "And there gave him a brutal whipping, because, as stated by Underwood, he had sworn out a warrant for a white man." Once again, Parsons politely sought permission to send a marshal to the area for an investigation.[31]

In December 1907, Judge Jones contacted Parsons with allegations he had received that a lumberman named Henry Stephenson was holding large numbers of black workers in forced labor at a cross-tie camp near Enterprise, Alabama. An anonymous informer wrote Judge Jones that when one black worker ran away and then refused to return to the camp after being tracked down, Stephenson told him: "If you don't cut ties for me you won't cut them for any one unless you cut them in hell." The white man then put a pistol to the head of the unnamed black man and fired "probably a fatal wound." At least one other white man was present, and reported nothing of the killing to police authorities.[32]

A year later, on December 22, 1908, William Armbrecht, the U.S. attorney in Mobile, Alabama, wrote a disappointed letter to the U.S. attorney general. Armbrecht had presented the evidence to a federal grand jury in Selma related to an allegation that a white man named Pete Nevers was holding debt slaves. "I did every thing I could to secure an indictment but failed. I can not understand why an indictment was not found except that, the country members of the Grand Jury in that section of Alabama are not disposed to find true bills in cases of peonage. The failure to secure indictments was not due to any lack of investigation on the part of the Special agents who investigated this case, nor do I think it was due to any failure on my part to present the case properly."[33]

Indeed, even after a U.S. Supreme Court ruling upholding the laws against peonage, Alabama's judicial system continued to routinely assist in the holding of black workers to involuntary servitude. Armbrecht, the mystified failed prosecutor in Mobile, learned in January 1909 that the deputy sheriff in Selma had wired the sheriff in Mobile to grab a local black man named L. McIlwane and hold him on any charge until he could be picked up. McIlwane's alleged crime was that he had broken a labor contract with a white employer near Selma. The local sheriff duly arrested McIlwane for "vagrancy" and then turned him over to the other sheriff when he arrived.

"This appears to be a clear case of peonage," committed by the sheriffs of two of the state's largest towns, Armbrecht wrote.[34]

In 1909, an internal review of all peonage prosecutions in Alabama in the first decade of the century found that of forty-three indictments issued—including those of Pace and his co-conspirators, all ended in acquittals, dismissals, suspended sentences, or presidential pardons. A total of $300 in fines had been collected from the defendants; four of those convicted served short periods in jail.[35]

Evidence of widespread peonage in Alabama and elsewhere in the Black Belt sections of other southern states barely slowed. In 1913, two Alabama men, Butler and John Searcy, were finally tried on peonage cases—having first delayed their trial by several years by kidnapping the primary witness against them, a black man named Wash Gardner, and shipping him to Cuba. The jury refused to convict.

It was plainly apparent that convictions on peonage charges would be nearly impossible to obtain. As cases collapsed, U.S. attorneys in various districts continued to go through the motions of investigating allegations of slavery. But indictments grew rare. More and more often, federal officials—citing a highly technical reading of the peonage statute—asserted that they had jurisdiction only in cases in which a slave was being held specifically to repay a debt. Adopting the same legal rationale put forward by the defense lawyers in the trials of 1903, officials increasingly took the position that merely forcing a man or woman to labor for nothing—or buying them for that purpose—was not a federal crime. Responsibility for any "action" to combat it "lies entirely within the state," said the Department of Justice.[36]

The new slavery reached a critical plateau. The resubjugation of southern blacks was achieved in such broad totality—and reaffirmed with such crushing consequences for millions of individuals, that codes and statutes were increasingly unnecessary for its preservation.

African Americans had virtually no political representation in any place in the South—even those where blacks of voting age made up the overwhelming majority of the population. Public education for African Americans was a threadbare reflection of that provided for whites—limited to half the number of days provided for white children in most cotton-producing counties. Only 5 percent of whites were entirely illiterate in 1910; nearly a third of blacks were. Nearly 69 percent of white children attended school; 37 percent of African Americans did so. Laws written and unwritten barred African Americans from selling the produce of their farms to anyone but the most powerful white merchant in their worlds and prohibited them from buying goods from anyone else as well.

A local grand jury in Birmingham reported that the bartering of African Americans for sale into the state's coal mines and the collusion of local justices of the peace in the system were only increasing. "The dockets of the justices of the peace in this county would convict many of them for peonage should the federal government choose to enforce its laws," read the final report of the grand jurors, issued in September 1911. It cited thousands of unwarranted arrests and instances of cruelty, such as seventeen men penned into a fourteen-square-foot holding cell without food for up to two days.

"It would be far better for the state of Alabama that every misdemeanant in the county of Jefferson should go unpunished than for a court to be run for the oppression of those unable to protect themselves," the jurors concluded. The U.S. attorney in Birmingham forwarded the report to Justice Department officials in Washington, but no federal action was ever undertaken in response.[37]

Desperate for traction in the face of the forces coalescing against African Americans, W. E. B. DuBois launched what would be the NAACP's seminal organ, *The Crisis*, in 1910. But the same year, Baltimore, followed by a host of cities across the South, enacted the first local ordinances delineating the geographic boundaries of black and white neighborhoods.

The election in 1912 of Woodrow Wilson, an openly white supremacist Democrat from Virginia, precipitated a dramatic expansion of Jim Crow restrictions on African Americans. In the nearly half century since the Civil War, the federal government had been the one province of American public life where black officials could still be appointed to important public positions, such as postmasters, customs officers, and other administrative roles. The Washington government hired thousands of black workers, and within federal buildings, African Americans maintained a measure of civil equality with whites.

Wilson, narrowly elected in a split election among himself, Republican William Howard Taft, and Theodore Roosevelt running on an independent Bull Moose platform, aggressively reversed the federal government's traditions of at least modest equity for African Americans. In paradoxical contrast with the "Wilsonian" reputation the president developed after World War I for his pursuit of the visionary League of Nations, Wilson dramatically curtailed the number of black appointees in his own government. His administration largely introduced to Washington, D.C., the demeaning southern traditions of racially segregated work spaces, office buildings, and restrooms.

Wilson strongly backed the demands of southern leaders that their states be left alone to deal with issues of race and black voting without interference from the North, ensuring there would be no challenge to the raft of laws passed to disenfranchise African Americans across the region.

Another half century would pass before the civil rights movement could crack the anti-black legal regime consolidated during Wilson's tenure.

After being named president of Princeton University in 1902, Wilson openly discouraged African Americans from applying to the school. In his academic writings as a political scientist, he blamed the existence of slavery not on American leaders but on England's imposing the institution upon its colonies despite England's abolition three decades before the Civil War.

Wilson accepted the most distended idealization of the antebellum South and demonization of the black political participation that followed. "Domestic slaves were almost uniformly dealt with indulgently and even affectionately by their masters," he wrote. The Reconstruction era of African American governance in states with black majorities was "an extraordinary carnival of public crime." Wilson called the eventual suppression of black political activity "the natural, inevitable ascendancy of the whites."[38]

In 1910, the vast majority, more than 93 percent, of the 10.2 million African Americans living in the United States continued to reside in the South. Nearly 60 percent of adult black men and nearly 50 percent of black women worked in farming.[39]

Among whites, farming was a path to or an established form of economic independence. More than 3.7 million white men, more than two thirds, owned their own farms. Conditions were more than reversed for blacks. Fewer than one third of nearly 900,000 farms operated by African Americans were owned by the black men who tilled the land. The rest worked at the behest of white men.

There is little empirical evidence on which to establish the precise economic arrangements between most black families and the landlords who so dominated their lives—especially on the question of how many black families lived in a form of uncompensated, de facto involuntary servitude. But what record survives indicates that the desperate plight of black farmers captured in DuBois's loosely fictionalized account of Lowndes County, Alabama, was only worsening. When federal census takers questioned every farmer in the United States in 1910, they calculated that nearly 700,000 black men, along with at least 2.5 million wives and children, lived and worked in the murky limbo of sharecroppers and rent farmers. Tenants ostensibly paid some form of rent for the land they farmed; sharecroppers gave up most of their crops at the end of each season to a landlord in return for use of his property, a house, and supplies. But under the South's regime of legal restrictions on black mobility and job freedom, the vast majority of those African Americans lived in a state of subjection to the white land-owners or employers. Federal enumerators were unable to classify tens of thousands more men for whom the nature of their relationship to white landowners was unclear.

A separate federal survey of farmers in 1909 gave a telling clue to the true status of African Americans who whites would have claimed were free laborers. Of nearly 2.5 million farms in the eleven states of the old Confed-eracy, the owners of almost 1 million farms reported giving some form of compensation to workers during the previous year. On most of the farms— a total of more than 850,000—the entire compensation to "laborers" for the year was less than seventy-nine dollars.[40]


When *The Birth of a Nation*, the movie version of the racially vitriolic stage play *The Clansman* starring the former deputy sheriff from Shelby County, Alabama, appeared in 1915, President Wilson enthusiastically embraced it. The best-selling creator of the play, Thomas Dixon, who had proclaimed in Atlanta less than a decade earlier that the duty of every southern white man was to preserve "Aryan supremacy," was a classmate from Johns Hopkins University and longtime friend of the president.

Swept up by the movie's romanticization of the Ku Klux Klan's savage war on black political involvement in the 1870s, white audiences thrilled to the silent movie, the first full-length American film. It became Hollywood's first true theatrical blockbuster. Its screening for President Wilson was the first showing of a moving film at the White House. Wilson helped arrange previews for other elected officials, members of his cabinets, and justices of the Supreme Court. "My only regret," he reportedly said, "is that it is all so terribly true."

As discomfiting for blacks as the president's embrace of a film that depicted their participation in public life as no less than venal was an extra-ordinary combination of applause and silence from other white Americans. Even in the most distant left-wing reaches of white political activism in the

North, the embryonic movements to create socialist and communist parties in the United States, many succumbed to the lure of a caricatured view of African Americans as an inferior class capable of comic relief but little more. *The Masses* magazine, a groundbreaking socialist journal published in Greenwich Village, routinely ran cartoons and spoofs depicting large-lipped, buffoonish blacks. "Your pictures of colored people . . . depress the negroes themselves and confirm the whites in their contemptuous and scornful attitude," wrote a critical reader in a 1915 letter to the editor.[41]

In Alabama's forced labor coal mines, more than three thousand prisoners were at work by 1915.[42] A study commissioned by Alabama's governor three years later concluded that the state's convict system remained an "extraordinary hazard to the life and limbs" of anyone pulled into it. He recommended abolishing the labor system entirely.[43]

As thousands of black soldiers returned to the United States after the end of World War I in 1918, anticipating that their service overseas would earn some relief from racial animosity at home, whites across the country rampaged again, with gruesome riots in South Carolina, Texas, Washington, D.C., Illinois, and Arkansas, and a new wave of lynchings.

In the spring of 1920, a white farmer in rural Jasper County, Georgia, visited the prison stockade on Bryan Street in Atlanta—the same one James W. English had relied on as a supply of slave labor for Chattahoochee Brick two decades earlier. He spotted a strong, young black man whose nickname was "Iron John," and paid his fine in return for a contract on the prisoner's labor, probably for one year.

Repeating the ritual that played out hundreds of thousands of times in hundreds of counties across the South over more than half a century since the end of the Civil War, the farmer, John S. Williams, took the man back to his sprawling plantation and ordered him to get to work or expect to be brutally punished. He was locked into a bunkhouse with about forty other black men acquired by similar means and held against their will.

It wasn't long before Iron John drew the wrath of Williams's grown son Leroy—who believed the new laborer wasn't working hard enough on a crew of black laborers ordered to build a fence. Iron John was stretched across a gasoline barrel, naked from the waist up, and whipped long and hard with a buggy whip. At some point, he cried out angrily, "Don't hit me no more . . . I'd rather be dead than treated this way."[44]

Leroy Williams drew his pistol, stepped forward, and shot the striped and bleeding black man in the shoulder. "Do you want any more?" he asked.

"Yes . . . shoot me," he answered.

The white man raised the pistol to Iron John's head and fired into his skull. He died instantly. At the instructions of the white man, other laborers attached Iron John's body to a heavy log with wire, rowed it to the middle of a farm pond, and allowed it to sink.

The murder—and certainly the whippings that preceded it—were hardly unusual. There had been many of the former and thousands of the latter by the time a black laborer named Gus Chapman escaped from the Williams plantation in November 1920. Early in 1921, he made his way to the federal courthouse in Atlanta. Two weeks after Chapman told his story to federal officials, two agents from the Department of Justice's still new Bureau of Investigation visited Williams to inquire about conditions.

They found eleven black forced laborers working in a field, all of them evidently there to work off criminal fines supposedly paid on their behalf by Williams. The African American men were supervised by Clyde Manning, a black overseer long entrusted by Williams to keep the men on the farm while he was away. While the agents were there, the plantation owner returned home. Williams, a thin fifty-four-year-old with a drawn face and slight mustache, invited the two officers to sit and have a glass of tea. Reclining on chairs on the porch, the agents asked if the black field workers were being held in "peonage." Williams asked them to explain exactly what the "peonage" law was about.

"If you pay a nigger's fine or go on his bond and you work him on your place, you're guilty of peonage," replied George W. Brown, one of the Bureau of Investigation agents, using the time-honored southern signal that his questions didn't indicate any particular regard for black people.

Williams laughed softly, according to later testimony. "Well, if that is the case, me and most of the people who have done anything of the sort were guilty of peonage," the farmer replied. "I don't keep any of my niggers locked up. Of course, I do tell some of them they shouldn't leave before paying the fine they rightly owe me."

Brown and his partner seemed satisfied with the answer. The farmer relaxed. But then Williams began to talk more about the farm. He described how he sometimes hunted down escapees and forced them to return. The agents asked if they could look around the plantation. They saw the slave quarters, where shackles and chains were clearly used to restrain forced laborers at night. Every black worker they quizzed, while appearing terrified and reluctant to talk, nonetheless said they were satisfied with their treatment on the farm. None of the workers spoke of the murder of Iron John or other acts of violence on the farm.

By the end of the day, the agents were convinced that Williams had committed at least a technical violation of the peonage statute. But to a pair of experienced field agents, both native to the South, the situation looked typical for most big southern farms. The anxiety and mumbling of the workers were routine, given the unwavering social custom of blacks showing absolute deference to all whites and open fear to law enforcement. After all the years of investigations and failed peonage prosecutions in the South, Brown knew no Georgia jury would convict a white man for practices engaged in by tens of thousands of other white farmers across the region— especially since Williams's laborers appeared relatively well fed and clothed. This wasn't a case worth wasting time on. The agents explained the anti-peonage statute to the farmer again, warning him not to violate it further.

"I don't think you need to have any fear of any case before the federal grand jury," Brown told him as they departed.

That assurance wasn't enough for Williams. He was an intelligent and relatively worldly man. Now that he understood the peonage law more clearly—and knew that federal agents had identified him as a violator— Williams recognized his vulnerability, and that of his adult sons. The property he and his oldest sons farmed stretched for miles across Jasper County. In Williams's big house at the center of the plantation lived his wife and eight minor children.

He had built a comfortable and influential life, and a farm admired for its size and profitability. Williams had the distinction of owning an early automobile, and the ear of white county leaders. He would not risk seeing a personal empire built over twenty years ruined. Williams resolved that no African American would ever testify of the slavery on his plantation.

Just after dawn the next morning, Williams found Manning, the black overseer, in the early chill and told him the other workers could "ruin" them all. "You have to get rid of all the stockade niggers," Williams said. "We'll have to do away with them."

Two days later, Williams and Manning attacked Johnnie Williams, one of the forced laborers, in a remote pasture and bludgeoned him to death with the flat side of an axe. The following morning, John Will Gaither was ordered to begin digging a new well. Once it was a few feet deep, he was killed with a pickaxe blow to the head and buried in the hole.

On the evening of Friday, February 25, 1921, a week after the federal agents visited, Williams entered the slave quarters and told the stunned men they were free to go. He said John Browne and Johnny Benson should get in his car to go to the train station that night. Instead, Williams drove them to an isolated spot, where Manning wrapped chains around their bodies and attached a heavy iron wheel from a cotton press. The pair were thrown alive off a bridge into the Alcovy River, where they sank into the murk and drowned.

As darkness fell on Saturday night, Willie Preston, Lindsey Peterson, and Harry Price climbed into the car under the same ruse. They were chained to bags filled with bricks, and Preston and Peterson were thrown off a different bridge. Price, resigned to his fate, jumped in on his own. Before the church hour on Sunday morning, Manning split Johnny Green's skull with an axe. The white farmer watched as Manning attacked and then instructed him to keep hitting Green's shattered skull until all signs of life ceased.

After a Sunday dinner of fried chicken and biscuits, Williams called for Willie Givens, another black slave worker, to join him and Manning for a walk into the nearby woods. At the edge of the forest, Manning sank his axe in Givens's back. A week later, Williams drowned Charlie Chisolm, the other African American who had been ordered to assist in the killings, and then shot to death Fletcher Smith, the last of the other forced laborers.

A total of eleven African Americans were murdered to conceal slavery on the Williams farm. Men who had grown to adulthood in a South steeped in terror of physical harm, or even more brutal forms of involuntary servitude, in which they had no cause to expect justice or equity from any white person, passively resigned themselves to violent death, unwilling or unable to resist.

Only after decomposing bodies began to surface in the rivers of Jasper County did the federal agents who had been willing to ignore Williams's slave farm a few weeks earlier grow suspicious. Williams and Manning were eventually tried and convicted for murder in connection with the killings. Williams—the only white man found guilty in Georgia of killing a black man during the ninety years between 1877 and 1966—died in prison.[45]

The Williams farm was exceptional in the level of violence used to conceal its use of slave labor—and the degree to which the revolting details of that violence came to be revealed. But as John Williams easily admitted to the federal agents when they first arrived at his property, forced labor remained as ubiquitous as cotton in the South, an endemic feature of the landscape and economy.

During the investigation of Williams, a government prosecutor brought charges against Arthur Farmer, Dr. James T. Tyner, and Charles Madares for holding slaves in central Alabama. After the indictment in March 1921, the primary witness in the case, a black man named Jim Stenson, was kidnapped—twice—and spirited out of the state. The white men eventually pleaded no contest to the charges and received a nominal penalty. There was no prosecution for having intimidated their victim into refusing to testify.[46]

Increasingly, after years of absolute political hegemony by the white supremacist southern wing of the Democratic Party, federal officials in the South wanted as little as possible to do with the political and social inflammation that came with investigations into any racially oriented crime. An accusation in 1924 that the logging camp and sawmill of S. J. Wilkins on Alabama's Tombigbee River had held a twenty-two-year-old African American man and his fifteen-year-old brother for more than nine months—claiming they owed the owner $150 each—went nowhere.[47]

U.S. attorneys and field offices of the Department of Justice abrogated their role in such cases, knowing full well that virtually no act of violence by whites against African Americans—and certainly no cases of involuntary servitude whatsoever—would ever be prosecuted by sheriffs or state officials in the South. In April 1926, federal authorities in Birmingham were told of a brutal whipping given to a black man working in a textile mill as a signal to other African Americans that they shouldn't seek work above the level of floor sweepers or janitors. The following month, J. Edgar Hoover, director of what was then called the Department of Justice's Bureau of Investigation, wrote Assistant Attorney General O. R. Luhring blithely asserting that the facts surrounding an attack on a black worker by whites in the Birmingham, Alabama, textile mill didn't merit a federal investigation. "We have an enormous amount of work on hand involving undoubted violations of Federal statutes and I can see no reason for proceeding with this matter," Hoover wrote.[48] The case was ignored.

· Two months later, a black woman in Birmingham named Rebecca Jones mailed a letter to the White House, asking President Calvin Coolidge to help her free her teenage daughter, Carolina Dixon. The mother said two men claiming to be sheriffs had seized her daughter on a country road when she was just thirteen years old and then held her in collusion with the Butler County judge for five years—forcing her to work and abusing her sexually. When Jones went to the farm of Tom Couch, the man holding her daughter, "I was met with threats under the point of high powered rifles, stating that I could not take my daughter back," Jones wrote. My "child was scarred unmerciful in several places on her body." A federal agent was dispatched to investigate, and the facts of the kidnapping were put before a grand jury. It refused to indict Couch. The matter was dropped.[49]

Yet even as the federal government did little to check the breadth of the new slavery, the economic logic of the system weakened. Crude industrial enterprises to which slave labor lent itself so effectively for fifty years were being eclipsed by modern technologies and business strategies. Mechanized coal mining—using hydraulic digging tools, electric lights, modern pumps, and transportation—made obsolete the old manual labor mines of Alabama, packed with thousands of slave workers and mules.

When cotton prices fell drastically after World War I, and the new scourge of the boll weevil ravaged millions of acres of cotton fields, depression set in across the rural landscape. The cost of labor plunged yet further. Prisoners offered for sale by state officials who expected the returns on their business in labor to steadily increase grew too expensive for some market conditions. Buying and selling them was less and less sensible. As financial incentives for the states faded, political scandals and abuse outrages gained traction. In even the most notorious states, public cries to end the leasing of convicts to private contractors arose for the first time.

In the winter of 1921, Martin Tabert, a twenty-two-year-old white man from a middle-class farm family in Munich, North Dakota, decided to take a walk-about through the United States, traveling by train, sleeping in railroad camps with tramps, and working to support himself as he crossed the West, Midwest, and finally the South. Running short of money in December, Tabert, along with a group of other itinerant men, hopped aboard a freight train without a ticket.

Unbeknownst to Tabert, the sheriff of Leon County, just south of the Georgia state line, maintained a rich trade from spying on the freight rails that crossed into his territory, seizing men from the train, charging them with vagrancy or "beating" a ride on a railroad, and selling them into slavery. Tabert was arrested, fined $25 for vagrancy, and then sold for three months' work to a turpentine camp owned by Putnam Lumber Company— then a vast enterprise headquartered in Wisconsin but engaged in the harvest of hundreds of thousands of swampy Florida forestland. Within days, Tabert's family wired more than enough to pay the fine, but their son had already been shipped into the maw of Putnam's forced labor system. In sixty-five years, the southern turpentine camp—desperate, hungered, sadistically despotic—had changed hardly at all.

Young Tabert did not last long in the putrid swamp. He was given ill-fitting shoes, and his feet became blistered and swollen. A boil formed in his groin. Accused of shirking work in January 1922, the slight-framed Tabert was forced by the camp whipping boss, Walter Higginbotham, to lie on the ground as eighty-five other prisoners watched. Higginbotham pulled up Tabert's shirt and applied to his back more than thirty licks with a seven-and-a-half-pound leather strap. By the time the beating concluded, Tabert was "twitching on the ground," according to one witness. Higginbotham placed his foot on Tabert's neck to keep him from moving, and then hit him more than forty more times with the strap. The boss ordered Tabert to stand, and when he moved too slowly, the guard whipped him two dozen more times, witnesses later testified. When the young North Dakota man, a thousand miles from home and an immeasurable distance from any measure of sanity or decency, finally made it to his feet, Higginbotham chased him in a circle, striking him over the head and shoulders, shouting repeatedly: "You can't work yet?"

When the beating finally ended, Tabert collapsed into his cot and never stood again. A terrible odor rose from his body. He died the following night. A Putnam Lumber executive wrote to Tabert's family a few days later, informing him that their son had died of malaria and expressing the company's sympathy.

Unconvinced of the explanation for their son's death, the Tabert family triggered a series of legal inquiries and a Pulitzer Prize–winning journalistic investigation by the *New York World*. Higginbotham was tried and convicted of second-degree murder. But his conviction was later overturned by a Florida court. He was never retried or punished.[50] Still, public disclosure of the gruesome killing and its subsequent cover-up stirred a wave of outrage—especially as a demonstration that the excesses of the South's new slavery could even extend to a white boy from a family of distinction. The following year, the Florida legislature, after an extended debate, voted to ban the use of the whip on any prisoners in the state.[51]

Alabama officials were also under growing humanitarian and union pressures to end the worst abuses of the convict leasing system. Over time, state agencies took more direct control of the supervision and punishment of convicts—though through every purported reform, black prisoners continued to be driven beyond reasonable human limits under the cold mandates of the businessmen and companies who captured them.

Most reforms were cursory and superficial, such as requiring that men be clothed during their lashings. The fee system and its profit motivation to encourage sheriffs to make as many arrests as possible remained in force. "Our jails are money-making machines," wrote a state prison inspector, W. H. Oates, in a 1922 report.

At the same time, the number of men being arrested and sentenced to some form of hard labor in Alabama ballooned. In the year ending September 30, 1922, total arrests nearly reached 25,000, driven partly by new prohibition laws. Within another five years, the figure was 37,701 for one twelve-month period.[52]

In 1924, another ghastly story of death in a slave mine surfaced. Like Martin Tabert's murder, it took on sensational proportions when the public realized that the young white man, James Knox, died while undergoing tortures that in the minds of most whites could only be justified as punishment for African Americans.

Working at Sloss-Sheffield's Flat Top prison outside Birmingham, Knox was first reported to have killed himself. Later, a grand jury collected evidence showing that the whipping boss in charge of Knox's crew punished him for slow work with the water cure so long in use in the slave camps of the South. "James Knox died in a laundering vat, located in the yard of the prison near the hospital, where he was placed by two negroes. . . . It seems likely that James Knox died as a result of heart failure, which probably was caused by a combination of unusual exertion and fear. . . . After death it seems that a poison was injected artificially into his stomach in order to simulate accidental death or suicide."[53]

Despite howls of protest that a white could die so ignominiously, Alabama's prisoners continued to struggle against medieval conditions. Monthly memos written by Glenn Andrews, a state medical inspector, recorded scores of routine lashings for offenses such as cursing, failure to dig the daily quota of coal, and "disobedience." One entry in March 1924 reported that in the previous month, "a negro woman was given seven lashes for cursing and fighting. On the same day, a negro man was given seven lashes for burning a hole in prison floor. On Feb. 14, a negro man was given seven lashes for cursing and fighting. On the same day and for the same offense two negro women were given six lashes each." In a 1925 report, two black inmates, Ernest Hallman and R. B. Green, received five lashes each for not obeying a guard. Others were put in chains and given up to a dozen lashes for "not working." White prisoners, now invested in larger numbers, were more often given solitary confinement.[54]

In March 1926, the front page of the *New York World* featured an exposé on southern slavery. The stories reported that in fifty-one of Alabama's sixty-seven counties, nearly one thousand prisoners had been sold into slave mines and forced labor camps the previous year—generating $250,000, or about $2.8 million in modern currency, for local officials. The state government pocketed $595,000 in 1925—or $6.6 million today—selling about 1,300 men to Sloss-Sheffield's Flat Top mine, the successor to Pratt Consolidated—now called Alabama By-Products Corp.—and the Aldrich mine in Montevallo, Alabama, the town where Green Cottenham's mother lived her last isolated years.

Once sold, the prisoners faced beatings with steel wire, hickory sticks, whips, and shovels. The stories described "dog houses"—rough-hewn boxes the size of coffins into which men were locked for up to forty-eight hours. Most prison camps had six to twenty such houses.[55]

Finally, in 1927, new Alabama governor Bibb Graves moved to stanch the long-running negative depiction of the state and its twentieth-century slavery. He began relocating a hundred prisoners out of the mines and other private businesses each month and sped up construction of new prison facilities and roadwork camps where county prisoners would soon be shackled into chain gangs—seeding the notorious scandals of the next generation.[56]

On June 1, 1928, the lungs of eight hundred men filled the damp air of the mine shafts at Flat Top with the sounds of "Swing Low, Sweet Chariot." The white prisoners held here and at Alabama's only other remaining prison mine had already been relocated to work on road gangs.

Only African Americans remained at Flat Top. They rose out of the mile-long manway in two columns—blinking at the sudden brightness of the summer sun. As the plaintive lyric "Coming for to carry me home" wafted into the daylight, the prisoners marched out of the shaft, surrounded by armed guards, and walked to a train platform. Within a few hours, they had been transported to the state's newly constructed Kilby Prison. No more men would be sold into slave mines by the state of Alabama.[57]

More than a year later, a thirty-six-year-old man born in Tallapoosa County and named Henry Tinsley arrived at the gates of Kilby Prison. Like Green Cottenham, he was born decades after Abraham Lincoln's emancipation of his parents and grandparents. Also like Green, all his years and every facet of his life were shaped and circumscribed by the slavery that succeeded the freedom of his forebears.

It was Henry Tinsley and his brother, Luke, who as children three decades earlier had been captured by John Pace and forced to work on his brutal Tallapoosa plantation.[58] They were the two young boys Warren

Reese had discovered still being held by Pace five years after taking them from their mother and long after Pace had been pardoned by President Roosevelt on a promise never to hold slaves again.

Henry had worked for a time in the warehouse of a grocery wholesaler in Birmingham. He had married and fathered a child more than a decade earlier. He had been a soldier too, called in 1917 to fight in the U.S. Army.[59] But the Alabama Henry returned to after World War I was the same state he was born into in 1892. And soon it returned him to the condition Alabama had reserved for him at birth.

His crime in 1929 was recorded as assault with intent to murder. The details of the case are lost, but the sentence of two years' imprisonment suggests a brawl in which the other man was injured.[60] Regardless of whether the man who had grown from that captive thirteen-year-old committed a real crime or whether it was his enslavement by John Pace that led him to do so twenty-three years later, deep into the twentieth century, Henry Tinsley wore chains again.

# XVII

## FREEDOM

*"In the United States one cannot sell himself."*

Two years after the last convicts emerged from Flat Top prison, a white writer named John Spivak visited the offices of the state Prison Commission in Georgia in September 1930. Presenting himself in Atlanta as a journalist seeking to document reforms in the convict system, Spivak was given a letter of introduction from none other than the state's top penal officer, directing the wardens of every prison camp in Georgia to give him full access to their stockades and inmates.

Spivak, born in Connecticut, had worked as a police reporter for a newspaper in his home state and as a writer of pulp fiction stories. His strong socialist leanings made him sympathetic to the plight of blacks held against their will in the South. His skill with the jocular techniques of insinuating into the comfort of sheriffs and wardens gave him the tools to render an astonishingly sharp portrait of what he found.

Contrary to the congratulatory pronouncements that followed Georgia's "abolition" of the practice of selling black prisoners in 1908, the state had more forced labor slaves than ever by 1930. In excess of eight thousand men—nearly all of them black—worked in chain gangs in 116 counties. Of 1.1 million African Americans in the state that year, approximately half lived under the direct control and force of whites—unable to move or seek employment elsewhere under threat that doing so would lead to the dreaded chain gang.[1]

Two years later Spivak published *Georgia Nigger*, a 241-page fictionalized account of his finds—built around the harrowing narrative of a young
black boy drawn inexorably and cynically into a lifetime of slavery—on a
county chain gang, as a debt slave to farmers, as a possession bought and
sold by white plantation men. The episodes that make up the narrative
could have just as easily been firsthand accounts of the fiery lynching disaster in Pine Apple, Alabama, the brutish violence and perversion of Lowndes
County three decades earlier, or the "murder farm" of John S. Williams.

Unlike the plethora of chain-gang-themed novels and movies that followed in the next four decades such as the 1967 film *Cool Hand Luke*—nearly
all of which assiduously labored to depict the southern penal barbarism as
something directed equitably at both whites and blacks—Spivak made no
effort to blunt the overtly racial character of involuntary servitude. He
unstintingly portrayed a system designed to enslave or intimidate black men
into obedience. That a small minority of white men were drawn in as well
was peripheral and inconsequential.

Spivak created a character named David Jackson, a black sharecropper's
son first sentenced to the chain gang of fictional Ochlockonee County
for no apparent crime. Still a teenager, he was released from the traveling
camp—in which prisoners were, as in actual life at the time, held in rolling
cages similar to circus wagons transporting exotic animals. The men were
perpetually chained to one another—eating, sleeping, working, bathing,
and defecating together, never freed from their heavy iron links.

After the character's release from the chain gang, David watched a game
of dice in an alleyway during a Saturday visit to town. A fight breaks out: "A
steel blade glinted in the yellow light. The burly nigger grunted and clutched
at his neck. The assailant dropped the knife and fled. Someone scooped up
the money and ran. Only the knife was left by the time the restaurant proprietor and his two customers rushed out. David instinctively turned to the
lighted streets, hoping to lose himself in the crowds. Dark forms scurried
by. A strong hand grasped the boy's arm and a voice demanded: 'What's yo'
hurry, nigger?'

" 'I didn't do nothing,' " he protested frantically.[2]

Rounded up with four other young black men, none of whom was connected to the fight, Jackson is convinced by the sheriff that he must allow the

county's largest landowner to buy him or sit in a vermin-infested jail for a year, awaiting trial. Sold to the white plantation farmer for $25—ostensibly to pay a fine for disturbing the peace—David is taken in chains to Jim Deering's remote plantation. There he is worked as a slave, and witnesses how Deering handles those blacks who resist any order—flogging men on their naked buttocks with straps dipped in syrup and sand, beating men with fists and clubs. As the farm falls behind during picking season—raising the prospect that some of the cotton in the field could be lost—Deering's methods of compelling the slaves to work harder grow even more sadistic. To teach others a lesson, he orders a man nicknamed "High Yaller" for his lighter skin to be whipped for stopping to get a drink of water.

> *A guard slipped handcuffs on him. Another appeared with a long, leather strap of knotted thongs. With a quick movement the guards threw him face down. One sat on his shoulders and the other on his feet. Charlie slipped the nigger's overalls down until the buttocks were exposed, took the strap and stepped back. It swished through the air and cracked like a pistol shot on the brown flesh.*
>
> *High Yaller screamed and squirmed, rubbing his face in the soil. The guards dug their feet into the earth to keep from being thrown off. Red welts showed on the skin.*
>
> *The strap swished through the air again. High Yaller ceased screaming before the twentieth stroke. He moaned and his body jerked spasmodically. His face was scratched and bleeding. He tried to spit the red clay from his mouth but it stuck to his lips and chin. The exposed flesh was a mass of welts and criss-crossed lines of blood. . . . Flies settled on the raw buttocks.*[3]

Another morning a sick prisoner named Limpy—for his injured hip—begs in the road to be allowed to rest. Ordered to begin picking cotton again, Limpy has the audacity to resist. He accuses the farmer of trying to work him to death, of treating the prisoners worse than "real" slaves before the Civil War. "If I was yo' slave an' you paid a t'ousan' dollar fo' me you'd tek care o' me when I git de mis'ries but you kin git plenty mo' niggers cheap if I die,' " Limpy yelled from the pages of the book.

*Deering turned on him white with fury. His fist smashed against the nigger's face. Limpy sank to the ground, blood running from his nose and mouth. . . .*

*"Get up and go to work!" Deering ordered tersely. "Get up, or I'll give you something to get sick over!"*

*"Sho," he growled, "why doan you kill me now instead o' sendin' me out in de fiel's to die!"*

*The planter's face turned apoplectic. For a moment he tried to restrain himself. Then with a swift movement his hand darted to his hip and drew his pistol.*

*With a hoarse scream Limpy tried to scramble to his feet, his hands half raised in supplication.*

*"Mist' Deerin'—" he cried.*

*Deering fired twice. Limpy slumped to the ground, his head on his chest. . . .*

*"You asked for it, you black bastard! . . . I want no impudence around here!" he shouted to the terrified niggers at the tables. "Remember that!"*

*He turned to the gigantic nigger beside him. "Weight the son of a bitch and bury him in the swamp!"*[4]

Spivak's protagonist eventually escaped Deering's farm, but his freedom leads only to a series of pathetic and ever more desperate efforts to avoid returning to his slave status under Deering or another white man. Finally finding a way out of his home county and the feudal dominion of Deering and the sheriff he controlled, Jackson discovers that every other town in Georgia is another vortex of police coercion and involuntary servitude. He is quickly arrested and sold to other white men. Hunted down by bloodhounds after another escape—betrayed by a prisoner who had been "stretched" on a rack by guards—Jackson is finally resigned to his fate. Spikes riveted to his ankles and an iron collar padlocked to a five-foot chain, Jackson accepts that he will die a slave.[5]

To underscore the veracity of Spivak's description of black life in Georgia, the author published as a visual epilogue to the book a series of photographs taken in Georgia's labor camps. He reprinted reports detailing whippings, extra chains, and "put in barrel"—a variation of the sweatbox.

One document—titled "Official Whipping Report"—listed fifty beatings at one camp in August 1930. A gallery of photographs showed bloodhounds baying at an escapee in a tree. Guards proudly demonstrated to their visitor the latest techniques of punishment and torture—colonial-era stocks, black men trussed around pick handles like pigs ready for slaughter, the "stretching" rack.[6]

Across the South, despite claimed reforms in many states, more prisoners than ever before were pressed into compelled labor for private contractors—but now almost entirely through local customs and informal arrangements in city and county courts. The state of Alabama was no longer selling slaves to coal mines, but thousands of men continued to work on a chain gang or under lease to a local owner. The total number of men arrested on misdemeanor charges and subject to sale by county sheriffs in 1927 grew to 37,701. One out of every nineteen black men over the age of twelve in Alabama was captured in some form of involuntary servitude.

The triviality of the charges used to justify the massive numbers of people forced into labor never diminished. More than 12,500 people were arrested in Alabama in 1928 for possessing or selling alcohol; 2,735 were charged with vagrancy; 2,014 with gaming; 458 for leaving the farm of an employer without permission; 154 with the age-old vehicle for stopping intimate relations between blacks and whites: adultery.[7]

Roughly half of all African Americans—or 4.8 million—lived in the Black Belt region of the South in 1930, the great majority of whom were almost certainly trapped in some form of coerced labor like that described in Spivak's chilling account.

Two Mississippi sheriffs reported making between $20,000 and $30,000 each during 1929 in extra compensation for procuring black laborers and selling them to local planters. After a plea for more cotton pickers in August 1932, police in Macon, Georgia, scoured the town's streets, arresting sixty black men on "vagrancy" charges and immediately turning them over to a plantation owner named J. H. Stroud. A year later, *The New York Times* reported a similar roundup in the cotton town of Helena, Arkansas.[8]

Otto B. Willis, a forty-six-year-old white farmer living near Evergreen,

Alabama, deep in the Black Belt, wrote the Department of Justice in 1933, describing the desperate system under which black families were held as de facto serfs on the land of the county's white landowners. Why Willis— an Alabama-born farmer with a wife and six children, living on land they owned—would be moved to defend the plight of the tens of thousands of black laborers who shared rural Hale County with him is a mystery. But in an elegant longhand, he described point by damning point how black men and their wives and children were compelled to remain at work for years upon years to retire so-called debts for their seed, tools, food, clothing, and mules that could never be extinguished, regardless of how much cotton they grew in any year. Little had changed since Klansmen in Hale County shipped R. H. Skinner to the Alabama slave mines in 1876.

"The negro is worse than broke. . . . His family goes ragged and without medical attention and the women are attended by ignorant colored midwives at childbirth and many die from blood poison," Willis wrote. "The negro is half starved and half clothed, yet he sees no hope of ever being out of debt, cause many landowners tell them if they move off his land he will have them put in jail or threatened bodily harm. Colored people have little standing in court here. So he is *afraid* to *move*. So they are forced to remain on and start another crop for the landlord. . . . These are the facts. . . . Is it right?"[9]

Whatever motivation Willis had in penning his detailed litany of the mechanics of slavery in the 1930s, federal officials weary of the issue had little interest. Writing on behalf of the attorney general, Joseph B. Keenan replied with the timeworn explanation for why slavery was not a matter meriting the attention of the Department of Justice—that only narrowly defined debt slavery would be examined by federal agents.

"Peonage is a condition of compulsory service based upon the indebtedness of the peon to the master; the basal fact being indebtedness," Keenan wrote, in bored, boilerplate language. Ignoring that Willis's letter explicitly described a system of holding laborers against their will until claimed debts were paid off, the Justice Department official dismissed Willis with a patronizing bureaucratic directive. "If you have any specific facts showing that the matter falls within the above definition, it is suggested that you report the same." The case was closed.[10]

By the middle of the decade before World War II, federal investigations into peonage all but stopped except in the most egregious cases. Even those resulted in the rarest convictions. Even more rare was meaningful punishment. On October 13, 1941, Charles E. Bledsoe pleaded guilty in federal court in Mobile, Alabama, to a charge of peonage for holding a black man named Martin Thompson against his will. Using the same technique as John Pace in 1903, Bledsoe didn't resist the charge and trusted that federal officials and the U.S. District Court judge would not deal harshly with a white man holding slaves. He was correct. Bledsoe's punishment was a fine of $100 and six months of probation. The status of new black slavery appeared complete. The futility of combating it was clear.

Less than two months after the slap on the wrist of Charles Bledsoe, the naval forces of imperial Japan launched their attack on Pearl Harbor. Caught flat-footed and unprepared for war, U.S. officials frantically planned for a massive national mobilization. President Franklin D. Roosevelt instinctively knew the second-class citizenship and violence imposed upon African Americans would be exploited by the enemies of the United States. Attorney General Francis Biddle called together his top assistants and shared the president's concern. Biddle was informed that federal policy had long been to cede virtually all allegations of slavery to local jurisdiction—effectively guaranteeing they would never be prosecuted. Biddle—favorite son of an elite Northern family in Philadelphia—was shocked. He could not comprehend that forced labor continued in America on more than "a few plantations."[11]

Nonetheless, Biddle knew that in an all-out war, in which millions of African Americans would be called upon to sacrifice in a struggle to protect freedom and liberty in Europe and Asia, the U.S. government had to make clear that anyone who continued to practice slavery, in violation of 1865's Thirteenth Amendment, would be prosecuted as a criminal.

Five days after the Japanese attack, on December 12, 1941, Biddle issued a directive—Circular No. 3591—to all federal prosecutors acknowledging the long history of the unwritten federal law enforcement policy to ignore most reports of involuntary servitude. "A survey of the Department files on alleged peonage violations discloses numerous instances of 'prosecution declined,'" he wrote. "It is the purpose of these instructions to direct the attention of the United States Attorneys to the possibilities of successful prosecutions stemming from alleged peonage complaints which have heretofore been considered inadequate to invoke federal prosecution." Biddle proceeded to lay out a series of federal criminal statutes that could be used to prosecute slavery—all of which had long been available to federal officials.

He ordered that instead of relying on the quirks of the old anti-peonage statute as an excuse for not attacking instances of forced labor, prosecutors and investigators should embrace "building the cases around the issue of involuntary servitude and slavery."[12]

Biddle descended from extensive antebellum Virginia slaveholders in his mother's family and from the most pedigreed line of lawyers in the country on his father's. His great-great-grandfather, Nicholas Biddle, had served as president of the Bank of the United States under President James Monroe. Like virtually every white American who considered themselves racially moderate in 1941, Biddle was more than a petty racist as well. In his memoirs, Biddle chuckled at the speech of a "colored boy" testifying in a trial early in his legal career. His "vocabulary, from a generous estimate, could not have contained more than a few hundred words." He described black babies born in a clinic for unwed mothers as "exhibiting, like Indians, the glowing beauty of primitive children." His "colored man, Benjamin . . . polished brass with the ardor with which his race always approaches brass and with a grave friendly dignity helped our guests with their coats and hats after a dinner party."[13]

Yet Biddle—especially when faced with the harsh but truthful depiction of black life as it would be suddenly projected through the propaganda of Japan and Germany—fundamentally grasped that African Americans, no matter how condescendingly he viewed them, had been denied the compact of freedom forged in the Civil War. "One response of this country to the challenge of the ideals of democracy made by the new ideologies of Fascism and Communism has been a deepened realization of the values of a government based on a belief in the dignity and rights of man," Biddle said in one major wartime speech.[14] He mounted the first modest legal attack on the southern states' successful expulsion of blacks from political participation. Unlike any prior U.S. attorney general, he recognized the federal government's duty to admit that African Americans were not free and to assertively enforce the statutes written to protect them. "We determined to breathe new life" into the dormant civil rights laws, Biddle later wrote.[15]

The Justice Department's recently formed Civil Rights Section, created primarily to investigate cases related to anti–organized labor cases, began shifting its focus to discrimination and racial abuse.

Less than a week into the ravages of World War II, Biddle explicitly repudiated the legal rationale laid out by Judge Thomas Jones in the 1903 trials that had unwittingly facilitated so much slavery across the South in the intervening half century.

"In the United States one cannot sell himself as a peon or slave—the law is fixed and established to protect the weak-minded, the poor, the miserable. Men will sometimes sell themselves for a meal of victuals or contract with another who acts as surety on his bond to work out the amount of the bond upon his release from jail. Any such sale or contract is positively null and void and the procuring and causing of such contract to be made violates [the] statutes," argued Biddle in his memo. Henceforth, he ordered all Department of Justice investigators to entirely drop reference to peonage in their written reports. They were to instead label every file as related to what it truly was—what it had always been for the past seven decades: "Involuntary Servitude and Slavery."[16]

In August 1942, a letter from a sixteen-year-old black boy arrived at the Department of Justice alleging that Charles Bledsoe—the Alabama man who received a $100 fine for peonage prior to Biddle's memo—was still holding members of the boy's family as slaves. Despite the Biddle directive, FBI director J. Edgar Hoover initially saw no need to mount another aggressive investigation. The U.S. attorney in Mobile, Francis H. Inge, was similarly disinterested. "No active investigation will be instituted," Hoover wrote to Assistant Attorney General Wendell Berge, attempting to close the file.[17]

That would have been the end of the matter even a year earlier. But seven months into World War II, with the nation anxious to mobilize every possible soldier and counter every thrust of Japan's and Germany's propaganda machines, Berge directed Hoover to look further. "In accordance with the request of the Attorney General that we expedite cases related to Negro victims, it will be appreciated if this matter is given preference," Berge wrote in a terse letter ordering Inge into action.[18]

"The matter complained of in the instant case is but one of many in which members of the Negro race have been the victims. Enemy propagandists have used similar episodes in international broadcasts to the colored race, saying that the democracies are insincere and that the enemy is their friend," Berge wrote. "There have been received from the President an instruction that lynching complaints shall be investigated as soon as possible; that the results of the investigation be made public in all instances, and the persons responsible for such lawless acts vigorously prosecuted. The Attorney General has requested that we expedite other cases related to Negro victims. Accordingly, you are requested to give the matter your immediate attention."[19]

Biddle's civil rights lawyers began to reassess fundamentally the legal breadth of the constitutional amendments ending slavery, the Reconstruction-era statutes passed to enforce them, and other largely forgotten laws such as the antebellum Slave Kidnapping Act, which made it illegal to capture or hold forced laborers in U.S. territory where slavery was prohibited.

As the war progressed, the Department of Justice vigorously prosecuted U.S. Sugar Company in Florida for forcing black men into their sugarcane fields. Sheriffs who colluded with the company were brought to trial. Before the end of World War II, the federal courts would rule that slaveholders could be prosecuted for peonage, even if the debt they claimed a worker owed them was fictitious. It was a subtle change. But the decision eliminated what had been a standard defense against the crime—the assertion that no evidence of a debt between the slave and slave driver existed.

Finally, early in September 1942, a team of FBI agents, highway patrolmen, and deputies descended on a remote farm near Beeville, Texas, to arrest a white farmer, Alex Skrobarcek, and his adult daughter, Susie Skrobarcek. They were initially charged in a state court with maiming a mentally retarded black worker named Alfred Irving. But a month later, lawyers at the Department of Justice drew a federal indictment alleging that the pair had held Irving in slavery for at least four years. They were accused of repeatedly beating the man with whips, chains, and ropes—so much so that he was physically disfigured from the abuse.[20]

Signaling the special significance of the case, a special assistant to Attorney General Biddle actively participated in prosecuting the trial. He later wrote that investigators found "overwhelming" evidence that the Skrobarceks "repeatedly horsewhipped the victim . . . starved him and otherwise held him in fear."[21]

The attorneys argued that the century-old Slavery Kidnapping Act applied to this case of abject involuntary servitude, in apparently the first such prosecution since the Civil War. The defendants were found guilty and sentenced to federal prison. Federal officials made clear that the case was intended to send a message that despite any claims by U.S. enemies, the federal government was finally serious about ending involuntary servitude for African Americans.

"The Skrobarczyk [sic] trial and its conclusion undoubtedly will be said . . . to have given a decisive setback to the enemy propaganda machine . . . urging . . . negroes that their proper place in this conflict is with the yellow race," editorialized the *Corpus Christi Times.*[22]

Two years later, President Harry Truman's Committee on Civil Rights recommended bolstering the anti-slavery statute to plainly criminalize involuntary servitude. In 1948, the entire federal criminal code was dramatically rewritten, further clarifying the laws against involuntary servitude. Finally, in 1951, Congress passed even more explicit statutes, making any form of slavery in the United States indisputably a crime.

Reports of involuntary servitude continued to trickle in to federal investigators well into the 1950s. But America—however deeply racist it remained—had begun a profound change. Millions of soldiers—black and white—had witnessed the horror of racial ideology exalted to its most violent extremes in Nazi Germany. Thousands of African American men who returned as fighting men, unwilling to capitulate again to the docile state of helplessness that preceded the war, abandoned the South altogether or joined in the agitation that would become the civil rights movement. Throughout the region, tractors, new chemicals, and cotton pickers began to radically reduce the need for manual labor in fields of cotton, soybeans, and tobacco. In 1954, the U.S. Supreme Court's ruling in *Brown v. Board of Education* desegregating public schools and reversing the cynical logic of

1896's *Plessy v. Ferguson*, sealed forever that the terror regime which had dominated black life over the previous ninety years was ending.

It was a strange irony that after seventy-four years of hollow emancipation, the final delivery of African Americans from overt slavery and from the quiet complicity of the federal government in their servitude was precipitated only in response to the horrors perpetrated by an enemy country against its own despised minorities.

# EPILOGUE

*The Ephemera of Catastrophe*

Still the voice of Green Cottenham would not speak. For six years I sought signs of him. Nowhere was there more than the faintest trace. A flicker here that a brother, Sam, almost ten years his elder, died in 1953. Musty evidence that his sisters married and remarried. A last glimpse of Mary, his mother, living her final years at an address on Block Street in the town of Montevallo, a few blocks from where she and Henry moved long before, still in the shadow of the old slavery world. There, sometime in the 1930s, Mary Cottenham, the girl born a slave and married at the dawn of freedom, died alone. In the place of the little house she occupied for so long, only weeds grow.

The black Cottinghams descended from the old plantation on Six Mile Road were scattered, in variant spellings and skin tones, across the United States. I found a woman my own age in Shelby County named Molly Cottenham. She knew little of her family's past.

Molly is descended from Gabe, a toddler in the Cottingham Loop house of Milt Cottingham when he was saved by his brothers from arrest and re-enslavement in 1893. Gabe grew to manhood and scratched together enough to eventually buy land in Shelby County, near a community of farms called Keywater. Nearby, a ferry transported goods across the Coosa River from Fayetteville. A contemporary of Green, living in the same county, Gabe almost certainly would have known of his cousin's fate at Slope No. 12.

Gabe's sons, Edgar, Charlie, and Abraham, joined in the heavy labor of poorly educated workers of the time. Abraham died pouring iron in a foundry, according to the few stories passed down to Molly, who still lives not far from the old Keywater homeplace. Edgar worked in a quarry before retiring and then dying in the 1980s.

Gabe was forced to flee Shelby County after a fight with a white man, Molly was told. Edgar and Charlie lived most of their lives without their father, reared by their mother.

Little else of the context or human familial foundation survives for the descendants of the black Cottingham line. Molly, forty-five years old in 2008, and the mother of two grown children, doesn't remember her grandmother's name. She never knew the identities of her great-grandparents.[1]

In some respects, it is little surprise that the long-lingering persistence of American slavery has been so largely ignored. Its longevity mars the mythology most white Americans rely upon to explain our past and to embroider our present. At the same time, it grieves and shames the descendants of its victims. They recoil from the implication that emancipated black Americans could not exercise freedom, and remained under the cruel thumb of white America, despite the explicit guarantees of the Constitution, the Fourteenth and Fifteenth amendments, and the moral resolve of the Civil War.

Harold Cottingham lives in a modest house on a quiet street in Centreville, Alabama. In an office he built onto his workshop in the backyard, piles of newspaper clippings and letters are heaped where he left them years ago—while piecing together the genealogy of all the acknowledged descendants of Elisha Cottingham. He is Elisha's grandson, four generations removed. Every summer, Harold visits the old family burial ground to make sure the grass has been properly cut back from the tombstones. Today, age and health challenge his dedication to the family plot. Already, the forest has overtaken the sunken unmarked graves of many of those who died black on the Cottingham farm.

On a chilly day, Harold and his wife take me to lunch at Oliver's, a little

restaurant in a historic home across the street from the Bibb County courthouse and its monument to Confederate war dead. They know by verse the
heroic accounts of how Elisha extracted a legacy from the Alabama wilderness, and each of the succeeding white generations that followed.

Nowhere in the stories is there reference to Scip, the man who worked
beside Elisha for most of fifty years, who carved the farm from the forest
with him. Harold, a gentle man, is not responsible for the washing away of
the memories of the family's partners and likely cousins of the past. They
had vaporized long before Harold became the Cottingham storyteller. "I
knew there was some slaves out there," he told me. "But I never knew there
was so many."[2]

The residual wealth of W. D. McCurdy's baronic slave farm in
Lowndes County still dominates a cluster of fabulous white-columned
mansions in the old cotton town of Lowndesboro, Alabama. A family mansion sits at the end of McCurdy Lane. W. D. McCurdy's great-great-
grandchildren still hold much of the family land, but cotton died here long
ago. The county's overwhelming black majority elected the first African
American sheriff in the 1970s.

The vast wealth of John T. Milner began to dissipate with his death in
the early twentieth century. The dynasty that grew from his partnership
with the Flowers family collapsed in a 1920s bank failure. By 2007, however, a Massachusetts-reared grandson three generations removed, Chris
Flowers, had resurrected and exponentially eclipsed the family's prior fortunes. His firm, J. C. Flowers & Co., emerged as one of the most dynamic
financiers in the private equity boom on Wall Street.[3]

Like Elisha Cottingham's antebellum slavery, few others of the thousands of plantation dynasties forged with the modern forced labor of John
W. Pace survived its final abolition. The big houses of the great Kinderlou
slave farm in Georgia all burned before World War II. The McRee family
fell into obscurity. Pace died within a decade of his pardon by President
Roosevelt. In 1926, a hydroelectric dam was completed by a Southern
Company subsidiary on the Tallapoosa River, several miles south of the
convergence with Big Sandy Creek. The rich river-bottom plantation of
John Pace, along with many of the other slaveholding farms along Red
Ridge Road, was swallowed under 44,000 acres of water, much of it more
than one hundred feet deep. Pace's schoolteacher son, Fulton, became a

civil engineer for the town of Goodwater and died sometime after World War II. His grandson, Fulton Jr., retired to Florida and died there in 1976. On a hilltop, near the lake's edge, a Cosby family cemetery plot clings to existence amid a cluster of vacation homes.[4]

The legacy of this slavery is stronger among the corporations that relied on it. In 1969 Walter Industries, Inc., acquired an ailing company called U.S. Pipe & Foundry Company in Birmingham. Seventeen years earlier, that company had merged with Sloss-Sheffield Iron and Steel, the company with the longest record of operating slave mines in Alabama. The purchase included Flat Top mine, where so many black laborers perished under the whip. Later, the company changed the name of the mine and bulldozed the old prison stockade. The sprawling town that surrounded the shafts was abandoned when the mine shut down. In the 1980s, Walter Industries strip-mined the land—consuming the earth and coal with massive machines that obliterated the landscape for miles. Only an abandoned stretch of rail line and the old commissary, its windows blown out, survive.

The old Sloss-Sheffield today is a subsidiary called Sloss Industries. Its parent's best-known enterprise is another division called Jim Walter Homes—a famous maker of inexpensive, prefabricated homes. A sign of aspiration and success among low-income African Americans all across the Black Belt is to leave behind public housing or broken-down trailer homes and purchase the comfort of a Jim Walter home. Descendants of the South's forced laborers are a critical market.

On the Web site of Sloss Industries, the company heralds its long and rich history as a titan of southern industry that helped "launch Birmingham's rise to fame as a major industrial center."[5] There is no reference to the human engines that fueled so much economic activity over Sloss's nearly fifty-year reliance on slaves after the Civil War.

In the 1960s, U.S. Steel published a 100th anniversary commemorative book to honor Tennessee Coal, Iron & Railroad Co.'s history dating to the 1860s. But the volume says nothing of the tens of thousands of slave workers who passed through its mines, the armies of broken miners, the hundreds buried or burned in its graveyards and ovens.

The executives of Walter Industries in the twenty-first century say they know nothing of that past. "Obviously, this was a dark chapter for U.S. business," Kyle Parks, a spokesman for the company, told me in 2001. "Certainly no company today could even conceive of this kind of practice."

In Atlanta, the fortunes generated at slave mines, plantations, and the nightmarish Chattahoochee Brick became pillars of the economic transformation and social orbits of the city that would outpace all others in the South. A daughter of James W. English married a bank executive named James Robinson Sr., who grew the Fourth National Bank into the most prosperous in the South. The family guided the bank through a series of mergers and acquisitions ending in 1985, when it was purchased by a company that is now part of Wachovia Bank Corp.—the fourth largest in the United States as measured by assets. English's great-grandson, James Robinson III, was the chief executive officer of American Express from 1977 to 1993 and became a member of the board of Coca-Cola Co., where he serves today.

Joel Hurt, who believed the slaves in his coal mines could never be whipped too much, was also chairman of Atlanta's Trust Company Bank. In 1893, Hurt installed as head of his streetcar company his younger brother-in-law Ernest Woodruff. Leveraging his interests in real estate and slave mines, Hurt and his enterprises became Atlanta's most energetic deal makers and buyout artists. Beginning with a sale in 1902, the streetcar company evolved over time into Georgia Power Company—flagship of Southern Company, one of the largest electric utilities in the United States today. In 1919, after succeeding Hurt as chairman of Trust Company, Woodruff engineered the purchase of Coca-Cola for $25 million and the current incarnation of that company. Suntrust Bank, the modern version of Trust Company, remains one of the largest holders of stock in Coca-Cola. Woodruff's son, Robert Woodruff, was named president of Coke in 1923, and ran the company until 1954, becoming the era's most influential business figure in the South. He died in 1985.

But what do these threads to a terrible past tell us? Every figure who chose to continue slavery is dead. None of the actions, however cruel, of long-dead companies or men can be interpreted as a reflection on their current corporate manifestations or on distant lines of familial descent. I wanted to know, though, how the heirs to slave-dependent corporations and the pools of wealth they sometimes left behind perceive that history today—or whether they knew of it at all.

When I contacted descendants of Atlanta's former mayor and extraordinary early entrepreneur James W. English, who died in 1925, the family asked me to speak with Rodney Mims Cook Jr., the son-in-law of James Robinson III. It was obvious that even nine decades after his death, English's descendants are drenched in the lore of his remarkable life and achievements.

Cook is an elite architect, an ardent preservationist, and the driving force behind an ambitious plan to build a dramatic seventy-three-foot-high monument in downtown Atlanta as a tribute to the great families of the city, including the family of Captain English. Once it is completed, exhibition space at the classical stone archway will house the personal papers of English, Joel Hurt, and other pioneering builders of the city. Some black entrepreneurs of later in the twentieth century will be featured as well. Cook told me the museum space is expected to become the primary institution for presenting the positive history of Atlanta and its emergence as a major American city and commercial center.

After a long lunch with Cook and English Robinson, another family member, I was uncertain, however, about how the museum will present the crucial role of the new slavery in building Atlanta and the fortunes of their forebear. "In the proper context, we don't object to it being discussed," Cook told me.[6] But they were insistent that no significant abuses of African Americans had ever occurred at the brick factory, coal mines, and lumber camps of a century ago. They cited an admirable account of English's unsuccessfully attempting to calm and disperse the white mobs that rampaged in Atlanta during the bloody race riot of 1906 and a nineteenth-century newspaper article extolling the food and fellowship offered to the forced laborers at the family brick factory. They knew nothing of the real history. I sympathized with their discomfort in encountering my contradictions to the heroic, tutelary portrait of English handed down through generations. But I left our dialogue worried that the slaves who made the bricks with which Atlanta was built would yet be denied their place in the city's history.

Most corporations say it would be terribly wrong to associate their current manifestations with the abuses of convict leasing and twentieth-century forced labor—particularly for actions committed by companies they acquired or merged into decades after the fact.

Drummond Coal Company, founded in 1935,[7] says it has no meaningful connection to the use of convict labor, despite its merger in 1985 with Alabama By-Products Corp.,[8] a company created through a merger in 1925 with Pratt Consolidated Coal, one of the biggest users of forced labor during the previous two decades and owner of the deadly Banner Mine.

Drummond today is a family-owned coal and real estate company based in Jasper, Alabama, with mining operations in Alabama and South America. "I don't know how we could be tied back to something that happened in the early part of the century," Drummond spokesman Mike Tracy said when I called to inquire about the company's roots. "Drummond wasn't even founded then."[9]

U.S. Steel executives say that while convict leasing was clearly "abhorrent," their company shouldn't be associated with it—especially events that predated the acquisition of Tennessee Coal, Iron & Railroad in late 1907. "When it comes to the question of burden, I don't think anybody here at this company today would feel burdened at all by anything that happened before 1908," Richard F. Lerach, assistant general counsel to U.S. Steel, told me in 2001. "If we in fact knew that the people who were there between 1908 and 1911 were forced to work in obviously unsafe conditions, which we don't know that was true, we would feel badly about that."[10]

Legally, there are few grounds on which to argue that a modern corporation inherits any liability of a predecessor's civil rights violations or other crimes that might have occurred in the distant past. A federal judge in 2004 denounced the horrors of a 1921 rampage by whites in Tulsa, Oklahoma, who killed between one hundred and three hundred African Americans and destroyed more than a thousand homes.[11] But at the same time he dismissed a lawsuit brought by elderly plaintiffs whose families were attacked in the riot, saying the statute of limitations had passed for any legal claims and that the passage of time would make it impossible for the truth ever to be fully revealed.

Yet U.S. law is unequivocal that the deaths of executives who were responsible for dubious actions don't end a company's legal obligations. And in the specific area of hazardous waste, the United States has adopted laws forcing companies to take responsibility for contamination by predecessor companies, regardless of the passage of time. "It doesn't matter whether you had nothing to do with this toxic stuff. If you buy a company that failed to clean up this stuff, you're responsible," says Martha Minow, a professor at Harvard University Law School who has written extensively about reparations for social abuses. "Why have we done that on environmental matters, but not race?"[12]

Indeed, the commercial sectors of U.S. society have never been asked to fully account for their roles as the primary enforcers of Jim Crow segregation, and not at all for engineering the resurrection of forced labor after the Civil War. The civil rights movement focused on forcing government and individual citizens to integrate public schools, reinstate full voting rights, and end offensive behavior.

But it was business that policed adherence to America's racial customs more than any other actor in U.S. society. American banks maintained ubiquitous discriminatory lending practices throughout the country that until the 1960s prevented millions of working-class African Americans from obtaining the lines of credit that millions of white families used to accumulate wealth and move from lower- to middle-class status. Indeed, the opportunity for blacks to pursue the most basic American formula for achieving middle-class status—buying a home in desirable neighborhoods where real estate values were likely to appreciate over time—was openly barred by legions of real estate agents in every city and region. Until the 1950s, rules of the National Association of Realtors made it a violation of the organization's code of ethics for an agent to sell a home in a white neighborhood to an African American, or vice versa. It was hundreds of thousands of individual businesses that refused to give blacks jobs, equal pay, or promotions. It was wealthy men on Wall Street and in the executive suites of southern banks that financed the organized opposition to passage of the Civil Rights Act of 1964.[13]

U.S. Steel executives say that whatever happened at the company's Alabama mines long ago, it would be impossible to appropriately assign responsibility for any corporation's actions in so remote an era. "Is it fair in fact to punish people who are living today, who have certain assets they might have inherited from others, or corporate assets that have been passed on?" said Lerach. "You can get to a situation where there is such a passage of time that it simply doesn't make sense and is not fair."

U.S. Steel said it knew almost nothing about the cemeteries in Pratt City, where so many are buried. It still owns the properties, and obtained a cemetery property tax exemption on the largest burial field in 1997. But officials say they are unable to locate records of burials there, or of the company prisons that once stood nearby, or for that matter any other aspect of the company's history of leasing forced laborers. The only reference to the graveyards in surviving corporate documents, they say, is a map of the property marked with the notation "Negro Cemetery." Company officials theorize that the graveyard was an informal burial area used by African American families living nearby, with no formal connection to U.S. Steel.

"Are there convicts on that site? Possibly, quite possibly," said Tom Ferrall, the company spokesman. "But I am unable to tell you that there are."[14]

A striking contrast to U.S. Steel's approach is that of Wachovia Bank, the North Carolina financial institution that in 1985 acquired FirstAtlanta Corp., the bank born of the wealth created by James W. English's slave-driven brick factory in Atlanta. Prompted by an ordinance passed by the Chicago City Council, Wachovia disclosed in 2005 that two predecessor banks in Georgia and South Carolina owned or held as collateral at least 691 slaves before the Civil War. It formally apologized to "all Americans and especially to African Americans and people of African descent," established scholarship funds for minorities, and promoted a broad discussion of racial issues inside the company.[15]

Wachovia's chief executive officer, Ken Thompson, a fifty-seven-year-old native of Rocky Mount, North Carolina, was an enlightened white southerner but had never much considered if the racial climate of earlier eras related to the present. Like many Americans, he was vaguely uncomfortable with the idea of delving into sensitive discussions of race or the past.

"I had the attitude that this was something that happened five generations ago, and we have no responsibility for it," Thompson told me. But he was convinced by a close adviser that the disclosure requirement ought to be taken seriously, both to ensure the bank's ongoing business relationship with the city of Chicago and to demonstrate its willingness to probe a difficult issue honestly.

A team of historians was hired to investigate the past records of Wachovia, all the banks it had acquired, and all their corporate predecessors. Once the results were back, Thompson and other top managers began meeting with employee groups to discuss the findings and repeatedly apologizing for the company's ties to events more than 150 years earlier. What initially felt like a rote "diversity" relations process to fulfill a government regulation quickly became something more profound.

"I was overwhelmed by the emotional impact our apology had . . . for African American employees," Thompson said. Workers cried, held hands, embraced one another regardless of company rank, and, in an unprecedented way, began speaking to one another.

"Just by going through the act of acknowledging something that happened one hundred fifty years before and talking about it galvanized that group. . . . It was cathartic," Thompson said. "African American employees at our company in my view all of a sudden are always willing to give us the benefit of the doubt on our intentions about anything that's race related. There's a deeper trust. . . . What you get is more understanding and more 'Okay, let's go forward and figure out solutions for this in the future. Let's not rehash this forever.' "[16]

By frankly confronting a past that Wachovia didn't know existed and then expected to stir anger and tumult, an old southern bank found a kind of peace.

I found something similarly gratifying in the life of Judge Eugene Reese, the grandson of the federal prosecutor who worked so assiduously—and unsuccessfully—to beat back slavery in 1903. The contemporary Reese actually knew nothing about that surprising crusade by his grandfather, who died before the eventual judge was born. But like his grandfather, Eugene Reese, a Democrat, is neither a bleeding heart nor willing to shy away from the vestiges of slavery. "Some people say we *still* have slavery," he said to me. Reese's most controversial ruling was in a 1990s case in which he declared unconstitutional Alabama's system for funding public schools, under which schools serving children in poor areas receive dramatically less than those in more affluent areas. The racial implications of the system, a vestige of the same constitution that ended black voting in 1901, are obvious. Reese was excoriated in conservative circles in his home state.

"We've come a long way in Alabama," he told me. "But we still have a ways to go."[17]

That most American corporations and families would rather not reopen the details of how they profited from the racial attitudes in the early twentieth century is perhaps to be expected. More puzzling is that as badly as many young African Americans want answers to the question of what truly happened in the century after the Civil War, many others do not.

When Earl Brown[18] became a young miner in Birmingham in the 1940s, he was sent to the remains of Flat Top mine. Where once two train lines into the shafts had been used to separate felony prisoners from misdemeanor prisoners, the company by then used the double-track system to separate white miners from black. Among the African Americans, many of the oldest laborers were former prisoners who had taken jobs as free workers in the mine after being freed from bondage. Those men still called the bosses in the shaft "Captain," and told stories to younger men of the brutalizations that had occurred underground there. When Brown became a union activist, they warned him about the dangers of white managers and they told him stories of how they had been drawn into the mines as slaves on the basis of trumped-up charges and kidnappings by county sheriffs.

Brown listened. But he didn't believe. "I never found it credible," he told me.

Instead, Brown and so many other African Americans accepted a rationale that whites had long foisted upon them. There were "good" black people and "bad" black people. Those who ended up as slave laborers were bad or weak—adding further to the terror of being forced to join them and to share their social stain. Their injuries, and the fear they fostered among all other African Americans, were attributed to them—not their white masters. Whites repeatedly tried to stir this internal black tension. When Martin Luther King Jr. arrived in Selma, Alabama, in 1965 to tour the terrorized surrounding counties of the Black Belt, he was accused of pitting good blacks versus bad. When he drove to Lowndes County—which a full century after the end of slavery remained a place of desolate black powerlessness and unchecked white brutality—King and his activists were warned not to agitate the docile "good Negroes" of the county. Despite a population over-whelmingly majority-black, whites controlled virtually all the land, and every aspect of politics and economics. The Calhoun School had all but col-lapsed. Most African Americans remained tenants and sharecroppers, living in unplumbed hovels little changed from the desperate conditions recorded by DuBois in 1906.

No African American had cast a vote there in the twentieth century. Galvanized by the work of civil rights ministers, dozens of young Afri-can Americans attempted unsuccessfully during the spring and summer of that year to register to vote outside the Lowndes County courthouse in Hayneville. On August 20, 1965, after releasing from the local jail a group of civil rights workers who had attempted a peaceful march in the county, Deputy Sheriff Tom Coleman—a man cut from the same crude cloth as Sheriff J. W. Dixon, who drove out federal investigators six decades ear-lier—followed the activists down a sunny street, raised a 12-gauge shotgun, and at point-blank range gunned down two white ministers working with the group. One, Jonathan Daniels, was killed instantly, his body all but cut in half by the force of the blast.[19]

Reading Charles Silberman's *Crisis in Black and White* after its publica-tion the prior year, Martin Luther King scribbled a long note in the mar-gins of his personal copy: "The South deluded itself with the illusion that the Negro was happy in his place; the North deluded itself with the illusion that it had freed the Negro. The Emancipation Proclamation freed the slave, a legal entity, but it failed to free the Negro, a person."[20] In every aspect and among almost every demographic, how American society di-gested and processed the long, dark chapter between the end of the Civil War and the beginning of the civil rights movement has been delusion.

In my quest to find Green Cottenham, I also discovered an unsettling truth that when white Americans frankly peel back the layers of our commingled pasts, we are all marked by it. Whether a company or an individual, we are marred either by our connections to the specific crimes and injuries of our fathers and their fathers. Or we are tainted by the failures of our fathers to fulfill our national credos when their courage was most needed. We are formed in molds twisted by the gifts we received at the expense of others. It is not our "fault." But it is undeniably our inheritance.

I never expected to discover my own family lines as characters in the narrative of this book. Yet to my great surprise, I learned that the branch of black Cottinghams who left the old farm in Alabama during the Civil War and made their way to Louisiana settled in the parish of my mother's birth, the place where I spent countless summer days on the modest farm of my grandparents. The Cottingham descendants expired generations in the backwoods black settlements of Jackson Parish through the cruel decades of the twentieth century, as my family migrated from arch-poverty to blue-collar stability and finally to the comfort of white middle-class sanctity. Today, an ebullient woman named Margaret Cottenham, my mother's peer, writes a regular column for the parish newspaper on the social life of African Americans in and around Jonesboro, Louisiana. Black Cottenhams are celebrated athletes in the schools of an adjacent town. The law firm of my eldest cousin has represented young Cottenhams who find their way into trouble with the law. There is a measure of relief in that justice.

But there was more. Many times in my childhood, my grandmother Myrtie Wiggins Blackmon told me the epic story, passed down to her by my great-great-grandmother, of the family's passage after the Civil War from a place she called New Light, Alabama, to the hill country of northern Louisiana. Morris Foshee, my great-great-great-grandfather, had returned from four years of fighting with the 48th Infantry to a devastated Alabama. An inconspicuous private who had fought with his brother Wiley from 1861 until their surrender with Lee at Appomattox, he had been too poor to own slaves before the war, and poorer still in its aftermath. But in my visits to Alabama, searching for the shards with which to reconstruct the evil visage of John Pace, I found in the Tallapoosa County courthouse, among the slave deeds, mortgages, and convict contracts, the wedding license signed by Morris and my great-great-great-grandmother. I found the place of their farm, a few miles upstream on the Coosa River from the horrific Threat slave plantation. New Light was actually a tiny misremembered and mispronounced town called Newsite. I discovered that a distant Foshee line invested in a sawmill once operated with forced labor.

As I tugged further at the tightly threaded shrouds of the past, I learned that Morris and Wiley served in gallant, if misguided, company—the Tal-lapoosa County men who famously charged the hill called Little Round Top and were repulsed by a hailstorm of Union gunfire and bayonets in the Bat-tle of Gettysburg on July 2, 1863. They attacked that day under the direct command of Lt. Col. Michael J. Bulger, the man who thirty years later rose in defense of John Pace as he climbed to power in Tallapoosa County. Another decade hence, it was Bulger's son—by then the town's most promi-nent lawyer—who represented Pace in his trial for slavery in 1903.

I had no hand in the horrors perpetrated by John Pace or any of the other twentieth-century slave masters who terrorized American blacks for four generations. But it is nonetheless true that hundreds of millions of us spring from or benefit as a result of lines of descent that abided those crimes and benefited from them.

Over the decades, Birmingham spread to surround the cemetery where convicts in the first Pratt Mines prisons were buried. Low-rent apartments on one side of the graveyard, shabby storefronts on another, an industrial site, a city park designated for "colored" use when it was created. In 1994, industrial archaeologist Jack Bergstresser found the cemetery while con-ducting a survey for the federal government to map the remains of nearby coke ovens, mine shafts, and railroad lines.

As a boy in the 1930s, Willie Clark, a lifelong resident of Pratt City, already knew what lay deep in the thick underbrush. He and other young-sters played among the unmarked graves of the first cemetery, picking blackberries from the thorny vines that grew wild between the plots. Buri-als were rare by then. The older graves had begun to collapse, he says, exposing jumbles of human bones.

"The convicts were buried out there," Clark told me, sweeping his arm toward the overgrown field. "I heard my daddy talking about how they would beat the convicts with pick handles. If they didn't like them, they would kill them. . . . They would put them under harsh punishment. It was gruesome back then."[21]

Though in his ninth decade, Clark, more than six feet tall, could still walk with me to the site from his nearby home and point out where old mine shafts reached the surface and where dozens of company houses once stood. He told me his father also said that when convicts were killed in the shafts, company officials sometimes didn't take the time to bury them, but instead tossed the bodies into the red-hot coke ovens glowing nearby.

"What can you do about it now?" he says, stepping gingerly through the trees and undergrowth. "But the company . . . ought to clean that land up, or turn it back over to the city or somebody else who can make some use of it, take care of it."

On a cool fall night, Pearline Danzey, the eighty-eight-year-old matriarch of the extended family of Martin Danzy, who died as a slave worker in a turpentine camp in 1916, welcomed me to her home. She presided from a worn vinyl recliner in her living room over a parade of nieces, nephews, and children. Across the room, her bewhiskered grandfather—one of Martin's older brothers—squints from a faded photograph above the television set. After all these years, it is hard for Mrs. Danzey to stay focused on the story of Uncle Martin—now commingled with so much time, struggle, and memories of the other privations and violence that came with life as a young black girl on a sharecrop farm. Whether the companies that played a hand in the abuse and death of her uncle and other African Americans should be held accountable today is an abstraction she can't or won't waste time contemplating.

"To kill a colored person then, it wasn't nothing," she says. "We was slaves too in a way."[22]

For most of the Danzeys gathered that night, this is the first time they have heard "Pearl," as Mrs. Danzey is known to them all, tell the harsh tales of her childhood. Her daughter Ida was of the generation in their country town that as teenagers integrated the local schools and defied the Ku Klux Klan in the 1960s. They are filled with a sense of righteous victory over the segregation of their childhoods. But until this night, Ida Hogan and most of the others had never inquired—never considered really—that the childhood Pearline was born into had been one vastly more difficult than their own.

"Our daddy and momma never taught us to hate white people. . . . We just got taught who always got the job, who had authority, and we were supposed to address them with respect," explained Ida, one of Pearline's nieces. "Until the civil rights movement we didn't know" life could be any other way, she said.

The racial disparities of the 1950s and 1960s were the routine, rarely commented-upon backdrop of rural black life. "We had to pick cotton to buy books, so we picked cotton," said Cynthia James, a great-niece of Pearline's in her late forties. "It was much later on that we realized that the raggedy old books we were getting were just being passed on."

Inspired by Martin Luther King's historic visit to Selma, Ida and six other black children in Abbeville in 1966 insisted on being served in the town's whites-only diner. It was a turning point for the community. Her generation became the family's bridge between the desperate farm life Pearl was born into and today's mystifying era, when relative prosperity, lingering racial tensions, and the occasional biracial marriage all coexist in Henry County.

The Danzeys live in a place where cotton has been grown for most of two centuries and where Mrs. Danzey's family traces its history back to 1832 and a slave, Frank, brought to the county by a local white farmer named John Danzey. Pearline remembered her uncle Martin mostly as a man who spelled his last name without an "e," as did one line of white Danzys who lived nearby. She said she no longer remembered his alleged crime.

"My granddaddy used to talk about him. He went off to prison and died there," she says. "They was real sad about it."

In years past, Pearline had told her granddaughter, Melissa Danzey Craddock, that Uncle Martin and another local man were arrested after a brawl among men gambling outside a rural church. By the end of the fight, one man was dead. It wasn't clear whether the elder Mrs. Danzey's recollection had failed or, as was the case in many black families in Alabama, the stigma of imprisonment makes her uncomfortable discussing the subject. One thing is certain: after his arrest, Uncle Martin never came back.

Pearl's father sharecropped all his life. "The man would take everything that was made," she says of the white man on whose land her father worked. "I worked in the fields for $1 a day." Her three sisters and three brothers worked alongside her. "If a colored man hit a white man, they could come in and kill him."

She told the story of a childhood friend murdered by a white mob after allegedly speaking to a white woman. She tells of another night, when one of her brothers, Henry Edward Danzey, was seized by a mob after an argument at the town movie theater. The sheriff took him to the jail to stop the lynching and then let the black teenager go in the dark. He made his way home, and Pearline's father and uncles waited all night with pistols, sticks, and rocks, expecting the mob to arrive. The whites never came, and Pearl's brother left town to join the army.

Only after Dr. King, she says, did "people see how colored people were treated," and the terror began to subside.

The younger Danzeys aren't sure what to make of the story of Uncle Martin. "You can't go back and change the past. Just don't let it happen again," says Cynthia James. Pearline's granddaughter, Melissa Craddock, disagrees. The companies that made money off the forced labor of Uncle Martin owe something, she says. "If there was something that came out of that, then there ought to be compensation," she says. "That was after slavery ended."

Cynthia's brother, James Danzey, a deeply religious forty-five-year-old, has listened intently as his great-aunt unspooled her stories. James Danzey brings up the talk of slave reparations he has heard recently and of other long-ago abuses of African Americans that have come to light in recent years.

"I believe it's God's hand," says James Danzey, who works as a counselor at a center for behaviorally disturbed children in a nearby town. "I believe there are some good true white people of God, who realize that their ancestors did bad, and they have to make right."

The indictments of white people, despite her own contributions, begin to make Pearline uneasy, though. "There've always been some good white people," she interjects. The younger people nod heads in deference.

But James Danzey doesn't waver. "Think about all the money those companies made on those people," he says later. "Those companies should be investigated for doing that. They should have to pay something."[23]

The Danzeys were as close as I would ever come to the heart of Green Cottenham. But I did find a version of his voice. Louis Cottingham lives in Montevallo, Alabama, the same small town where Green Cottenham's mother went to live on Block Street after her son's death at the Pratt Mines. Until I called out of the blue in the winter of 2003, he had never heard of Green Cottenham.

Cottingham's wife answered the phone. She was uncertain at the sound of an unknown white man's voice seeking her husband. Admittedly, my appearance in the lives of descendants of twentieth-century slaves was for many akin to the arrival of some unidentifiable creature dropped from the sky. It was, for many, an unnatural, un-credible event. As I explained who I was, where I was calling from, and my interest in the genealogy of the black Cottinghams, she grew impatient. No, I don't want to sell anything, I tried to reassure her. I'm a newspaper reporter in Atlanta, writing a book about African Americans and your husband's family.

My words, increasingly quick and pleading, were disintegrating in the telephone line on the way to Alabama. Mrs. Cottingham was hearing none of it. Finally, I blurted that the book was about a man in their family who had been forced into slavery long after slavery was supposed to have ended.

"Slavery?" she screeched. "You can talk to my husband. But don't nobody round here have anything to say about slavery."

Finally, her husband took the receiver, as his wife continued a querulous mutter in the background. "Slavery! Nothing to say about some slave!"

Louis Cottingham's voice is strong and crisp. It resonates not with the jowly dialect of rural Alabama blacks but the smoothly defiant lilt of urban Birmingham. "*Who* are you asking about?" he wanted to know. "Green Cottenham. I don't know who that is."

"No, he wasn't a brother to my daddy. I know all the names of my daddy's brothers and sisters."

"My grandfather? No, he wasn't named Henry. His name was Elbert."

"No, not Edgar! Elbert. E-L-B-E-R-T."

Each of his sentences ended with a successively heavier tone of finality, the signal that at any moment, still baffled as to why this young white voice was quizzing him about long-dead family, Cottingham was going to say an absolute goodbye. Asking him to bear with me just a moment more, I scanned the genealogical chart of the Cottenham family I'd constructed over the previous fourteen months. Finally, I spotted Elbert, at a dead end of one branch of the family. His father had been a brother of Green Cottenham's father.

"I see it now, Cottingham," I said. "Elbert Cottingham. Yes. His father was George, born on a plantation in Bibb County in 1825. Your daddy must have been named for him. That was your great-grandfather."

Louis Cottingham went silent for a moment, and then spoke slowly. "Well I never knew that. I never knew past my granddaddy and my grand-mother."

His tone was still uninflected. He was curious, for an instant. Perhaps he would talk to me, would help me unlock the enigma of Green Cotten-ham. I dropped what I knew was my only real bombshell.

"I know the name of your great-great-grandfather too," I said. "He was Scip, and he spelled his name Cottinham. He was born in 1802, in Africa. He's the African slave you and your family are descended from."

"You say his name was Scip?" Cottingham said.

"Yes, I think that's short for Scipio."

"A slave named Scip. Born in, when did you say? 1802?"

"Yes sir. That's right."

Cottingham turned away from the phone and repeated to his wife, "Says there was a slave named Scip Cottinham, born in 1802." There was wonder in Cottingham's voice as he relayed the words. But not the wonder I had hoped for. Instead of astonishment, and gratitude, that a stranger had offered up the connection to Africa and lost generations of souls that mil-lions of American blacks claim a visceral, but ultimately almost never requited, need to find, the wonder in Cottingham's voice was flat and heavy and sorrowful. Sorrowful that a past escaped still lived at all. I thought to myself, he's glad to know, but he doesn't want to know anything else. His wife had been right from the first instant. Nobody around here wants to talk about slavery.

Still, I tried again. "Could you help me contact your older brothers who are still alive? Perhaps they remember more," I pressed gently.

"No, I couldn't do that," he said.

Could I come to your home, I offered, and share all that I've found? Perhaps it would jog a recollection. Perhaps there's a younger person with an interest in history. "I could be there in a few days," I said.

"No. No. I don't think so."


As painful as it may be to plow the past, among the ephemera left behind by generations crushed in the wheels of American white supremacy are telling explanations for the fissures that still thread our society. In fact, these events explain more about the current state of American life, black and white, than the antebellum slavery that preceded.

Certainly, the great record of forced labor across the South demands that any consideration of the progress of civil rights remedy in the United States must acknowledge that slavery, real slavery, didn't end until 1945— well into the childhoods of the black Americans who are only now reaching retirement age. The clock must be reset.

Even more plain, no one who reads this book can wonder as to the origins, depth, and visceral foundation of so many African Americans' fundamental mistrust of our judicial processes.

Most profoundly, the evidence moldering in county courthouses and the National Archives compels us to confront this extinguished past, to recognize the terrible contours of the record, to teach our children the truth of a terror that pervaded much of American life, to celebrate its end, to lift any shame on those who could not evade it. This book is not a call for financial reparations. Instead, I hope it is a formidable plea for a resurrection and fundamental reinterpretation of a tortured chapter in the collective American past.

We should rename this era of American history known as the time of "Jim Crow segregation." How strange that decades defined in life by abject brutalization came to be identified in history with the image of a largely forgotten white actor's minstrel performance—a caricature called "Jim Crow." Imagine if the first years of the Holocaust were known by the name of Germany's most famous anti-Semitic comedian of the 1930s. Let us define this period of American life plainly and comprehensively. It was the Age of Neoslavery. Only by acknowledging the full extent of slavery's grip on U.S. society—its intimate connections to present-day wealth and power, the depth of its injury to millions of black Americans, the shocking nearness in time of its true end—can we reconcile the paradoxes of current American life.


A few months before the publication of this book, as I studied a century-old map of coal mines near Birmingham, it dawned on me that the name of an old mining camp town called Docena was a Spanish translation of "dozen"—as in Slope No. 12, the prison mine where Green Cottenham died. I quickly confirmed that Docena, at the top of the long hill above the graveyard at Pratt Mines, was the site of the No. 12 shaft, renamed after U.S. Steel finally stopped using slave laborers to avoid association with the company's last forced labor mine.

I drove there on a Saturday morning, with my wife and young children in the car. On the way we stopped near the ruins of Tennessee Coal, Iron & Railroad's Ensley furnaces. The giant smokestacks have been dead for decades but still own the sky—like lightning streaks of rust or a frightening amusement park ride, the kids said.

Nearby was Docena. The old mine had long been abandoned. Its opening at the center of the little town was collapsed and unrecognizable. Trees and brush crowded a streambed flowing from the site of the entrance. A disabled white man in a crumbling house nearby told me he remembered an old plot of unmarked graves a short distance down the hill, in a hollow where his father had kept pigs in his childhood. It was the mine burial ground. I knew Green's body was almost certainly buried there, just outside what had been the walls of the Pratt No. 12 prison.

We drove to the site. It was densely covered with undergrowth and pine trees. A path into the forest led from one heap of garbage and refuse to another. A forest fire had opened the way through another part of the woods. The children and I picked our way through the litter and foliage. We found the brick and concrete foundation of a shower room built for free miners after the company lost its slaves. The graves were supposed to be a few feet away. I pressed into the thicket of scrub and briars. We studied the ground for the telltale slumps in the earth like those scattered by the hundreds in the burial field at the bottom of the hill. I searched for the remains of a fence delineating a plot, rocks in the symmetry of graves, a crude headstone, any sign. But there was nothing. Too much time had passed. Too much had been done—or gone undone. The last evidence of Green Cottenham's life and death was obliterated by the encroachment of nature and the detritus of man.

# ACKNOWLEDGMENTS

∎

As a young seventh grader in the public schools of Leland, Mississippi, in 1977, I decided to enter an essay contest sponsored by the Washington County Historical Society. For reasons no longer remembered, I settled for a topic on the story of an all but forgotten civil rights incident on the outskirts of our Mississippi Delta town a little more than a decade earlier. A group of African American farmworkers on a plantation there had gone on strike, defended themselves against the Klan, and ultimately built a desperate but defiant encampment called Strike City—one that persists precariously even in 2008.

The two-page essay won a second-place certificate during the county fair and a promise that it would be included in a future journal of the historical society. A year later, I gave a speech based on the essay in an oratorical contest held by a local men's fraternal organization. Standing before that group of middle-aged white men during a springtime lunch hour, I told a story that to my twelve-year-old thinking was ancient history—but to my listeners was a searing lightning bolt from the near past. I experienced for the first time that day the combustible response that can come with unearthing history that a community would just as soon forget. My English teacher, Freida Inmon, who unbeknownst to me had fought behind the scenes to make sure my speech was heard that day, applauded loudly and then rescued me from an angry critic. Later I learned that the wrathful man who berated me that day had been one of the violent white suprema-cists. (For the record, I did not win the contest.)

Afterward, despite the turmoil of that day, my mother, Sarah Avery Blackmon, urged me to "finish the story" on Strike City—to go back and talk to even more participants, to get to the bottom of what happened in 1965, to study the results of that incident on the people involved and the community surrounding it. I have been doing so ever since—for thirty years attempting to plumb the forgotten or withheld chapters of history that shape the ever larger communities that have fascinated me. *Slavery by Another Name* still doesn't finish the story, but with the help of many extra-ordinary friends, colleagues, historians, and researchers, it hopefully begins to bridge a gaping omission in American history.

The book, and the July 21, 2001, article in *The Wall Street Journal* that preceded it, would never have occurred without the guidance and passion of Jack Bergstresser, director of the museum at Tannehill Ironworks His-torical State Park in McCalla, Alabama.

The research for this book has also been made much easier by the expert staffs of the departments of history and archives in Alabama, Geor-gia, Mississippi, and Arkansas, the Atlanta History Center, and countless clerks, sheriffs, and local historical society volunteers in county seats across Alabama, Georgia, and Florida. Of particular help were Jim Baggett, direc-tor of the Birmingham Public Library Archives, and Bobby Joe Seales, the indefatigable president of the Shelby County Historical Society, where I spent many days over many years. The staffs of the libraries of Emory Uni-versity in Atlanta, Duke University in Durham, North Carolina, and the Harry Ransom Center at the University of Texas at Austin were gracious and patient with my overlong borrowings from their shelves and searches for obscure images. My thanks as well to A. S. Williams III, of Birmingham, who generously granted access to his unrivaled private collection of mate-rials related to Alabama history.

I am also indebted to the many historians and scholars whose work guided aspects of my research. Pete Daniel, curator in the Division of Work and Industry at the Smithsonian National Museum of American History, who in 1972 authored the seminal work on twentieth-century peonage in the South, was kind enough to share a dinner and wise suggestions with me midway through the project. For the years prior to 1900, no work rivals the research of Mary Ellen Curtin, now a lecturer at the University of Essex, and the author of *Black Prisoners and Their World, Alabama, 1865–1900*. My effort on this book was also inspired by the incomparable southern historian Dan T. Carter, now at the University of South Carolina, whose 1964 thesis on convict leasing set the groundwork for dozens of historians who have followed.

The book would never have been completed without the support of many colleagues and editors, especially at *The Wall Street Journal*. My editor, John Blanton, sharpened and elevated the original story. Managing editor Paul E. Steiger offered invaluable support for that article, as well as all of my other work at the *Journal* since then and for the completion of this book. The reporters of the *Journal*'s Atlanta bureau have inspired me with their devotion and talent—especially in their unrivaled coverage of hurricanes in recent years. My fellow journalists and friends Nikhil Deogun, Rick Brooks, Glenn Ruffenach, Ken Wells, Catherine Williams, Carrie Teegardin, and Ken Foskett have pushed me forward many times. I was often inspired by the late Manuel Maloof and my wise friend Angelo Fuster. My thanks as well to Doubleday's Bill Thomas, who suggested that I write this book; Stacy Creamer, the editor who has gently asked for it ever since then; and David Black, my agent and friend.

Finally, even though it is a writer's cliché, I am most grateful to my family for their unwavering enthusiasm and patience for this project. This book has hovered, a seemingly immovable background, over every weekend, holiday, and beach trip in most of my remarkable son Michael's young life and for every one of them in my extraordinary daughter Colette's. Yet they have urged me on without fail and with my only penance being a periodic update to their classmates. My wife, Michelle Jones Blackmon, has supported and assisted me in more ways than I could ever record here while at the same time founding and nurturing the amazing neighborhood school where our children learn. This book is dedicated to them, Michelle, Michael, and Lettie.

# NOTES

■

Abbreviations:

ADAH           Alabama Department of Archives and History, Montgomery, Ala.

AHC            Atlanta History Center, Atlanta, Ga.

BCC            Bibb County Courthouse, Centreville, Ala.

BPLA          Birmingham Public Library Archives, Birmingham, Ala.

BTW Papers    *Booker T. Washington Papers, Volumes 1–14*

EPRRC        National Archives, Regional Records Center, East Point, Ga.

GDAH         Georgia Department of Archives and History, Atlanta, Ga.

NA             National Archives, Washington, D.C.

RG60, NA      Department of Justice, Peonage Files, Record Group 60, National Archives, Washington, D.C.

SCHS          Shelby County Historical Society, Columbiana, Ala.

TCC           Tallapoosa County Courthouse, Dadeville, Ala.

## INTRODUCTION

1. "Sheriff's Prisoners Register," 1906–1910, SCHS.
2. Willie Clarke, Leroy Bandy, Verdell Wade, interviews by the author with former miners and witnesses, January 2002.

3. Ibid.

4. Carrie Kinsey to Theodore Roosevelt, July 31, 1903, RG60, NA.

## CHAPTER I: THE WEDDING

1. Rhoda Coleman Ellison, *Bibb County, Alabama: The First Hundred Years, 1818–1918* (Tuscaloosa: University of Alabama Press, 1984), p. 15.

2. Deed of Sarah Cotard to Charles Cottingham, Dec. 5, 1825; deed of Malcolm McCray to Charles Cottingham, Jan. 8, 1831, BCC. In 1825, Charles Cottingham paid $200 for land and lots in the town of Centreville. In 1831, he bought more property on the east side of the Cahaba River.

3. United States of America, Bureau of the Census. *Eighth Census of the United States, 1860. East Side Cahaba River (Free Inhabitants), Bibb, Alabama,* p. 157.

4. Anna Blanche Cottingham, *The Cottingham's of Bibb County: Vol. 1* (Ada, Okla.: Pontotoc County Historical and Genealogical Society, 1970), p. 10.

5. Deed of Elisha Cottingham to Rebecca Battle, May 22, 1852, BCC.

6. Ibid.

7. Marriage license of Albert Cottingham and Laura Pratt, Sept. 8, 1866, by J. W. Starr, *Bibb County Marriages,* SCHS, F-115.

8. Congress enacted a bill on March 3, 1865, creating the Bureau of Refugees, Freedmen, and Abandoned Lands, with a mandate to provide food, clothing, and other assistance to victims of the Civil War, white and black.

9. Edward Royce, *The Origins of Southern Sharecropping* (Philadelphia: Temple University Press, 1993), p. 101.

10. See Edward Magdol, "Local Black Leaders in the South, 1867–1875: An Essay Toward the Reconstruction of Reconstruction History," *Societas—A Review of Social History* 4 (Spring 1974), cited in Royce, pp. 103–5.

11. Mary Ellen Curtin, *Black Prisoners and Their World, Alabama, 1865–1900* (Charlottesville: University Press of Virginia, 2000), p. 48.

12. James R. Bennett, *Old Tannehill: A History of the Pioneer Ironworks in Roupes Valley (1829–1865)* (Birmingham: Jefferson County Historical Commission, 1986), pp. 27–28.

13. Ethel Armes, "Adventures in Early Iron Country," 1910, SCHS.

14. Doris Fancher Farrington, unpublished typescript of oral history, in possession of author, n.d.

15. David L. Nolen, "Wilson's Raid on the Coal and Iron Industry in Shelby County" (thesis, University of Alabama in Birmingham, Spring 1988), pp. 2–3.

16. Bennett, *Old Tannehill*, p. 22.

17. Ibid., p. 26.

18. Deed of purchase by the Confederate States of America of Bibb County Iron Co., Sept. 7, 1863, BCC.

19. Bennett, *Old Tannehill*, p. 29.

20. Joseph Hodgson, ed., *The Alabama Manual and Statistical Register for 1869* (Montgomery: Montgomery Daily Mail, 1869), p. 105.

21. Advertisement in *The Sunday Mississippian*, Jan. 24, 1864, ADAH.

22. Ellison, p. 134.

23. Eugenia Wallace Logan, copy of typescript of oral history, in possession of author, 1935.

24. Cirrenia Langston, "Childhood Memories of the War Between the States," *Centreville Press*, March 14, 1934, in Fern Langston, ed., *Echoes of Six Mile* (privately published, 1994), p. 107; Ellison, pp. 128–29.

25. Nolen, p. 1.

26. James Pickett Jones, *Yankee Blitzkrieg: Wilson's Raid Through Alabama and Georgia* (Athens: University of Georgia Press, 1976), p. 3.

27. Gov. T. H. Watts to Lt. Gen. Polk, April 2, 1864, *The War of Rebellion: A Compilation of the Official Records of the Union and Confederate Armies* (Washington, D.C.: U.S. Government Printing Office, 1880–1901), pp. 734–35.

28. *The War of Rebellion*, pp. 404–16.

29. Frank E. Vandiver, "Josiah Gorgas and the Brierfield Iron Works," *Alabama Review*, January 1950, citing Walter L. Fleming, *Civil War and Reconstruction in Alabama* (New York, 1905), p. 254.

30. Ellison, p. 144.

31. Mary Ann (Cobb) Johnson McNeill, copy of unpublished typescript, in possession of author, n.d.

32. Ellison, p. 144.

33. Ibid., p. 147.

34. Royce, p. 72.

35. Ibid.

36. Ibid., p. 75.

37. Deed of Elisha and Nancy Cottingham to John P. Cottingham, James M. Cottingham, Moses L. Cottingham, and Harry P. Cottingham, Feb. 8, 1868, BCC.

38. Deed of Rebecca Battle to Elisha Cottingham, Feb. 22, 1868, BCC.

39. Deed of Moses Cottingham to John G. Henry, Feb. 27, 1868, BCC.

40. Deed of Moses Cottingham to P.W., Feb. 27, 1868, BCC.

41. Deed of Moses L. Cottingham to J. W. Pruit, Jan. 21, 1869, BCC.

42. Deeds of Elias Bishop to McSpaden, Aug. 28, 1869; to Jasper Thompson, Aug. 21, 1869, BCC.

43. Deed of Sarah Bishop to John C. Henry, July 6, 1870, BCC.

44. Ellison, p. 92.

45. Deed of Purchase by Elias Bishop, filed December 27, 1836, BCC. Bishop acquired nearly two hundred acres on the east side of the Cahaba River, Township 22, Section 11, Range 9.

46. *1860 U.S. Census*, Slave Schedule, Bibb County, Ala.

47. Langston, *Echoes*, pp. 107–11.

48. Ellison, p. 29.

49. In *Uncle Tom's Cabin*, Harriet Beecher Stowe's landmark abolitionist novel published in 1852, the character Augustine St. Clare tells the story of a powerful slave named Scipio who despite repeated beatings remained obstinate and disobedient. After Scipio escapes and is shot by a search party, St. Clare nurses him back to health and then gives him papers setting him free. Scipio, now devoted and gentle, rips the documents in half in gratitude to his master, and soon dies, after embracing Christianity.

50. "Manifest of Brigantine Arethusa," arriving Port of New Orleans, Nov. 6, 1821; Inward Slave Manifests of the Port of New Orleans, Roll 2, January–March 1821, Entry #360, transcribed by Dee Parmer Woodtor, http://www .afrigeneas.com/slavedata/background.html (April 1999). A twelve-year-old slave, height four feet three inches, named Scipio is listed among slaves owned by Townes L. Webb of Petersburg, Virginia.

51. *1850 U.S. Census*, Slave Schedule, Bibb County. The Cottingham slave quarters were likely similar to those of John E. Green, on a 3,400-acre plantation near the town of Woodstock, Alabama: "The place required numerous slaves and mules to work it. The old slave cabins were located about a hundred feet north of the present well on the southeast side of the house. Across the present highway was a large mule lot, cotton gin, sorghum mill, and a few other smaller buildings." See Ellison, p. 85.

52. Record of Incorporation, Bibb Steam Mill Company, Nov. 26, 1850, BCC.

53. "Minutes of the Mobile Conference," Methodist Church Records, pp. 37–38, transcribed at http://homepages.rootsweb.com/~marykozy/text_files/starfile .shtml. Methodism was not a faith for those who enjoyed even modest worldly pastimes. Early in Starr's years of service, pastors of his Alabama conference met to decry the dangers and immorality of "dram drinking," viewing races, attending "dancing parties," circuses, or theaters, and "the indulgence of superfluous ornaments." Starr prided himself on his "rule" over his wife and chil-

dren and the believers to whom he ministered. So visceral was his passion for stern, orderly church and family hierarchy that Starr lived much of his adult life agonizing over his shameful pliancy as a young minister to the leaders of a congregation that wished to allow its young people to dance. Starr confided to another pastor late in life that as a result he "never afterwards had the same power and influence over a congregation." On his deathbed, Starr implored his fellow preachers to remember that "the old fashioned doctrine of holiness, as taught by our fathers, is true; it is the doctrine of the Bible . . . preach it to the people."

54. Reynolds E. Wallace Jr., "Recollections of the Past: Wesley Chapel," copy of unpublished typescript, in possession of author, 1996.

55. Deed of J. W. and Hannah Starr to J. S. Hansberger, Nov. 24, 1868, BCC.

Rev. Starr and Hannah in November 1868 agreed to sell more than two hundred acres east of Ridge Road to Hansberger, owner of an adjacent tannery, reserving to themselves access to a spring on the property. Harry P. Cottingham bought a total of 161 acres in May 1865 from the longtime family neighbor Pulaski Wallace; the land was adjoined by two ninety-foot-wide lots sold near the same time to J. W. Starr for $2,502. Deed of Harry P. Cottingham to P. Wallace, May 18, 1865, BCC.

56. Marguerite Starr Crain and Janell Turner Wenzel, *They Followed the Sun: The Story of James Penn Starr and Georgian Theus: Their Ancestors and Their Progenies* (Dallas: Suburban Tribune, 1971), cited at http://members.aol.com/InmanGA/family.starr.html.

57. Vandiver, "Josiah Gorgas," p. 12, citing Gorgas diary entry, Aug. 3, 1865.

58. Marriage license of Henry Cottinham and Mary Bishop, Jan. 8, 1868, by J. W. Starr, *Bibb County Marriages*, SCHS.

## CHAPTER II: AN INDUSTRIAL SLAVERY

1. *1860 Census.*

2. Rhoda Coleman Ellison, *Bibb County, Alabama: The First Hundred Years, 1818–1918* (Tuscaloosa: University of Alabama Press, 1984), pp. 82–83.

3. Ibid.

4. Donald E. Collins, ed., "A Georgian's View of Alabama in 1836," *Alabama Review*, January 1972, p. 221.

5. *Harper's Weekly*, July 13, 1861, p. 442.

6. Ellison, p. 69.

7. Frederick Law Olmsted, *A Journey in the Back Country* (New York: Mason Brothers, 1860), p. 64.

8. Cited in Olmsted, *The Cotton Kingdom: A Traveller's Observations on Cotton and Slavery in the American Slave States* (New York: Mason Brothers, 1862), p. 439.

9. James C. Cobb, *The Most Southern Place on Earth: The Mississippi Delta and the Roots of Regional Identity* (New York: Oxford University Press, 1992), p. 22.

10. Ibid., p. 13.

11. Ibid., p. 23.

12. Ibid., pp. 13, 20–23.

13. Ibid., p. 26.

14. Ellison, p. 97.

15. Ethel Armes, *The Story of Coal and Iron in Alabama* (Birmingham: Chamber of Commerce, 1910), p. 73.

16. Ellison, p. 100.

17. Armes, p. 72.

18. Ibid., p. 71.

19. Frank E. Vandiver, "The Shelby Iron Company in the Civil War: A Study of a Confederate Industry," *Alabama Review* (January 1948), p. 14.

20. Armes, pp. 67–68.

21. James R. Bennett, *Old Tannehill: A History of the Pioneer Ironworks in Roupes Valley (1829–1865)* (Birmingham, Ala.: Jefferson County Historical Commission, 1986), p. 18.

22. Ibid., p. 22.

23. Ibid., p. 18.

24. The South Carolina Railroad reported in its corporate records at the end of 1861 the ownership of nearly ninety slaves, at a total investment of $77,566. Similar records from the North Carolina Railroad during 1862 show the company leasing 273 slaves from owners scattered across the state. By 1864, the number had grown to nearly four hundred. The Richmond & Petersburg Railroad owned 118 slaves in that year, employing a dozen as firemen and train hands, two dozen in their mechanics shops, and a score of slaves repairing tracks. The Virginia Central relied on more than three hundred slaves during the Civil War, primarily for the building and repair of rail lines but also assigning dozens of blacks as brakemen and firemen on railroad cars. Also see Kenneth M. Stampp, *The Peculiar Institution: Slavery in the Ante-bellum South* (New York: Alfred A. Knopf, 1956).

25. Armes, pp. 76, 66, 68.

26. Ibid., p. 74.

27. Ibid., p. 78.

28. Bennett, p. 27.

29. Ibid., p. 28.

30. Armes, p. 169.

31. Anderson to Ware, Feb. 12, 1859, Shelby Iron Co. Papers, University of Alabama Library, cited in Vandiver, "The Shelby Iron Company," p. 15.

32. John W. Lapsley, a "militant industrialist" and early Alabama railroad builder, was associated with the Shelby Coal Co. and the Shelby Lime Co., both essential to the Shelby Iron Works. On March 18, 1862, to provide capital for the Confederate expansion, Lapsley, another major slave owner named John M. McClanahan, and Henry H. Ware, John R. Kenan, Andrew T. Jones, and James W. Lapsley each bought a one-seventh interest in the Shelby Works. Cited in ibid., pp. 14–16.

33. *1860 Census,* Shelby County Slave Schedules.

34. Referring to A. N. DeWitt & Co., Columbus, Miss., making two hundred barrels a week; Griswold & Gunnison, pistol makers in Griswoldville, Ga. See Vandiver, "The Shelby Iron Company."

35. Bennett, *Old Tannehill,* p. 24.

36. Vandiver, "The Shelby Iron Company," p. 20.

37. J. Michael Bunn, "Slavery in the Shelby Iron Works During the Civil War," *Shelby County Historical Society Quarterly* (March 2003), pp. 24–29.

38. Ibid.

39. Bennett, *Old Tannehill,* p. 17.

40. Armes, pp. 162–64.

41. Justin Fuller, "History of the Tennessee Coal, Iron and Railroad Company, 1852–1907" (Ph.D. diss., University of North Carolina, 1966), p. 280.

42. W. David Lewis, *Sloss Furnaces and the Rise of the Birmingham District: An Industrial Epic* (Tuscaloosa: University of Alabama Press, 1994), p. 34; also see Alex Lichtenstein's review, *Alabama Review* 51 (April 1998), pp. 106–13.

43. John T. Milner, "Report to the Governor of Alabama on the Alabama Central Railroad" (Montgomery: Advertiser Book and Job Steam Press Print, 1859), pp. 44–45, ADAH.

44. Arney R. Childs, ed., *The Private Journal of Henry William Ravenel, 1859–1887* (Columbia, S.C., 1947), p. 256, cited in William Cohen, "Negro Involuntary Servitude in the South, 1865–1940," *Journal of Southern History* (February 1976), p. 34.

45. Matthew J. Mancini, *One Dies, Get Another: Convict Leasing in the American South, 1866–1928* (Columbia: University of South Carolina Press, 1996), p. 100.

46. Ibid., p. 169.

47. Ibid., pp. 82, 117.

48. Ibid., pp. 133, 154–55, 161, 169, 202.

49. Mary Ellen Curtin, *Black Prisoners and Their World, Alabama, 1865–1900* (Charlottesville: University Press of Virginia, 2000), pp. 14–15, 66–67.

50. *Annual Report of the Inspectors of the Alabama Penitentiary for the Year Ending Sept. 30, 1877* (Montgomery: Barrett & Brown, 1878), ADAH.

51. *Convict Legislation and Rules, 1882–1883*, Department of Corrections, ADAH.

52. *History of the Penitentiary*, Special Message of Gov. Cobb, 1882, ADAH.

53. *First Biennial Report of the Board of Inspectors of Convicts, September 1, 1894, to August 31, 1896* (Montgomery: Roemer Printing, 1896), ADAH.

## CHAPTER III: SLAVERY'S INCREASE

1. *1870 Census*, Bibb County.

2. Headstone of Elisha Cottingham, 1793–Nov. 10, 1870; headstone of Nancy Parker Cottingham, Feb. 3, 1796–July 22, 1873.

3. *1870 Census*, Bibb County, Six Mile Township.

4. *1870 Census*, Bibb County, Randolph Township, Brierfield Post Office.

5. *Shelby Sentinel*, Aug. 16, 1877.

6. *Docket of A. M. Elliott, Justice of the Peace*, 1878–1880, SCHS.

7. *Convicts at Hard Labor for the County in the State of Alabama on the First Day of March 1883*, microfiche, ADAH.

8. "Jefferson County Circuit Court Convict Docket, 1902–1903," BPLA.

9. Tallapoosa County Deed Book: "This agreement made and entered into between men Sevi Pearson of the first part, and John W. Pace of the second part, whereas Sevi Pearson of the first part has been convicted before Luke Davenport, a notary public of and ex officio J.P. on the 28th day of April 1885 for an assault and battery on Cora Iverson, and a fine of sixty dollars imposed and the further sum of ten and 50/100s cash, and whereas the said Sevi Pearson has confessed judgment for the above arrest and John W. Pace has become his security on payment for said conviction and upon becoming his security for said amount and paying the same for the said Sevi Pearson, bond himself to work faithfully for John W. Pace for eight dollars per month for nine months and further agrees that he will take such treatment as other convicts

this April 28 1885, signed in open court, Luke Davenport, NP, Sevi Pearson, John Pace."

10. Thomas L. Cochran to R. H. Dawson, Nov. 23, 1887, Administrative Correspondence, 1881–1897, Dawson Letter Books. Correspondence of the Inspectors of the Penitentiary, Department of Corrections, ADAH.

11. Shelby County Record of Prisoners, April 11, 1878, to October 11, 1878, SCHS.

12. *History of the Penitentiary,* Special Message of Gov. Cobb, 1882, pp. 357–58, ADAH.

13. For an excellent examination of the dialogue between Archey and Dawson, see Mary Ellen Curtin, *Black Prisoners and Their World, Alabama, 1865–1900* (Charlottesville: University Press of Virginia, 2000).

14. Ezekiel Archey to R. H. Dawson, Pratt Mines, Jan. 18, 1884, Dawson Letter Books, ADAH.

15. Curtin, p. 69.

16. Testimony of Jno. D. Goode, *Testimony Taken by the Joint Special Committee of the Session of 1880–81 to Enquire into the Condition and Treatment of Convicts of the State* (Montgomery, Ala., 1881), ADAH.

17. Curtin, p. 69.

18. Ethel Armes, *The Story of Coal and Iron in Alabama* (Birmingham: Chamber of Commerce, 1910), p. 110.

19. Marjorie Longenecker White, *The Birmingham District: An Industrial History and Guide* (Birmingham: Birmingham Publishing, 1981).

20. *New York Times,* Dec. 17, 1882; cited in Curtin, p. 70.

21. Curtin, p. 75.

22. *Biennial Report of the Board of Inspectors of Convicts, 1880–1882* (Montgomery, Ala.: Barrett & Brown, 1882), ADAH.

23. Cobb, *Penitentiary,* pp. 357–58.

24. Dawson to B. F. Porter, June 21, 1883; to B. H. Warren, June 30, 1883, Dawson Letter Books, ADAH.

25. Armes, p. 196.

26. Curtin, p. 83.

27. Dawson to Simon O'Neal, Judge of the Probate, Russell County, May 23, 1883, Dawson Letter Books, ADAH.

28. Dawson to Judge Allston, Aug. 27, 1883, Dawson Letter Books, ADAH.

29. *Annual Report of Inspectors,* 1878.

30. Lewis McCurdy, of Lowndesboro, Ala., telephone interview with the author, Aug. 29, 2003.

31. Dawson diary entries, *Diary of Reginald Heber Dawson, 1883–1906*, July 5, 13, 1883, folder 1, ADAH.

32. Dawson to Simon O'Neal, Sept. 10, 1883, A. S. Williams Collection, Eufaula Athenaeum; Dawson to L. A. J. Cumlie, Sept. 25, 1883, Dawson Letter Books, ADAH.

33. Curtin, pp. 84–88.

34. *Convicts at Hard Labor, 1883.*

35. *Dawson Diary*, July 10, 1885, ADAH.

36. Curtin, p. 88.

37. Minutes of the Board of Inspectors, 1883–1913, Department of Corrections, ADAH.

38. *Dawson Diary*, July 11, 1883, ADAH.

39. Ibid., Nov. 14, 21, 1883.

40. Ibid., May 22, 1887.

41. Convict Legislation and Rules, 1882–1883, ADAH.

42. Testimony of Pratt payroll agent Justin Collins, Nov. 16, 1883, U.S. Congress, Senate, Committee on Education and Labor, 49th Cong., 2nd Session, *Testimony Before the Committee to Investigate the Relations Between Capital and Labor* 4:441, cited in Curtin, p. 86.

43. A. T. Henley to R. H. Dawson, Dec. 7, 1883, Dawson Letter Books, ADAH.

44. Ezekiel Archey to R. H. Dawson, Jan. 18, 1884, Dawson Letter Books, ADAH.

45. Milner to Dawson, June 10, 1885, Dawson Letter Books, ADAH.

46. Minutes of the Shelby County Commission, December 1880, SCHS.

47. Shelby County Record of Prisoners, April 18, 1879, to Oct. 1, 1888, SCHS.

48. Shelby County Commission Minutes, July 9, 1883, SCHS.

49. Shelby County Commission Minutes, Feb. 2, 1883, SCHS. Elliott received approval for $43.50 for fees related to state cases he had adjudged; warrants totaling $94.65 for work in circuit court cases were also approved.

50. Shelby County Minutes, Feb. 11, 1884, SCHS.

51. J. A. MacKnight, "Columbiana: The Gem of the Hills" (Columbiana, Ala.: Shelby County Sentinel, circa 1907), pp. 5–6.

52. Shelby County Record of Prisoners, Aug. 17, 1884, to May 16, 1886, SCHS.

53. *1880 Census*, Bibb County; Bibb County Commission Minutes, July 1881, BCCH.

54. Ibid.

55. Bibb County Commission Minutes, Oct. 8, 1881, BCCH.

56. Bibb County Commission Minutes, Oct. 31, 1881, BCCH.

57. Bibb County Commission Minutes, Feb. 13, 1893; Feb. 11, 1895, BCCH.

## CHAPTER IV: GREEN COTTENHAM'S WORLD

1. Allan Nevins, *Hamilton Fish: The Inner History of the Grant Administration* (New York: Dodd, Mead, 1936), 2: 853–54.
2. *Nation*, April 5, 1877.
3. C. Vann Woodward, *Reunion and Reaction* (New York: Little, Brown, 1951).
4. *1890 Census.*
5. *Second Annual Report of the Commissioner of Labor, 1886: Convict Labor* (Washington, D.C.: U.S. Government Printing Office, 1887).
6. Investigations regarding James M. Smith, Peonage Files, Cases 10935, 16214, 18205, RG60, NA (5280).
7. "Interview with John Hill, April 27, 1938," *Slave Narratives: A Folk History of Slavery in the United States* (Washington, D.C.: Library of Congress, 1941), Georgia Narratives, Vol. 4, Part 2.
8. Alex Lichtenstein, *Twice the Work of Free Labor: The Political Economy of Convict Labor in the New South* (London: Verso, 1996), p. 48; William Andrew Todd, "Convict Lease System," *New Georgia Encyclopedia*, December 2005.
9. *Proceedings: Joint Committee of the Senate and House to Investigate the Convict Lease System of Georgia*, Vol. 1, 1908, GDAH.
10. *Augusta Chronicle*, Jan. 3, 1891.
11. Robert Perkinson, "Hell Exploded: Prisoner Writing and the Fall of Convict Leasing in Texas," unpublished, Sept. 2002.
12. David W. Blight, *Race and Reunion: The Civil War in American Memory* (Cambridge: Harvard University, 2001), p. 308.
13. Ibid., p. 309.
14. Ethel Armes, *The Story of Coal and Iron in Alabama* (Birmingham: Chamber of Commerce, 1910), p. 422.
15. Ibid., p. 423.
16. *Second Biennial Report of the Inspectors of Convicts, Oct. 1, 1886, to Sept. 30, 1888* (Montgomery: W. D. Brown & Co., 1888), ADAH.
17. *First Biennial Report of the Inspectors of Convicts, October 1, 1884, to October 1, 1886* (Montgomery: Barrett & Co., 1886), ADAH.
18. *Proceedings: Joint Committee of the Senate and House to Investigate the Convict Lease System of Georgia*, Vol. 1: 4, 9, GDAH; also *Atlanta Constitution*, June 24, 1891, p. 6.
19. *Second Biennial Report of Inspectors, 1888.*
20. *Birmingham Daily News*, May 23, 1891.

21. *Third Biennial Report of the Inspectors of Convicts, Oct. 1, 1888, to Sept. 30, 1890* (Montgomery: Brown Printing, 1890), pp. 14–15.

22. Ibid., p. 15.

23. Ibid., pp. 20–21.

24. Ibid., pp. 242–45.

25. 1904 map of site, BPLA.

26. *Third Biennial Report*, 1890, pp. 242–45, 262.

27. Ibid., p. 53. Nicholson, the chaplain, boasted of the 197 sermons he had given in the prior year at various convict camps and attendance of more than one hundred regularly for a Sunday school at the Pratt Mines. A separate school at Slope No. 2 prison attracted even larger crowds, he said.

28. Ibid., p. 226.

29. Ibid., pp. 78, 227.

30. Message of Thos. E. Kilby, Governor, Relative to Feeding of Prisoners, Legislative Document No. 3, Alabama Legislature, Jan. 15, 1923 (Montgomery: Brown Printing, 1923), author's collection; Bush citation, p. 5; "Starvation" reference is from Dr. Glenn Andrews, quoted p. 6.; "Pale and anemic" reference from Dr. C. H. Smith, quoted p. 7.

31. Author's analysis of *Convict Record*, Barbour County, Barbour County Courthouse, Clayton, Ala.

32. G. Bridges to Lewis Grant, Feb. 24, 1891, Sheriff's Loose Papers File, SCHS.

33. Grant to Bridges, undated, Sheriff's Loose Papers File, SCHS.

34. J. McMillan to Grant, undated; P. J. Rogers to Grant, April 9, 1891, Sheriff's Loose Papers Files, SCHS.

35. Postcard dated April 21, 1891, Sheriff's Loose Papers File, SCHS.

36. F. E. Burfitt to Grant, May 26, 1891; J. Rowland to Grant, May 27, 1891; W. B. Fulton to Grant, Nov. 23, 1891, Sheriff's Loose Papers File, SCHS.

37. By the end of 1892, Sheriff Grant had amassed scores of such letters and telegrams, enough to stuff six file folders.

38. P. J. Rogers to L. T. Grant, April 10 and May 6, 1891, SCHS.

39. John Milner, "White Men of Alabama Stand Together," Pamphlet Collection, 1890, ADAH.

40. *Montgomery Advertiser*, Feb. 2, 1889.

41. Horace Mann Bond, *Negro Education in Alabama: A Study in Cotton and Steel* (Tuscaloosa: University of Alabama Press, 1994), p. 142, citing H. Paul Douglass, *Christian Reconstruction in the South* (Boston: Pilgrim Press, 1909), pp. 122–23.

42. Bond, pp. 160–61.

43. Ibid., p. 162.
44. Annual Report, Tennessee Coal, Iron & Railroad Company, Reports to Board of Directors: Dec. 19, 1892. Cahaba Coal Mining Company conveyed to Tennessee Coal, Iron & Railroad 44,000 acres in lower Cahaba coal basin, fifteen miles of standard gauge railroad track with appurtenant equipment, 467 coke ovens, 575 tenement houses, stores, and telephone lines, and seven coal mines in active operation with a daily capacity of 3,000 tons; Rogers to G. B. McCormack, April 14, 1894, *Letterbooks of Tennessee Coal, Iron & Railroad, 1893–1895*, A. S. Williams Collection, Eufaula Athenaeum, Eufaula, Ala.
45. *First Biennial Report of Inspectors, 1896.*
46. Shelby County Record of Prisoners, Oct. 19, 1890, to Aug. 20, 1906, SCHS.
47. *Third Biennial Report of Inspectors, 1890*, pp. 54–65.
48. Ibid., pp. 242–45.
49. Thomas D. Parke, "Report by Dr. Thos. D. Parke, MD," and the subsequent exchange of claims by Judson Davie and Thomas Seddon regarding Sloss-Sheffield's Coalburg prison are compiled in *First Biennial Report of Inspectors, 1896.*
50. *Report of Special Committee to Investigate Convict System*, Alabama Legislature, 1897, ADAH.
51. *Second Biennial Report of the Board of Inspectors of Convicts, September 1, 1896, to August 30, 1898* (Montgomery: Roemer Printing, 1898), ADAH.
52. *Fourth Biennial Report of the Board of Inspectors of Convicts, September 1, 1900, to August 31, 1902* (Montgomery: Brown Printing, 1904), ADAH.
53. "Jefferson County Circuit Court Convict Docket, 1902–1903," BPLA.
54. Ibid.
55. *Fifth Biennial Report of the Board of Inspectors of Convicts, September 1, 1902, to August 31, 1904* (Montgomery, Ala.: Brown Printing, 1904), ADAH.
56. *Shelby County Poll Tax Book*, 1890, SCHS.
57. *1900 Census*, Alabama, Shelby County, ED 120, Precinct No. 4 (June 20, 1900).

## CHAPTER V: THE SLAVE FARM OF JOHN PACE

1. *Montgomery Advertiser*, May 30, 1903, p. 1.
2. *1900 Census*, Coosa County, Nixburg beat.
3. *Official Proceedings of the Constitutional Convention of the State of Alabama*, May 21–Sept. 3, 1901 (Wetampka, Ala.: 1940).

4. Horace Mann Bond, *Negro Education in Alabama: A Study in Cotton and Steel* (Tuscaloosa: University of Alabama Press, 1994), p. 175.

5. Affidavit of John Davis, May 9, 1903, RG60, File 76904, EPRRC.

6. Affidavit of J. L. London, May 14, 1903, RG60, File 76904, EPRRC.

7. Davis affidavit.

8. Robert Crew Smith, *The Coming of the Railroad*, privately published compilation of family historical material, Goodwater, Ala., Goodwater Public Library, Genealogy Section, n.d., p. 103.

9. Dana David White, "An Unforgettable Character," in *Coming of the Railroad*, p. 113.

10. *Montgomery Advertiser*, July 3, 1903.

11. Deed of Property, Known as "Old Dorster Edwards place," 1900, Tallapoosa County Deed Books, TCC.

12. C. A. Abernathy, "The Birth of Calcis: Founding of Calcis, Turner Brothers, Justice Store, and Our 'Historical' House: The Community, Its Historical Importance, and Our Family Ties to It," copy of unpublished typescript, Nov. 1, 1992, in possession of author.

13. Compilation by the author, based on affidavits in *U.S. v. Pace; U.S. v. Franklin; U.S. v. Turner; U.S. v. Cosby;* EPRRC.

14. *Montgomery Advertiser*, May 30, 1903, p. 1.

15. Affidavit of J. W. Pace, May 11, 1903, Department of Justice, File 76904, EPRRC.

16. Sevi Pearson contract, April 28, 1885.

17. Text from April 24, 1902, contract with a man name Patterson: "I further agree to be locked up in the cell at night and that I will be obedient and faithful in the discharge of every duty required of me by the said Pace or his agents, and that should the said Pace advance me anything over and above what he had already furnished me, I agree to work for him under this contract until I have paid for same in full, working at the rate of five dollars per month. I agree that if I fail to comply fully with all the obligations on my part under the contract that I will pay the said Pace for all the cost and trouble he is put to in forcing to comply with the same, including a reasonable attorney's fee for prosecuting or making me company with this contract. I agree that should I fail to comply with all the requirements of this contract on my part that said Pace is hereby authorized to hire me out to any person, firm or corporation in the state of Alabama—at such sum as he may be able to hire me at for a term sufficient to pay him all that I may owe him, including all cost and

expense in making me do the work or apprehending and arresting me if I escape."

18. "Interview with Jim Threat, Nov. 4, 1937," conducted by Jessie R. Ervin, McAlester, Okla., Oklahoma Writers' Project, Oklahoma Historical Society.

19. *Convict Record*, Autauga County Probate Clerk's Office.

20. Booker T. Washington, "Southern Prisons," Feb. 18, 1886, letter to editor of *Southern Workman*, BTW Papers, *Vol. 2: 1860–1889* (Urbana: University of Illinois Press, 1972), p. 296, http://www.historycooperative.org/btw.

21. *Montgomery Daily Dispatch*, Feb. 18, 1886.

22. Tallapoosa County Deed Books, August 1879. Pace paid $200 for two hundred acres in Section 2. On Christmas Eve of 1883, he bought 200 acres for $200 in Township 21. In November of 1886, Pace purchased 130 in Section 19, Township 21, Range 22. October 1886, he paid $200 to buy from J.B. and his wife another portion of Section 28 in Township 21. In 1891, Pace paid $1,200 for four lots facing the main street in Dadeville, Broadnax Street, one block away from the antebellum county courthouse. Two years later, he bought a half interest in two more lots on Broadnax, for $200. In 1893, he paid $1,000 for several lots in Dadeville.

23. As part of a mining venture, late in May 1894 Pace paid for a half interest in the minerals contained in a section of Section 16, Township 21.

24. Affidavit of J. M. Kennedy, May 30, 1903, File 76904, EPRRC.

25. Ibid.

26. *Tallapoosa Voice*, April 7, 1892.

27. Reprinted from *Alliance Herald*.

28. Ibid., Oct. 6, 1892.

29. Ibid., July 7, 1892: "The negro politicians have all been in town this week. A majority of them will vote for Kolb for governor. . . . Stand firm to the nominees and break down this effort that is being made to have another '80 campaign in our county. A majority of the Democrats of our county have named their choice for officers—if you are a democrat vote that ticket.; there will be a picnic on R.S. Patillos' place in Red Ridge beat on the 20th of July. Everybody invited to come. The men who have suffered their names to go before the people as independent candidates have deliberately committed political suicide. Politically speaking the four men put out on the 5th are as dead as door nails—funeral ceremonies will occur on the first Monday in August."

30. *1900 Census*, Alabama, Tallapoosa County, Red Ridge District, pp. 1–27.

31. *1900 Census*, Alabama, Tallapoosa County, Red Ridge District, p. 12. Mary

Smith was initially entered as a boarder but changed later to "servant," thirty-seven years old, married ten years, two children, listed as a cook; Maurice Cunningham, initially entered as boarder but changed later to "servant," nine years old, water carrier with no schooling and unable to read or write; S. J. Harriet, convict, twenty-eight; William Riddle, convict, twenty-eight years old; Archer Wiggins, convict, thirty-two years old, married five years; Jack Armour, convict, twenty.

32. Warren S. Reese Jr. to Attorney General, March 22, 1905, Department of Justice, Peonage Files, ff 5280-3, RG60, NA.
33. Affidavits, 1903, File 76904, EPRRC.
34. Affidavit of Joe Patterson, May 7, 1903, File 76909, EPRRC.
35. Affidavit of M. J. Scroggins, undated, Peonage Files, EPRRC. Dadeville Mayor's Docket, Miscellaneous Papers, Peonage Files, File 76904, EPRRC.
36. Affidavit of Wheeler Stone, 1903, File 76904, EPRRC.
37. Compilation by the author of personal ledgers, bank records, and sworn statements of African Americans who were seized and white men who captured them.
38. Pace affidavit: "I paid . . . for him and I kept him ten months." Thompson's mother eventually appeared and paid to set her son free. "There was no commitment paper from any court given me at that time," Pace said.
39. Affidavit of Note Turke, June 30, 1903, File 76909, EPRRC.
40. Town of Goodwater, Acts of Board of Aldermen, Sept. 2, 1904.
41. *1900 Census*, Laray A. Grogan, born May 1872, with a wife, daughter, six, son, five, son, three.
42. Affidavit of Dock Crenshaw, May 25, 1903, File 76909, EPRRC.
43. Affidavit of Charley Williams, May 25, 1903, File 76909, EPRRC.
44. Affidavit of Pat Hill, May 12, 1903, File 76909, EPRRC.

## CHAPTER VI: SLAVERY IS NOT A CRIME

1. *Montgomery Advertiser*, May 27, 1903.
2. Alabama voted to secede January 11, 1861; the Confederate Constitutional Convention convened in Montgomery; Jefferson Davis was sworn in on the state capitol portico; the Confederate capital moved to Richmond, Virginia, in July 1861.
3. Charles W. Chesnutt, "Peonage, or the New Slavery," *Voice of the Negro* 1 (September 1904): 394–97.

4. Booker T. Washington, "To the Colored Citizens of Alabama," *Tuskegee Student*, Feb. 28, 1895, p. 2, BTW Papers.

5. Official Programme of Daily Events, Cotton States and International Exposition, Dec. 30, 1895 (Atlanta: C. P. Byrd), author's collection.

6. Theodore Roosevelt to Booker T. Washington, Washington, D.C., Nov. 9, 1901, BTW Papers.

7. TR to BTW, July 9, 1901, BTW Papers.

8. TR to BTW, March 21, 1901, BTW Papers.

9. Theodore Roosevelt, "Expansion of the White Races," Speech to Methodist Episcopal Church celebration of the African Diamond Jubilee, Washington, D.C., Jan. 18, 1909.

10. TR to BTW, Sept. 14, 1901, BTW Papers.

11. BTW to TR, Oct. 2, 1901, BTW Papers.

12. C. N. Dorsette to BTW, May 31, 1890, telegram, BTW Papers.

13. Thomas Goode Jones to BTW, June 28, 1901, BTW Papers.

14. BTW to TR, Oct. 2, 1901, BTW Papers.

15. William A. Sinclair, *The Aftermath of Slavery* (Boston: Small, Maynard & Company, 1905), pp. 187–90.

16. Ibid.

17. Edmund Morris, *Theodore Rex* (New York: Modern Library, 2002), p. 203.

18. *Dadeville Spot Cash*, March 13, 1903, reprinting editorial of *Birmingham Ledger.*

19. Ibid.

20. Ibid.

21. Sinclair, pp. 188–89.

22. *New York Times*, June 5, 1903.

23. Reese to Parsons, Jan. 27 and April 11, 1903, RG60, NA; typescript, "The Slave Traffic Today," Appointment and Credentials Files, Dept. of Justice, RG60, NA.

24. Jones to Philander C. Knox, March 21, 1903, ff 5280-03, RG60, NA:

Sir: Some witnesses before the Grand Jury here developed the fact that in Shelby county in this District, and in Coosa county in the Middle district, a systematic scheme of depriving negroes of their liberty, and hiring them out, has been practiced for some time.

The plan is to accuse the negro of some petty offense, and then require him, in order to escape conviction, to enter into an agreement to pay his accuser so much money, and sign a contract, under the terms of which his bondsmen can hire him out until he pays a certain sum. The negro is made to believe he is a convict, and treated as such. It is said that thirty negroes were in the stockade at one time.

Thursday, a negro witness who had been summoned here, and testified before the Grand Jury, was taken from the train by force, and imprisoned on account of his testimony; but finally his captors became frightened and turned him loose. The grand jury found indictments against nine of the parties. I deemed it essential to the safety of the negro that a deputy marshal should protect him while in that county, and while here giving testimony; and that the accused parties should be promptly arrested and held to bail, in order to deter them, at least, from further violence to the negro. . . . Yours truly, T. G. Jones

25. *United States v. William Eberhart*, indictment, U.S. District Court, Northern District of Georgia, April 19, 1898, Dept. of Justice, RG60, EPRRC; *Atlanta Journal*, April 21, 1898.
26. Angier to Attorney General W. H. H. Miller, April 19, 1898, RG60, NA.
27. *United States v. Eberhart*, Jan. 25, 1899 (127 F. 254), District Judge Newman.
28. Angier to Attorney General W. H. H. Miller, Jan. 17, 1899, RG60, NA.
29. Pete Daniel, *The Shadow of Slavery: Peonage in the South, 1901–1969* (Urbana: University of Illinois Press, 1972), p. 3.
30. Eagan to Attorney General Knox, July 13, 1901, RG60, NA.
31. Daniel, pp. 6–13.
32. Reese to Knox, April 7, 1903, ff 5280-03, #5664, RG60, NA.
33. Thomas R. Roulhac to Knox, April 9, 1903, ff 5280-03, #5762, RG60, NA:

The late Grand Jury at Birmingham Ala. made a careful investigation of the complaints as to the attempt to deprive citizens of African descent of their liberty and I am gratified to state that this investigation was not only closely and carefully made, but that the desire was universal among all its members, composed of as excellent material, in intelligence and character, as the district or State affords, to vindicate the State from such unlawful and disgraceful proceedings, and to bring to punishment every man who by the proof was shown to have had any connection with it. Indictments were found against nine persons, all that the testimony connected with the transaction but enough was disclosed to show that the same or like systems prevailed in other districts in the state. I do not think the present the most propitious time for employing the services of a secret Service operative. In my judgment after a comparatively short lapse of time, his investigation will not have so much attention attracted to them as they would have if begun immediately, and I think the participants and those who can impart any information will be more likely to do so when the present flutter has somewhat subsided.

It is equally gratifying to state that the said Grand Jury were aroused by an attempt to intimidate one of the witnesses before them, and that they promptly returned indictments against all who had any part in anything of that character. Indictments were found against all of these, arrests were promptly made, and such of them as were able to make bond were admitted to bail in the sum of the Two thousand Dollars each. . . . One was committed to jail in Birmingham. . . .

No effort will be spared to obtain a conviction of all of these parties, and it has been reported to us that already the effect has been most salutory [*sic*] resulting in the discharge of a number whose confinement has been illegal, or of questionable legality, and their restoration to liberty.

34. Affidavit of L. E. White, undated, File 76909, EPRRC.
35. Reese to Knox, April 25, 1903, ff 5280-03, RG60, NA.
36. Asa Stratton to Attorney General, Feb. 18, 1897, *Records Relating to the Appointment of Federal Judges, Marshals and Attorneys*, W. S. Reese Jr. file, #068849, RG60, NA.
37. Marielou Armstrong Cory, "History of the Ladies Memorial Association," 1902, http://www.monumentpreservation.com/monument/history.html.

## CHAPTER VII: THE INDICTMENTS

1. *Montgomery Advertiser*, June 9, 1903, p. 7.
2. Reese to Knox, June 15, 1903, RG60, NA.
3. Affidavit of Paul Hoffman, May 8, 1903; affidavit of Si Caldwell, May 9, 1903, File 76909, EPRRC.
4. Davis affidavit.
5. Affidavit of J. G. Dunbar, May 11, 1903, File 76909, EPRRC.
6. Affidavit of J. L. Purifoy, May 13, 1903; affidavit of Jim Caldwell, May 9, 1903, File 76909, EPRRC.
7. Affidavit of D. M. White, certifying copy of Mayor's Court Docket, May 29, 1903, File 76904, EPRRC.
8. Receipt, April 24, 1902, File 76904, Tallapoosa County Bank, EPRRC.

9. Purifoy affidavit.

10. White affidavit.

11. Affidavit of Esau Williams, May 25, 1903, File 76909, EPRRC.

12. Affidavit of Glennie Helms, May 25, 1903; affidavit of Dave Johnson, May 25, 1903, File 76909, EPRRC.

13. Johnson affidavit.

14. Helms affidavit.

15. E. Williams affidavit.

16. Dec. 1, 1955.

17. Affidavit of John W. Pace, May 11, 1903, File 76909, EPRRC.

18. Ibid.

19. Affidavit of Fletch Turner, May 12, 1903, File 76909, EPRRC.

20. Affidavit of George Cosby, May 15, 1903, File 76909, EPRRC.

21. Affidavit of J. M. Kennedy, May 30, 1903, File 76909, EPRRC.

22. Dunbar affidavit.

23. Affidavit of G. B. Walker, May 12, 1903, File 76909, EPRRC.

24. Affidavit of Mat Davis, May 9, 1903, File 76909; affidavit of Charles Davis, May 9, 1903, File 76909, EPRRC.

25. Kennedy affidavit.

26. Ibid.

27. Affidavit of J. W. Havalson, June 29, 1903, File 76909, EPRRC.

28. *Montgomery Advertiser*, May 30, 1903, p. 1.

29. Ibid.

30. Ibid.

31. *Cleveland Gazette*, Jan. 24, 1903, p. 2.

32. *New York Evening Post*, May 26, 1903, no page.

33. *Montgomery Advertiser*, June 13, 1903, p. 4.

34. Ibid., July 7, 1903, p. 4.

35. Ibid., June 9, 1903, p. 4.

36. *Dadeville Spot Cash*, June 5, 1903, p. 1.

37. *New York Herald*, June 8, 1903.

38. *Montgomery Advertiser*, June 12, 1903, p. 3.

39. Sinclair, p. 245.

40. Attorney General to Roosevelt, June 8, 1903, Executive and Congressional Letter Book 64, p. 341, NA.

41. Reese to Knox, June 10, 1903, RG60, NA.

42. Stanley W. Finch, Examiner, to Attorney General, Feb. 18, 1904, "Report on W. S. Reese Jr.," ff 5280-03, RG60, NA.

43. *1900 Census, 1870 Census, 1860 Census.*

44. *Montgomery Advertiser,* June 10, 1903, p. 3.

45. Judge Thomas G. Jones, "Charge to Jury," June 15, 1903, ff 5280-03, RG60, NA.

46. *Prattville Progress,* June 26, 1903, p. 2.

47. *Birmingham Age-Herald,* June 17, 1903.

48. *Montgomery Advertiser,* June 18, 1903, p. 4.

49. Reese to Knox, June 15, 1903, ff 5380-03, RG60, pp. 1–4, NA.

50. Ibid., p. 4.

51. Ibid., pp. 4–6.

52. Ibid., pp. 7–8.

53. Pete Daniel, *The Shadow of Slavery: Peonage in the South, 1901–1969* (Urbana: University of Illinois Press, 1972), p. 46.

54. Reese to Knox, June 15, 1903, p. 8.

55. *Nation,* June 11, 1903, p. 1.

56. *Montgomery Advertiser,* June 23, 1903, p. 7.

57. Ibid., June 25, 1903.

58. *Dadeville Spot Cash,* June 19, 1903, quoting *Atlanta Constitution.*

59. *Montgomery Advertiser,* June 25, 1903, p. 4.

60. Ibid., June 13, 1903, p. 4.

61. Ibid., June 19, 1903, p. 9.

## CHAPTER VIII: A SUMMER OF TRIALS, 1903

1. Stanley W. Finch to Frank Strong, General Agent, Department of Justice, June 23, 1903, Peonage Files (5280), ff 9927, RG60, NA.

2. Affidavit of Owen Green, no date, File 76909, EPRRC.

3. *1860 Census* (Pace month of birth: October 1853).

4. *Macon Telegraph,* June 25, 1903; Speer to Attorney General, June 25, 1903, EPRRC.

5. *Montgomery Advertiser,* June 28, 1903, p. 3.

6. Ibid., June 30, 1903, p. 2.

7. Ibid., July 1, 1908, p. 1.

8. Reese to Attorney General, June 30, 1903, ff 10157, RG60, NA.

9. Edward M. Adams to John E. Wilkie, Chief of Treasury Secret Service investigators, June 24, 1904, ff 13098, RG60, NA.

10. *Montgomery Advertiser,* July 5, 1903.

11. Affidavit of Fletcher Turner, May 12, 1903, EPRRC.

12. Helms affidavit.

13. *Montgomery Advertiser*, July 8, 1903.

14. Ibid., July 11, 1903.

15. Ibid.; *New York Times*, July 11, 1903.

16. *New York Times*, July 13, 1903.

17. *Montgomery Advertiser*, July 14, 1903, p. 1; *Dadeville Spot Cash*, July 17, 1903; *New York Times*, July 25, 1903, p. 2.

18. *Montgomery Advertiser*, July 21, 1903, p. 1.

## CHAPTER IX: A RIVER OF ANGER

1. Reese, the prosecutor, wrote to newspapers in response that Heflin had grossly understated the facts alleged in the indictments. Reese statement, July 21, 1903, Miscellaneous Papers, Peonage Cases, File 76904, EPRRC. Heflin replied, denouncing Reese, and Judges Jones and Speer in Alabama and Georgia, wrapping his condemnation in a defense of the jury system:

   I care not whether the Judge be named Jones or Speer; whether he lives in Alabama or Ohio. My contention is that no judge has the right, legal or moral, to coerce a jury into finding a verdict to his liking, that the jurors are the sole judges of the facts and they must find the verdict according to their own conviction and consciences that they are entitled to protection from insults and abuse of the presiding judge. We cannot be too strenuous in our efforts to guard the dignity and integrity of the jury system of our country. . . . It was only when, according to my honest convictions, he had invaded the sacred province of the jury, had used language if denunciation and intimidation that no judicial authority on earth could warrant, and had set a precedent fraught with the gravest danger to that ancient institution that great bulwark of the people's rights and liberties, the "right of trial by jury," that I excised the right that is mine as an American citizen to criticize his official conduct, and to speak publicly my views concerning this most remarkable occurrence in Alabama. *Montgomery Advertiser*, July 22, 1903, p. 2.

2. Ernest H. Hill to Reese, July 15, 1903, Miscellaneous Papers, Peonage Files, File 76904, EPRRC.

3. Thomas Dixon Jr., *The Leopard's Spots: A Romance of the White Man's Burden* (New York: P. F. Collier, 1902), pp. 381–84.

4. Thomas Nelson Page, *The Negro: The Southerner's Problem* (New York: Charles Scribner's Sons, 1904), p. 64.

5. *Montgomery Advertiser*, April 25, 1903, p. 1.

6. Ibid.; *Nation*, Aug. 19, 1903, p. 1.

7. William Hannibal Thomas, *The American Negro* (New York: Macmillan, 1901), cited in Page, p. 82.

8. *Montgomery Advertiser*, April 26, 1903, p. 1.

9. *Dadeville Spot Cash*, May 15, 1903.

10. *Montgomery Advertiser*, May 21, 1903, p. 4.

11. Ibid., June 5, 1903, quoting *Columbus Enquirer-Sun*, p. 4.

12. William A. Sinclair, *The Aftermath of Slavery* (Boston: Small, Maynard & Company, 1905), pp. 221–22.

13. Phillips Verner Bradford and Harvey Blume, *Ota: The Pygmy in the Zoo* (New York: St. Martin's, 1992).

14. *Montgomery Advertiser*, June 10, 1903, p. 1.

15. *Proceedings: Joint Committee of the Senate and House to Investigate the Convict Lease System of Georgia*, Vol. 1, transcripts of first meeting, Gaither testimony, pp. 187–97, GDAH.

16. *New York Times*, July 21, 1903.

17. *Montgomery Advertiser*, April 10, 1903, p. 1.

18. J. E. Sistrunk to Department of Justice, July 6, 1903, Peonage Files, EPRRC.

19. *Montgomery Advertiser*, April 16, 1903, p. 1.

20. Ibid., May 17, 1903, p. 1.

21. Ibid., May 16, 1903, p. 1.

22. *New York Times*, July 5, 1903.

23. Associated Press, July 5, 1903.

24. *New York Times*, July 13, 14, 1903.

25. W. E. B. Du Bois, *The Souls of Black Folk*, 1903 (New York: Dover, 1994), pp. 23, 65.

## CHAPTER X: THE DISAPPROBATION OF GOD

1. *New York Times*, July 25, 1903.

2. *Dadeville Spot Cash*, July 31, 1903.

3. Ibid., Aug. 14, 1903, publishing Tallapoosa County Grand Jury report, July 27, 1903.

4. Ibid., Aug. 28, 1903: "W. W. Pearson, who was one of the attorneys for the Cosbys, says he will petition Judge Jones to commute their sentence. It will be remembered that they plead guilty to charges of peonage against them and were sent to the U.S. Penitentiary in Atlanta to serve a year and a day. It is agreed that their penalty is too severe and the late deliverances of the court show it to be inclined to mercy and it is thought that the petition will meet with favor. . . . The citizens of Tallapoosa county are signing petitions for the release of the Cosbys now in prison in Atlanta . . . claimed that the petition will go up with at least 3000 names signed to it."

5. *Montgomery Advertiser,* Dec. 14, 1903: "The state convict inspectors are surprised at the county commissioners of Tallapoosa county in awarding the convict labor contract of that county to J. W. Pace. Pace had the county convicts at the time he was arrested for peonage. He is now under sentence of five years but the sentence has been suspended by Judge Jones of the US court."

6. *Nation,* Aug. 19, 1903, p. 1; *New York Times,* Nov. 23, 1903.

7. M. D. Wickersham to Attorney General, Sept. 21, 1903, File 5280, ff 14901, Peonage Files, RG60, NA.

8. Catherine McRee Carter, "History of Kinderlou, Georgia, 1860–1940," unpublished typescript, December 1940, in possession of author.

9. "The New Slavery in the South, An Autobiography," *Independent,* February 25, 1904, pp. 409–14.

10. Affidavit of Henry C. Dickey, Nov. 24, 1903, EPRRC.

11. Kinsey File, Department of Justice, Peonage Files, RG60, NA.

12. Affidavit of Edward McRee, Nov. 24, 1903, EPRRC.

13. Opinion of Judge Emory Speer, *U.S. v. McClellan and Crawley,* March 17, 1904, EPRRC.

14. Akerman to Attorney General, March 27, 1905, EPRRC.

15. Sternfeld to Reese, Nov. 12, 1903, ff 5280-17119, Peonage Files, RG60, NA.

16. L. R. Farmer to Attorney General, Nov. 17, 1903, ff 3098-1902, Peonage Files, RG60, NA:

Morganton N.C., Dear Sir, i write you for information i have a little girl that has been kidnapped from me and is now under bondage in Ga and I cant get her out only her but no of others i want ask you is it law for people to whip (col) people and keep them and not allow them to leave without a pass my reason for writing you is the people in Ga wont do any

thing with him and if the negroes tell any thing they will beat them to
death and they are a fraid to testfie against him because cary them write
back and beat them to death and some of them has beened killed trying
to get away from their and i got a little girl there and get her a way from
their if you could inform me please to write me how can tell me the
proper one

over p.s.   you pleas ans me at once this little of mine is begging me
to come after and i write you for information i have tried to get outte a
write of habeaus corpus and that could not get her you will find stamp for
the ans

Rev. L.R. Farmer pastor of Baps of this place

17. Attorney General to Farmer, Nov. 18, 1903, Peonage Files, ff 3098-1902,
RG60, NA.

18. *New York Times*, Dec. 4, 1904.

19. *Wilcox Progressive Era*, Jan. 14, 1904, transcribed by Stephen Lee, Dec. 2003,
http://ftp.rootsweb.com/pub/usgenweb/al/wilcox/vitals/marriages/gmr12melton
.txt.

20. J. R. Adams to Attorney General, Feb. 23, 1904, Peonage Files, RG60, NA.

21. Ibid.

22. U.S. Commissioner to W. H. Armbrecht, Feb. 13, 1904, Peonage Files,
RG60, NA.

23. *Galveston News*, Dec. 27, 1903; *Atlanta Constitution*, Dec. 29–31, 1903.

24. *Nation*, Jan. 14, 1904; BTW to Edward Henry Clement, Dec. 30, 1903, BTW
Papers.

25. Finch to Attorney General, Feb. 18, 1904, File 5280-03, ff 29562, RG60, NA.

26. Reese to Attorney General, March 2, 1904, File 5280-03, ff 29606, RG60, NA.

27. Indictment of Alex D. Stephens, Miscellaneous Papers, Peonage Files, File
76904, EPRRC.

28. Akerman to Attorney General, April 14, 1904, Peonage Files, RG60, NA.

29. Acting Attorney General to Reese, June 24, 1904, Peonage Files, RG60, NA.

30. Reese to Attorney General, Aug. 23, 1904, Peonage Files, RG60, NA.

31. *Clyatt v. U.S.*, 197 U.S. 207 (1905).

32. *Jamison v. Wimbish*, 130 F. 351, 355–57 (S.D. Ga. 1904) (Speer, J.).

33. Reese to Attorney General, March 25, 1905; Attorney General to Reese,
March 27, 1905; File 5280-03, ff 53321, Peonage Files, RG60, NA.

34. Reese to Attorney General, March 27, 1905, File 5280-03, ff 53574, Peonage
Files, RG60, NA.

35. "Susanna" to Jones, July 3, 1905, Miscellaneous Papers, Peonage Files, File 76904, EPRRC. Susanna said a store clerk named C. L. Waldrup had detailed information on the slavery ring; one of the black laborers being held was Dick Gray, the same name of one of the men captured in the John Pace slavery network five years earlier. Susanna didn't know the names of others, but said all were held against their will, tracked down if they attempted to leave, and forced back to the turpentine operation at gunpoint.

36. Reese to W. H. Moody, March 27, 1905, Peonage Files, RG60, NA.

37. Reese to BTW, Feb. 1, 1905, BTW Papers.

38. Attorney General to Reese, April 5, 1905, File 5280-03, ff 53574, Peonage Files, RG60, NA.

39. *Atlanta Constitution*, March 18, 1905, p. 3.

40. Ibid., Oct. 29, 1905, p. 2; Aug. 12, 1906, p. 6.

41. Ibid., Oct. 26, 1905.

42. Ibid., Oct. 31, 1905, p. 2; Nov. 1, p. 5.

43. Author's collection.

44. *Atlanta Constitution*, March 16, 1906, p. 7.

45. Ibid., Nov. 6, 1905, p. 7.

46. Ibid., Oct. 16, 1905, p. 1; Oct. 29, 1905, p. 2.

## CHAPTER XI: SLAVERY AFFIRMED

1. David Levering Lewis, *W. E. B. Du Bois: Biography of a Race, 1868–1919* (New York: Henry Holt, 1993), pp. 354–59, 436–39.

2. R. H. Ellis, "The Calhoun School, Miss Charlotte Thorn's 'Lighthouse on the Hill' in Lowndes County, Alabama," *Alabama Review* 37, no. 3 (1984): 183–201.

3. Jonathan Grossman, "Black Studies in the Department of Labor, 1897–1907," *Monthly Labor Review*, June 1974.

4. W. E. B. Du Bois, *The Autobiography of W. E. B. Du Bois: A Soliloquy on Viewing My Life from the Last Decade of Its First Century* (New York: International Publishers, 1968), pp. 226–77.

5. Du Bois to Charles P. Neill, Nov. 2, 1906, Du Bois Papers, University of Massachusetts, cited in Lewis, *W. E. B. Du Bois: Biography of a Race*, p. 354.

6. Du Bois, *Autobiography*, p. 227.

7. *Atlanta Constitution*, Sept. 20, 21, 22, 1906.

8. For the definitive account of the Atlanta race riot, see Mark Bauerlein, *Negrophobia: A Race Riot in Atlanta, 1906* (San Francisco: Encounter, 2001).

9. *Atlanta Constitution*, Oct. 12, 1906, p. 7.

10. Lewis, p. 355.

11. Du Bois, *Autobiography*, p. 227.

12. W. E. B. Du Bois, *The Quest of the Silver Fleece* (Chicago: A. C. McClurg & Co., 1911).

13. *Jamison v. Wimbish*; *Atlanta Constitution*, Oct. 17, 1905.

14. Pete Daniel, *The Shadow of Slavery: Peonage in the South, 1901–1969* (Urbana: University of Illinois Press, 1972), p. 62.

## CHAPTER XII: NEW SOUTH RISING

1. Born Sept. 1885, *1900 Census*.

2. *Fourth Biennial Report of the Board of Inspectors of Convicts, September 1, 1900, to August 31, 1902* (Montgomery: Brown Printing, 1902), ADAH.

3. Register of Prisoners Committed to the County Jail of Shelby County, 096-1, p. 172, SCHS; Schedule of Convicts obtained by Tennessee Coal, Iron & Railroad Co. from Shelby County, second quarter 1904, SCHS.

4. J. A. MacKnight, "Columbiana: The Gem of the Hills," c. 1907, published by the *Shelby County Sentinel*, SCHS.

5. In June 1892, George W. Vines, superintendent of town schools, posted a notice inviting "all white persons interested in the welfare of the Dadeville High School" to assemble at the courthouse to select new leadership of the public school system.

6. Photograph file, SCHS.

7. MacKnight, p. 20.

8. Will Lewis was taken before Judge A. P. Longshore in February 1908. He had taken $25 to sign a contract in the fall of 1906 agreeing to work in another local lime kiln, this one owned by C. L. O'Neal. Three months later, he tried to leave, and O'Neal took out a warrant for false pretense.

9. "Contract on Confession of Judgment Record," 1903–1913, SCHS.

10. Register of Prisoners Committed to Jail, 1890–1906, SCHS, analysis by author.

11. "Contract on Confessions of Judgment Record."

12. MacKnight's publicity pamphlet for Columbiana captured a full portrait of the town's mercantile, legal, and political elite, all of which benefited in some respect from the county's active trade in forced labor. D. R. McMillan, predecessor of Longshore as probate judge, was another of the town's most promi-

nent attorneys. The son of a cotton planter ruined by the Civil War, he studied law during Reconstruction and arrived in Columbiana in 1886 to form a law practice with former Alabama governor Rufus Cobb. By 1907, he was in partnership with J. J. Haynes, the rising young man among lawyers in the province. The people of Columbiana were particularly proud of their new "free school," funded by the town council and available to any white children living in the city limits. Milner & Armstrong operated a steam-powered sawmill near the rail line on the outskirts of Columbiana. Rufus Lester had arrived in Shelby as a young farmer and then taken work in a general store, weighing sugar and measuring out calico for yeoman families. He had risen to become owner of the business and a major buyer of cotton for mills he owned. John S. Pitts was the county's longtime tax collector, the right-hand man in politics of Judge Longshore. W. R. A. Milner, deputy to Sheriff Fulton, was a respected Confederate veteran.

13. *Sixth Biennial Report of the Board of Inspectors of Convicts, September 1, 1904, to August 31, 1906* (Montgomery, 1906), ADAH.

14. *Fifth Biennial Report of the Board of Inspectors of Convicts, September 1, 1902, to August 31, 1904* (Montgomery, Ala.: Brown Printing, 1904), ADAH.

15. *Sixth Biennial Report*, 1906.

16. Ibid.

17. W. David Lewis, *Sloss Furnaces and the Rise of the Birmingham District: An Industrial Epic* (Tuscaloosa: University of Alabama Press, 1994), p. 310.

18. *Birmingham Age-Herald*, Aug. 2, 1900, cited in Lewis, *Sloss Furnaces*, p. 251.

19. Justin Fuller, "History of Tennessee Coal, Iron and Railroad Company, 1852–1907" (Ph.D. diss., University of North Carolina, Chapel Hill, 1966), pp. 273–74.

20. *Birmingham Age-Herald*, Aug. 2, 1900, cited in Lewis, *Sloss Furnaces*, p. 251.

21. W. F. Tyler to Eagle & Phoenix Mfg. Co., Oct. 18, 1899, original in possession of author.

22. Erskine Ramsey to H. C. Frick, Aug. 7, 1903, File 1.1.11, p. 88, BPLA.

23. *1900 Census*, Jefferson County, Precinct 29.

24. Fuller, p. 331.

25. *Wall Street Journal*, May 16, 1905.

26. Annual Report, U.S. Steel Corp., Dec. 31, 1907; C. A. Abernathy, "The Birth of Calcis: Founding of Calcis, Turner Brothers, Justice Store, and Our 'Historical' House: The Community, Its Historical Importance, and Our Family Ties to It," copy of unpublished typescript, Nov. 1, 1992, in possession of author.

27. Fuller, pp. 148–52; Lewis, *Sloss Furnaces*, p. 290.

28. Ron Chernow, *The House of Morgan: An American Dynasty and the Rise of*

*Modern Finance* (New York: Atlantic Monthly Press, 1990), pp. 124–28; Edmund Morris, *Theodore Rex* (New York: Modern Library, 2002), pp. 497–99; Lewis, *Sloss Furnaces*, pp. 288–93; Fuller, pp. 153–54.

29. Agreement entered into by J. Craig Smith, President of the Board of Convict Inspectors of the State of Alabama and Tennessee Coal, Iron & Railroad Company, Nov. 26, 1907, copy in possession of author.

## CHAPTER XIII: THE ARREST OF GREEN COTTENHAM

1. Analysis by the author of charges and sentencings in central and southern Alabama, 1900–1910.

2. Report of Persons Sentenced to Hard Labor for Shelby County, March 1908, SCHS.

3. Ibid.

4. Criminal Court Records, Bibb County and Shelby County, Ala.

5. Report of Shelby County Grand Jury, Spring Term, 1908, published in *Shelby County People's Advocate*, April 23, 1908.

6. Photographs on file, SCHS.

7. *1900 Census.*

8. References appear frequently in archival material of women sexually abused by police officials and, in the case of female prisoners, other convicts. For the most complete treatment of the conditions of female prisoners, see Mary Ellen Curtin, *Black Prisoners and Their World, Alabama, 1865–1900* (Charlottesville: University Press of Virginia, 2000), pp. 113–29.

9. Leon F. Litwack, *Trouble in Mind: Black Southerners in the Age of Jim Crow* (New York: Alfred A. Knopf, 1998), p. 269, citing *Statement of Pardons, Paroles and Commutations Granted by Cole L. Blease, 1913* (Columbia, S.C.: 1914).

## CHAPTER XIV: ANATOMY OF A SLAVE MINE

1. Shelby M. Harrison, "A Cash-Nexus for Crime"; "The Human Side of Large Outputs, Steel and Steel Workers in Six American States, Part IV, Birmingham District: Labor Conservation," both in *The Survey*, Jan. 6, 1912, pp. 1526–47.

2. Ramsey to G. B. McCormack, General Manager, on Pratt Division, Feb. 13, 1896, Erskine Ramsey Papers, File 1.1.1D, BPLA.

3. TCI company photographs, in possession of author.

4. *Miles College: The First Hundred Years* (Charleston, S.C.: Arcadia, 2005), pp. 15–18.

5. *Birmingham Age-Herald,* Feb. 21, 1908.

6. "County Convict Contracts," internal memorandum of Tennessee Coal, Iron & Railroad Co., Aug. 28, 1908, copy in possession of author.

7. *Quadrennial Report of the Board of Inspectors of Convicts, Sept. 1, 1910 to Aug. 31, 1914* (Montgomery: 1914), ADAH.

8. "Statement of State and County Convicts at Pratt Mines Division as of Month of August, 1908," U.S. Steel Corp., copy in possession of author.

9. Sheriff's Prisoners Register (1908), Shelby County, SCHS.

10. Tennessee Coal, Iron & Railroad Co. photograph, labeled "Muscoda Ore Mines, Hospital in Use in 1901 and 1902," in possession of author.

11. John N. Reynolds, *Twin Hells* (Chicago: M. A. Donahue & Co., 1890), pp. 86–87.

12. Alvaran Snow Allen, "The Story of a Lie: By Convict No. 2939, Himself 15 Years in Prison," pamphlet printed by Mission Printing Company, Tulsa, c. 1926, in possession of author.

13. Harvey R. Hougen, "The Impact of Politics and Prison Industry on the General Management of the Kansas State Penitentiary, 1883–1909," 1977, citing Carl "Cork" Arnold, *A Life Prisoner,* 1906.

14. Allen, "Story of a Lie."

15. Ibid.; Reynolds, p. 94.

16. Interview by the author of Willie Clark, 2001, 2002, 2003.

17. "Registry of Convict Deaths," *Quadrennial Report of the Board of Inspectors of Convicts, September 1, 1906, to August 31, 1910* (Montgomery: Brown Printing, 1910), ADAH.

18. Brian Kelly, *Race, Class, and Power in the Alabama Coalfields, 1908–21* (Urbana: University of Illinois Press, 2001), pp. 1–8.

19. *Atlanta Constitution,* Aug. 6, 1908, p. 2.

20. Death Certificate—County Convict: Green Cunningham [*sic*], Aug. 15, 1908.

## CHAPTER XV: EVERYWHERE WAS DEATH

1. *Atlanta Constitution,* July 13, 1908, p. 1; July 15, 1908.

2. "The Lynching Century: African Americans Who Died in Racial Violence in the United States, 1865–1965," Tuskegee Institute Lynching Inventory, www

.geocities.com/Colosseum/Base/8507/NLists.htm; *Atlanta Constitution*, July 16, 1908.

3. *Atlanta Constitution*, July 29, 1908, p. 5.

4. Ibid., July 30, 1908, p. 1.

5. Ibid., Aug. 2, 1908.

6. *New York Times*, Aug. 16, 1908, p. 1.

7. Brian Kelly, *Race, Class, and Power in the Alabama Coalfields, 1908–21* (Urbana: University of Illinois Press, 2001), pp. 23–24.

8. Ibid.

9. *Birmingham Age-Herald*, Nov. 11, 1908, p. 1.

10. Ibid., Nov. 18, 1908, p. 5.

11. *Quadrennial Report of the Board of Inspectors of Convicts, September 1, 1906, to August 31, 1910* (Montgomery: Brown Printing, 1910), ADAH.

12. Jefferson County Coroner's Record, Preliminary Investigation Reports, Record of B. L. Brasher, Coroner; Office of Coroner/Medical Examiner, Jefferson County, Ala.

13. Sentenced to life for first-degree murder, his first criminal charge.

14. Ethel Armes, *The Story of Coal and Iron in Alabama* (Birmingham: Chamber of Commerce, 1910), pp. 493–95; James Saxon Childers, *Erskine Ramsey: His Life and Achievements* (New York: Cartwright & Ewing, 1942), pp. 160–65, 264.

15. *Montgomery Advertiser*, April 12, 1911.

16. Jefferson County Coroner's Record, Preliminary Investigation Reports, Jefferson County Coroner's Office.

17. *Atlanta Constitution*, Aug. 7, 1908, p. 1.

18. *Clayton Record*, Jan. 20, 1911, p. 1.

19. Barbour County Jail Registry, undated, Sheriff R. B. Teal, Barbour County Courthouse.

20. *Clayton Record*, April 28, 1911, p. 1.

21. A prison inspector report from 1915 says building prior to 1913 had been condemned.

22. Barbour County Jail Registry, 1911; *Clayton Record*, May 12, 1911, p. 1.

23. Jail Registry, 1911; author's analysis.

24. Jail Registry, 1911, Barbour County Courthouse.

25. *Clayton Record*, May 31, 1912, p. 1.

26. *State Convicts Descriptive Record, 1913–1916*, Vol. 8, Alabama Department of Corrections, ADAH; Demas, p. 175; Miller, p. 488.

27. *State Convicts Descriptive Record, 1913–1916,* Vol. 8, Alabama Department of Corrections, ADAH.

28. Registry of Convict Deaths.

29. Ida M. Tarbell, *The Life of Elbert M. Gary: The Story of Steel* (New York: D. Appleton, 1925), pp. 310–11.

30. *Transcript of Public Investigation into Affairs and Conduct of the Convict Department, March 1913,* Vol. 2, Alabama Department of Corrections, ADAH, testimony of Walker Percy, pp. 690–91.

31. Ibid., pp. 693–98.

32. Internal U.S. Steel legal memo, May 1913, in possession of author.

33. *Transcript: Public Investigation,* testimony of E. H. Coxe, pp. 675–77.

34. Ibid., Coxe to Oakley, Sept. 25, 1911.

35. "Report of Persons Sentenced to Hard Labor for Shelby County," December 1913, SCHS.

## CHAPTER XVI: ATLANTA, THE SOUTH'S FINEST CITY

1. *Twentieth Annual Report of the Commissioner of Labor, 1905: Convict Labor* (Washington, D.C.: U.S. Government Printing Office, 1906), p. 206.

2. *Atlanta Constitution,* July 11, 1908, p. 1.

3. Ibid., July 23, 1908.

4. *Proceedings: Joint Committee,* Daniel Long testimony, pp. 501–5, GDAH.

5. *Proceedings: Joint Committee,* Susan Long testimony, pp. 506–9, GDAH.

6. *Proceedings: Joint Committee,* R. A. Keith testimony, pp. 162–87, GDAH.

7. *Proceedings: Joint Committee,* Will Wynne testimony, pp. 1582–91, GDAH.

8. James W. English Personality File, AHC; also, Clement A. Evans, *Confederate Military History* (Atlanta: 1899), 4: 635–38.

9. Memoirs of Georgia (Atlanta: Southern Historical Association, 1895), Vol. 1, Ch. 4, pp. 766–69.

10. *Proceedings: Joint Committee,* James W. English testimony, pp. 1209–40, GDAH; Annual Statement of Brickyard Account, June 1, 1906, to May 31, 1907, Chattahoochee Brick Company File, AHG.

11. *Proceedings: Joint Committee,* Arthur Moore testimony, no page number, July 23, 1908; Ed Strickland testimony, p. 479, GDAH.

12. *Proceedings: Joint Committee,* J. A. Cochran testimony, pp. 64–105, GDAH.

13. Ibid.; *Atlanta Constitution,* July 24, 1908, p. 1.

14. Alex Lichtenstein, *Twice the Work of Free Labor: The Political Economy of Convict Labor in the New South* (London: Verso, 1996), p. 122.

15. Joel Hurt to J. W. Callahan, Dec. 24, 1904, and Dec. 29, 1904, GDAH.

16. J. W. Callahan to Hurt, Jan. 6, 1905, GDAH.

17. Hurt to Callahan, Jan. 5, 1905, GDAH.

18. *Proceedings: Joint Committee*, Joel Hurt testimony, pp. 418–48.

19. *Proceedings: Joint Committee*, Jake Moore testimony, Aug. 4, 1908, GDAH.

20. *Proceedings: Joint Committee*, George Hurt testimony, pp. 724–42, GDAH.

21. Ibid.

22. *Atlanta Constitution*, July 13, 1908.

23. Ibid., Aug. 3, 4, 5, 1908.

24. Annual Statement of Brickyard Account, June 1, 1909, to May 31, 1910, Chattahoochee Brick Company File, AHC.

25. Matthew J. Mancini, *One Dies, Get Another: Convict Leasing in the American South, 1866–1928* (Columbia: University of South Carolina Press, 1996), p. 221.

26. H. Gibson to E. J. Parsons, May 7, 1906; Thomas Jones to Attorney General, May 11, 1906; E. J. Parsons to Attorney General, June 18, 1906, Peonage Files, RG60, NA.

27. Gibson to Parsons, May 7, 1906, Peonage Files, RG60, NA.

28. Parsons to Attorney General, May 11, 1906, File 50-87, Peonage Files, RG60, NA.

29. Parsons to Attorney General, June 18, 1906, Peonage Files, RG60, NA.

30. Johnson to Department of Justice, March 30, 1907, Peonage Files, RG60, NA.

31. Parsons to Attorney General, Sept. 18, 1907, Peonage Files, RG60, NA.

32. Jones to Parsons, Dec. 24, 1907; "Law Abiding Citizen" to Jones, Dec. 19, 1907; Parsons to Attorney General, Dec. 26, 1907, Peonage Files, RG60, NA.

33. W. Armbrecht to Attorney General, Dec. 22, 1908, File 50-92, Peonage Files, RG60, NA.

34. Armbrecht to Attorney General, January 1909, RG60, NA.

35. "Statement of All Peonage Cases Since May 1, 1902," J. W. Dimmick to M. H. Smith, March 3, 1909, Peonage Files, RG60, NA.

36. Attorney General to Herman Perkins, undated note, Sept. 1923, 50-1-6, File 5280-03-02, Peonage Files, RG60, NA.

37. "Copy of Report of the September 1911 Grand Jury of the Criminal Court of Jefferson County: Justice of the Peace"; Oliver Street to Attorney General, Jan. 24, 1912, File 50-112, RG60, NA.

38. Woodrow Wilson, *Division and Reunion, 1829–1889* (New York: Longmans, Green, 1893), pp. 124, 125, 268, 273; Lawrence J. Friedman, *The White Savage: Racial Fantasies in the Postbellum South* (Englewood Cliffs, N.J.: Prentice-Hall, 1970); Arthur Link, *Wilson: The Road to the White House* (Princeton: Princeton University Press, 1947); James Chace, *1912: Wilson, Roosevelt, Taft & Debs— the Election That Changed the Country* (New York: Simon & Schuster, 2004).

39. Bureau of the Census, Bulletin 129, *Negroes in the United States* (Washington, D.C.: Government Printing Office, 1915), pp. 7, 36–39.

40. Bureau of the Census, *Plantation Farming in the United States* (Washington, D.C.: Government Printing Office, 1916), pp. 36, 37.

41. William L. O'Neill, ed., *Echoes of Revolt: The Masses, 1911–1917* (Chicago: Quadrangle, 1966), p. 232.

42. *Quadrennial Report of the Board of Inspectors of Convicts, September 1, 1910, to August 31, 1914* (Montgomery, Ala., 1914), p. 180, ADAH.

43. Hastings H. Hart, *Social Problems of Alabama: A Study of the Social Institutions and Agencies of the State of Alabama as Related to Its War Activities* (Montgomery: Russell Sage Foundation, 1918).

44. See Pete Daniel, *The Shadow of Slavery: Peonage in the South, 1901–1969* (Urbana: University of Illinois Press, 1972), pp. 110–31, citing trial transcript, *Georgia v. John S. Williams*, Newton Superior Court, March term, 1921. For the definitive treatment of the Williams case, see Gregory A. Freeman, *Lay This Body Down: The 1921 Murders of Eleven Plantation Slaves* (Chicago: Chicago Review Press, 1999); *1920 Census*, Jasper County, Ga.

45. Ibid.

46. Thomas D. Sanford to Attorney General, April 11, 1921, 50-80-5, Peonage Files, RG60, NA.

47. Joseph John to Attorney General, July 28, 1924, 50-30-1, Peonage Files, RG60, NA.

48. J. Edgar Hoover to O. R. Luhring, May 13, 1926, 50-2-2-1, Peonage Files, RG60, NA.

49. O. R. Luhring to Rebecca Jones, Aug. 6, 1926; Jones to Calvin Coolidge, July 26, 1926; affidavit of Rebecca Jones, July 26, 1926; Assistant Attorney General Nugent Dodds to Hon. Oscar DePriest, July 25, 1932; 50-1-2-2, Peonage Files, RG60, NA.

50. N. Gordon Carper, "Martin Tabert, Martyr of an Era," *Florida Historical Quarterly* 52 (October 1973): 115–31.

51. *Jacksonville Florida Times-Union*, May 24 and 25, 1923.

52. *Report of the State Prison Inspector of Alabama, for the Period of Two Years End-*

*ing Sept. 30, 1928* (Montgomery: Birmingham Printing, 1928), in author's collection.

53. Mancini, p. 115.
54. *County Camp Inspection Records*, Department of Corrections, ADAH.
55. *New York World*, March 22, 23, 24, 27, 1926.
56. Mancini, pp. 115–16.
57. Associated Press, July 2, 1928.
58. *1930 Census*, Alabama Census of Kilby Prison; *1900 Census*, Tallapoosa County.
59. Draft Registration Card of Henry Tinsley, June 5, 1917, *World War I Selective Service System Draft Registration Cards, 1917–1918* (Washington, D.C.: NA M1509), online data accessed at www.ancestry.com.
60. *State Convict Record*, Vol. 14, Sept. 1929–Jan. 1931, p. 217, ADAH; Tinsley died in 1971, at the "Negro" veterans' hospital at Tuskegee Institute.

## CHAPTER XVII: FREEDOM

1. *1930 Census*, Georgia.
2. John Spivak, *Georgia Nigger* (New York: Brewer, Warren and Putnam, 1932), pp. 61–65.
3. Ibid., pp. 104–5.
4. Ibid., pp. 97–99.
5. Ibid., p. 240.
6. Ibid., unnumbered pages.
7. *Report of the State Prison Inspector of Alabama, for the Period of Two Years Ending September 30, 1928* (Birmingham: Birmingham Printing, 1928), in author's collection.
8. Walter Wilson, *Forced Labor in the United States* (New York: International Publishers, 1933), pp. 92–94.
9. O. B. Willis to Department of Justice, Nov. 20, 1933; Joseph B. Keenan to O. B. Willis, Dec. 8, 1933, 50-1-0, Peonage Files, RG60, NA.
10. Ibid.
11. Francis Biddle, *In Brief Authority* (Garden City, N.Y.: Doubleday, 1962), p. 155.
12. Francis Biddle to All United States Attorneys, Dec. 12, 1941, "Circular No. 3591, Re: Involuntary Servitude, Slavery, and Peonage," File 50-821, RG60, NA.
13. Francis Biddle, *A Casual Past: The Reminiscences of a Former Attorney General of the United States* (Garden City, N.Y.: Doubleday, 1961), pp. 339, 374, 376–77.

14. Biddle, "Civil Rights and the Federal Law," Speech at Cornell University (Oct. 4, 1944) (on file with the *Duke Law Journal*), cited in Risa L. Goluboff, "The Thirteenth Amendment and the Lost Origins of Civil Rights," *Duke Law Journal* 50, no. 6 (2001): 1609.

15. Biddle, *Brief Authority*, pp. 154–60.

16. Biddle to All U.S. Attorneys.

17. J. Edgar Hoover to Wendell Berge, July 18, 1942, Re: Charles Edward Bledsoe; W. F. Lanier—Involuntary Servitude and Slavery, File 50-843, Peonage Files, RG60, NA.

18. Wendell Berge to J. Edgar Hoover, Director Federal Bureau of Investigation, Aug. 8, 1942, File 50-843, Peonage Files, RG60, NA.

19. Berge to Francis H. Inge, Aug. 8, 1942, File 50-843, Peonage Files, RG60, NA.

20. *Galveston Daily News*, Oct. 2, 1942, p. 14.

21. Frank Coleman to U.S. Board of Parole, March 15, 1945; Douglas McGregor to Attorney General, June 28, 1943; "Judgment, United State Circuit Court of Appeals for the Fifth Circuit, Extract from the Minutes of June 19th, 1943," File 50-74-6, RG 60, NA.

22. *Corpus Christi Times*, March 23, 1943, quoted in Goluboff, p. 38.

## EPILOGUE

1. Interview by the author of Molly Cottenham, Feb. 2002.

2. Interview by the author of Harold Cottingham, Feb. 2002.

3. Interview by the author of J. Christopher Flowers, Oct. 9, 2007.

4. *Census, 1900, 1910, 1930*; U.S. Social Security Administration Death Index.

5. http://www.sloss.com/coke/history.asp.

6. Interview by the author of Rodney Mills Cook Jr., and English Robinson, Oct. 2, 2007.

7. Speech by Gary N. Drummond, Oct. 2000, posted at www.drummondco.com.

8. Corporate records, Secretary of State's Office, State of Alabama, Montgomery, Ala.

9. Douglas A. Blackmon, "Hard Time: From Alabama's Past, Capitalism and Racism in a Cruel Partnership," *Wall Street Journal*, July 16, 2001, p. 1.

10. Ibid.

11. Hearing before U.S. District Court Judge James Elicon, Feb. 13, 2004, Tulsa.

12. Interview by the author of Martha Minow, June 2001.

13. Blackmon, "Silent Partner: How the South's Fight to Uphold Segregation Was Funded Up North," *Wall Street Journal*, June 11, 1999, p. 1.

14. Interview by the author of Tom Ferrall, 2001.

15. "Wachovia Announces National Partnerships in Support of African Americans," July 28, 2005, www.wachovia.com.

16. Interview by the author of Ken Thompson, chairman and chief executive officer, Wachovia Bank, Sept. 14, 2007.

17. Interview by the author of Eugene Reese, Sept. 19, 2007.

18. Interview by the author of Earl Brown, John Burt, April 23, 2002, Birmingham, Ala.

19. Taylor Branch, *At Canaan's Edge: America in the King Years, 1965–68* (New York: Simon & Schuster, 2006), pp. 303–5.

20. Martin Luther King Jr., notes in margins of Charles Silberman, *Crisis in Black and White*, 1964, p. 6, Papers of Dr. Martin Luther King, AHC.

21. Blackmon, "Hard Time."

22. Interviews by the author of Pearline Danzey, Ida Hogan, Cynthia James, Melissa Danzey Craddock, and James Danzey, Sept. 28, 2000.

23. Ibid.

# SELECTED BIBLIOGRAPHY

■

## BOOKS

Adams, Charles Edward. *Blockton: The History of an Alabama Coal Mining Town.* Brierfield, Ala: Cahaba Trace Commission, 2001.

Allen, Ivan. *Atlanta from the Ashes.* Atlanta: Ruralist Press, 1928.

Armes, Ethel. *The Story of Coal and Iron in Alabama.* Birmingham: Chamber of Commerce, 1910. Reprint, Cambridge, Mass.: University Press.

Atchison, Ray M., and G. Benton Towry. *Richard Hopkins Pratt and the Six Mile Academy.* Birmingham: Banner, 1965.

Bauerlein, Mark. *Negrophobia: A Race Riot in Atlanta, 1906.* San Francisco: Encounter, 2001.

Bayor, Ronald H. *Race and the Shaping of Twentieth-Century Atlanta.* Chapel Hill: University of North Carolina Press, 1996.

Bennett, James R. *Old Tannehill: A History of the Pioneer Ironworks in Roupes Valley (1829–1865).* Published by the Jefferson County Historical Commission in cooperation with the Birmingham-Jefferson Historical Society and the Tannehill Furnace and Foundry Commission, Birmingham, Ala., 1986.

———. *Tannehill and the Growth of the Alabama Iron Industry, Including the Civil War in West Alabama.* Published by the Alabama Historic Ironworks Commission in cooperation with the Appalachian Regional Commission, the West Alabama Planning and Development Council, the Jefferson County Historical

Commission, and the Birmingham-Jefferson Historical Society. Printed in McCalla, Ala., 1999.

Berney, Saffold. *Hand Book of Alabama: A Complete Index to the State, with Map.* Birmingham: Roberts and Son, 1892.

*Bibliography of Birmingham, Alabama, 1872–1972.* Birmingham: Oxmoor, 1973.

Biddle, Francis. *A Casual Past: The Reminiscences of a Former Attorney General of the United States.* Garden City, N.Y.: Doubleday, 1961.

———. *In Brief Authority.* Garden City, N.Y.: Doubleday, 1962.

———. *The World's Best Hope: A Discussion of the Role of the United States in the Modern World.* Chicago: University of Chicago Press, 1949.

Blight, David W. *Race and Reunion: The Civil War in American Memory.* Cambridge, Mass.: Harvard University Press, 2001.

Bond, Horace Mann. *Negro Education in Alabama: A Study in Cotton and Steel.* Tuscaloosa: University of Alabama Press, 1994.

Botkin, B. A. *Lay My Burden Down: A Folk History of Slavery.* Chicago: University of Chicago Press, 1945.

Bradford, Phillips Verner, and Harvey Blume. *Ota: The Pygmy in the Zoo.* New York: St. Martin's Press, 1992.

Branch, Taylor. *At Canaan's Edge: America in the King Years, 1965–68.* New York: Simon & Schuster, 2006.

Brands, H. W. *The Reckless Decade: America in the 1890s.* Chicago: University of Chicago Press, 1995.

Buck, Paul H. *The Road to Reunion, 1865–1900.* Boston: Little, Brown, 1937.

Burns, Robert E. *I Am a Fugitive from a Georgia Chain Gang!* Athens: University of Georgia Press, 1997.

Cable, George W. *Bonaventure: A Tale of Louisiana.* New York: International Association of Newspapers and Authors, 1901.

———. *The Silent South: Together with The Freedman's Case in Equity and the Convict Lease System.* New York: Charles Scribner's Sons, 1885.

Carr, Robert K. *Federal Protection of Civil Rights: Quest for a Sword.* Ithaca: Cornell University Press, 1947.

Chace, James. *1912: Wilson, Roosevelt, Taft & Debs—the Election That Changed the Country.* New York: Simon & Schuster, 2004.

Chernow, Ron. *The House of Morgan: An American Banking Dynasty and the Rise of Modern Finance.* New York: Atlantic Monthly Press, 1990.

Childers, James Saxon. *Erskine Ramsey: His Life and Achievements.* New York: Cartwright & Ewing, 1942.

Cobb, James C. *The Most Southern Place on Earth: The Mississippi Delta and the Roots of Regional Identity.* New York: Oxford University Press, 1992.

Cohen, William. *At Freedom's Edge: Black Mobility and the Southern White Quest for Racial Control, 1861–1915.* Baton Rouge: Louisiana State University Press, 1991.

Coulter, E. Merton. *James Monroe Smith: Georgia Planter: Before Death and After.* Athens: University of Georgia Press, 1961.

Curtin, Mary Ellen. *Black Prisoners and Their World, Alabama, 1865–1900.* Charlottesville: University Press of Virginia, 2000.

D'Angelo, Raymond. *The American Civil Rights Movement: Readings and Interpretations.* Guilford, Conn.: McGraw-Hill/Dushkin, 2001.

Daniel, Pete. *The Shadow of Slavery: Peonage in the South, 1901–1969.* Urbana: University of Illinois Press, 1972.

Diouf, Sylviane A. *Dreams of Africa in Alabama: The Slave Ship* Clotilda *and the Story of the Last Africans Brought to America.* New York: Oxford University Press, 2007.

Dixon, Thomas, Jr. *The Clansman.* New York: Doubleday, Page, 1905.

———. *The Leopard's Spots: A Romance of the White Man's Burden.* New York: Doubleday, Page, 1902.

———. *The Southerner: A Romance of the Real Lincoln.* New York: D. Appleton, 1913.

Dray, Philip. *At the Hands of Persons Unknown: The Lynching of Black America.* New York: Random House, 2002.

DuBois, W. E. B. *The Autobiography of W. E. B. Du Bois: A Soliloquy on Viewing My Life from the Last Decade of Its First Century.* New York: International Publishers, 1968.

———. *Darkwater: Voices from Within the Veil.* Mineola, N.Y.: Dover, 1999.

———. *The Quest of the Silver Fleece.* Chicago: A. C. McClurg & Co., 1911.

———. *The Souls of Black Folk.* 1903. Repr. New York: Dover, 1994.

Ellison, Rhoda Coleman. *Bibb County, Alabama: The First Hundred Years, 1818–1918.* Tuscaloosa: University of Alabama Press, 1984.

Evans, Matthew S. *The Soil Runs Red.* Chicago: Van Kampen, 1948.

Fierce, Milfred C. *Slavery Revisited: Blacks and the Southern Convict Lease System, 1865–1933.* New York: African Studies Research Center, Brooklyn College, City University of New York, 1994.

Flynt, Wayne. *Poor but Proud: Alabama's Poor Whites.* Tuscaloosa: University of Alabama Press, 1989.

Foner, Eric. *Reconstruction: America's Unfinished Revolution, 1863–1877.* New York: Harper & Row, 1988.

Franklin, John Hope. *Reconstruction: After the Civil War.* Chicago: University of Chicago Press, 1961.

Franklin, John Hope, and Alfred A. Moss Jr. *From Slavery to Freedom: A History of African Americans.* Seventh edition. New York: McGraw-Hill, 1994.

Fredrickson, George M. *The Inner Civil War: Northern Intellectuals and the Crisis of the Union.* New York: Harper Torchbooks, 1965.

Freeman, Gregory A. *Lay This Body Down: The 1921 Murders of Eleven Plantation Slaves.* Chicago: Chicago Review Press, 1999.

Freese, Barbara. *Coal: A Human History.* Cambridge, Mass.: Perseus, 2003.

Friedman, Lawrence J. *The White Savage: Racial Fantasies in the Postbellum South.* Englewood Cliffs, N.J.: Prentice-Hall, 1970.

Gates, Henry Louis, Jr., and Cornel West. *The African American Century: How Black Americans Have Shaped Our Country.* New York: Free Press, 2000.

Hale, Grace Elizabeth. *Making Whiteness: The Culture of Segregation in the South, 1890–1940.* New York: Pantheon, 1998.

Hart, Albert Bushnell. *The Southern South.* New York: D. Appleton, 1910.

Hochschild, Adam. *King Leopold's Ghost: A Story of Greed, Terror, and Heroism in Colonial Africa.* New York: Houghton Mifflin, 1998.

Hodgson, Joseph, ed. *The Alabama Manual and Statistical Register for 1869.* Montgomery: Montgomery Daily Mail, 1869.

Hoole, William Stanley. *Alias Simon Suggs: The Life and Times of Johnson Jones Hooper.* Tuscaloosa: University of Alabama Press, 1952.

Hooper, Johnson Jones. *Adventures of Captain Simon Suggs, Late of the Tallapoosa Volunteers.* Philadelphia: Carey & Hart, 1845.

Jones, James Pickett. *Yankee Blitzkrieg: Wilson's Raid Through Alabama and Georgia.* Athens: University of Georgia Press, 1976.

Kelly, Brian. *Race, Class, and Power in the Alabama Coalfields, 1908–21.* Urbana: University of Illinois Press, 2001.

Kennedy, Stetson. *Southern Exposure.* New York: Country Life Press, 1946.

Kolchin, Peter, *First Freedom: The Responses of Alabama's Blacks to Emancipation and Reconstruction.* Westport, Conn.: Greenwood Press, 1972.

Langston, Fern, ed. *Echoes of Six Mile.* Privately published collection of genealogical histories and documents.

Larson, Erik. *The Devil in the White City: Murder, Magic, and Madness at the Fair That Changed America.* New York: Vintage, 2004.

Lewis, David Levering. *W. E. B. Du Bois: Biography of a Race, 1868–1919*. New York: Henry Holt, 2003.

———. *W. E. B. Du Bois: The Fight for Equality and the American Century, 1919–1963*. New York: Henry Holt, 2000.

Lewis, David Levering, and Deborah Willis. *A Small Nation of People: W. E. B. Du Bois and African American Portraits of Progress*. New York: HarperCollins, 2005.

Lewis, W. David. *Sloss Furnaces and the Rise of the Birmingham District: An Industrial Epic*. Tuscaloosa: University of Alabama Press, 1994.

Lichtenstein, Alex. *Twice the Work of Free Labor: The Political Economy of Convict Labor in the New South*. London: Verso, 1996.

Link, Arthur. *Wilson: The Road to the White House*. Princeton: Princeton University Press, 1947.

Litwack, Leon F. *Trouble in Mind: Black Southerners in the Age of Jim Crow*. New York: Alfred A. Knopf, 1998.

Malcomson, Scott L. *One Drop of Blood: The American Misadventure of Race*. New York: Farrar, Straus & Giroux, 2000.

Mancini, Matthew J. *One Dies, Get Another: Convict Leasing in the American South, 1866–1928*. Columbia: University of South Carolina Press, 1996.

Maunder, Elwood, and Estelle McGowin Larson. *James Greely McGowin—South Alabama Lumberman: The Recollections of His Family*. Santa Cruz, Calif.: Forest History Society, 1977.

McKiven, Henry M., Jr. *Iron and Steel: Class, Race, and Community in Birmingham, Alabama, 1875–1920*. Chapel Hill: University of North Carolina Press, 1995.

McPherson, James M. *The Most Fearful Ordeal: The Original Coverage of the Civil War by Writers and Reporters of* The New York Times. New York: St. Martin's Press, 2004.

McWhorter, Diane. *Carry Me Home: Birmingham, Alabama: The Climactic Battle of the Civil Rights Revolution*. New York: Simon & Schuster, 2001.

Morris, Edmund. *Theodore Rex*. New York: Modern Library, 2002.

Myers, Martha A. *Race, Labor, and Punishment in the New South*. Columbus: Ohio State University Press, 1998.

Nevins, Allan. *Hamilton Fish: The Inner History of the Grant Administration*. New York: Dodd, Mead, 1936.

Norrell, Robert J. *James Bowron: The Autobiography of a New South Industrialist*. Chapel Hill: University of North Carolina Press, 1991.

Novak, Daniel E. *The Wheel of Servitude: Black Forced Labor After Slavery*. Lexington: University Press of Kentucky, 1978.

Olmsted, Frederick Law. *The Cotton Kingdom: A Traveller's Observations on Cotton and Slavery in the American Slave States*. New York: Mason Brothers, 1862.

———. *A Journey in the Back Country*. New York: Mason Brothers, 1860.

O'Neill, William L., ed. *Echoes of Revolt: The Masses, 1911–1917*. Chicago: Quadrangle, 1966.

Oney, Steve. *And the Dead Shall Rise: The Murder of Mary Phagan and the Lynching of Leo Frank*. New York: Pantheon, 2003.

Oshinsky, David M. *"Worse Than Slavery": Parchman Farm and the Ordeal of Jim Crow Justice*. New York: Free Press, 1996.

Packard, Jerrold M. *American Nightmare: The History of Jim Crow*. New York: St. Martin's Press, 2002.

Page, Thomas Nelson. *The Negro: The Southerner's Problem*. New York: Charles Scribner's Sons, 1904.

———. *The Old Gentleman of the Black Stock*. New York: Charles Scribner's Sons, 1900.

———. *Red Rock: A Chronicle of Reconstruction*. New York: Charles Scribner's Sons, 1899.

Poe, Clarence H. *A Southerner in Europe*. Raleigh, N.C.: Mutual Publishing Company, 1908.

Powell, J. C. *The American Siberia: Or, Fourteen Years' Experience in a Southern Convict Camp*. Chicago: Homewood, 1893.

*Proceedings of the Annual Congress of the National Prison Association of the United States Held at Cincinnati, September 25–30, 1890*. Pittsburgh: Shaw Brothers Printers, 1891.

*Proceedings of the Annual Congress of the National Prison Association of the United States Held at Nashville, November 16–20, 1889*. Chicago: Knight & Leonard Co., 1890.

Reed, John. *Ten Days That Shook the World*. New York: Boni & Liveright, 1919.

Reynolds, John N. *Twin Hells*. Chicago: M. A. Donahue & Co., 1890.

Rosengarten, Theodore. *All God's Dangers: The Life of Nate Shaw*. New York: Alfred A. Knopf, 1974.

Royce, Edward. *The Origins of Southern Sharecropping*. Philadelphia: Temple University Press, 1993.

Sapiro, Karin A. *A New South Rebellion: The Battle Against Convict Labor in the Tennessee Coalfields, 1871–1896*. Chapel Hill: University of North Carolina Press, 1998.

*Shelby County: Historical Images—The Early Years.* Presented by the *Shelby County Reporter* with the Shelby County Historical Society. Piedmont Publishing, 2005.

Sinclair, William A. *The Aftermath of Slavery.* Boston: Small, Maynard & Company, 1905.

Smith, Lillian. *Strange Fruit.* New York: Reynal & Hitchcock, 1944.

Spivak, John L. *Georgia Nigger.* New York: Brewer, Warren & Putnam, 1932.

Stampp, Kenneth M. *The Peculiar Institution: Slavery in the Ante-bellum South.* New York: Alfred A. Knopf, 1956.

Steiner, Jesse F., and Roy M. Brown. *The University of North Carolina Social Study Series: The North Carolina Chain Gang.* Westport, Conn.: Negro University Press, 1970. Originally published in 1927 by the University of North Carolina Press.

Stuart, Ruth McEnery. *The River's Children.* New York: Century, 1904.

Suitts, Steve. *Hugo Black of Alabama: How His Roots and Early Career Shaped the Great Champion of the Constitution.* Montgomery: NewSouth Books, 2005.

Sullivan, Larry E., ed. *Bandits and Bibles: Convict Literature in Nineteenth-Century America.* New York: Akashic, 2003.

Tarbell, Ida M. *The Life of Elbert H. Gary: The Story of Steel.* New York: D. Appleton, 1925.

Thomas, William Hannibal. *The American Negro.* New York: Macmillan, 1901.

Thompson, Stith. *One Hundred Favorite Folktales.* Bloomington: Indiana University Press, 1974.

Tourgee, Albion W. *Bricks Without Straw.* New York: Fords, Howard & Hulbert, 1880.

———. *A Fool's Errand and the Invisible Empire.* New York: Fords, Howard & Hulbert, 1880.

Trelease, Allen W. *White Terror: The Ku Klux Klan Conspiracy and Southern Reconstruction.* Baton Rouge: Louisiana State University Press, 1971.

Walker, Donald R. *Penology for Profit: A History of the Texas Prison System, 1867–1912.* College Station: Texas A&M University Press, 1988.

Ward, Robert David, and William Warren Rogers. *Convicts, Coal, and the Banner Mine Tragedy.* Tuscaloosa: University of Alabama Press, 1987.

Warren, Kenneth. *Big Steel: The First Century of the United States Steel Corporation, 1901–2001.* Pittsburgh: University of Pittsburgh Press, 2001.

Warren, Louis S. *Buffalo Bill's America: William Cody and the Wild West Show.* New York: Alfred A. Knopf, 2005.

Wharton, Vernon Lane. *The Negro in Mississippi, 1865–1890.* New York: Harper & Row, 1965.

White, Marjorie Longenecker. *The Birmingham District: An Industrial History and Guide*. Birmingham: Birmingham Publishing, 1981.

Wilson, Bobby M. *America's Johannesburg: Industrialization and Racial Transformation in Birmingham*. Lanham, Md.: Rowman & Littlefield, 2000.

————. *Race and Place in Birmingham: The Civil Rights and Neighborhood Movements*. Lanham, Md.: Rowman & Littlefield, 2000.

Wilson, Walter. *Forced Labor in the United States*. New York: International Publishers, 1933.

Wilson, Woodrow. *Division and Reunion, 1829–1889*. New York: Longmans, Green, 1893.

Winik, Jay. *April 1865: The Month That Saved America*. New York: Harper-Collins, 2001.

Wood, Forrest G. *Black Scare: The Racist Response to Emancipation and Reconstruction*. Berkeley: University of California Press, 1970.

Woodward, C. Vann. *The Burden of Southern History*. New York: Vintage, 1960.

————. *Origins of the New South, 1877–1913. Volume 9*. Baton Rouge: Louisiana State University Press, 1951.

————. *Reunion and Reaction: The Compromise of 1877 and the End of Reconstruction*. Boston: Little, Brown, 1951.

————. *The Strange Career of Jim Crow*. New York: Oxford University Press, 1966.

Work, John W. *American Negro Songs and Spirituals*. New York: Crown, 1940.

## ARCHIVAL COLLECTIONS

*The Peonage Files of the U.S. Department of Justice, 1901–1945*. Department of Justice, Record Group 60, National Archives, Washington, D.C.

*Booker T. Washington Papers, Volumes 1–14*. Urbana: University of Illinois Press, 1972, http://www.historycooperative.org/btw.

## ARTICLES, PAMPHLETS, MANUSCRIPTS, SPEECHES

Abernathy, C. A. "The Birth of Calcis: Founding of Calcis, Turner Brothers, Justice Store, and Our 'Historical' House: The Community, Its Historical Importance, and Our Family Ties to It." Unpublished typescript, Nov. 1, 1992. Author's collection.

Allen, Alvaran Snow. "The Story of a Lie: By Convict No. 2939, Himself 15 Years in Prison." Pamphlet printed by Mission Printing Company, Tulsa, c. 1926. Author's collection.

Armes, Ethel. "The Ironmasters of Alabama." *Advance Magazine* 3, no. 15 (November 17, 1906).

Blackmon, Douglas. A. "Hard Time: From Alabama's Past, Capitalism and Racism in a Cruel Partnership." *Wall Street Journal,* July 16, 2001, p. 1.

———. "Silent Partner: How the South's Fight to Uphold Segregation Was Funded Up North." *Wall Street Journal,* June 11, 1999.

Bunn, J. Michael. "Slavery in the Shelby Iron Works During the Civil War." *Shelby County Historical Quarterly,* March 2003.

Carper, N. Gordon. "Martin Tabert, Martyr of an Era." *Florida Historical Quarterly* 52 (October 1973).

Carter, Catherine McRee. "History of Kinderlou, Georgia, 1860–1940." Unpublished typescript, Dec. 1940. Author's collection.

Cohen, William. "Negro Involuntary Servitude in the South, 1865–1940: A Preliminary Analysis." *Journal of Southern History,* February 1976.

Collins, Donald E., ed. "A Georgian's View of Alabama in 1836." *Alabama Review,* January 1972.

Cory, Marielou Armstrong. "History of the Ladies Memorial Association," 1902, http://www.monumentpreservation.com/monument/history.html.

Cottingham, Anna Blanche. *The Cottingham's of Bibb County: Vol. 1.* Ada, Okla.: Pontotoc County Historical and Genealogical Society, 1970.

Drobney, Jeffrey A. "Where Palm and Pine Are Blowing: Convict Labor in the North Florida Turpentine Industry, 1877–1923." *Florida Historical Quarterly* 72, no. 4 (1994), pp. 411–34.

Ellis, R. H. "The Calhoun School, Miss Charlotte Thorn's 'Lighthouse on the Hill' in Lowndes County, Alabama." *Alabama Review* 37, no. 3 (1984).

Goluboff, Risa L. "The Thirteenth Amendment and the Lost Origins of Civil Rights." *Duke Law Journal* 50, no. 6 (2001).

Graves, John Temple, ed. "Bibb County History," in *The Book of Alabama and the South.* Birmingham: Protective Life Insurance Co., 1933.

Grossman, Jonathan. "Black Studies in the Department of Labor, 1897–1907." *Monthly Labor Review,* June 1974.

Harrison, Shelby M. "A Cash-Nexus for Crime"; "The Human Side of Large Outputs, Steel and Steel Workers in Six American States, Part IV, Birmingham District: Labor Conservation." *The Survey,* Jan. 6, 1912.

"Keystone Lime Company." *Columbiana Sentinel,* Sept. 7, 1905. SCHS.

Langston, Cirrenia. "Childhood Memories of the War Between the States." Centreville Press, March 14, 1934.

Logan, Eugenia Wallace. Copy of typescript of oral history, 1935. Author's collection.

MacKnight, J. A. "Columbiana: The Gem of the Hills." Published by the *Shelby County Sentinel*, c. 1907. SCHS.

McNeill, Mary Ann (Cobb) Johnson. "Cobb History and Stories." Unpublished manuscript, n.d., http://www.mytree.net/gen/showhistory .php?docID=53.

"The New Slavery in the South, an Autobiography." *Independent*, Feb. 25, 1904.

Official Programme of Daily Events, Cotton States and International Exposition, Dec. 30, 1895 (Atlanta: C. P. Byrd). Author's collection.

Roosevelt, Theodore. "Expansion of the White Races." Speech to Methodist Episcopal Church celebration of the African Diamond Jubilee, Washington, D.C., Jan. 18, 1909.

Seales, Bobby Joe. "Shelby Iron Company: Brief History of Shelby Iron Co." Shelby County Historical Society *Quarterly* 7, no. 2 (May 1980), http://www .rootsweb.com/~alshelby/shelbyironco.html.

————. "Siluria Cotton Mill Company." SCHS, http://www.rootsweb.com/ ~alshelby/SiluriaMills.html.

Smith, Robert Crew. "The Coming of the Railroad." Privately published compilation of family historical material, n.d., Goodwater, Ala., Goodwater Public Library, Genealogy Section.

Teague, E. B. "Sketches of the History of Shelby County." Typescript, 84 pp. SCHS.

Vandiver, Frank E. "Josiah Gorgas and the Brierfield Iron Works." *Alabama Review*, January 1950.

————. "The Shelby Iron Company in the Civil War: A Study of a Confederate Industry." *Alabama Review*, January 1948.

Wallace, Reynolds E., Jr. "Recollections of Wesley Chapel." Copy of unpublished manuscript, 1996. Author's collection.

Walthall Family History. Typescript, 16 pp. SCHS.

Washington, Booker T. "To the Colored Citizens of Alabama," *Tuskegee Student*, Feb. 28, 1895, p. 2, BTW Papers.

Wells, Ida B. "The Convict Lease System"; "Lynch Law." Chapters in *The Reason Why the Colored American Is Not in the World's Columbian Exposition*. Chicago, 1893.

## DISSERTATIONS AND THESES

Carter, Dan T. "Prisons, Politics and Business: The Convict Lease System in the Post–Civil War South." M.A. thesis, University of Wisconsin, 1964.

Day, James Sanders. "Diamonds in the Rough: A History of Alabama's Cahaba Coal Field." Ph.D. diss., Auburn University, 2002.

Fuller, Justin. "History of the Tennessee Coal, Iron and Railroad Company, 1852–1907." Ph.D. diss., University of North Carolina, Chapel Hill, 1966.

Nolen, David L. "Wilson's Raid on the Coal and Iron Industry in Shelby County." Thesis, University of Alabama, Birmingham, Spring 1988.

## CORPORATE RECORDS AND REPORTS

Agreement Entered into by J. Craig Smith, President of the Board of Convict Inspectors of the State of Alabama and Tennessee Coal, Iron and Railroad Company, Nov. 26, 1907. Author's collection.

Annual Report, Tennessee Coal, Iron & Railroad Company, Reports to Board of Directors, Dec. 19, 1892.

Letterbooks of Tennessee Coal, Iron & Railroad, 1893–1895, A. S. Williams Collection, Eufaula Athenaeum, Eufaula, Ala.

*Mechanical Mining Handbook.* Tennessee Coal and Iron Division, United States Steel Corp., 1956. Author's collection.

*Pocket Companion Information and Tables for Engineers and Designers and Other Data Pertaining to Structural Steel.* Pittsburgh, Penn., and Chicago, Ill.: Carnegie-Illinois Steel Corporation, 1936. Birmingham, Ala.: Tennesse Coal, Iron and Railroad Company, 1936. San Francisco, Calif.: Columbia Steel Company, 1936.

*Rules and Regulations, Tennessee Coal, Iron and Railroad Company.* Ensley Works, May 1921. Author's collection.

*Sixth Annual Report of the United States Steel Corporation,* for the Fiscal Year ended Dec. 31, 1907.

*Steel Making at Birmingham, Ala.* Fairfield, Ala.: Published by Tennessee Coal & Iron Division of United States Steel Corp., 1954. An official company history.

*Story of Tennessee Coal, Iron Railroad Company.* As told in *Blast Furnace and Steel Plant,* Aug. 1939. Author's collection.

"Tennessee Coal, Iron and Railroad Company." *U.S. Steel News*, Aug. 1937. Author's collection.

Wiebel, A. V. *Biography of a Business. Tennessee Coal & Iron Division.* United States Steel Corporation, 1960.

## GOVERNMENT DOCUMENTS

Administrative Correspondence, 1881–1897, Dawson Letter Books. Correspondence of the Inspectors of the Penitentiary, Department of Corrections. ADAH.

*Annual Report of the Inspectors of the Alabama Penitentiary, for the Year Ending Sept. 30, 1877.* Montgomery: Barrett & Brown, 1878. ADAH.

*Annual Report of the Inspectors of the Alabama Penitentiary, October 1, 1873, to September 30, 1874.* Montgomery: W. W. Screws, 1874. Author's collection.

Bibb County Commission Minutes, BCCH.

*Biennial Report of the Adjutant-General of Alabama, to Thos. G. Jones, Governor and Commander-in-Chief.* Montgomery: Brown Printing, 1894.

*Biennial Report of the Board of Inspectors of Convicts, 1880–1882.* Montgomery: Barrett & Brown, 1882. ADAH.

"Circular No. 3591, Re: Involuntary Servitude, Slavery, and Peonage." Francis Biddle to All United States Attorneys, Dec. 12, 1941, File 50-821, Record Group 60, Department of Justice, National Archives.

Commissioner of Labor. *Twentieth Annual Report of the Commissioner of Labor 1905: Convict Labor.* Washington, D.C.: U.S. Government Printing Office, 1906.

"Contract on Confession of Judgment Record, 1903–1913." SCHS.

Convict Legislation and Rules, 1882–1883, Alabama Department of Corrections. ADAH.

*Convict Record,* Autauga County Probate Clerks Office, Prattville, Ala.

*Convict Record,* undated, Barbour County. Sheriff R. B. Teal, Barbour County Courthouse, Clayton, Ala.

*Convicts at Hard Labor for the County in the State of Alabama on the First Day of March 1883,* microfiche. ADAH.

Dawson, R. H. *Diary of Reginald Heber Dawson, 1883–1906.* ADAH.

Deed of Purchase by the Confederate States of America of Bibb County Iron Co., Sept. 7, 1863, BCC.

*Docket of A. M. Elliott, Justice of the Peace, 1878–1880,* SCHS.

Feeding Accounts, 1908, Shelby County. SCHS.

*Fifth Biennial Report of the Board of Inspectors of Convicts, September 1, 1902, to August 31, 1904.* Montgomery: Brown Printing, 1904. ADAH.

*First Biennial Report of the Board of Inspectors of Convicts, September 1, 1894, to August 31, 1896.* Montgomery: Roemer Printing, 1896. ADAH.

*First Biennial Report of the Inspectors of Convicts, October 1, 1884, to October 1, 1886.* Montgomery: Barrett & Co., 1886. ADAH.

*Fourth Biennial Report of the Board of Inspectors of Convicts, September 1, 1900, to August 31, 1902.* Montgomery: Brown Printing, 1902. ADAH.

Hart, Hastings H. *Social Problems of Alabama: A Study of the Social Institutions and Agencies of the State of Alabama as Related to Its War Activities.* Montgomery: Russell Sage Foundation, 1918.

Henry County Convict Record, Henry County Courthouse, Abbeville, Ala.

*History of the Penitentiary.* Special Message of Gov. Cobb, 1882. ADAH.

Jail Record, May 1888 to December 1890, Shelby County. SCHS.

Jail Register, 1907, Shelby County. SCHS.

"Jefferson County Circuit Court Convict Docket, 1902–1903." Birmingham Public Library Archives.

Jefferson County Coroner's Record, Preliminary Investigation Reports, Record of B. L. Brasher, Coroner, Office of Coroner/Medical Examiner, Jefferson County.

Kilby, Thomas E. "Message Relative to Convict Lease System." Jan. 10, 1923. Montgomery: Brown Printing, 1923. Author's collection.

———. "Message Relative to Feeding of Prisoners." January 15, 1923. Montgomery: Brown Printing, 1923. Author's collection.

Kolb, R. F. *Annual Report of Department of Agriculture and Industries for the Fiscal Year 1912–1913.* Montgomery: Brown Printing, 1913.

*Land Atlas and Plat Book*, Bibb County, Alabama. Rockford, Ill.: Rockford Map Publishers, 1989.

Lee, A. Frank. "Historical Review of the Alabama Prison System." Department of Corrections. Montgomery, 1960. ADAH.

Message of Thos. E. Kilby, Governor, Relative to Feeding of Prisoners, Legislative Document No. 3, Alabama Legislature, Jan. 15, 1923 (Montgomery: Brown Printing, 1923). Author's collection.

Milner, John T. "Report to the Governor of Alabama on the Alabama Central Railroad." Montgomery: *Advertiser* Book and Job Steam Press Print, 1859. ADAH.

Minutes of the Board of Inspectors, 1883–1913, Department of Corrections. ADAH.

Minutes of the Shelby County Commission, Dec. 1880, 1881, 1882, 1883, 1884. SCHS.

Oates, W. H. *Report of the State Prison Inspector of Alabama, for the Period of Two Years Ending September 30th, 1916.* Montgomery: Brown Printing, 1917. ADAH.

*Official Proceedings of the Constitutional Convention of the State of Alabama,* May 21–Sept. 3, 1901. Wetumpka, Ala.: 1940.

*Proceedings: Joint Committee of the Senate and House to Investigate the Convict Lease System of Georgia.* Vols. 1 and 2, 727 pp. GDAH.

*Quadrennial Report of the Board of Control and Economy: Convict Department, 1919–1922.* Montgomery: Brown Printing, 1922. ADAH.

*Quadrennial Report of the Board of Inspectors of Convicts, September 1, 1906, to August 31, 1910.* Montgomery: Brown Printing, 1910. ADAH.

*Quadrennial Report of the Board of Inspectors of Convicts, September 1, 1910, to August 31, 1914.* Montgomery, 1914. ADAH.

*Quadrennial Report of the Board of Inspectors of Convicts, Sept. 1, 1914, to Aug. 31, 1918.* Montgomery: Brown Printing, 1918. ADAH.

Record of Incorporation, Bibb Steam Mill Company, Nov. 26, 1850. BCC.

Register of Prisoners Committed to the County Jail of Shelby County. SCHS.

"Report of Persons Sentenced to Hard Labor for Shelby County." December 1913. SCHS.

*Report of the State Prison Inspector of Alabama, for the Period of Two Years Ending September 30th, 1916.* Montgomery: Brown Printing, 1917.

*Report of the State Prison Inspector of Alabama, for the Period of Two Years Ending September 30, 1920.* Montgomery: Brown Printing, 1920. ADAH.

*Report of the State Prison Inspector of Alabama, for the Period of Two Years Ending September 30th, 1926.* Birmingham: Birmingham Printing, 1926. ADAH.

*Report of the State Prison Inspector of Alabama, for the Period of Two Years Ending September 30th, 1928.* Birmingham: Birmingham Printing, 1928. Author's collection.

*Report of the State Prison Inspector of Alabama, for the Period of Two Years Ending September 30th, 1930.* Montgomery: Wilson Printing Co., 1930. Author's collection.

Schedule of Convicts Obtained by Tennessee Coal, Iron & Railroad Co. from Shelby County, 2nd Quarter 1904. SCHS.

*Second Annual Report of the Commissioner of Labor, 1886: Convict Labor.* Washington, D.C.: U.S. Government Printing Office, 1887.

*Second Biennial Report of the Board of Inspectors of Convicts, September 1, 1896, to August 31, 1898.* Montgomery: Roemer Printing, 1898. ADAH.

*Second Biennial Report of the Inspectors of Convicts, Oct. 1, 1886, to Sept. 30, 1888.* Montgomery: W. D. Brown, 1888. ADAH.

*Shelby County Poll Tax Book,* 1890. SCHS.

Shelby County Record of Prisoners, April 11, 1878, to October 11, 1878, SCHS.

Shelby County Record of Prisoners, April 18, 1879, to October 1, 1888. SCHS.

Shelby County Record of Prisoners, Aug. 17, 1884, to May 16, 1886. SCHS.

Shelby County Record of Prisoners, Oct. 19, 1890, to Aug. 20, 1906. SCHS.

Shelby County Sheriff's Office, Loose Papers File, Columbiana, Ala., SCHS.

Sheriff's Feeding Account, 1899–1907, Shelby County. SCHS.

Sheriff's Feeding Accounts, 1907, Shelby County. SCHS.

Sheriff's Prisoners Register, 1908, Shelby County. SCHS.

*Sixth Biennial Report of the Board of Inspectors of Convicts, September 1, 1904, to August 31, 1906.* Montgomery, 1906. ADAH.

Tallapoosa County Probate Clerk's Records, Dadeville, Ala.

*Testimony Taken by the Joint Special Committee of the Session of 1880–81 to Enquire into the Condition and Treatment of Convicts of the State,* Testimony of Jno. D. Goode. Montgomery, Ala., 1881. ADAH.

*Third Biennial Report of the Board of Inspectors of Convicts, September 1, 1898, to August 31, 1900.* Montgomery: A. Roemer, 1900. ADAH.

*Third Biennial Report of the Inspectors of Convicts, Oct. 1, 1888, to Sept. 30, 1890.* Montgomery: Brown Printing, 1890. ADAH.

*The War of Rebellion: A Compilation of the Official Records of the Union and Confederate Armies.* Washington, D.C.: U.S. Government Printing Office, 1880–1901.

Wilcox County Probate Clerk's Records, Camden, Ala.

## NEWSPAPERS

*Atlanta Constitution*
*Atlanta Journal*
*Augusta Chronicle*
*Birmingham Age-Herald*
*Birmingham Daily News*
*Centreville Press*

*Cleveland Gazette*
*Dadeville Spot Cash*
*Galveston Daily News*
*Jacksonville Florida Times-Union*
*Montgomery Advertiser*
*Montgomery Daily Dispatch*
*New York Evening Post*
*New York Herald*
*New York Times*
*New York World*
*Prattville Progress*
*Shelby Sentinel*
*Sunday Mississippian*
*Tallapoosa Voice*
*Wall Street Journal*
*Wilcox Progressive Era*

# INDEX

■

*Photography Credits*

| | |
|---|---|
| 5 (top right) | Courtesy of the Alabama Department of History and Archives |
| 5 (bottom) | Courtesy of the Alabama Department of History and Archives |
| 6 (top left) | Author's collection |
| 6 (top right) | Author's collection |
| 6 (bottom) | Courtesy of Library of Congress |
| 7 (top) | Courtesy of Birmingham Public Library and Archives |
| 7 (bottom) | Author's collection |
| 8 (top) | Courtesy of the Library of Congress, LC-USF344-007S41-ZB |
| 8 (bottom) | Courtesy of the Library of Congress, LC-USZ62-58998 |